# COUNSELING: THEORY AND PRACTICE

# COUNSELING: THEORY AND PRACTICE

## SECOND EDITION

RICKEY L. GEORGE
THERESE S. CRISTIANI
*University of Missouri, St. Louis*

Prentice-Hall, Inc., Englewood Cliffs, New Jersey 07632

**Library of Congress Cataloging-in-Publication Data**

George, Rickey.
COUNSELING THEORY AND PRACTICE.

    Rev. ed. of: Theory, methods & processes of counseling & psychotherapy. c1981.
Bibliography.
Includes index.
1. Counseling. 2. Psychotherapy. I. Cristiani,
Therese Stridde. II. George, Rickey. Theory,
methods & processes of counseling and psychotherapy.
III. Title.
BF637.C6G42  1985        158'.3        85-12468
ISBN 0-13-181298-X

Editorial/production supervision: Jeanne M Hoeting
Cover design: Lundgren Graphics, Inc.
Manufacturing buyer: Barbara Kelly Kittle

BF
637
.C6
G42
1985

This book was previously published under the title of
*Theory, Methods, & Processes of Counseling & Psychotherapy.*

Printed in the United States of America

10   9   8   7   6   5   4   3   2   1

ISBN 0-13-181298-X  01

Prentice-Hall International (UK) Limited, *London*
Prentice-Hall of Australia Pty. Limited, *Sydney*
Prentice-Hall Canada Inc., *Toronto*
Prentice-Hall Hispanoamericana, S.A., *Mexico*
Prentice-Hall of India Private Limited, *New Delhi*
Prentice-Hall of Japan, Inc., *Tokyo*
Prentice-Hall of Southeast Asia Pte. Ltd., *Singapore*
Editora Prentice-Hall do Brasil, Ltda., *Rio de Janeiro*
Whitehall Books Limited, *Wellington, New Zealand*

*TO OUR CHILDREN WITH LOVE*

*Amanda Kathleen George*      *Katharine Goodwin Cristiani*
*Laura Michelle George*        *Jeffrey Michael Cristiani*
*Susan Nicole George*

# CONTENTS

# PART II
# THEORETICAL APPROACHES TO COUNSELING   22

## 2   FOUNDATIONS OF COUNSELING   22

## 3   PSYCHOANALYTIC FOUNDATIONS   37

# PART III
# COUNSELING PROCESSES AND METHODS

## 7 CHARACTERISTICS OF A HELPING RELATIONSHIP   118

## 8 COUNSELING PROCEDURES/SKILLS: I   134

## 13  DIAGNOSIS AND ASSESSMENT  220
### James T. Hurley

## PART IV
## ISSUES & TRENDS  234

## 14  CHANGING ROLE OF THE COUNSELOR: COUNSELOR AS CONSULTANT  234

# PREFACE

Several major changes were made in the second edition of this text. First, two totally new chapters were added. One of these focused on the psychoanalytic traditions which have played an influential role in the formulation of other theoretical viewpoints. The second is a chapter on diagnosis and assessment written by James Hurley, to meet the needs of counselors who are regularly involved in testing clients. Other major changes include the integration of chapters 1 and 2 from the first edition into one chapter as well as a reorganization of the chapters on group counseling, counseling for special concerns, and counseling special populations. In addition, much of the remaining material was revised to include new ideas and research, including sections on family systems therapy, holistic counseling, hypnotherapy, cognitive therapy, and crisis counseling.

As before, the goal of this counseling text is to present a comprehensive overview of the field of counseling. Although the book is written for use as a major textbook in beginning counseling courses and should be particularly useful in methods classes, it should also be a valuable resource and reference for more advanced readers. It is designed to address a wide audience including counselors and counseling psychology majors preparing to work in a variety of settings.

Our intent is to present a broad view of the foundations, theories, and practices of counseling without emphasizing a particular theoretical orientation, thus giving the reader a well-balanced foundation for further study. It is also our objective to integrate fundamental counseling research with practical implications in a meaningful and useful way. Therefore, we examine the major findings of those who have studied counseling theory, methods and processes.

While the material presented is current and thorough, we have been selective regarding the material and ideas included. The book does not contain every important research finding or concept; rather, it gives wide enough coverage to introduce the reader to the major ideas and includes a comprehensive list of references to provide direction for those students who seek greater depth.

We believe this book differs from other existing textbooks in several fundamental ways. It places greater emphasis on theory and includes a description of the major theoretical orientations used by contemporary counselors; these theories are presented in such a way that their application in the work setting is clear. It devotes an entire chapter to career counseling and it discusses in depth the counselor's role as consultant. It is contemporary in its coverage of special populations and client concerns, and it is presented in a highly readable style.

We wish to express our gratitude to our spouses, Kathy and Michael, for their support and encouragement in completing this revision. Special thanks goes to Jim Hurley for writing the chapter on diagnosis and assessment. As with the first edition, it has been a pleasure to work with the people at Prentice-Hall, especially Wayne Spohr and Susan Katz Willig. Finally, we express thanks to those individuals who reviewed the manuscript and provided useful feedback: Dr. James Bray, Texas Woman's University, Dr. Jerry Davis, University of Wisconsin, Dr. Harold Engen, University of Iowa, and Dr. James O'Neil, University of Connecticut, and Dr. Kenneth W. Wegner, Boston College.

# 1

# AN OVERVIEW TO COUNSELING

**DEFINITIONS OF COUNSELING**

**DISTINCTIONS BETWEEN COUNSELING AND PSYCHOTHERAPY**

> **Differences in Goals**
> **Differences in Clients and Settings**
> **Differences in Training**

**GOALS OF COUNSELING**

> **Five Major Goals**
> **Commonality of Goals**
> **Client Expectations**

**HISTORICAL DEVELOPMENT OF THE COUNSELING PROFESSION**

> **Vocational Guidance Movement**
> **Mental Health Movement**
> **Standardized Testing**
> **Federal Legislation**

**PROFESSIONAL ORGANIZATIONS**

Although the profession of counseling is a relatively new field, still in its growing stages, its overall impact on society is growing at a tremendous rate. Increasing numbers of individuals are turning to counselors for help in dealing with the sometimes overwhelming concerns of everyday living, including job-related difficulties or unemployment, marital and family problems, lack of self-confidence, inability to make decisions, educational problems, difficulties in establishing and maintaining relationships, and many others. Thus, the vitality and potential of the counseling profession has never been greater.

At the same time, the relative youth of the profession means that the organization is still changing, redefining its basic goals and purposes as well as its role in our society. Even in defining counseling, one is faced with the fact that various authorities have seen it in different lights. These differences result not only from differences in point of view and in philosophy among the practitioners but also from historical changes and more general perceptions of this process.

## DEFINITIONS OF COUNSELING

Several elements are common to the many definitions of counseling. One is the notion that counseling is aimed at helping people make choices and act on them. A second is the notion of learning, although there are some sharp differences as to what facilitates learning and how learning occurs. Still another element is that of personality development, with relatively little agreement as to how personality development is best facilitated.

Certainly one of the most novel definitions of counseling is that of Krumboltz (1965), who states that "counseling consists of whatever ethical activities a counselor undertakes in an effort to help the client engage in those types of behavior which will lead to a resolution of the client's problems" (p. 384). This definition clearly emphasizes what the counselor is trying to accomplish—the attainment of client goals—rather than the counseling methods used.

The 1980 American Personnel and Guidance Association (APGA) Licensure Commission's licensing bill, developed to persuade state legislators to license counselors for private practice, defined counseling as ". . . the application of counseling procedures and other related areas of the behavioral sciences to help in learning how to solve problems or make decisions related to careers, personal growth, marriage, family, or other interpersonal concerns" (p. 23).

A final definition is that of Burks and Stefflre, one that seems most appropriate to us. This definition is the following:

> Counseling denotes a professional relationship between a trained counselor and a client. This relationship is usually person-to-person, although it may sometimes involve more than two people. It is designed to help clients to understand and clarify their views of their lifespace, and to learn to reach their self-determined goals through meaningful, well-informed choices and through resolution of problems of an emotional or interpersonal nature. (1979, p. 14)

This definition, although similar to many previously quoted, indicates that counseling is a relationship, is a process, and is designed to help people make choices and solve problems.

## DISTINCTIONS BETWEEN COUNSELING AND PSYCHOTHERAPY

One problem facing the counseling practitioner is that of distinguishing between counseling and psychotherapy. Indeed, efforts to distinguish between the two have not met with universal approval. Some practitioners think that such a distinction need not be made and use the two terms synonymously. Others, however, feel that such a distinction must be made. This is particularly true of those who train school counselors, since few would hold that school counselors are ordinarily trained psychotherapists.

However, once the decision to make a distinction between counseling and psychotherapy has been made, the problems begin; the edges of the distinction may blur and agreement on all the particulars is unlikely. The problem is clearly posed by Hahn (1953), who writes, "I know few counselors or psychotherapists who are completely satisfied that clear distinctions have been made" (p. 232). Hahn goes on to point out that the most complete agreements are that counseling and psychotherapy cannot be clearly distinguished; counselors practice what psychotherapists consider psychotherapy, and psychotherapists practice what counselors consider to be counseling, and despite the above, they are different.

Although the difficulty in reaching a commonly accepted definition of psychotherapy is similar to the difficulties in reaching a common definition of counseling, some attempts have been made. Blocher (1966) distinguishes between counseling and psychotherapy by pointing out that the goals of counseling are ordinarily developmental-educative-preventive, and the goals of psychotherapy are generally remediative-adjustive-therapeutic. Although Blocher suggests that there is a great deal of overlap between the two, he lists five basic assumptions about clients and counselors which he believes further differentiate counseling from psychotherapy:

1. Counseling clients are not considered to be "mentally ill," but are viewed as being capable of choosing goals, making decisions, and generally assuming responsibility for their own behavior and future development.
2. Counseling is focused on the present and the future.
3. The client is a client, not a patient. The counselor is not an authority figure but is essentially a teacher and partner of the client as they move toward mutually defined goals.
4. The counselor is not morally neutral or amoral but has values, feelings, and standards of his/her own. Although the counselor does not necessarily impose these on clients, he or she does not attempt to hide them.
5. The counselor focuses on changing behavior, not just creating insight.

It seems more likely that rather than attempting to make clear distinctions between the two, they might be best viewed as points on a continuum in regard to various elements: goals, clients, settings, practitioners, and methods. Various theorists have examined this concept of a continuum from counseling to psychotherapy. Brammer and Shostrom (1982) indicate that while the two activities may overlap, counseling in general can be characterized by such terms as "educational, vocational, supportive, situational, problem-solving, conscious awareness, normal, present time, and short-term"; psychotherapy can be characterized by such terms as "supportive (in a crisis setting), reconstructive, depth emphasis, analytical, focus on the past, emphasis on 'neurotics' or other severe emotional problems, and long-term" (pp. 6–7).

### Differences in Goals

In comparing the goals of counseling to the goals of psychotherapy, it seems apparent that a frequent goal of counseling is to help individuals deal with the developmental tasks appropriate to their age. The adolescent who is being helped with problems of sexual definition, emotional independence from parents, career decision making and preparation, and the other tasks typical of that age in our culture would be receiving counseling. A middle-aged person grappling with these same problems might appropriately be the concern of a psychotherapist.

Within the context of the continuum, the goals of psychotherapy are more likely to involve a quite complete change of basic character structure; the goals of counseling are apt to be more limited, more directed toward aiding growth, more concerned with the immediate situation, and more aimed at helping the individual function adequately in appropriate roles.

### Differences in Clients and Settings

When attempts have been made to distinguish counseling from psychotherapy on the basis of the clients each serves, the traditional view has been that the counselor deals with normal persons and the psychotherapist deals with neurotic or psychotic persons. Such a distinction, of course, has many of the same built-in problems in the definition of "normal" as are involved in the distinction between counseling and psychotherapy.

Perhaps part of the difficulty in distinguishing on the basis of the clients served occurs because of the differences in settings. Psychotherapists are more apt to work in hospital settings or in private practice; counselors are more apt to work in educational settings. However, as counselors become employed in a wider range of settings and more psychotherapists are employed in school systems and colleges, such a distinction becomes less meaningful. Thus, although counseling may occur more often in educational institutions and psychotherapy more often in medical settings, we cannot always determine which activity is going on by knowing where it is happening.

We take the view that both counseling and psychotherapy utilize a common base of knowledge and a common set of techniques. Both involve a therapeutic process but they differ in terms of the severity of the client's situation, in terms of the client's level of problem and/or functioning. Since the process does not change—only the situation or the client's concern may—we use the terms interchangeably, although we general-ly use the term *counseling* in this book.

### Differences in Training

Some practitioners of counseling may be trained at the doctoral level with a supervised internship, as psychotherapists are. But many counselors have less train-ing, with relatively little psychology and little or no formal supervised internship. Such individuals may think of themselves as psychotherapists and see little distinction be-tween the two fields. However, more objective observers distinguish between counsel-ing and psychotherapy on the basis of the extent of training in personality theory, in research methods, and in the formal internship.

## GOALS OF COUNSELING

What is the expected result from counseling? Certainly individuals have different per-ceptions of what can be expected. Individuals preparing to become counselors, those who seek counseling, parents, teachers, school administrators, and governmental agen-cies all differ in what they hope will result from the counseling experience. Such expec-tations are, of course, germane to the counseling process. However, the ultimate decision about what the goals of counseling shall be must rest with the counselor and the client as a team.

### Five Major Goals

As you will discover in the chapters on the various counseling theories, counsel-ing theorists have not always agreed on appropriate counseling goals. Statements of counseling goals are often general, vague, and saturated with implications. However, the following five major goals are often stated: (1) facilitating behavior change, (2) im-proving the client's ability to establish and maintain relationships, (3) enhancing the client's effectiveness and ability to cope, (4) promoting the decision-making process, and (5) facilitating client potential and development. These goals are not mutually ex-clusive, and some are emphasized more often by some theorists than by others.

*Facilitating Behavior Change*   Almost all theorists indicate that the goal of counseling is to bring about a change in behavior which will enable the client to live a more productive, satisfying life as the client defines it within society's limitations. The way theorists talk about behavior change varies greatly, however. Rogers (1961) sees behavior change as a necessary result of the counseling process, although specific behaviors receive little or no emphasis during the counseling experience.

Dustin and George (1977), on the other hand, suggest that the counselor must establish specific counseling goals. They believe that a shift from general goals to specific goals enables both the client and the counselor to understand precisely the specific change

**Figure 1-1**   A man discusses his problem with a family counselor    (Color Image Inc., Jim Trotter)

that is desired. They point out that specific behavioral goals have an additional value: The client is better able to see any change that occurs.

Krumboltz (1966) suggests three criteria for judging counseling goals. They are the following: (1) The goals of counseling should be capable of being stated differently for each individual client; (2) The goals of counseling for each client should be compatible with, though not necessarily identical to, the values of his counselor; and (3) The degree to which the goals of counseling are attained by each client should be observable.

*Enhancing Coping Skills*    Almost all individuals run into difficulties in the process of growing up. Few of us completely achieve all of our developmental tasks, and the various unique expectations and requirements imposed on us by significant others often lead to problems. Certainly, inconsistency on the part of significant others can result in children's learning behavior patterns that are inefficient, ineffective, or both. These learned coping patterns may serve the individual well in most situations, but in time, new interpersonal or occupational role demands may create an overload and produce excessive anxiety and difficulty for the individual. Helping individuals learn to cope with new situations and new demands is an important goal of counseling.

*Promoting Decision Making*    To some, the goal of counseling is to enable the individual to make critical decisions. It is not the counselor's job, they say, to decide which decisions the client should make or to choose alternate courses of action. The decisions are the client's, and the client must know why and how the decision was made.

The client learns to estimate the probable consequences in personal sacrifice, time, energy, money, risk, and the like. The client also learns to explore the range of values that are related to the situation and to bring these values into full consciousness in the decision-making process.

Counseling helps individuals obtain information and clarify and sort out personal characteristics and emotional concerns that may interfere with or be related to the decisions involved. It helps these individuals acquire an understanding not only of their abilities, interests, and opportunities but also of the emotions and attitudes that can influence their choices and decisions.

*Improving Relationships*  Much of one's life is spent in social interaction with other individuals, yet many clients have a major problem relating to other people. This problem may be conceptualized as the result of the client's poor self-image, which causes him or her to act defensively in relationships, or it may be seen as the result of inadequate social skills. Whatever the theoretical approach, counselors work with clients to help them improve the quality of their relationships with others. Difficulties with relationships can range from the family and marital problems of adults to the peer group interaction difficulties of the elementary school child. In every case the counselor is striving to help the clients improve the quality of their lives by becoming more effective in their interpersonal relationships.

*Facilitating the Client's Potential*  Developing the client's potential is a frequently emphasized, although ambiguous, counseling goal. Certainly few theorists would disagree with the idea that counseling seeks to promote the growth and development of clients by giving them the opportunity to learn ways to use their abilities and interests to the maximum. This goal can be viewed as one of improving personal effectiveness. Blocher (1966) suggests that first, counseling seeks to maximize an individual's possible freedom within the limitations supplied by himself and his environment, and second, counseling seeks to maximize the individual's effectiveness by giving him control over his environment and the responses within him that are evoked by the environment.

Such an emphasis means that counselors work to help people learn how to overcome excessive smoking or drinking, to take better care of their bodies, and to overcome shyness, stress, and depression. They help people to learn how to overcome sexual dysfunctions, drug addiction, compulsive gambling, overweight, and fears and anxieties. At the same time, counselors can help people with their interpersonal problems, with emotional problems, and with the development of learning and decision-making skills (Krumboltz & Thoresen, 1976).

### Commonality of Goals

The previous description of the kinds of goals that various counselors emphasize fails to recognize certain points about counseling goals. First, as Shertzer and Stone

(1974) point out, the goals expressed by differing counseling theorists may reflect their own needs rather than those of the clients. Blackham (1977), however, suggests that while the counselor does provide some direction for the counseling process, both counselor and client decide which goals are to be pursued and how.

Second, perhaps there are more likenesses than differences among the statements of counseling goals. Certainly all of the theorists seem to recognize the broader goal of helping the client to feel better, to function at a higher level, to achieve more, and to live up to his or her potential.

Third, the focus of all counseling goals is the achievement of personal effectiveness that is both satisfactory to the individual and within society's limitations. Thus many of the presumed differences in counseling goals shrink in importance and become simply differences in terms of the criteria used to judge the counselor's effectiveness. In addition, the differences in the way counseling goals are formulated may result from the differences in the way counselors attempt to help clients.

### Client Expectations

Before leaving the subject of counseling goals, it is important to note that whether or not a particular counseling experience will be worthwhile to the client will depend on the client's expectations. The client's lack of clearcut understanding of the nature of counseling is a widespread source of inadequate readiness to attack problems. Along with knowing such practical information as length of interviews, probable length of the process, or how to make appointments, the client should understand the limitations and possibilities of counseling. Moreover, the counselor must be aware of his or her own expectations and should encourage clients to talk about their expectations for the counseling experience.

The majority of clients expect counseling to produce personal solutions for them. Those in stressful situations expect that counseling will bring relief. Those who are having difficulty making a particular decision expect counseling to result in a choice. Those who are lonely expect solace and expect to discover ways of improving their interactions with others. Those who want to go to college may view counseling as guaranteeing them admission or even financial aid. Those who are about to fail, either in school or in other ventures, expect failure to turn into success as the result of counseling. Those who seek employment counseling expect quick placement, job satisfaction, and easy promotion (Shertzer & Stone, 1974).

Many clients expect to have something done *to* or *for* them as part of the counseling process. Counselors must communicate to clients that ultimately it is the client who acts, decides, changes, becomes. In addition clients often seek counseling in crisis situations, hoping to find remediation, whereas counselors operate with goals that imply that counseling should be preventive or growth inducing. In these situations counselors must learn to respond to the immediate needs of the client while working toward some intermediate or ultimate goals through the counseling process.

## HISTORICAL DEVELOPMENT
## OF THE COUNSELING PROFESSION

Counseling has emerged and developed as an American product of the twentieth century. Its acceptance and widespread use in the United States far exceeds that of other countries, partially because of the American emphasis on the importance of the individual and partially because of American affluence, which allows our society to afford it.

### Vocational Guidance Movement

Although no single date can mark the beginning of the counseling movement, counseling may well have begun in 1898 when Jesse B. Davis worked as a counselor with high school students in Detroit. His work with these students' educational and vocational problems is a clear illustration of the early ties of counseling to vocational guidance. Another early pioneer of the movement was Frank Parsons, who founded a vocation bureau in 1908 in Boston, which eventually led to the National Vocational Guidance Association in 1913. One year after Parsons's vocation bureau opened its doors, it established a direct connection with the Boston schools, allying counseling with education as the schools used the services of the new bureau (Rossberg & Bond, 1978). During this same period dozens of other schools were experimenting with counseling concepts.

### Mental Health Movement

During the same period, other professional developments evolved independently and merged to help form the modern approach to counseling. In particular, the development of the mental health movement became an important part of the whole emphasis on counseling. A book by Clifford Beers, *A Mind That Found Itself,* was published in 1908 and made a profound impression on an awakening society and on the counseling movement. The book sparked concern for the individual; school children came to be viewed as growing, developing organisms and as pliable receptacles for rote memory tasks. In 1909 Beers also supplied the leadership for the formation of the National Committee for Mental Hygiene, which was responsible for or contributed to significant innovations in legislative reform, aftercare, and free clinics for the mentally ill.

During the 1920s and 1930s scientific journals and organizations and child study centers designed to promote the well-being of children came into existence, primarily as the result of the work of G. Stanley Hall of Clark University. Hall, who was a leader in collecting data related to different phases of the mental life of all ages, was also credited with introducing Freudian concepts of child development into American education and psychology. This child-study movement was fourfold: (1) it emphasized the individual as the focal point of study; (2) it stressed the importance of the formative years as the foundation for mature personality development; (3) it pointed out the need for reliable, factual knowledge about children; and (4) it led to better controlled, more analytical and accurate methods of child study (Shertzer & Stone, 1974).

### Standardized Testing

In many ways, developments in mental measurements and other types of human assessment formed the basis for the early technology of counseling practice. Prior to World War I technical efforts in human assessment were basically restricted to the work of individual researchers attempting to measure individual differences in performance on a variety of tasks. The Binet Scales and the American revisions, the appearance of group intelligence tests, and the administration of the first standardized achievement tests are examples of the kind of work that was done to predict success in areas such as academic performance. Interest inventories such as the Strong Vocational Interest Blank emerged. Testing of special aptitudes in music, mechanics, and art was initiated and refined.

Following World War II test ''batteries'' and large-scale testing programs emerged. But by 1960 many had become highly critical of the practice of using such tests for educational and job selection, believing that current tests penalized members of minority groups who had not had equal educational opportunities.

The testing movement has had a profound influence on counseling: It led to the objective study of individual differences; it enabled scientific investigations to be made into the problems of intelligence; and it facilitated prediction, classification, and placement of individuals. Standardized testing gave the new profession tools that were practical and usable at a time when the tools were needed.

### Federal Legislation

Legislation affecting the profession began with the 1917 Smith-Hughes Act and the 1918 Vocational Rehabilitation Act. Both contained provisions either explicitly or implicitly providing for the vocational preparation, education, and guidance of young men and women and veterans. A number of acts passed in the late 1920s and 1930s dealt with vocational education and paved the way for establishing guidance divisions within state departments of education. In 1938 the U.S. Office of Education created the Occupational Information and Guidance Services Bureau. Its publications and research efforts consistently stressed the need for school counselors and the services they provide. Other federal acts gave support to counseling in settings ranging from rehabilitation centers to community agencies.

Two significant pieces of legislation at about midcentury gave still stronger impetus to counseling. The first was the extension of the Vocation Rehabilitation Legislation in 1954, which itself was an extensive revision of the earlier vocational rehabilitation acts. Among other things, it provided enabling legislation and financial support for an extensive program to educate rehabilitation counselors. It provided a legislative mandate for the development of counselors who specialized in assisting the disabled and created a federal source of support that since its inception has provided direct assistance for the education of several thousand counselors and has indirectly affected an equal number in the field.

The second piece of legislation, the National Defense Education Act (NDEA) of 1958, provided funds to strengthen school guidance programs and train school counselors. In 1964 Congress amended Title V of the NDEA to include the preparation of elementary school counselors in institute programs, and financial support was given to elementary school guidance programs at the local level. This amendment also provided funds for the preparation of counselors for higher education settings. Other notable pieces of legislation include the Vocational Education Act of 1963, the 1968 amendments, and subsequent amendments.

## PROFESSIONAL ORGANIZATIONS

The primary organization representing counselors is the American Association for Counseling and Development (formerly the American Personnel and Guidance Association), organized in 1951 by merging the National Vocational Guidance Association, the American College Personnel Association, and the National Association of Guidance Supervisors and Counselor Trainers. The organization currently has thirteen divisions, allowing counselors to belong to the one or more divisions that relate to their work. Another professional group is the Division of Counseling Psychology of the American Psychological Association. Professional organizations also exist at the state and local area levels.

Involvement in professional groups permits counselors to support the standards and policies of these organizations. In addition, counselors can meet with and learn from other members, take part in conferences and in-service workshops, and benefit from publications, placement services, and public relations efforts, including lobbying for relevant legislation. Membership and participation in professional organizations is a primary way for counselors to remain up-to-date and to actively support their profession.

## THE COUNSELOR AS A PERSON

Before we can focus on what happens with the client during the counseling process, we should consider the other person involved in therapeutic intervention—the counselor. In their professional behavior, counselors draw on three somewhat different areas: personal qualities, professional knowledge, and specific counseling skills. These three areas combine to determine counseling effectiveness. Thus, the qualities of the counselor as a *person*, as opposed to what he actually does during counseling, require special attention. Are certain individual characteristics likely to enable the counselor to become more effective? If so, what are these qualities?

Counseling theorists and researchers have given these questions as much attention as any other question in the field of counseling. Despite the vast amount of research, the exact qualities that distinguish an effective counselor from an ineffective one still remain somewhat uncertain. Part of the difficulty is semantic. Words to identify clearly the specific human traits essential in effective counseling are still lacking. Such words as *accepting, open, warm, genuine, flexible,* and *sincere* are the closest we can come, and the meanings of these words have been polluted by their everyday use to convey a large variety of qualities. Such terms no longer have specific meanings; the meanings often overlap and are ambiguous.

We also continue to have difficulty defining and measuring counselor effectiveness. As we will see in Chapter 14, no universally accepted method for measuring effectiveness has been devised, largely due to the many different conceptualizations of counseling goals. Attempts to construct a widely accepted objective rating scale have had only limited success.

Despite these problems, a great deal is known about qualities that significantly contribute to counselor effectiveness. The basic premise is that while effective counseling requires certain behaviors or core conditions, the personal traits of the counselor are also extremely important variables.

### Personal Characteristics of Counselors

Several years ago, the National Vocational Guidance Association (1949) proposed that general characteristics of counselors include a deep interest in people and patience with them, sensitivity to the attitudes and the actions of others, emotional sta-

**Figure 1-2**   The influence of the peer group must be recognized by the counselor (Color Image, Inc., Jim Trotter)

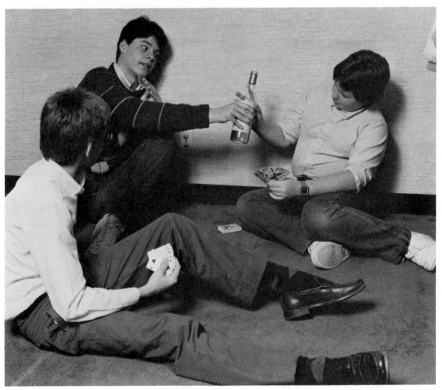

bility and objectivity, a capacity for being trusted by others, and respect for facts. Later, the Association for Counselor Education and Supervision (1964) indicated that the counselor should have six basic qualities: belief in each individual, commitment to individual human values, alertness to the world, open-mindedness, understanding of self, and professional commitment.

Combs and his coworkers (1969) concluded from a series of studies that the major differences between effective and ineffective counselors were their personal beliefs and traits. These findings led Combs to conclude that the major "technique" of counseling was the "self-as-instrument"; the counselor's self or person became the major facilitator of positive growth for clients. In addition, Combs studied some basic beliefs that counselors held concerning people and their ability to help themselves. He found that effective counselors perceived other people as *able* rather than unable to solve their own problems and manage their own lives. Effective counselors also perceived people as *dependable, friendly,* and *worthy.* They were also more likely to identify with *people* rather than things, to see people as having an adequate *capacity to cope* with problems, and to be more *self-revealing* than self-concealing.

Combs and Soper (1963) found that effective counselors perceived their clients as capable, dependable, friendly, and worthy, and perceived themselves as altruistic and nondominating. Rogers (1961) concluded from his experiences and his reviews of research that the counselor's theory and methods were far less important than the client's perception of the counselor's attitudes. Rogers was pointing out that the effective counselor must be an attractive, friendly person, someone who inspires confidence and trust.

The research suggests that one approach to determining counselor effectiveness would be to look for characteristics of personal effectiveness. Allen found that "the effective counselor is a person who is on relatively good terms with his own emotional experience and that the ineffective counselor is one who is relatively uneasy in regard to the character of his inner life" (1967, p. 39).

## A Composite Model of Human Effectiveness

Thus an analysis of personal characteristics of effective counselors must begin with an analysis of the characteristics of effective persons. Over the years, a number of models of human effectiveness have been presented (See ASCD, 1962); a composite model can be drawn from these models of effectiveness. This is not a "perfection" model; rather, these are characteristics that are generally found in effective counselors and that counselors are continually striving to attain. The list is incomplete and still evolving. The model is proposed as a stimulus for present and prospective counselors to examine their own ideas of what personal qualities they need to become effective counselors. These same qualities may also be seen as goals for clients to attain as a result of the counseling process. What are these personal characteristics of effective counselors?

*Effective counselors are open to and accepting of their own experiences.* Such individuals do not try to control their emotional reactions but are able to accept their feelings as they are. *Openness,* as used in this context, means being open to oneself, not necessarily revealing oneself to everyone with whom one comes in contact.

Much of our experience teaches us to deny our feelings. Small boys are told,

"There, there, now, big boys don't cry!" Even adults are admonished, "Now, don't cry!" or "Don't be nervous! You have nothing to worry about." Pressures are applied not to feel depressed or not to be angry or not to be frustrated. Effective counselors can accept within themselves feelings of sadness, anger, resentment, and other feelings ordinarily considered negative. By accepting these feelings as they are, without denying or distorting them, effective counselors have greater control of their behavior. Because they are aware of their emotional reactions, they can choose how they wish to act, rather than permitting their feelings to affect their behavior without their conscious awareness.

Persons learn to be accepting of their experiences (1) if the significant individuals in their lives model such acceptance and (2) if they are not punished for such acceptance. Counselors have a positive effect on clients when their clients see them as accepting of both their own and the clients' undesired emotional reactions—boredom, anger, anxiety, depression. Accepting the idea that clients have the right to hold negative feelings is far more effective in promoting positive growth than telling clients that they are foolish to feel the way they do, logical though such arguments may be.

*Effective counselors are aware of their own values and beliefs.* They know what is important to them and have determined the standards by which they wish to live. Thus, they can make decisions and choose alternatives that are consistent with their value systems. More important, a clear value system allows individuals to find a meaningful role for their lives and gives them guidelines for relating to the people and things around them. They can avoid ineffective and inconsistent patterns of behavior and instead engage in more positive, purposeful, and rewarding behavior.

---

**Box 1-1**  *Personal Characteristics of Effective Counselors*

1. Are open to, and accepting of, their own experiences
2. Are aware of their own values and beliefs
3. Are able to develop warm and deep relationships with others
4. Are able to allow themselves to be seen by others as they actually are
5. Accept personal responsibility for their own behaviors
6. Have developed realistic levels of aspiration

---

*Effective counselors are able to develop warm and deep relationships with others.* They can prize other individuals—their feelings, their opinions, their persons. This feeling is caring, but a nonpossessive caring with little evaluation or judgment; the other person is accepted with few conditions. Such warmth or caring is not widespread. Most people experience a certain amount of fear toward feeling warmth toward another person. We fear that if we let ourselves freely experience such positive feelings toward another, we will become trapped and therefore vulnerable. Other persons may take advantage of us; they may make demands that we are unable to reject; they may reject our feelings by failing to reciprocate. So we keep our distance, rarely permitting ourselves to get close to someone.

Effective counselors are less vulnerable to such fears because they recognize that the risk involved is worth the value to be gained. They therefore respond to other people more freely, developing close relationships with those who share their interests and values. They have wide freedom of choice in developing such relationships because of their ability to care and their relative lack of fear towards caring.

*Effective counselors are able to allow themselves to be seen by others as they actually are.* This characteristic results in an attitude of realness or genuineness. When individuals gain awareness of and accept the feelings they are experiencing, they need not impose feelings on others nor put up a facade to make people think they are something they are not. Authentic persons are willing to be themselves and to express, in their words and in their behavior, the various feelings and attitudes they hold. They do not need to present an outward facade of one attitude while holding another attitude at a deeper level. They do not pretend to know the answers when they do not. They do not act like loving persons at moments when they feel hostile. They do not act as though they are confident and full of assurance when they are actually frightened and unsure. On a simpler level, they do not act well when they feel ill.

Part of the difficulty for most individuals is that energy spent on playing a role or presenting a facade prevents them from using that energy for accomplishing tasks and solving problems. In addition, effective persons, by presenting their authentic selves to others, are more able to develop cooperative relationships with others, thus gaining support for problem-solving tasks. They have less need to puff up their own importance, to blow their own horn. They can share the limelight; therefore, they are able to secure the help of others.

*Effective counselors accept personal responsibility for their own behaviors.* Rather than denying the way they are and blaming others, effective counselors can handle their failures and weaknesses. They recognize that, while many situations are largely caused by factors beyond their control, they are responsible for their actions in these situations. Recognizing that they can determine, in large part, their own behavior gives them the freedom to consciously choose either to conform to external group control or to ignore those controls, with that choice based on well-considered reasons.

This acceptance of personal responsibility also means that these individuals are able to accept criticism in a much more constructive way. Instead of constantly defending themselves, effective counselors view criticism as a desirable feedback mechanism permitting them to lead more effective, constructive lives. They stand by their behaviors rather than "passing the buck" or blaming others.

*Effective counselors have developed realistic levels of aspiration.* Ordinarily, persons raise their goals slightly as a result of success and lower their goals after failure. In this way they protect themselves from both too easy achievement and continued failure. Sometimes this self-protective mechanism is thrown out of balance, and individuals either set their goals too high, which results in inevitable failure, or too low, which robs them of a sense of achievement, no matter what they do.

Effective counselors, on the other hand, are able to set obtainable goals and take failure in stride. Because they are aware of their own skills and abilities, they can accurately estimate what to expect from themselves. Their acceptance of their experiences—both positive and negative—enables them to evaluate previous goals realistically and to use this evaluation to establish future goals.

## THE COUNSELOR'S VALUES

As was previously pointed out, counselors must understand their own values and the values of others. No one set of values is superior to others. Every person has a set of beliefs that determines the decisions they make, their ability to appreciate the things around them, their consciences, and their perceptions of others. Since the counselor's values are an integral part of his personality and, therefore, a part of his professional role, we are particularly concerned with how those values contribute to the counseling process (Belkin, 1984).

Values serve as reference points for individuals. They provide a basis for determining which course of action an individual should take. Individuals have always needed these guidelines to provide structure and meaning in their lives and to avoid an existence of "running around in circles."

### Influence of Counselor's Values on Client's Values

A key issue is whether or not counselors can avoid conveying their values to their clients. Some maintain that the counselor should remain neutral while counseling and communicate no value orientation to the client. In such a situation counselors would strive to appear nonmoralizing and ethically neutral in their counseling; they would focus on the client's values. Such counselors would know their own value systems but would avoid introducing these values into the counseling interview. They would not indicate their own position on any of the moral or value areas that arise. The basic belief supporting this position is that in any counseling situation the client must move from a position of outside evaluation by others to a position of internalized self-evaluation. Any value input by the counselor would work against this objective.

Williamson (1958) called for an abandonment of this position in favor of an open and explicit value orientation in counseling. He suggested that attempts to be neutral in value situations could easily lead the client to believe that the counselor accepted unlawful behavior and even condoned it. Such a situation could lead to the client's feeling that the counselor supported behavior that is completely unacceptable by any social, moral, or legal standards.

In support of Williamson's position, Samler (1960) states that a change in values constitutes a counseling goal and that counselor intervention in the client's values is an actuality to be accepted as a necessary part of the counseling process. He urges counselors to develop an awareness of their own values and to clarify how these values might relate to their own counselor-client interaction.

Patterson (1958) points out that the counselor's values influence the ethics of the counseling relationships, the goals of counseling, and the methods employed in counseling. Patterson cites evidence for the assertion that, no matter how passive and valueless the counselor appears, the client's value system is influenced and gradually becomes more similar to the counselor's value system. However, Patterson suggests that counselors are not justified in consciously and directly imposing their values on clients, for these reasons:

1. Each individual's philosophy on life is different, unique, and unsuited to adoption by another.
2. All counselors cannot be expected to have a fully developed, adequate philosophy on life.
3. The appropriate places for instruction in values are the home, school, and church.
4. An individual develops a code of ethics, not from a single source or in a short period of time, but over a long time and from many influences.
5. No one ought to be prevented from developing her or his own unique philosophy since it will be more meaningful to her or him; and
6. The client must have the right to refuse to accept any ethic or philosophy of life. (1958, pp. 216–223)

Such disagreements have led to extensive research into the nature and desirability of the influence of counselor values upon clients. Rosenthal (1955) contended that some types of counselor values invariably influence the client. He suggested that most counselors believe that the counselor's values should be kept out of therapy as much as possible, but his own research results indicated that those clients who improved most changed their moral values to conform more closely with the values of their counselor. In an experiment using the *Study of Values* test, Cook, (1966) found that differences in the counselors' and clients' value systems affected counseling outcome. He found that when clients were grouped by how similar their values were to the values of the counselor, clients who were in a medium similarity group improved more than those in either high similarity or low similarity groups. These findings suggest that when the counselor or client perceives his world as being too similar to or too different from that of the other, it has an adverse effect upon their interactions.

In another area of values, Lee (1968) found that social class bias influenced psychiatric residents' diagnosis of patients; however, a subsequent study by Routh and King (1972) questioned these findings. Fitzgibbons and Shearn (1972) also found that the professional background of the therapist had an important influence on whether the therapist judged a patient schizophrenic or not. Thus, some evidence suggests that what might be considered a cognitive value is in fact culturally relative.

Counselors do expose their values to clients. Since counselors are in an intimate relationship with their clients, their values will be a part of that interaction, either consciously or unconsciously (Rokeach & Regan, 1980). Counselors cannot pretend that they do not possess a value system or that they are something other than what they really are. The issue is to what degree counselors expose those values and influence the client.

### Importance of Valuing Human Freedom

Counselors must be committed to some values in order to maintain meaningfulness in their lives. Belkin (1984) suggests that the primary value to which counselors must commit themselves is freedom. Freedom is an ideal that propels the individual to certain types of actions. Freedom allows the individual to determine what direction in which to move. It allows the individual to be creative, to make choices and be responsible for them. Freedom also commits the client to assuming responsibility for his action and its consequences.

## THE ROLE OF THE COUNSELOR

A lack of understanding about the counselor's role has unquestionably reduced the counselor's effectiveness in our schools and agencies. Much of this lack of understanding has come about because counselors fail to define clearly the roles they fill, perhaps because of an extreme desire to please others and to meet whatever needs others may bring to them. Yet much of what happens during counseling is a result of what the client expects the counselor to do. Frequently, clients seek counseling because they expect the counselor to solve their problems—to tell them whether to get a divorce, quit school, or attend the state university. But counselors have generally recognized that they cannot tell others how to live their lives. Thus, at the very beginning conflict arises between the clients' expectations and the counselors' in terms of the goals of their relationship.

The school or agency where the counselor works also has some expectations concerning the role the counselor will assume. Frequently the school or agency expects the counselor to represent that institution and to interact with clients in a way that meets the goals of the institution, even at the expense of neglecting the needs and goals of the individual client. Counselors in such situations often feel a great deal of frustration and guilt. They complain bitterly about the failure of the administration to permit them to perform their role in the most effective way. However, if counselors are to be able to operate most effectively, they must recognize the need to clarify their roles and communicate those roles to both the clients and the institution they serve.

In any institution counselors may attempt to fill varied counseling roles. These roles are not mutually exclusive; in fact they are often supportive. However, the counselor must determine which role or roles seem most plausible in that particular situation. As an example of this multiplicity of roles, Gibson and Mitchell (1981) present an excellent analysis of the various roles of the school counselor.

Counselors in many settings share similar frustrations in defining their role and functions. However, the basic function of all counselors, regardless of setting, was clearly stated by Wrenn:

> the function of the counselor in any setting is a) to provide a *relationship* between counselor and counselee, the most prominent quality of which is that of mutual trust of each other in the other; b) to provide *alternatives* in self-understanding and in the courses of action open to the client; c) to provide for *some degree of intervention* of the situation in which the client finds himself and with "important others" in the client's immediate life; d) to provide leadership in developing *a healthy psychological environment* for his clients, and finally e) to provide for *improvement of the counseling process* through constant individual criticism and (for some counselors) extensive attention to improvement of process through research. (1965, p. 327)

Thus, counselors must work toward a personally defined role that takes into account the expectations of their clients, the regulations of their institution, and their own personal understanding of their professional role. This role definition can best be facilitated by discussing differences in expectations with appropriate institutional personnel, then providing clear communication of the counselor's roles to staff and clients alike.

## SUMMARY

Counseling is viewed as a relationship, as well as a process, and is designed to help people make choices and resolve problems.

Although the distinction between counseling and psychotherapy is difficult to state clearly, differences between the two exist and may best be analyzed by viewing the activities of the two as taking place along a continuum. Counseling is most characterized by terms such as *educational, preventive, short-term,* and *problem-solving;* psychotherapy is more often characterized by terms such as *reconstructive, emphasis on severe emotional problems, remediation,* and *long-term.*

Five general goals of counseling are (1) facilitating behavior change, (2) improving the client's ability to establish and maintain relationships, (3) enhancing the client's ability to cope, (4) promoting the decision-making process, and (5) facilitating client potential and development.

Counseling as a professional activity can be traced back to 1898, when it began as a vocational guidance movement. Other mental health movements contributed to the growth of counseling, as did the development of testing programs. Legislation in the 1950s was particularly important in giving stronger impetus to counseling.

Counseling services are provided by individuals involved in a number of different professions, including social work, psychiatry, clinical psychology, and clergy.

A composite model identified six personal characteristics of effective counselors. Such counselors

1. Are open to, and accepting of, their own experiences
2. Are aware of their own values and beliefs
3. Are able to develop warm and deep relationships with others
4. Are able to allow themselves to be seen by others as they actually are
5. Are accepting of personal responsibility for their own behavior
6. Have realistic levels of aspiration

The importance of valuing the personal freedom of clients underlies the values issue. This emphasizes the importance of clients' determining the directions in which they wish to move, making their own choices, and accepting responsibility for their choices and resulting action. In so doing, counselors must avoid insensitivity to cultural differences and personal life-styles that may differ from social norms.

Counselors must work toward giving the institutions in which they work and the clients they serve a better understanding of their role. This role must be personally defined within the institutional guidelines and clearly communicated both to the institution and to the clients.

# REFERENCES

ALLEN, T. (1967). Effectiveness of counselor trainees as a function of psychological openness. *Journal of Counseling Psychology, 14,* 35–40.

American Personnel and Guidance Association. (1980). *Licensure Committee action packet.* Washington, D.C.

Association for Counselor Education and Supervision. (1964). The counselor: Professional preparation and role. *Personnel and Guidance Journal, 42,* 536–541.

BELKIN, G. (1984). *Introduction to counseling.* (2nd ed.). Dubuque, Iowa: Wm. C. Brown.

BLACKHAM, G.J. (1977). *Counseling: Theory, process and practice.* Belmont, Calif.: Wadsworth.

BLOCHER, D.H. (1966). *Developmental counseling.* New York: Ronald Press.

BRAMMER, L.M., and SHOSTROM, E.L. (1982). *Therapeutic psychology: Fundamentals of Counseling and Psychotherapy,* (4th ed.). Englewood Cliffs, N.J.: Prentice-Hall.

BURKS H.M. and STEFFLRE, B. (1979). *Theories of counseling* (3rd ed.). New York: McGraw-Hill.

COMBS, A.; SOPER, D.; GOODING, C.; BENTON, J.; DICKMAN, J.; and USHER, R. (1969). *Florida Studies in the helping professions.* Gainesville: University of Florida Press.

COMBS, A., and SOPER, D. (1963). The perceptual organization of effective counselors. *Journal of Counseling Psychology, 10,* 222–226.

COOK, T. (1966). The influence of client-counselor value similarity on change in meaning during brief counseling. *Journal of Counseling Psychology, 13,* 77–81.

DUSTIN, R., and GEORGE, R. (1977). *Action counseling for behavior change.* (2nd ed.). Cranston, R.I.: Carroll Press.

FITZGIBBONS, D., and SHEARN, C. (1972). Concepts of schizophrenia among mental health professionals: A factor-analysis study. *Journal of Consulting and Clinical Psychology, 38,* 228–295.

GIBSON, R., and MITCHELL, M. (1981). *Introduction to guidance.* New York: Macmillan.

HAHN, M.E. (1953). Conceptual trends in counseling. *Personnel and Guidance Journal, 31,* 231–235.

KRUMBOLTZ, J.D. (1965). Behavioral counseling: Rationale and research. *Personnel and Guidance Journal, 44,* 383–387.

KRUMBOLTZ, J.D. (1966). Behavioral goals of counseling. *Journal of Counseling Psychology, 13,* 153–159.

KRUMBOLTZ, J.D., & THORESEN, C.E. (Eds.). (1976). *Counseling methods.* New York: Holt, Rinehart & Winston.

National Vocational Guidance Association. (1949). *Counselor preparation.* Washington: National Vocational Guidance Association.

PATTERSON, C. (1958). The place of values in counseling and psychotherapy. *Journal of Counseling Psychology, 5,* 216–223.

PATTERSON, C.H. (1980). *Theories of counseling and psychotherapy* (3rd ed.). New York: Harper & Row.

ROGERS, C. (1961). *On becoming a person.* Boston: Houghton Mifflin.

ROKEACH, M., and REGAN, J.F. (1980). The role of values in the counseling situation. *Personnel and Guidance Journal, 58,* 576–582.

ROSENTHAL, D. (1955). Changes in some moral values following psychotherapy. *Journal of Consulting Psychology, 19,* 431–436.

ROSSBERG, R.H., and BAND, L. (1978). Historical antecedents of counseling: A revisionist point of view. In J.C. Hansen (Ed.), *Counseling process and procedures.* New York: Macmillan.

ROUTH, D., and KING, K. (1972). Social class bias in clinical judgment. *Journal of Consulting and Clinical Psychology, 38,* 202–207.

SAMLER, J. (1960). Change in values: A goal in counseling. *Journal of Counseling Psychology, 7,* 32–39.

SHERTZER, B., and STONE, S.C. (1974). *Fundamentals of counseling* (2nd ed.). Boston: Houghton Mifflin.

WILLIAMSON, E. (1958). Value orientation in counseling. *Personnel and Guidance Journal, 36,* 520–528.

WRENN, C. (1965). Crisis in counseling: A commentary and a contribution. In J. McGowan (Ed.). *Counselor development in American society.* Washington: U.S. Department of Labor and U.S. Office of Education.

# 2

# FOUNDATIONS
# OF COUNSELING

**PHILOSOPHICAL FOUNDATIONS**

> Importance of an Integrated Philosophical System
> Belief in the Dignity and Worth of the Individual
> Arbuckle's Philosophical Model
> Blocher's Grouping of Relevant Philosophical Systems

**SOCIOLOGICAL FOUNDATIONS**

> Influence of Social Organizations on Individuals
> Socialization Processes
> Development of Social/Cultural Values

**PSYCHOLOGICAL FOUNDATIONS**

> Social Psychology
> The Concept of Self
> Goal-Directed Behavior
> Learning Principles

**DEVELOPMENTAL PSYCHOLOGY**

> Stages of Development

**SUMMARY**

As a relatively new discipline, the theory and practice of counseling has drawn on insights from other disciplines, including philosophy, psychology, sociology, and the other social sciences. These disciplines have provided both data and comprehensive hypotheses that counselors have used to clarify the theoretical structures underlying the whole counseling process. Before reviewing the major counseling approaches, a brief summary of some of the relevant ideas and characteristics of these disciplines will be presented.

# PHILOSOPHICAL FOUNDATIONS

## Importance of an Integrated Philosophical System

Although counseling theorists often refer to the counselor's philosophical orientation, they rarely discuss it in depth. There is, however, reason to compare the integrated philosophical system to the integrated personality. Most theorists agree that in a healthy personality the different aspects of the individual are integrated. In a healthy personality the individual has a realistic perception of himself, his desires are in keeping with his moral code, and he has defined and clarified his values—he knows what he wants and how much he wants it. Such an individual has developed a harmonious relationship between all aspects of his needs and desires. From a philosophical standpoint, this means that a goal of counseling is to help individuals to reach their maximum potential, which can occur only when they develop consistent philosophical outlooks.

Psychologists have often argued that philosophy has no place in the scientific study of human behavior, though it seems to be a pervasive aspect of the individual. However, May (1967) points out that every scientific method rests on philosophical presuppositions. These presuppositions determine not only how much reality the scientist can observe with his particular method, but also whether what is observed is relevant to real problems and therefore whether any scientific work will endure.

## Belief in the Dignity and Worth of the Individual

One theme is found consistently in the literature discussing the philosophy of counseling: belief in the dignity and worth of the individual, in the recognition of the individual's freedom in determining his own values and goals, and in the client's right to pursue his own life-style. Two writers as different in orientation as Patterson (1958) and Williamson (1958) agree that counselors inevitably influence their clients' values. For counselors to attempt to deny responsibility for changes that occur in their clients would be to admit their total ineffectiveness. Research by individuals such as Rosenthal (1955) tends to support the position that clients' values and attitudes do change during counseling and even suggests that they become increasingly similar to the counselor's own values. This information, rather than denying the idea of individual freedom and responsibility, points out the concern counselors must have regarding their unplanned, inadvertent impact on the client.

Philosophical positions of interest to counselors have long historical roots. A number of beliefs, more correctly described as attitudes than positions, have emerged from Western civilization philosophies. These beliefs center around the concept of *individualism.* Its first aspect is the importance accorded the individual. Over the past several thousand years, the idea has evolved that the individual has value in and of himself, not just because of what the person can accomplish. This attitude provides the basis for the idea that an individual may develop uniqueness and emphasize individuality. Thus, in our culture a counselor is encouraged to help the client to become more independent, more autonomous (Hershenson, 1983).

### Arbuckle's Philosophical Model

Arbuckle (1975) illustrates this philosophical stand by suggesting a few of the philosophical elements that are crucial to his counseling theory:

1. Every human being is, to a high degree, an obviously conditioned product of an environmental milieu, which at any point in time is itself a product of conditioning.
2. The reality of outside negative pressures often clouds the equal reality that basic individual change comes from the inside out, not from the outside in.
3. Individual responsibility is the creator of individual freedom, rather than the other way about.
4. Too frequently, too, in the "freedom" literature, we find indignant statements regarding bigotry and prejudice when the so-called "evidence" is no evidence at all.
5. A responsible and free individual is one who has narrowed the gap between attitudes and behaviors.
6. Another thought is that the literal meaning of freedom and responsibility changes as the culture changes.
7. And, finally, a responsible individual is one who has no need to impose himself or his ideas on others.

### Blocher's Grouping of Relevant Philosophical Systems

Blocher (1966) has proposed grouping contemporary philosophical systems into three major categories that seem to have relevance for counseling. He terms these three groups *essentialism, progressivism,* and *existentialism.*

***Essentialism*** Under essentialism can be grouped the approaches usually termed *rationalism, idealism,* and *realism.* Essentialistic philosophies assume that humans are the only creatures endowed with reason and that their chief function is to use this reason in order to know the world in which they live. It therefore follows that truth is universal and absolute, and the individual's destiny is to discover truth by distinguishing between the essential and the accidental.

Although the essentialistic systems do have differences, all share a belief in the existence of fixed, unchanging absolutes of the good, the true, and the beautiful. The search for values is essentially not personal but universal, and it can be finalized when these absolutes are understood.

Arbuckle (1975) points out that belief in absolute values can pose some difficulties for counselors. He asks whether the counselor who is firmly committed to absolutistic concepts of right and wrong, truth and error, beauty and ugliness, can allow a client the freedom to develop values in the client's own unique way. The key question for the counselor is probably not whether he believes in the theoretical existence of absolutes, but whether he believes that he himself has indeed finally reached full understanding of what those absolutes are. Does the counselor have knowledge of absolute right and absolute wrong, absolute truth and absolute error, absolute beauty and absolute ugliness?

*Progressivism*   Blocher's (1966) second set of systems, termed *progressivistic,* came about through a steady erosion of the old certainties that formed the basis of essentialistic philosophies. As new scientific findings undermined the ideas that the classical thinkers had considered self-evident, less confidence could be placed in the existence of absolutes themselves. Progressivistic philosophies, including such approaches as experimentalism, pragmatism, and instrumentalism, have as a central feature the notion of the continuity between the knower and what is unknown, between object and observer. Since the scientist has less immediate interest in a general theory of knowledge than in understanding an immediate, specific phenomenon, he operates in the context of a specific problem and an immediate solution to that problem.

Such systems begin not with the assumptions of universal truths but with specific and particular experiences. The present and the future are stressed, rather than the past. The question "What is true?" is less important than "What will work?" A fact is valued for its usefulness, not its universality. As a result, values have no existence in themselves. Values are individual to the observer, and truth is dynamic in a world that is always changing.

Certainly such a view describes the philosophy that underlies behaviorism. The behavioral approach is primarily pragmatic; that which works is good; that which does not is discarded. Since an action is evaluated purely in terms of its consequences, no absolutes exist.

Progressivistic philosophies create some difficulty for the counselor. Although they do not carry the problem of the troublesome absolutes involved with essentialism, the progressivistic philosophies provide societal sanctions that can be just as tyrannical. These views suggest that maturity and mental health can be measured in terms of adjustment and conformity to some individual or group. Therefore, they allow little room for individuality and autonomy.

*Existentialism*   Blocher's third major category of philosophical systems is that of existentialism (Blocher, 1966). Existentialism is concerned with human longing and with seeking for importance within the individual's self. The existential philosophies emphasize the view of reality most meaningful to individuals—own existence. As a result, existentialistic philosophy provides a basis for describing an attitude and an approach to human beings rather than to a formal system or group. It suggests a radical stress on the concept of identity and the experience of identity as the major core of human nature and of any philosophy or science of human nature.

Counseling from an existential philosophy involves applying key existentialist concepts to the treatment of problems. It involves the attempt by the counselor to experience along with the client. In a sense, it represents an approach that stresses a total empathic response by the counselor, as the counselor attempts to reconstruct the personal meaning structure of the client.

Beck (1963) has formulated a number of assumptions that seem to offer one basis for a philosophy of counseling. Drawn largely from existentialistic philosophy, these include:

1.  The individual is responsible for his own actions.
2.  Man must regard his fellow men as objects of value, as part of his concern.
3.  Man exists in a world of reality.
4.  A meaningful life must remove as much threat from reality as possible, both physical and psychological.
5.  Every person has his own heredity and has had unique experiences.
6.  Man behaves in terms of his own subjective view of reality, not according to some externally defined objective reality.
7.  Man cannot be classified as ''good'' or ''evil'' by nature.
8.  Man reacts as a total organism to any situation.

The whole idea of a philosophical foundation to counseling is important to counselors. Philosophy is in part an analysis of what people do—not of their actions at any particular time and place, but rather of the generalized meaning of those actions. To analyze human behavior in philosophical terms is to ask serious questions about what a person values, whether he or she should value it, whether this value fits in with a pattern of values, whether the valuing of something hampers or assists other important values.

Philosophical questions are directly involved when an individual faces a problem, whether personal, vocational, or interpersonal. ''What vocation should I choose that will satisfy my values and meet my needs?'' demands an answer to the same philosophical questions as a question such as, ''What can I do to make my life more meaningful?'' As individuals deal with the important problems of living, they begin to work out their own pattern of beliefs, which may or may not prove adequate in helping them live their lives. A pattern of beliefs may be self-defeating, or it may lead to choices that result in a rich and meaningful life.

## SOCIOLOGICAL FOUNDATIONS

Sociology is basically a study of social group behavior; hence, it frequently emphasizes factors that influence group interactions as well as conditions that control social life. A basic premise of sociology is that people's behavior is largely determined by their social interactions, their relationships as individuals and as group members. These interactions tend to become stabilized into a pattern of relationships, which is a social organization. Within these organizations the behavior of one person tends to exert increasingly significant effects on the life of another.

### Influence of Social Organizations on Individuals

Counselors must be very much aware of the patterns of social organization within which the growing human being interacts. They must understand how the patterns and purposes of the social units exercising social control over the individual merge or conflict in their impact on that individual. Counselors need to understand how social control processes in the workplace, in the neighborhood, in the school, in the peer group, and in the family reinforce or conflict with each other and how each individual copes with these influences.

Sociologists have examined what impact the social structure has on the individual and how the individual adapts to these social controls. Merton (1957) suggests that individuals can cope through five general means: conformity, innovation, ritualism, retreatism, or rebellion. He hypothesizes that deviant behavior is frequently the result of the individual's being unable to resolve goal-blocking frustrations through conformity.

### Socialization Processes

Social control is exerted on new members of social organizations through a process called *socialization*. This process transmits values and purposes of the group to the individual, teaching the individual how to fit into the pattern of that social organization. Socialization does not typically deal with the uniqueness of individuals; rather, it focuses on those aspects of an individual's development that concern the adaptations and adjustments to the culture or society. In effect, the socialization processes work primarily to further the goals of the group rather than to further the development of the individual.

The same socialization processes that further group goals also significantly affect the individual: The individual gains a sense of personal identity as well as a set of individual ideas, values, and goals from this experience. In effect then, socialization not only regulates behavior, but it also supplies the context within which individuality, self-awareness, and identity can develop. This two-sided nature of socialization processes must be recognized by counselors who would understand the nature of individual development and individual choice. Counselors must be particularly sensitive to the possibility of conflicting and irreconcilable objectives and values imposed on a client by such socialization groups as the family, school, church, or peer group in order to help clients develop a real sense of personal identity.

Because the counselor's primary commitment is to individual growth and development rather than to the facilitation of group ends, the counselor is particularly concerned with those socialization processes that help the individual develop identity, self-awareness, values, and goals. These socialization factors can never be completely separated from those that lead to conformity, mediocrity, and other-directedness. The counselor is not concerned with helping the individuals adjust to or resist these socialization forces, but rather with helping them learn to harness those forces in ways that will bring about maximum personal development in terms of a personal value system derived in a humanizing context of an open and pluralistic society.

A major focus of the socialization process is development of the personal values around which the individual organizes his or her own identity. These values are largely learned within the primary groups with which the individual is associated. From a cultural standpoint, Du Bois (1955) suggests that American values are based on three central premises: first, that the universe is mechanistically conceived and the human race is its master; second, that humans are essentially equal; and third, that humans are perfectible.

These premises have resulted in three sets of value types. One is materialism, which emphasizes material well-being. This set of values presumes that individuals can control and master their environment and create conditions for their own material comfort and well-being.

The second set of values is conformity, which emphasizes conforming to modal ways of behaving. Although class and cultural differences exist, they are deemphasized and devalued. Assimilation is the valued norm as the society moves toward equality.

The third set of values is called effort-optimism; it emphasizes achievement, self-improvement, and hard work. Since humans are perfectible, they should perfect themselves. Since the world is controllable, hard work and effort will pay off. In this value set, youthfulness, energy, and enthusiasm are valued. Aspirations should be high and achievement a prime virtue.

### Development of Social/Cultural Values

Effective counselors need some objective way of looking at cultural values and value formation. They need to be able to conceptualize how cultural values impinge upon the individual's freedom to move toward individual development. They should be able to understand how an individual's cultural influences his value structure and how conflicts between individual and cultural values influence development. Such conflicts occur when the individual or the individual's subcultural group resists the values of a dominant culture (Lee, 1983).

Such conflicts do cause problems. One example is the middle-class dilemma of confused gender roles. The behavior expected of a boy or girl varies from one culture to another and over time. Within our own culture in past years, the woman was supposed to be a subservient wife, a demure helpmate who raised children and patiently submitted to her husband. The husband was expected to be the breadwinner and the head of the household. But the roles of men and women have changed drastically. Our culture has gone through world wars in which women were needed outside the home; divorce rates have risen, making a much larger percentage of women heads of households. Girls are now encouraged to pursue an academic program of study, to go to college and graduate school, to choose ''exciting'' careers, and to carve out for themselves an existence wholly independent of motherhood. As these roles have changed, individual females have often been caught in the middle. While a young girl may be encouraged to develop her talent by going to college and preparing for a career, she may also be pushed toward an engagement, marriage, and children. Whether she chooses to pursue a career or raise a family, judged by one set of values, she is wrong. At fault is what sociologists call a *cultural lag;* that is, habits and beliefs from previous times conflict with the cultural patterns brought about by new technology.

## PSYCHOLOGICAL FOUNDATIONS

Although counseling frequently attempts to identify itself with the discipline of psychology—and in a sense there is a direct relationship—psychology is a much broader discipline. Psychology does study the individual's interaction with the environment, but it also studies many aspects of that individual's interaction that are not directly related to counseling. Psychologists may specialize in physiological psychology, experimental psychology, social psychology, or any of a large number of other areas. Still, the ideas developed from the many psychology emphases have greatly influenced counseling.

### Social Psychology

Contemporary social psychology has been greatly concerned with perceptual processes in human beings. Psychologists have long known that considerable individual variations occur in perception of similar stimuli. These studies of perception have led to the belief, emphasized more strongly than others, that the individual's behavior is largely governed by how that individual perceives a particular situation, not by the actual situation. For example, when an individual views a situation as threatening, he or she acts as if that situation were indeed threatening. Therefore, the person will behave defensively or aggressively, depending on what he sees as the best reaction to the perceived threat. Whether or not the threat indeed exists is not important in determining the individual's behavior (Snyder, 1982).

Psychologists focusing on this area of perception have done extensive research to try to determine exactly what influences the way people perceive various situations. One example of how perceptual theory has affected counseling is the "directive state" theory. This theory suggests that the direction of perceptual experience is influenced by such factors as sex, attitudes, values, needs, and similar intervening variables. Other studies have shown that a number of factors operate to make us organize stimuli in a particular way. Some factors are intrinsic to the stimulus object or situation—for example, the nearness of various elements to each other or their physical likeness, the inclusiveness of one perceptual pattern as opposed to another, the tendency to see a complete object (closure), and the context, or part-whole relationships, of the situation. The way we perceive things is also influenced by personal factors—our tendency to create and maintain a stable structure, our particular past experience, our organic condition, and our needs and values. Social and cultural factors encourage us to develop certain perceptions and discourage us from developing others. Likewise, our deep-rooted, basic classifications of experience strongly influence our perceptions, as do our previous successes or failures.

The basic idea that behavior is a product of the perceptual field of the individual at the moment of action points out the need to understand the nature of the individual's perceptual field. If the counselor is to have a positive effect on the client, then the counselor must understand the nature of the individual's perceptual experiences. Only then can the counselor create conditions that will facilitate changes in that client's behavior and personality. Snygg and Combs (1949) have developed a whole perceptual view of personality based on the idea that the growth and development of individuals is determined by their perception of the experiences they have with other people. An individual's perception in any given situation may be directly related to that individual's need satisfaction. The individual perceives what he needs to perceive. When needs are not satisfied, the individual's perception becomes narrow and rigid. Thus, needs must be satisfied before an individual can develop a more fluid, open field of perception.

### The Concept of Self

Psychology has also influenced counseling by revealing that human behavior is much more complex than was originally believed. Much of this complexity was uncovered as the concept of self was explored. This concept was introduced as psychologists learned that the way individuals perceive themselves strongly influences their behavior. Field theory psychologists went on to discover that whether some kind of reality exists independent of individual perceptions is simply not of psychological relevance. How a person perceives reality constitutes reality for him. Individuals act for reasons that may be difficult to describe, and any simple, unqualified generalization about behavior is probably either wrong or incomplete.

### Goal-Directed Behavior

Psychologists have also pointed out that human beings have purposes and goals that cannot be explained simply by reference to physiological makeup. Almost any behavior, however bizarre or irrational it may at first appear, is performed to reach a particular goal. Even though the individual may not realize the purpose or goal of the behavior until later or until given some help in analyzing the behavior, the goal or purpose was there. Sometimes called "private logic," this idea suggest that for every behavior, the individual has his or her own private logic which makes that behavior meaningful in terms of achieving a goal. The counselor may wish to probe beyond the obvious to determine what kind of payoff or goal the individual is hoping to achieve through the behavior.

### Learning Principles

Certainly psychology has made a major contribution to counseling in the area of learning. Although different theories of learning can be identified, the behavioristic theories, the field theories, and the cognitive theories are probably most applicable to counseling. The behavioral theories tend to emphasize the idea that learning is essentially a mechanical matter. Thorndike, for instance, believed that learning takes place as an organism responds to a stimulus. As the response forms a groove through the neural pathway, the individual may be said to have learned.

*Behavioristic Theories* Skinner (1961) considerably refined Thorndike's ideas and focused on two major parallel forms of learning: respondent and operant. Respondent learning, sometimes called classical conditioning, occurs when a stimulus elicits a response. Operant learning occurs when a response is emitted in order to obtain an outcome that reinforces the learner. Thus, respondent behavior is controlled by its antecedent whereas operant behavior is controlled by its consequences.

In operant learning the consequences which strengthen behavior are called reinforcers. A reinforcer is any event which, instead of eliciting a specific class of behaviors, increases the probability of any resulting behavior occurring. Thus an individual who behaves in a particular way and is immediately rewarded will have that behavior strengthened. An activity or an event is reinforcing simply because it has an effect on behavior. If a reinforcing stimulus is pleasant—for example, one that provides the opportunity for some novel activity—then the event or stimulus is positive reinforcement, increasing the likelihood that a particular act with which it is associated will be repeated. The initial act may have been learned as the result of previous consequences or may be a random, somewhat spontaneous action. In both cases, the action is more likely to reoccur because of the subsequent pleasant consequences.

However interesting Skinner's experiments and findings, some counseling theorists object to them because they make the learner a passive object who has little insight or control over behavior. In addition, the ideas are criticized because the individual is manipulated and has lost the freedom to comprehend the significance of what is being done to him.

*Field Theories*    Field theory proponents include the gestaltists, who emphasize the idea of insight, a realization or awareness of a certain relationship. Their emphasis on perception eventually forced the behaviorists to stop speaking as if the stimuli were purely objective and therefore equivalent for everyone. Experiments devised by field theory psychologists indicated that sometimes complex learning occurred through insight.

In a typical experiment, apes would be placed in an unfamiliar situation where desirable food was in sight but could not be reached. After giving up on trying to reach it by stretching or jumping, the apes often engaged in what appeared to be thinking. Then, when they suddenly perceived the solution, they behaved very much as humans do when they have an "aha" experience, and they proceeded to solve the problem immediately. This early experimentation suggested that when an individual gets an insight, he "catches on" in a rapid, almost dramatic fashion. An insight may occur quickly or it may arrive slowly; it may be deep or shallow, and it is not necessarily accurate.

The counselor who sees learning from a field theory point of view would not condition new behavior by reinforcing correct responses; rather, he or she would attempt to get clients to utilize their own intellectual and emotional resources to become aware of certain feelings, relationships, or attitudes. Such an approach assumes that clients have sufficient intelligence to solve their own problems and that the counselor simply provides an assisting environment for this purpose. When clients gain insight into themselves and their problems, then they are free to decide what is to be done and how to do it.

*Cognitive Theories*    The cognitive theories of learning are based to a large extent on the work of the field theorists. Cognitive theorists conceptualize learning as an active restructuring of perceptions and concepts, not as passive responses to stimuli and reinforcement. They stress the conceptual aspects of learning, resulting from the unique abilities of humans. The cognitive theorists hold that the ability to use language to mediate learning is too basic and important to allow many general laws of behavior. While recognizing the importance of reinforcement, they tend to stress its role in providing feedback rather than its role as a motivator. Cognitive theorists place greater stress on mental processes believed to be involved in the active perception and exploration of the environment. These include the strategies learners use in processing information and developing new insights, as well as changes in existing conditions brought about by new learning.

The field of psychology has had and will continue to have a profound impact on the field of counseling. Along with the work already discussed, psychologists have provided counselors with useful data on motivation, the nature of anxiety, personality theory, and abnormal psychology.

## DEVELOPMENTAL PSYCHOLOGY

Because of its extreme importance to counseling, developmental psychology requires a separate discussion. Facilitating human development is a major goal of all counseling approaches, and counselors should be aware of major findings in developmental psychology that are applicable to counseling. Counselors must understand the complex processes through which human behaviors are acquired and modified so that they can intervene to facilitate their smooth and orderly operation (Blocher, 1980).

Development is a lifelong set of psychological, social, and physiological processes that encompass the entire scope of human existence from birth to death. The physiological processes that define the physical organism, and the environmental forces, including culture, that act on the individual are mediated by a set of psychological processes. Thus, development combines growth, maturation, and learning. It is influenced by environmental factors, and developmental processes must be understood within this context.

### Stages of Development

Such theorists as Erikson (1950), Bruner (1964), and Piaget (1962) have attempted to determine whether development is smooth and continuous or whether it indeed occurs in recognizably discrete stages. Some physiological processes that are developmental catalysts—the onset of puberty, for example—are relatively discrete events. Other physiological processes take place very gradually and continuously. Our society reinforces stages of development by organizing social institutions around them: grade levels in school, legal ages for driving, drinking, and marriage.

Blocher (1966) has identified five major life stages—organization, exploration, realization, stabilization, and examination. He analyzes each in terms of expected social

**Figure 2-1** Counselors must be aware that children at different ages have different social and physical skills to learn (Color Image, Inc., Jim Trotter)

roles, coping behaviors, and developmental tasks. Such an approach is useful to the counselor who accepts the general concept that cultural forces and maturational changes acting at particular times in the lives of human beings will result in particular kinds of problems, crises, and behavior patterns. The interaction between the culture and the developing individual can best be understood in terms of these life stages.

From this point of view, development is seen as a patterned, orderly, lifelong process that leads to effective behavior, behavior that permits long-term control of environment, where possible, and control of the individual's affective responses when the environment cannot be controlled. This process of development includes gaining understanding, assigning meanings, and organizing behavior. Development, then, is orderly, but each individual develops in a unique way.

*Organization* Although Blocher divided the organization stage into four substages—infancy, early childhood, later childhood, and early adolescence—the stage is seen as a single one because it is dominated by the phenomena of the physiological unfolding of the individual. The development crises of this period are dictated primarily by the individual's struggle to meet the emerging physical and emotional needs within a society that defines how these needs may be met.

Development of the ability to trust takes place during the infancy period (birth to three years). This sense of trust is formed in the primary relationship between the parent and child and is then generalized toward others. By demonstrating sensitivity, consistency, and self-confidence, parents and significant persons in the child's life help the child to trust others. Such a development enables the infant to begin to defer immediate gratifications and to begin to behave as a separate but secure individual.

As the infant emerges into early childhood (ages three to six), his world rapidly becomes more complex. New roles are thrust on the child, often including those of sibling and playmate; he is also expected to assume sex-appropriate roles. Most important, however, is the development of a sense of autonomy, the basis for a sense of separateness and responsibility essential in achieving independence. The individual must learn to make choices, assume responsibility for them, and accept the consequences that those choices imply. The coping behaviors to be learned during this stage can be broken down into three areas: (1) cooperative behaviors, (2) control behaviors, and (3) substitution behaviors.

The later childhood (ages six to twelve) stage of development sees the child's social world becoming rapidly more complex. The new social roles—student, helper, big brother or sister—require the mastery of new developmental tasks. Failure to master these tasks has drastic consequences to future development. The key developmental tasks are those of initiative and industry—learning to plan and attack tasks. The child must learn these skills to gain success and mastery experiences. His mastery leads others to accept him for being himself, and increases his self-esteem and self-acceptance. Out of such experiences the child can gradually develop a sense of personal responsibility and pride. The coping behaviors learned at this stage can be grouped into the categories of mastery behaviors, value-relevant behaviors, and work-relevant behaviors.

Early adolescence (ages twelve to fourteen) is known as a critical and painful stage in human development. The drastic physiological changes of puberty cause a profound disequilibrium in the life of the early adolescent. At the same time the adolescent is confronted with a frightening new cluster of social role expectations that are often ambiguous and about which he may be ambivalent.

Two role expectation changes of major importance occur at this stage: peer roles and heterosexual roles. In early adolescence the peer expectations begin to shape the youngster's behavior to ever-increasing degrees. Peer expectations begin to carry more weight than family or school expectations—formerly the primary shapers of behavior—often putting the adolescent in a position of acute choice anxiety. The adolescent is also beginning to become involved in heterosexual relationships, with which he has had little experience but which are activated by powerful new biological needs. Thus, the primary development task for this adolescent period involves the conflict between identity and role confusion. Certainly the most critical phase of this process in early adolescence is the development of a sexual identity.

The adolescent seeks increased clarification or identity through peer groups and through new heterosexual relationships. Within the relative intimacy of such relationships, he is able to get some increased definition of his own identity by projecting and reflecting it upon others. Thus, the sense of belonging with the group and belonging to someone of the opposite sex helps the adolescent clarify his or her personal identity. The resulting coping behaviors that need to be learned at this time are social behaviors, sex-appropriate behaviors, and achievement-oriented behaviors.

*Exploration*    The exploration stage begins in midadolescence and moves the individual through later adolescence and early adulthood. It is characterized by a reaching out for new values, ideals, motivations, and purposes. During this stage, individuals are intent on reaching out into the environment to find the elements to which they can relate their new-found sense of physical maturity. Working from the identity formation of adolescence to the central task of developing intimacy and commitment, young adults reach out to establish new reciprocal relationships in friendship, courtship and dating, educational achievement, and career development. They must learn to give and receive in situations that call for mutuality and cooperation. In particular, young adults need to develop effective sexual behaviors, risk-taking behaviors, and value-consistent behaviors.

*Realization*    Following the exploration stage is the realization stage (ages thirty to fifty), which represents culmination of effective human development. Physical maturation is complete; psychological growth has established a set of personality structures and patterns of behavior that can support a high level of functioning. At this stage individuals can fulfill leadership roles, helping roles, creative roles, and accomplishment roles as they accept their responsibility to their families and the groups that are important to them. The chief focus is the development of unity and integration, a harmony between the individual's life-style and values of the individual's culture. Such a harmony can give meaning to life and overcome the existential despair that arises from the inevitability of death. The mature adult needs to learn such coping behaviors as discrimination, selective awareness, sensitivity, and time reversal.

*Stabilization*    The stabilization stage (ages fifty to sixty-five) is that stage of development at which an already high level of functioning is continued and refined. Controlled growth continues to enhance the behavior of the individual who now reaps the rewards of previous experiences. A frequent developmental task of this period is recognizing the inevitability of change and developing a time perspective for observing and evaluating problems that go beyond the limits of one's own life span. Coping behaviors to be learned include change-oriented behaviors, value-relevant behaviors of a self-transcending nature, and sensitivity behaviors.

*Examination*    The examination stage (sixty-five plus) is characterized by reflection, active disengagement from events, and taking on the roles of observer and mentor rather than active participant. The real dangers in this stage are isolation and detachment, which can deprive life of its meaning and reality. Giving up roles of authority and responsibility to take on the new social role of retired person can produce devastating consequences in self-perception. Learning to cope with retirement and with the death of spouse and friends becomes extremely important. Coping behaviors for dealing with these tasks include affiliative behaviors, productive leisure-time behaviors, and personal enhancement behaviors.

## SUMMARY

Both the theory and practice of counseling have been strongly influenced by such other disciplines as philosophy , sociology, and psychology. These disciplines have provided both data and comprehensive hypotheses useful in clarifying the underlying theoretical structures of the counseling process.

Philosophical input has been chiefly in the areas of the emphasis on the worth of the individual and of the analysis of values as being absolute or relative.

Sociology has provided information regarding the impact of the social structure on the individual and the process by which individuals learn to cope with this structure.

Psychology is especially relevant for counseling, providing insight into perceptual processes, the concept of the self, the process by which individuals learn, and the developmental periods through which they pass.

## REFERENCES

ARBUCKLE, D.S. (1975). *Counseling and psychotherapy* (3rd ed.). Boston: Allyn and Bacon.

BECK, C.E. (1963). *Philosophical foundations of guidance.* Englewood Cliffs, N.J.: Prentice-Hall.

BLOCHER, D.H. (1966). *Developmental counseling.* New York: Ronald Press.

BLOCHER, D.H. (1980). Some implications of recent research in social and developmental psychology for counseling practice. *Personnel and Guidance Journal, 58,* 334–336.

BRUNER, J.S. (1964). The course of cognitive growth. *American Psychologist, 19,* 1–15.

DuBOIS, C. (1955). The dominant profile of American culture. *American Anthropologist, 57,* 1232–1240.

ERIKSON, E.H. (1950). *Childhood and society.* New York: W.W. Norton & Co.

HERSHENSON, D.B. (1983). A Viconian interpretation of psychological counseling. *Personnel and Guidance Journal, 62,* 3–9.

LEE, D.J. (1983). Philosophy and counseling: A metatheoretical analysis. *Personnel and Guidance Journal, 61,* 523–526.

MAY, R. (1967). *Psychology and the human dilemma.* New York: Van Nostrand.

MERTON, R.K. (1957). Social theory and social structure. (Rev. ed.). New York: Free Press.

PATTERSON, C.H. (1958). The place of values in counseling and psychotherapy. *Journal of Counseling Psychology, 5,* 216–223.

PIAGET, J. (1962). *The moral judgement of the child.* New York: Collier Books.

ROSENTHAL, D. (1955). Changes in some moral values following psychotherapy. *Journal of Consulting Psychology, 19,* 431–436.

SKINNER, B.F. (1961). *Cumulative record.* Englewood Cliffs, N.J.: Prentice-Hall.

SNYDER, D.M. (1982). Some foundations of counseling and psychotherapy from a phenomenological perspective. *Personnel and Guidance Journal, 60,* 364–367.

SNYGG, D., & COMBS, A.W. (1949). *Individual behavior: A new frame of reference for psychology.* New York: Harper & Row.

WILLIAMSON, E.G. (1958). Value orientations in counseling. *Personnel and Guidance Journal, 36,* 520–528.

# 3

# PSYCHOANALYTIC FOUNDATIONS

**FREUD**

> Structure of Personality
>
> View of Human Nature
>
> Layers of Personality
>
> Ego—Defense Mechanisms
>
> Stages of Development
>
> The Therapeutic Process
>
> Contributions
>
> Criticisms

**NEO-FREUDIAN THEORISTS**

**ALFRED ADLER**

> View of Human Nature
>
> Striving for Superiority
>
> Feelings of Inferiority and Compensation
>
> Life-Style
>
> Family Constellation
>
> Early Memories
>
> The Counseling Process
>
> Contributions
>
> Criticisms

**KAREN HORNEY**

   Ten Neurotic Needs

**HARRY STACK SULLIVAN**

**NEW DIRECTIONS**

   The Ego Analysts

**SUMMARY**

Chapters 3, 4, and 5 give a brief overview of the theoretical foundations of some of the counseling approaches in use today. The approaches summarized in these chapters have been chosen because they are clear-cut and unique, and have attained significant support in the field.

The impact of psychoanalytic thought on the field of counseling and psychotherapy is summarized to provide insight into the way the study of human behavior has developed over the years. Chapters 4 and 5 are divided according to the emphasis of the theories—feelings or thoughts and behaviors. Each approach recognizes and deals with both aspects, but places a primary emphasis on one of the two.

Only an introduction to these approaches is given in these chapters; prospective counselors are urged to study each approach in much greater depth and to explore other approaches that seem relevant.

Chapter 6 discusses theory in greater detail—its nature, function, and purpose—and will provide some comparisons of these theories as a beginning point for the counselor in developing a personal theoretical model.

## SIGMUND FREUD

While Freudian theory is not considered to be entirely relevant to present counseling practice, it is essential to understand the influential role it has played in current theoretical conceptualizations. A close examination of the theories presented here will reveal that many are extensions or modifications of Freudian thought. Here we will explore the basic constructs of Freud, and we will summarize the significant contributions of his followers Adler, Horney, and Sullivan, and the ego analysts. Due to the limitations of space in this text, interested readers are encouraged to read the original works of each of these important theorists.

Sigmund Freud, in an effort that spanned more than forty years, developed what is thought to be the first comprehensive theory of personality. This theory was revised over the years as a result of Freud's experience in his clinical practice. Psychoanalysis, then, is not only a theory, but also a method of therapy.

Freud's views of the importance of the unconscious were at odds with previously held views of behavior. These views, which emphasized conscious processes, were thought to be totally inadequate by Freud, who viewed the unconscious as a huge region of feelings, urges, and passions which exerted control over conscious behavior. Thus he developed techniques, such as free association and dream interpretation, to enable the therapist to tap these unconscious but powerful determinants of behavior.

The works of Freud are far too numerous to list. Important introductions to Freudian thought would include Brenner's (1974) *An Elementary Textbook of Psychoanalysis,* and Hall's (1954) *A Primer of Freudian Psychology.*

### Structure of Personality

Personality, according to Freud, is composed of three systems: the id, ego, and superego. These systems are interrelated, and behavior is a function of the interaction among them.

***The Id***   Freud regards the id as the original system of personality, consisting of all that is inherited at birth, including the instincts. Within the id lies the reservoir of psychic energy which fuels the other two systems, the ego and the superego. The id is in direct contact with bodily processes, represents the inner world of subjective experience, and operates to reduce tension. Because the id cannot tolerate tension, it discharges it immediately and returns the organism to a homeostatic state. This principle of tension reduction is called the *pleasure principle*. Thus, the id functions to satisfy the needs of the organism by decreasing pain and increasing pleasure, with no concern for external realities or morality.

***The Ego***   Because the id is the driving force of the personality and functions at an unconscious level with no concern for external reality, the ego exists to make transactions with the objective world of reality. That is, it is the responsibility of the id to make decisions about which instincts to satisfy and to somehow mediate between the conflicting demands of the id, the superego, and the real world. The ego is thus in control of the actions of the organism, and it employs intellect and reason to satisfy the organism's needs. The ego is said to operate by the *reality principle*.

***The Superego***   The superego represents the moral and traditional values of society which are communicated to the child by the parents. As children, we are rewarded by our parents for good behavior and punished by them for wrongdoing. Thus the behavior for which we are punished becomes part of our ''conscience,'' and positive behavior becomes part of our ego-ideal. The superego, then, is comprised of these two subsystems: the ''conscience,'' which punishes us with guilt, and the ''ego-ideal,'' which rewards us with pride. The functions of the superego include restraining the impulses of the id, convincing the ego to substitute moralistic goals for realistic ones, and striving for perfection.

In summary, personality, according to Freud, is a complex energy system consisting of the interaction between the driving forces of the id and the restraining forces of the ego and superego. The id, which houses the reservoir of psychic energy, strives to satisfy its needs according to the pleasure principle, while the ego seeks to mediate the impulses of the id with the superego and the external world.

## View of Human Nature

Freud viewed the human organism as a complex energy system with psychic energy distributed among the three systems and behavior being a function of these unconscious forces. His view of human nature, then, is highly deterministic, since individuals are controlled by their biological drives and instincts; man is biological and, therefore, unsocialized and irrational.

The instincts consist of psychic energy, the reservoir of which is originally housed in the id. Freud classified the instincts into two broad categories, the life instincts and the death instincts. The *life instincts* include those which are necessary for the organism to survive, such as hunger, thirst, and sex. These instincts operate using a form of energy called *libido;* the term originally referred primarily to sexual energy but later was used more broadly to refer to all of the life instincts. The *death instincts* are related to aggression and destruction. While Freud knew less about the death instincts, he believed that they were motivating forces in behavior.

### Layers of Personality

One of Freud's most significant contributions was his emphasis on the unconscious. Freud likened the mind to an iceberg, with consciousness being represented by the small part above the water and the unconscious region being the large area beneath the surface. Thus the unconscious houses all memories, experiences, reactions, feelings, and needs that are not in our awareness. Freud thus believed that most of our psychological functioning is not in our awareness; hence the need for a therapeutic model that could gain access to these important influences on behavior (Corey, 1982). The unconscious is a critical construct in psychoanalytic thought; it is essential to therapeutic growth that motivations and other repressed material be brought to a conscious level of awareness, so that the person can understand the roots of the symptoms and decide whether or not to change. In other words, to understand human behavior the therapist must be able to reveal the unconscious (Nye, 1981).

Thus the layers of personality in Freud's "topography of the mind" are the unconscious, the preconscious, and the conscious. The preconscious includes material that is just beneath the surface and is reasonably accessible if we give it some thought. The conscious includes material that is at an immediate level of awareness, and the unconscious houses the basic determinants of personality (Nye, 1981).

### Ego-Defense Mechanisms

One of Freud's most important contributions to psychology was his conceptualization of the ego-defense mechanisms. As previously discussed, Freud viewed personality as an energy system with psychic energy being distributed among the id, ego, and superego. The id originally had all of the psychic energy. Because the ego needs psychic energy to function, a state of conflict exists between the driving forces of the id and the restraining forces of the ego and superego. Most of the time the outer world functions to satisfy the wishes of the ego. Sometimes, however, the outer world threatens the ego, and when the ego receives this excessive stimulation, it is flooded with anxiety.

Anxiety may exist in three forms: reality anxiety, neurotic anxiety, and moral anxiety. *Reality* anxiety is caused by real dangers in the external world. *Neurotic* anxiety results from fear that the instincts will get out of control and cause the individual to do something for which he will be punished. *Moral* anxiety is a fear of the conscience. In other words, people with strong superegos feel guilty when they do something that violates the moral code. (Hall & Lindzey, 1978).

Anxiety serves an important function: It warns the individual of impending danger by signaling the ego that unless appropriate measures are taken, the ego may be overthrown (Hall & Lindzey, 1978). Anxiety, therefore, is a state of tension that can motivate the individual to action. When the ego cannot deal with anxiety through appropriate and rational methods, it resorts to unrealistic measures—the ego-defense mechanisms.

We employ defense mechanisms when we are in situations in which the ego is threatened. These mechanisms are, therefore, essential for helping us to cope with failure and to maintain a positive self-image. In fact, in a traumatic situation in which the experience is repressed, the repression serves to protect the ego from severe damage. In this situation the defense mechanisms are fundamental to the individual's psychological survival. In other instances, however, such as a succession of job-related failures, the ability to rationalize these failures may actually prevent the individual from taking appropriate measures to improve his behavior and enhance his success. Thus, the ego-defense mechanisms can operate to protect the individual, or they can serve as blocks to the self-growth that occurs when one faces problems or mistakes and learns to adequately cope with them.

While there are many ego-defense mechanisms, Anna Freud (1946) states that there are four principal defense mechanisms: repression, projection, reaction formation, and fixation and regression. Here we will define these four and seven others.

1. *Repression*   Repression is one of the earliest Freudian concepts. It involves the removal of painful or dangerous thoughts and experiences from consciousness. Thus a highly traumatic event, such as witnessing one's mother's murder, is not forgotten but is removed from one's awareness, producing amnesia. Often the repression of an event or experience is not complete, and such repressed desires may be revealed through dreams or slips of the tongue. In certain instances, such as the traumatic incident cited above, repression may be temporary and may protect the individual until other resources or methods of coping are available. Unfortunately, repression can also be used to enable the individual to deceive himself and evade learning more effective methods of dealing with the problem. Thus energy that could be used to enable the individual to cope effectively on a daily basis is tied up in maintaining the defensive posture.

2. *Projection*   Projection involves transferring blame for our own shortcomings onto others as well as attributing to others our unacceptable desires or impulses. A student who fails an exam attributes the failure to the poor quality of the test. Or, the sibling who pushes and shoves her brother exclaims that the brother actually started the fight.

3. *Reaction Formation*   This is a defensive reaction in which a dangerous impulse is replaced by a feeling or behavior pattern that is just the opposite. Thus a mother who hates her child might ''smother'' the child with love and affection. Another example might be someone who crusades against various vices or exhibits other forms of extreme intolerance. A reaction formation is characterized by compulsiveness and extravagant showiness (Hall & Lindzey, 1978).

4. *Fixation and Regression*   Personality development involves passage through a series of well-defined stages. At each stage there is a certain amount of frustration

and anxiety. If the anxiety of the next stage is too great, the individual's development may be halted (Hall & Lindzey, 1978). A related mechanism of defense is that of regression. Regression is a reaction to stress that involves reverting back to a less mature level of adjustment in order to feel safe and secure and to get one's needs met. For example, an older child at the birth of a sibling will sometimes revert to bed wetting or request a bottle in order to acquire attention. In severe forms of regression, the individual retreats from reality to a developmental stage that is less demanding or stressful. An illustration might involve a woman in her early twenties who, unable to meet the demands of her marriage and family, regresses to infantile levels of behavior and assumes a fetal position.

5. *Denial*   Denial involves the refusal to acknowledge unpleasant realities by ignoring their existence. Many of us refuse to acknowledge the reality of death; some deny criticism; others ignore a physician's diagnosis or prognosis. Denial is used to protect ourselves from the stress, but it also prevents us from facing the very real conflicts and problems of our daily existence.

6. *Rationalization*   Rationalization involves coming up with logical, ethical, or socially approved reasons for our behavior; this enables us to do things that are sources of conflict for us. For example, after we've had a stressful experience, we might spend money on a glamorous trip rather than spending the savings on home repairs. When turned down for a position, we convince ourselves that the job really was not what we wanted. In this sense, rationalization softens the blow of disappointments and enables one to deal with experiences without serious damage to one's ego.

7. *Sublimation*   Channeling aggressive or sexual impulses into socially acceptable activity is the basic principle of sublimation. Thus someone who has a lot of aggressive feelings might choose to play football. Some cultural achievements are attributed to sublimation of sexual urges.

8. *Identification*   While identification as a defense occurs as part of the individual's normal development, it is used to enhance self-worth. Individuals who have poor self-concepts or who feel basically inadequate might associate with successful organizations or causes in order to improve their sense of acceptability; for example, one might identify with athletic teams or with social clubs that impart status.

9. *Compensation*   Compensatory behavior can have either a positive or negative influence on one's adjustment. It involves masking weaknesses or feelings of inferiority by developing other aspects of one's physique or personality. A student who is slow academically might develop a pleasing personality, while someone who has suffered a physical disability might excel in another area of physical fitness. In other words, positive traits are exaggerated in order to make up for those that negatively influence the individual's self-concept.

10. *Displacement*   In this defensive reaction, there is a shift of emotion from the original target to a safer one. Work related stresses may be taken out at home. Children experiencing excessive family problems might act out their frustrations by abusing other children in the classroom. A father whose marriage is empty of emotional closeness and whose needs are not met in other ways might beat his child because the child is unable to satisfy him in an emotional sense.

11. *Introjection*   This reaction involves taking on the attitudes and values of others in an attempt to control one's own behavior and to act in an acceptable manner so as to protect oneself. In the German concentration camps, prisoners' previous values and identifications were broken down and new "Nazi" norms were adopted for survival's sake.

## Stages of Development

Freud considered the first five years of life to be quite important in the development of the child's personality. These first five years are followed by a latency period during which the dynamics are somewhat stabilized. At the onset of adolescence, the dynamics become active again (Hall & Lindzey, 1978).

Each developmental stage is dominated by a specific zone of the body. The first three stages, the oral, anal, and phallic, are referred to as the pregenital stage. The final stage of maturity, which occurs during adolescence, is the genital stage.

*Oral Stage*   The first year of life is called the oral stage. During this stage the primary source of gratification for the infant is through eating, which stimulates the lips and oral cavity, sensitive erogenous zones. Adult character traits are sometimes related to the two basic oral activities, incorporation of food and biting. That is, pleasure from oral incorporation may be displaced to the pleasure gained from acquiring possessions (Hall & Lindzey, 1978). Biting is sometimes displaced as sarcasm. Through the defenses of displacement and sublimation, modes of oral functioning provide the basis for the development of many attitudes and character traits (Hall & Lindzey, 1978). Additionally, the infant's relationship to the mother will influence the development of dependence/independence in adulthood.

*Anal Stage*   The anal region exerts considerable influence over personality development during the ages of one to three. With the onset of toilet training, typically during the second year of life, the infant experiences the external regulation of an impulse for the first time. That is, the child must learn to delay the gratification that comes from defecation. Parental attitudes toward toilet training are important and very influential in the development of future personality traits. Children learn to use their bodily functions to control their parents. Strict attitudes toward toilet training are said to produce retentive personalities—personalities, in other words, that are cruel or obstinate. If, on the other hand, the parents praise the child's bowel movements, the child may become creative and productive.

*Phallic Stage*   The focus of personality development from the age of three to the age of five or six is the genital area. During this time the child receives pleasure through masturbation, and there are several possible psychological developments, including castration anxiety, penis envy, and the Oedipus Complex, which Freud considered to be one of his greatest discoveries.

As the boy experiences increased tension and excitation in his genitals, masturbation increases. If his parents attempt to stop the masturbation, he may fear loss of his penis as a punishment; this is particularly possible if he observes a female, who does not have a penis. Castration anxiety is also related to the unconscious incestuous desires which children develop for parents of the opposite sex. As the male child experiences these desires for his mother, he fears that his father will punish him by cutting off his penis. This is the now-famous Oedipus Complex, which, if properly resolved, results in more acceptable forms of affection, as well as a strong identification with father (Corey, 1982).

The female counterpart to the Oedipus Complex is called the Electra Complex. Girls begin to transfer their feelings of love from mother to father during this stage. The absence of a penis in mother causes negative feelings or penis envy. The girl begins to compete with mother for father's attention and affection. Once she realizes she cannot compete, she begins to identify with her mother, taking on some of her behavioral characteristics (Corey, 1982).

Parental attitudes are, once again, most important during this psychosexual stage of development. Acceptance of the child's natural sexual curiosity lays the foundation for the development of adult attitudes toward sexuality, intimacy, and sex role identification.

*Latency Stage*    The latency period occurs between the ages of six to twelve and is basically a period of rest. The child moves from a narcissistic orientation to more socialized interaction. The focus during this period is on outside interests and relationships.

*Genital Stage*    During adolescence, children move into the genital stage, provided they are not fixated at an earlier stage of development. At this time the child begins moving into adulthood, replacing self-love with love of others. Heterosexual relationships become increasingly more important, as does the ability to form intimate relationships with members of the same sex. The adolescent begins to develop a sense of responsibility and moves gradually out of the realm of parental influence.

## The Therapeutic Process

*Role of Therapist*    The role of the therapist is to assume a neutral position with the patient so that the patient will develop a *transference relationship*. Thus, patients project onto the analyst feelings they have had toward significant others in their lives. It is felt that the transference relationship will provide more material for therapy as unresolved conflicts, feelings, and experiences are relived. Analysts, therefore, share very little about themselves with the patient. The session is characterized by the patient's deeply reflecting on past experiences while lying on a couch, with the therapist primarily remaining silent, except when making appropriate interpretations. The major therapeutic goal is to enable clients to gain insight into their problems through the uncovering of unconscious material.

***Therapeutic Techniques***  Several techniques—including interpretation, dream analysis, transference, and free association—are employed by psychoanalysts to uncover unconscious material.

*Interpretation,* which is used in the other techniques, has to do with the analyst's explaining to the patient the meanings associated with the uncovered unconscious material. These interpretations have a significant role in the patient's development of insight into problems and experiences.

*Dreams* are used by psychoanalytic therapists to gain access to the unconscious. The patient describes dreams to the analyst, and these dreams are then interpreted through the symbols that appear in them.

As has been described, the analyst strives to remain neutral in the relationship so that the patient will project onto the analyst unresolved feelings and experiences with others. The *transference relationship* allows patients to work out conflicts that are retarding their emotional and psychological growth.

Because it is necessary to tap the unconscious, analysts often use *free association* as a technique. Patients, while lying on a couch, are asked to spontaneously share whatever thoughts, words, expressions, or feelings come to mind, without censorship. These associations are interpreted by the analyst, who notes sequencing, blocking, and disruptions.

## Contributions

While Freudian theory has been the object of much attack, and while the application of Freudian thought to counseling per se is limited, the importance of Freud's contributions to both psychology and counseling must not be underestimated. Among the significant contributions are the following:

1.  The identification of the defense mechanisms has significantly influenced our understanding of abnormal behavior and the role of anxiety; this will be discussed in more detail at the conclusion of this chapter.
2.  The elaboration of both the developmental stages and the influence of early childhood experience has impacted contemporary views of development and child rearing.
3.  Freud's creativity, originality, and observations of human behavior gave us our first theory of personality.
4.  Psychoanalysis as an approach to therapy is the foundation from which many contemporary theoreticians have generated their approaches.
5.  Assessment instruments and techniques have been influenced by Freudian thought.

## Criticisms

The attacks against Freud and his theory have been numerous. Among the most common criticisms are the following:

1.  Freud's view of human nature was very negative and far too deterministic and mechanistic.

2. The strong emphasis on early childhood experiences makes it possible for patients to deny responsibility for their problems.
3. The role of interpersonal experiences and relationships was virtually ignored.
4. Women have strongly rejected the concept of penis envy.
5. Much criticism has been levied against the empirical procedures used by Freud, including the facts that he carried out no scientifically controlled studies and that his method of record keeping was incomplete.
6. Freud's emphasis on instinctual drives, particularly sex, was too strong.

Both the contributions and criticisms of Freudian thought are extensive. Here we have outlined a few of the most common of each. At the end of the chapter, we will explore in more depth the relationship between Freudian theory and other contemporary counseling approaches.

## NEO-FREUDIAN THEORISTS

Freud was surrounded by a group of followers, including Alfred Adler and Carl Jung, who eventually left the close circle and developed opposing views. Adler is said to have been the first analyst to reject Freud's view of sexuality in favor of an emphasis on the social nature of humans. Karen Horney, Eric Fromm, and Harry Stack Sullivan are the other psychoanalysts who developed a social-psychological view, which helped bridge the gap between Freud and contemporary psychoanalysts. While each of these theorists adapted and extended Freudian theory, they have made their own distinct contributions. Due to the limitations of space, we will discuss the theory of Alfred Adler, and review the significant contributions of Horney and Sullivan.

## ALFRED ADLER

Alfred Adler, a charter member of Freud's Vienna Psychoanalytic Society, split with Freud in 1911 because his views were at variance with Freud's. When he left the small group of followers who made up the Vienna Psychoanalytic Society, he formed his own group, known as Individual Psychology. The basic contention between Freud and Adler centered around Adler's disagreement with a sexual etiology of neuroses and belief that individuals were motivated by social responsibility and need achievement, not driven by the inborn instincts. Adler's views were well received initially, but later his popularity decreased. In the past twenty years, however, there has been a renewed interest in his views, and many counselors, particularly those working with children, have become ardent followers. Rudolf Dreikurs (1897–1972) contributed much to Adler's work, especially through the development of specific counseling techniques. Important sources of information about Adler's work are *The Practice of Individual Psychology* by Adler, and *The Individual Psychology of Alfred Adler* by Ansbacher and Ansbacher. Another excellent resource on Adlerian counseling is *Adlerian Counseling and Psychotherapy* by Dinkmeyer, Pew, and Dinkmeyer.

### View of Human Nature

Adler's view of human nature was much more positive than Freud's. Rather than viewing humans as being motivated by instinctual drives, Adler felt that humans were motivated by social, interpersonal factors. Adler saw people as having control over their lives, with each individual developing a unique life-style. Adler believed that behavior is goal directed and purposive, and that life goals motivate human behavior. The most important life goals involve overcoming feelings of inferiority and striving for security. The attempt to master feelings of inferiority provides the motivation for striving for perfection and creativity. From these basic concepts, it follows that Adler's emphasis is on conscious, rather than unconscious, process, with individuals assuming responsibility for their life decisions (Corey, 1982).

### Striving for Superiority

Adler believed that all human beings have "striving for superiority" as their life goal. The drive toward superiority is similar to the concept of self-actualization. It has nothing to do with achieving a position of status in society; rather it is, according to Adler, "the great upward drive." This upward drive pulls the individual through the developmental stages. It is important to note that individuals develop their own forms of achieving perfection which are related to the concept of feelings of inferiority (Hall & Lindzey, 1978).

### Feelings of Inferiority and Compensation

All individuals suffer from feelings of inferiority; these feelings, whether they stem from psychological or social problems or actual physical disability, motivate individuals to strive for perfection. Humans, then, are pushed by feelings of inferiority and pulled by feelings of superiority, and we tend to compensate for the areas of weakness or disability by developing a life-style that allows us to be successful.

### Life-Style

No two individuals develop the same style of life. As stated above, the life-style is based on the individual's feelings of inferiority and the particular way in which the individual strives to overcome a weakness. The life-style is a result of judgments the individual makes about the status of the self. The judgements of self in relation to one's perception of status in the world begin to form patterns of behavior that become one's life-style (Hansen, Stevic, & Warner, 1982). By the age of four or five, the style of life has been formed, and future experiences are merely integrated into it. Examples of life-style development would be a physical weakling becoming an athlete, or a withdrawn child developing his or her intellect.

### Family Constellation

One of Adler's most popular and useful contributions was his observation of family constellation and birth order. Adler placed a great deal of emphasis on early childhood experiences and, in line with his views on social determinants of personality, observed very carefully the influence of position in birth order on personality and life-style. In fact, he felt that birth order was an important determinant of the child's perceptions of the world outside the family.

Basically the concept of family constellation has to do with the child's interactions with and perceptions of the family group. The child is affected by others, just as he affects or influences them. The relationship is dynamic and interactive, and the child's perceptions of the family environment greatly influence how he comes to view himself.

Adler sought to associate characteristics with position in birth order. For example, many only children are pampered and are accustomed to having things their way. First children have to be first in order to maintain superiority over other children and may feel "dethroned" at the birth of the second child. Second children never have their parents' undivided attention and constantly have to look at the child ahead, who is more advanced. The second child is trying to catch up and, if the first child is very successful, may become discouraged. The youngest child resembles an only child and is usually spoiled.

### Early Memories

Adler used the adult's earliest recollections to help him understand style of life. He made interpretations of style of life based on these early memories. He felt that memory is biased and that only significant events are remembered; these recollections, then, are good indicators of present attitudes.

### The Counseling Process

The relationship between the counselor and the client received recognition by Adler. He believed that the counselor should feel warm and accepting toward the client; empathy was considered to be an important factor in the establishment of the therapeutic climate. The relationship was viewed as a collaborative one in which equal partners work out and agree upon specific goals.

The next stage of the counseling process is the assessment phase. During this stage, the counselor works to assess the client's style of life through an understanding of the client's beliefs, feelings, goals, and motives. Empathy enables the counselor not only to develop the relationship but also to understand the beliefs underlying the feelings. The counselor probes the client's early childhood to assess sibling relationships and the child's perception of his place in the family. Early recollections are used to further the life-style investigation. The assessment procedure enables the counselor to identify the client's "basic mistakes" and interpret how they are presently influencing the client.

In the third stage the counselor emphasizes the development of insight into problems through an awareness of mistaken goals and self-defeating behaviors. The counselor is confrontive in pointing out hidden purposes and using interpretation to facilitate insight. While insight is viewed as important, the emphasis is on changes in behavior. As the counselor interprets the clients' life-style, it is hoped that they will come to understand their role in creating their problems, so that they can see how to improve their present situation.

During the final stage of counseling, the counselor orients the client toward action. Clients are encouraged to take risks and try out new behaviors, to take responsibility for their lives, and to make new decisions that will enable them to reach their goals.

The above discussion is a summary of the phases of the counseling process as presented by Dinkmeyer, Pew, and Dinkmeyer (1979). For a more thorough description, counselors are encouraged to consult this important resource.

### Contributions

1. The Adlerian view of human nature is essentially positive.
2. The relationship between the counselor and the client is valued.
3. The concept of family constellation has been useful and has yielded important research investigations.
4. Adlerian theory is used by parent-education groups.
5. The concept of natural consequences has influenced child-rearing practices.

### Criticisms

1. Adlerian counseling is dependent on insight to influence change. That is, clients' experiences and life-styles are interpreted to them, and this intellectual understanding is supposed to result in behavior change.
2. The counseling process is basically educative rather than therapeutic. Clients' feelings, as related to insight, are not considered to be important.
3. Although it is done in the context of a supportive environment, Adlerian confrontation can be perceived as highly judgmental.
4. Counselors at the elementary level who use an Adlerian approach tend to limit their counseling to dealing with discipline problems, because Adlerian methods provide an efficient method for handling the misdirected goals of children, which result in behavior problems.

## KAREN HORNEY

Horney parted with Freud over his deterministic, mechanistic approach and his emphasis on instinctual drives. She emphasized, instead, the concept of anxiety, which she felt grew out of the child's feelings of isolation and helplessness. The real root of anxiety lies in the parent-child relationship, with anxiety being produced by anything that disturbs the child's fundamental security (Hall & Lindzey, 1978).

According to Horney, the insecure children handle their feelings by developing irrational (neurotic) solutions to the problem. These solutions compensate in some way for the emotional and psychological losses they've experienced, and may become permanent personality characteristics. The ten neurotic needs are listed; readers are encouraged to consult Horney's original writings listed in the reference section.

### Ten Neurotic Needs

1. The neurotic need for affection and approval.
2. The neurotic need for a partner who will take over one's life.
3. The neurotic need to restrict one's life within narrow borders.
4. The neurotic need for power.
5. The neurotic need to exploit others.
6. The neurotic need for prestige.
7. The neurotic need for personal admiration.
8. The neurotic need for personal achievement.
9. The neurotic need for self-sufficiency and independence.
10. The neurotic need for protection and unassailability.

It is important to understand that, for the neurotic, these needs are not easily met. In most cases, the need simply cannot be satisfied because of the deep inner conflict that lies at its source.

After defining the ten neurotic needs, Horney classified them into three basic orientations: moving toward people (need for love), moving away from people (need for independence), and moving against people (need for power). She distinguishes between normal individuals and neurotics by stating that normal individuals resolve their conflicts by integrating the three orientations, while neurotics rely exclusively on one of the orientations. Horney feels that all conflicts are avoidable if the child is reared in a loving, accepting home in which warmth, trust, and affection characterize the parent-child relationship (Hall and Lindzey 1978).

Horney parted significantly from Freud in her view that conflict is environmental and arises out of the individual's social surroundings. Possibly her greatest contributions were this awareness of the impact of environment in the role of psychological dysfunction, and her identification of neurotic needs and the psychological dynamics involved in neuroses.

## HARRY STACK SULLIVAN

Harry Stack Sullivan differs greatly from Adler and Horney both in his background and training and in his theoretical views. Sullivan was born and trained in America and never had direct contact with Freud. His unique approach to psychiatry was the first to emphasize the role of interpersonal relationships. He describes his approach and theory in *The Interpersonal Theory of Psychiatry* (Sullivan, 1953). His views of the importance both of interpersonal relationships and of the role of the therapist as an involved participant in the interview have significantly influenced present counseling theory and practice.

Personality, according to Sullivan, actually exists only through the individual's interactions with others. Processes such as thinking, perceiving, and even dreaming are considered to be interpersonal.

The self-system develops out of the anxiety experienced in interpersonal relationships, which originally stems from the mother-infant relationship. Individuals learn that if they please their parents, they will be praised (the good-me self), and that if they misbehave, they will be punished (the bad-me self). The self protects from anxiety and guards security. The self-system will avoid information that is not consistent with its organization, and thus it is protected from criticism. The self-system may lose its ability to be objective and may prevent the individual from accurately assessing his behavior. If the individual experiences much anxiety, the self-system will become inflated and will prevent the individual from growing and interacting with others in healthy relationships (Hall & Lindzey, 1978). Here we see some possible antecedents of Rogers' self theory and note the link between Freud's view that while anxiety stems from different sources, the ego (self) deals with it by distorting reality through use of the defense mechanisms.

Some believe that Sullivan's most unique contributions were in the area of cognitive processes. He delineated the following three modes of experiencing: *prototaxic, parataxic,* and *syntaxic.*

Prototaxic — involves experiences that have no connection or meaning for the experiencing individual. Infants undergo this kind of experiencing.

Parataxic — involves seeing a relationship between events that occur simultaneously, but that have no actual relationship. Superstitions are examples of parataxic thought processes.

Syntaxic — involves the use of language in which commonly agreed-upon verbal symbols enable communication.

Sullivan's theory of personality emphasized stages of development but differed from Freudian thinking with regard to the role of sexuality. His view of development emphasized social factors and consisted of the following six stages: infancy, childhood, juvenile era, preadolescence, early adolescence, and late adolescence.

One of Sullivan's major contributions was his view of the therapeutic interview. He made a significant departure from Freud and the so-called neoanalysts in viewing the interview as a highly personal and interpersonal experience in which the therapist functions as a "participant observer." The role of the therapist as conceptualized by Sullivan emphasizes the therapist as a person, with a focus on the communication between the therapist and patient. In other words, Sullivan acknowledged that the therapist's attitudes, feelings, doubts, or personal difficulties influence the interaction in the interview. Obviously, then, the therapist cannot assume a strictly observational stance.

The psychiatric interview consists of four stages—the formal inception, reconnaissance, detailed inquiry, and the termination. These stages are briefly summarized as follows:

1) *The Formal Inception* The therapist is viewed as an interpersonal relations expert. In the initial phase of therapy, the primary task is to determine the nature of the patient's problem and to begin a communication process in which the therapist is sensitive to nonverbal behavior, including voice tone, speech rate, and changes in volume. Sullivan emphasized that the patient has a right to expect to benefit from the experience, even from the initial session. Emphasis is placed on relationship building.

2) *Reconnaissance* During this phase the therapist structures sessions to gather factual information about the past, present, and future of the patient. The goal is to develop some hypotheses regarding the patient's problems.

3) *The Detailed Inquiry* Both questioning and listening are techniques that assist the therapist in sorting through tentative hypotheses and selecting the one that is most accurate. Information regarding the patient's functioning in all areas is collected.

4) *The Termination* A summary of the therapist's learnings about and observations of the patient characterizes this last stage. The therapist may also prescribe some guidelines for the patient following termination.

As previously stated, Sullivan's influence on contemporary counseling theory and practice is most obvious in his humanistic view of the psychiatric interview. He was a very creative thinker and was among the first to change the role of the therapist from a removed observer and interpreter of the patient's experience, to an active, involved participant in an interpersonal relationship. His emphasis on the therapist as a person and on the power of the relationship in facilitating client change was probably an antecedent of humanistic thinking, which resulted in the development of client-centered therapy.

## NEW DIRECTIONS

### The Ego Analysts

The ego analysts, while greatly influenced by Freud, have departed from Freudian theory in several significant ways. First, the ego analysts give consideration to the role of social and cultural influences on behavior. Second, they view the ego as functioning autonomously from the id. According to Heinz Hartmann (1958, 1964), a leader in ego psychology, the ego analysts believe that the ego develops separately from the id and is not dependent on the id for energy. Once developed, the ego resists reattachment to the id. Third, the ego analysts are concerned with normal functioning and believe that behavior is environmentally influenced and is relatively independent of instinctual impulses. And finally, the ego has at its disposal the cognitive processes of thinking, perceiving, and remembering, which help it adapt to the real world.

The stages of development from this view are best exemplified by Erik Erikson's (1963) psychosocial stages. The process, according to Erikson, goes through eight stages, the first four of which resemble Freud's, and the last four of which recognize the development of cognitive processes and the expanding role of the ego. Basically, Erikson states that each of the developmental stages consists of a crisis which must be successfully passed through. Success or failure at these critical points influences personality development.

According to Hall and Lindzey (1978), one of Erikson's greatest contributions is the psychosocial theory of development, which states that the life stages are formed by the interaction of social influences with the physically and psychologically maturing organism.

## SUMMARY

It has been the purpose of this chapter to explore Freudian theory, to summarize the contributions of Adler, Horney, and Sullivan, who are important links to present counseling practice, and to briefly explore the ego analysts as a contemporary extension of Freudian thinking.

In the section on Freud, we discussed his view that personality is a complex energy system consisting of the driving forces of the id and the restraining forces of the ego and superego. The reservoir of psychic energy is housed in the id, which functions by the pleasure principle. The instinctual impulses of the id are mediated by the ego and the superego, as well as by the external world. Personality, then, is a highly mechanistic and deterministic system, and behavior is largely a result of instinctual drives and unconscious processes. When the ego can no longer satisfy the demands of the ego and is flooded with anxiety, it employs defense mechanisms to enable it to cope. Repression, projection, reaction formation, fixation, and regression were discussed, along with several other commonly used defense mechanisms. Freud believed that personality developed in five psychosexual stages: oral, anal, phallic, latency, and genital. He utilized techniques such as interpretation, dream analysis, transference, and free association.

Each of the other theorists included in this chapter departed in some important way from Freudian thinking. Alfred Adler, Karen Horney, and Harry Stack Sullivan developed social-psychological views which rejected Freud's view of sexuality, placed greater emphasis on environmental and interpersonal factors, and bridged the gap with the ego-analytic view which is receiving attention today.

While Freudian theory differs in many ways from the contemporary affective approaches to counseling presented in the following chapters, there are some interesting linkages between Freud and Rogers, the counseling theorist who most significantly departed from Freudian thought.

The importance placed on feelings is the most obvious similarity between Freud and Rogers. Freud used techniques with both cognitive components (recall of early memories, interpretation, and making the unconscious conscious) and affective ones (transference and the corrective emotional experience) to facilitate client insight. It is important to note, however, that insight involved more than cognitive understanding.

It also involved the client's emotional reexperiencing of the event. Freud emphasized the emotional working through of feelings associated with past traumatic events. Blocked feelings had to be discharged through catharsis. Rogers also strongly emphasizes feelings and encourages clients to experience in the interview the very real feelings associated with their experiences. Thus, a goal of counseling, according to Rogers, is for clients to move from reporting feelings to actually feeling them with the therapist; Rogers uses empathy to accomplish this. It is interesting to note that empathy at its highest levels has both an affective and a cognitive component. That is, empathy involves the identification of feelings and a stimulus for the feelings; empathy not only brings feelings to awareness but, when most effective, also greatly facilitates clients' insight into their experiences. Here we see that change in the client, from both a Freudian and a Rogerian perspective, is most influenced not by cognitive or intellectual processes, but through feelings. This is an important similarity between the approaches.

Another interesting point of convergence between Freudian and Rogerian theory has to do with the importance of anxiety as it influences the self (ego). Freud believed that the ego coped with a flood of anxiety through use of the defense mechanisms. Rogers, without using the term *anxiety*, states that experiences that the self cannot integrate into the self-concept become denied or distorted. The denials and distortions of experience, according to self theory, result in defensive behavior. The self is coping through the use of defense mechanisms, but not in ways that are healthy and growth producing. Acceptance allows the self to be freed from anxiety and judgement, and the self-concept can change to integrate these previously threatening feelings and experiences. Thus, the goal of client-(person-) centered therapy is to relax the self-structure through empathy and unconditional positive regard in order to allow for the total integration of experience and the reduction of defensive behavior. The goal of psychoanalysis, according to Freud, is to reduce anxiety so that the ego can function without defenses.

While a comparison between Freud and Rogers can be drawn, the two were quite different in a number of important ways. Freud emphasized psychological dysfunction and held very deterministic and mechanistic views of personality and change processes; Rogers, on the other hand, emphasized psychological growth and healthy functioning with very positive views of the change process. While their therapeutic goals and their emphasis on the importance of feelings in the change process may be similar, their therapeutic approaches and techniques are quite different. That is, both seek to help individuals achieve a new level of integration; both encourage clients, through the therapist-patient relationship, to relive their experiences with an emphasis on feelings; and both enable clients to gain insight into themselves and their problems. Rogers accomplished this through accepting, understanding, listening, and empathizing; Freud used the techniques of transference, interpretation, early memory recall, and dream analysis.

Freud's influence on contemporary counseling theory and practice is apparent. One must appreciate the creativity and originality of his thinking. Indeed, he laid the foundation for all of the theories that will be discussed in the following chapters.

# REFERENCES

ADLER, A. (1925). *The theory and practice of individual psychology*, (trans. Paul Radin). London: Routledge and Kegan Paul Ltd.

ANSBACHER, H. & ANSBACHER, R. (1956). *The individual psychology of Alfred Adler*. New York: Basic Books.

BRENNER, C. (1974). *An elementary textbook of psycho-analysis*. Garden City, New York: Anchor Press.

COREY, G. (1982). *Theory and practice of counseling and psychotherapy*. (2nd ed.). Monterey, Calif.: Brooks/Cole.

DINKMEYER, D., PEW, W., DINKMEYER, D., JR. (1979). *Adlerian counseling and psychotherapy*. Monterey, Calif.: Brooks/Cole.

ERIKSON, E. (1963). *Childhood and Society*. (2nd ed.). New York: Norton.

FREUD, A. (1946). *The ego and the mechanisms of defense*. New York: International Universities Press.

HALL, C. (1954). *A primer of Freudian psychology*. New York: NAL (Mentor).

HALL, C., AND LINDZEY, G. (1978). *Theories of personality*. New York: John Wiley.

HANSEN, J., STIVIC, R., AND WARNER, R. (1982). *Counseling: Theory and Process*. (3rd ed.). Boston: Allyn & Bacon.

HARTMANN, H. (1958). *Ego psychology and the problem of adaptation*. New York: International Universities Press.

HARTMANN, H. (1964). *Essays on ego psychology: Selected problems in psychoanalytic theory*. New York: International Universities Press.

NYE, R. (1981). *Three psychologies*. (2nd ed.). Monterey, Calif.: Brooks/Cole.

SULLIVAN, H. S. (1953). The *interpersonal theory of psychiatry*. New York: W. W. Norton & Co.

# 4

# AFFECTIVE APPROACHES TO COUNSELING

**CLIENT-CENTERED THERAPY**

> Background
>
> View of Human Nature
>
> Key Concepts
>
> Process and Goals
>
> Implementation: Techniques and Procedures
>
> Contributions and Limitations

**GESTALT THERAPY**

> View of Human Nature
>
> Key Concepts
>
> Process and Goals
>
> Implementation: Techniques and Methods
>
> Contributions and Limitations

**EXISTENTIAL THERAPY**

**HOLISTIC COUNSELING**

**SUMMARY**

This chapter will focus on affective approaches to counseling, in which the counselor focuses on the client's feelings and gives secondary consideration to thoughts and behaviors. Client-centered therapy and Gestalt therapy will be discussed, along with a brief analysis of existential therapy and holistic counseling.

**Figure 4-1**   Carl Rogers
(The Bettmann Archive, Inc.)

## CLIENT-CENTERED THERAPY

### Background

Client-centered therapy was developed by Carl Rogers in reaction to the traditional, highly diagnostic, probing, and interpretive methods of psychoanalysis. *Counseling and Psychotherapy* (Rogers 1942) was the first attempt to present his new approach, one which emphasized the importance of the *quality* of the relationship between the client and the therapist. Rogers saw the therapist as the creator of a facilitative environment that would allow the client to move toward self-growth. Of his many books, *Client-Centered Therapy* (1951) and *On Becoming A Person* (1961) are considered classics.

Although client-centered counseling has evolved into a person-centered view with a wider range of applications—teaching, administration, organizational behavior, marriage and parenting, and interpersonal relations in general—the term *client-centered* will be used here both because it generally refers to counseling alone and because it is more frequently used in the literature.

### View of Human Nature

When Rogers began developing client-centered therapy, the basic belief among therapists was that individuals were basically irrational, unsocialized, and self-destructive, and had little control over themselves. Rogers rejected this view and emphasized that the individual can "guide, regulate, and control himself" (1959, p. 221). He pointed out that these views had been formed as a result of his experiences in psychotherapy; they did not precede his therapeutic experiences. Rogers's views can be organized into four basic areas: (1) a belief in the dignity and worth of each individual, (2) a perceptual view of behavior, (3) a tendency toward self-actualization, and (4) a belief that people are good and trustworthy.

*Belief in the Dignity and Worth of Each Individual*   Rogers is strongly committed to the belief that all persons should have the right to their own opinions and thoughts and should be in control of their own destiny, free to pursue their own interests in their own way as long as they do not trample on the rights of others. Rogers sees this democratic ideal, which underlies all his ideas about humanity, as having both practical utility and moral value. He also believes that a democratic society's needs are best served by social processes and social institutions that encourage the individual to be an independent, self-directing person.

*Perceptual View of Behavior*   Rogers clearly emphasizes that the ways in which individuals behave and adapt to situations are always consistent with their perceptions of themselves and their situations. He even states that "man lives essentially in his own personal and subjective world, and even his most objective functioning, in science, mathematics, and the like, is the result of subjective purpose and subjective choice" (1959, p. 191). As a result, the self-concept becomes an important aspect of one's perception. Since the self is the center of one's experiences with the environment, one's perceptions of, and interactions with, the environment change as the sense of self changes. Rogers feels that, in general, one's experiences are either (1) organized into the self-structure, (2) ignored because they are inconsistent with the sense of self, or (3) perceived distortedly because they are not harmonious with self-perceptions.

Thus those who are developing their full potential are able to accept the subjective aspects of self and to live subjectively, relying on their own subjective sense of evaluation rather than depending on external sources of evaluation.

*Tendency Toward Self-Actualization*   Rogers has gradually increased his emphasis on the inherent tendency of people to move in directions that can be described roughly as growth, health, adjustment, socialization, self-realization, and autonomy. He calls this directional tendency the *actualizing tendency*, and he defines it as "the inherent tendency of the organism to develop all its capacities in ways which serve to maintain or enhance the organism" (1959, p. 196).

This conception, while relatively simple, is all-encompassing. In fact, Rogers sees this actualizing tendency as applying to all life—animals and plants as well as people. Thus the essential nature of life is that it is an active process in which the organism interacts with its environment in ways designed to maintain, to enhance, and to reproduce itself.

Rogers emphasizes several ideas by his stress upon this actualizing tendency. First, the actualizing tendency is the primary motivating force of the human organism. Second, the actualizing tendency is a function of the total organism rather than of one or more parts of that organism. People do have specific needs and motives, but Rogers points out that the ways in which a person seeks to meet these needs enhances rather than diminishes self-esteem and other strivings of the total organism. In this sense Rogers's conception is similar though not identical to Maslow's hierarchy of needs.

Third, this stress on the actualizing tendency suggests a broad conception of motivation, including the usual needs and motives but emphasizing the individual's tendency to physical growth and maturation, the need for close interpersonal relationships, and the tendency of the individual to impose herself on her environment—that is, to move in directions of autonomy and away from external control.

Finally, individuals have both the capacity to actualize themselves and the tendency to do so. These capacities are released under the proper conditions. Hence, the counseling process is not aimed at doing something *to* or *for* the individual; rather it is aimed at freeing the individual's capacities for normal growth and development. The counseling theory developed by Rogers simply attempts to specify the conditions that allow this freeing process to occur.

***Belief that People are Basically Good and Trustworthy*** Throughout his writings Rogers uses such words as *trustworthy, reliable, constructive,* or *good* to describe the inherent characteristics of people. Rogers knows that people sometimes behave in untrustworthy ways, that they are capable of deceit, hate, and cruelty. But he believes that these unfavorable characteristics arise out of a defensiveness that has alienated individuals from their inherent nature. This defensiveness is the result of a widening incongruence between the individuals' ideal selves—the way they believe they ought to be, and their real selves—the way they think they are. As this incongruence becomes greater, individuals are less open to their own experiences, tending to distrust them, and they attempt to hide both from others and from themselves. However, Rogers points out that as defensiveness diminishes and individuals become more open to all of their experiences, they tend to behave in ways that are seen as being socialized and trustworthy, striving for meaningful and constructive relationships with others.

## Key Concepts

Rogers believes that client-centered therapy is on stronger theoretical ground than other kinds of therapy because of its close relationship to a well-developed theory of personality. In his writings Rogers has presented a series of nine formal propositions which clearly outline the underlying personality theory for a client-centered approach.

*All individuals exist in a continually changing world of experience of which they are the center* (Rogers 1951). This description of the private world of each individual's experience is sometimes called the *phenomenal field*. It includes all that the individual experiences, although these experiences are only occasionally conscious. The important aspect of this proposition is that only the individual can completely and genuinely perceive this world of experience. No one else can fully understand the experience of another who is rejected by a friend or unable to find a job. We can observe other individuals, even measuring their reactions to various stimuli, but we can never know in full and vivid detail how they are experiencing and perceiving any given situation.

*Individuals react to their phenomenal field as they experience and perceive it.* This perceptual field is, for the individual, "reality" (Rogers 1951). What this means, of course, is that individuals do not react to reality as it may be perceived by most people around them, but rather they react to reality as they perceive it. Such a proposition clearly supports the client-centered idea of understanding the individual's phenomenal field from his perception as a major part of the therapeutic process.

*Behavior is basically the goal-directed attempt of individuals to satisfy their needs as experienced, in their phenomenal field as perceived.* This proposition, then, ties in with the second proposition by emphasizing that individuals do not react to some absolute reality; they react to their perceptions of that reality. Rogers observed that a man dying of thirst in a desert, for instance, will struggle as hard to reach a mirage as he will to reach a real body of water. Thus, reality for any individual is that individual's perception of reality, regardless of whether or not it has been tested and confirmed.

*The best vantage point for understanding behavior is from the internal frame of reference of the individual.* Rogers includes within this *internal frame of reference* the full range of sensations, perceptions, meanings, and memories available to consciousness. Thus, to understand another individual from this internal frame of reference is to concentrate on a subjective reality that exists within that individual at any given time.

To achieve this understanding requires empathy. On the other hand, simply understanding another individual from an external frame of reference is to view the individual without empathy, as an object, usually with the intent of emphasizing objective reality. Persons become objects in that we make no empathic inferences about their subjective experiences. Even when the counselor's internal frame of reference may more closely approximate objective reality than the client's, it is still only the counselor's perception of objective reality, which tends to ignore the client's subjective experience of reality.

The student who feels that her teacher has treated her unfairly, for example, will act as though the teacher's treatment really was unfair. Whether or not an objective analysis of that treatment will agree with the student's perception is irrelevant, except perhaps for the self-satisfaction of the teacher. As long as the student believes that the teacher treated her unfairly, she will continue to behave as if the treatment really was unfair. To bring about a change in her behavior, Rogers suggests that her perception of that situation must first change, since her behavior is the result of her perception of the situation.

*Most ways of behaving adopted by the individual are consistent with the individual's concept of self.* The self-concept is basic to the client-centered system. For Rogers the self-concept describes an organized picture consisting of the individual's perception of himself alone and himself in relation to other persons and objects in his environment together with the values attached to those perceptions. Such a picture does not always exist at a level of awareness, but that picture is always available to awareness. Thus, by definition, the self-concept excludes unconscious self-attitudes that are not available to consciousness. In addition, the self-concept is considered to be fluid and changing, a process rather than a fixed entity.

*The incongruence that often occurs between an individual's conscious wishes and his behavior is the result of a split between the individual's self-concept and his experiences.* Rogers emphasizes some specific terms when he talks about this incongruence, particularly in referring to the development of certain needs. Rogers points out that as the individual gains an awareness of self, he also develops a need for positive regard and positive self-regard. Obviously these two needs are closely related. When the individual feels loved or not loved by significant others, he develops positive or negative feelings about himself.

*When the incongruence between the individual's self-picture and the individual's experiences is very wide, a state of anxiety exists.* Rogers believes that this state of anxiety can be best understood by seeing it as the result of the incongruence between the individual's ideal self and real self. As these two pictures of self diverge, the individual becomes more and more upset with herself and also fears that others will see her as inadequate and worthless. The anxiety comes from a fear that others will recognize her basic inferiority.

*To lower an individual's anxiety, the self-concept must become more congruent with the individual's actual experiences.* To state it differently, one's ideal self and real self must become more similar. One can change by creating conditions that are less threatening to one's self and that encourage one to assimilate denied and distorted experiences, and by sharing these with a significant person so that one can receive positive feedback that one is a worthwhile, able individual.

*The fully functioning individual is completely open to all experiences, exhibiting no defensiveness.* Such an individual experiences unconditional positive self-regard. The self-concept is congruent with the experiences, and the individual is able to assert his basic actualizing tendency.

### Process and Goals

Client-centered counseling can be described as an "*if, then*" approach to counseling: *If* certain conditions exist, *then* a definable process is set in motion, leading to certain outcomes or changes in the client's personality and behavior. The basic premise of client-centered counseling, then, is that once the proper conditions for growth is established, the client will be able to gain insight and take positive steps toward solving personal difficulties. In the client-centered view, the following conditions are both necessary and sufficient for counseling:

#### Conditions for Growth

PSYCHOLOGICAL CONTACT   Rogers suggests that the first essential condition for effective counseling is that two persons be in contact. He defines this contact as a situation in which each person makes a difference in the experiences of the other. From the very beginning, then, Rogers is setting the groundwork for a two-way interaction rather than a process where the counselor does something *to* or *for* the client.

MINIMUM STATE OF ANXIETY   The second necessary condition is that the client be in a state of incongruence, feeling vulnerable or anxious. As mentioned before, the client's incongruence between his self-concept and his actual experiences causes this anxiety. Rogers believes that the more anxious the individual is about this incongruence, the more likely successful counseling will take place. In effect, this means the individual must be uncomfortable enough to want to change.

COUNSELOR CONGRUENCE    The counselor must be congruent or genuine in the relationship. Rogers talks of the counselor's being authentic—or real—in the sense that what the counselor is experiencing internally must be consistent with the messages the counselor is communicating to the client externally. This allows the counselor to be aware of and honest about the kinds of feelings the client is eliciting.

UNCONDITIONAL POSITIVE REGARD    The counselor must experience unconditional positive regard for the client. This genuine acceptance of all aspects of the client's self-experiences is central to the client-centered counselor. Such unconditional positive regard for an individual means respecting the person, regardless of the different values the counselor might place on certain behaviors. To maintain such feelings for a person, counselors must be nonevaluative. They do not judge one behavior as being positive and another negative; rather, they accept the client as an individual, regardless of the client's behaviors. Rogers believes that when this condition is provided for the client, the client comes to believe that she is a person of worth, a person capable of growth.

EMPATHIC UNDERSTANDING    The counselor must experience empathic understanding of the client's internal frame of reference. Recognizing that no one can ever fully understand what an individual is experiencing internally, Rogers emphasizes that the counselor must develop a highly accurate understanding of the client's internal frame of reference. It is the counselor's attempt to put himself in the place of the client that is important. Although the counselor can never become the client, the counselor must try to understand as if he were the client himself.

CLIENT PERCEPTION    Finally, the client must perceive, at least to a minimal degree, the counselor's unconditional positive regard and empathic understanding. It is not enough that the counselor genuinely accept the client, and understand and empathize with the client's situation. Acceptance and understanding will have value only if they are communicated so that the client perceives that they are present.

*Outcomes*    In the client-centered view, the counselor must allow the client to set the goals. The client-centered counselor believes that individuals have an innate motivating force, the need for self-actualization, that will enable them to develop and regulate their own behavior. The counselor who sets goals for the client would be interfering with the basic nature of the individual. In Rogers's view, such a counselor is unable to help the individual learn self-reliance. In essence, the goal of the client-centered counselor is to establish the proper therapeutic conditions to allow the normal developmental pattern of the individual to be brought back into play.

In a more specific sense, the goal of client-centered counseling is to help the clients become more mature and to reinstitute the movement towards self-actualization by removing the obstacles. The objective, then, is to free individuals from anxiety and doubts that prevent them from developing their own resources and potential. Thus, counseling is simply a process of releasing an already existing force in a potentially adequate individual.

Rogers (1951) recognizes that the existence of those necessary and sufficient conditions for effective counseling do result in a process that leads to certain outcomes. As a result of these conditions, the client is less defensive and more congruent and open to his experiences. He is more realistic, objective, and extensional in his perceptions, and consequently, more effective in problem solving. The client's vulnerability to threat is reduced because of the increased congruence of self and experience.

The client's perception of his ideal self is more realistic, more achievable. As a result of the increased congruence of self and experience, his real self becomes more congruent with his ideal self; hence all tension is reduced and the degree of positive self-regard is increased.

The client perceives the locus of evaluation and the locus of choice to be within himself. He feels more confident and more self-directing; his values are determined by his own valuing process.

The client experiences more acceptance of others. He accepts more behaviors as belonging to himself and conversely has fewer behaviors that he denies as part of his own self-experience. Others see his behavior as more socialized and mature.

### Implementation: Techniques and Procedures

The development of client-centered therapy shifted the focus from *what* the therapist does, to *who* the therapist is, particularly her philosophy and attitudes. Certainly the primary emphasis is on the counseling relationship itself. As such, the "techniques" are simply ways of expressing and communicating genuineness, unconditional positive regard, and empathic understanding in such a way that the client knows that the therapist is attempting to fully understand the client's internal frame of reference. Thus techniques per se are unacceptable since they would destroy the genuineness of the therapist, by being applied self-consciously. Therefore the only acceptable techniques are those that represent implementation of the therapist's philosophy and attitudes in facilitating the client's personal growth.

There are, however, certain emphases within this counseling approach. One is an emphasis on the here-and-now of the individual's existence, both inside and outside of the counseling relationship. The counselor does not need a knowledge of the nature and history of the client's difficulties. What has happened in the individual's past to cause the present difficulties is not important to the counselor; how the client is now operating is. As a simple illustration, consider a client who feels hatred for her brother. The client-centered approach takes the position that it makes little difference that this hatred developed because of a particular situation. Rather, how the client now feels toward her brother and how her feelings affect her whole pattern of behavior are important. Thus one emphasis is to help the client focus on her present feelings by expressing them verbally.

This emphasis on the here-and-now replaces diagnosis in counseling. Diagnosis is considered undesirable because it suggests that certain individuals have the power to decide what is right for all individuals. It also violates the belief that all individuals are self-determining beings, responsible for their own actions. Likewise, diagnosis in counseling is inappropriate because only the client can diagnose the difficulty. Only the client can accurately see the internal frame of reference. It is dangerous for counselors to attempt diagnosis, no matter how accurate they feel their perception of the client's internal frame of reference may be. Finally, diagnosis implies a denial of the unique qualities of each person. To diagnose is to place individuals in categories, and the client-centered counselor wants to avoid this trap. Instead, the counselor responds to the individual as a unique person with a potential for self-diagnosis and remediation.

Another major emphasis of the client-centered approach is a concentration on the emotional rather than the intellectual elements in the relationship. Pure knowledge is not seen as helping the client; the impact of knowledge may be blocked from awareness by the emotional satisfactions that the individual achieves through the present behavior. Intellectually, the client may know what the real situation is but, because the client responds emotionally, this knowledge does not help to change behavior. Although clients ordinarily begin talking about particular situations and emphasize the factual content of those situations, client-centered counselors attempt to help clients focus on feelings about themselves, other people, and events that take place in their world. The counselor then feeds back to clients as accurately as possible the feelings they are expressing, in the hope that they will be able to view these feelings more objectively.

Since the emphasis of client-centered counseling is not on techniques but on the ability of the counselor to establish a relationship in which the necessary conditions outlined earlier are present, the counselor must be a patient and expert listener, one who fully accepts each individual by offering an atmosphere of unconditional positive regard and empathic understanding. The counselor attempts to help the client develop insight by encouraging free expression and then reflecting these feelings. In this process no specific problem, information, or other intellectual elements are emphasized; the focus is on the current state of the individual.

If the counselor follows this process, then the necessary and sufficient conditions for counseling are established. Clients will be able to go through the process of articulating their feelings, developing insight and self-understanding, and finally, developing new goals and modes of behavior. Counseling may end at this stage, but the process continues. The client has simply been returned to a state that allows the lifelong process towards self-actualization to continue. The individual is once again in control. The external conditions of worth have disappeared, and the organismic valuing process has taken its proper place as the evaluator of experiences and the controller of behavior.

Boy and Pine (1982), however, suggest that the client-centered viewpoint has been expanded and that there are two phases to this effective client-centered relationship. The first phase consists of those dynamics that have been traditionally identified by Rogers as essential in building a therapeutic, facilitative, and substantive relationship—empathy, acceptance, genuineness, liberality, involvement, sensitive listening, and equalizing. The second phase, which depends on the effectiveness of the relationship built in the first phase, centers on the needs of the client. Although they give but little emphasis and clarification to this phase and the needs of clients, they do point out that clients often need the intervention of counselors to obtain such basic needs as a job, adequate housing, and access to governmental agencies. Such an expansion, which is highly consistent with what client-centered counselors are doing, enables the counselor to be more flexible and concrete in meeting client needs once the therapeutic relationship has been fully established.

### Contributions and Limitations

The client-centered approach makes several unique contributions to counseling effectiveness. Its emphasis is on providing clients with the kind of facilitative environment in which the focus is fully on their concerns. As a result, they can sense that they are being listened to as they receive responses from the therapist that involve feedback of what they had communicated. Client-centered counseling emphasizes reflective listening, as the counselor adopts the internal frame of reference of the client. Further, if clients feel they are being heard without being judged or evaluated, they are likely to express even deeper feelings, thus leading to further self-exploration and self-understanding of attitudes, beliefs, and feelings. In addition, client-centered counselors consciously avoid taking responsibility for decision making by clients, leaving that responsibility with clients and thus helping them recognize their own power over themselves. Lastly, the client-centered concepts are applicable to a wide variety of helping situations, as well as to daily living itself.

Client-centered counseling does have some limitations. Some counselors oversimplify the major concepts of the theory and limit their own repertoire of responses to reflections and empathic listening. As a result, they often fail to distinguish between the use of techniques and the use of their own personality, their self-as-instrument. Another limitation: clients often fail to understand what the counselor is trying to accomplish. Such clients, since they are unaware of any positive effects resulting from their interactions with the counselor, may withdraw from the counseling process. In addition, client-centered therapy appears to be less effective with persons who do not voluntarily seek counseling, who have limited contact with reality, or who have difficulty communicating.

## GESTALT THERAPY

Gestalt therapy, developed by Frederick Perls, is a therapeutic approach in which the therapist assists the client toward self-integration and toward learning to utilize his energy in appropriate ways to grow, develop, and actualize. Perls's most important books include *Gestalt Therapy Verbatim* (1969a), *In And Out Of The Garbage Pail* (1969b), and *Gestalt Therapy: Excitement And Growth In The Human Personality* (Perls, Hefferline, & Goodman, 1951).

## View of Human Nature

Like client-centered therapy, Gestalt therapy views people as essentially phenomenological. Passons (1975) lists eight assumptions about the nature of humanity that form the framework for the Gestalt approach.

1. A person is a composite whole made up of interrelated parts. None of these parts, body emotions, thoughts, sensations, and perceptions can be understood outside the context of the whole person.
2. A person is also part of his own environment and cannot be understood apart from it.
3. A person chooses how to respond to external and internal stimuli, is an actor on his world, not a reactor.
4. A person has the potential to be fully aware of all sensations, thoughts, emotions, and perceptions.
5. A person is capable of making choices because of this awareness.
6. People have the capacity to govern their own lives effectively.
7. People cannot experience the past and the future, they can only experience themselves in the present.
8. People are neither basically good nor bad.

It is clear from these eight assumptions that Gestalt theorists share with Rogers an optimistic view that people are capable of self-direction. However, Perls also emphasized that individuals must take responsibility for their own lives. He believed that the motivation for this process was the result of an inherent goal of self-actualization. All other needs were viewed as stemming from and grounded in this basic need to actualize oneself (Perls, 1969a). Unlike Rogers, however, this striving for self-actualization is present-centered, rather than future-focused. Gestaltists believe that a healthy personality exists when a person's experiences form a meaningful whole (gestalt), where there is smooth transition between those sets of experiences that are immediately in the focus of awareness and those sets that are in the background. Thus, one has the capacity to know one's own balance and to attend to one's own needs as these needs emerge. Therefore, the purpose of Gestalt therapy is to increase the client's self-awareness, since awareness is, in itself, therapeutic. Perls believed that, with awareness, the most important unfinished business would emerge to be dealt with.

## Key Concepts

Probably the most significant concept in Gestalt therapy is the *now*. For Perls, this is related to awareness in that one becomes aware of what one does by becoming aware of what one is doing *now* and by remaining in this awareness, letting the experience flow through the total senses. By allowing oneself to fully experience the present moment, the individual is able to allow "organismic self-regulation" to take over and to eliminate self-manipulation, environmental control, and other factors that interfere with this natural self-regulating process. This attainment of awareness as it relates to the present is the basic goal of Gestalt therapy. Perls (1969a) in fact indicates that "awareness per se—by and of itself—can be curative" (p. 16).

This emphasis on experiencing the here-and-now is certainly a major contribution of the Gestalt approach, one which has greatly influenced other theories. Other affective approaches, as well as the major behavioral approaches and the cognitive approaches, have placed increasing focus on the present, either in terms of feelings, behaviors, or thinking.

Anxiety from the Gestalt point of view is the gap between the now and the later. Perls suggests that individuals experience anxiety because they leave the security of the present and become preoccupied with the future, frequently expecting bad things to happen. As a result, living with a focus on the future often results in not seeing what is at hand. Whether this leads to daydreams—fleeing from the present into better times—or catastrophizing—excessive worrying about what might happen—the impact on the present is real and can be dealt with only by "presentizing" these into current awareness (Passons, 1975).

Similar problems occur when individuals focus on the past. In particular, focusing on the past often relates to blaming the past as being responsible for what is happening now. By using past events and experiences as a scapegoat, clients place responsibility for their current behavior onto the past and thus avoid present responsibility. This avoidance of living in the present prevents individuals from having the energy or time for creative adjustments and changes that could make the present more satisfying. In addition, the past is over and cannot be reexperienced other than in fantasy and is usually dealt with in the past tense, leaving the past in the past. Gestalt therapists attempt to presentize the past by using fantasy to bring the past into the present. This is done by asking the clients to relate past events as if they were occurring at the moment. By reexperiencing the past as if it were happening now, clients are frequently able to reexamine those events and gain a new perspective for the meaning of those events for their lives.

This is particularly true in dealing with unfinished business or interrupted experiences of the past. Perls (1969a) emphasizes the need to relive or reexperience situations from the past about which clients have unexpressed feelings such as anger, pain, anxiety, grief, guilt, resentment, alienation, and so on. Even though these feelings are unexpressed, they are associated with distinct memories of specific events in which the client did not attain closure or did not resolve the matter. Perls points out that simply having an intellectual awareness of these events is not enough, but that clients must fully experience these events and work through the feelings involved.

Another key concept for the Gestalt view is that of *growth* or *maturation,* which Perls (1971) defined as ". . . the transcendence from environmental support to self-support" (p. 30). Thus maturity is seen in terms of process rather than in terms of product and involves the individual's taking on the functions necessary for self-support and learning to mobilize her own resources for dealing with the environment effectively. This necessitates learning to make creative adjustments, in which an active, dynamic, and changing self is able to respond both to environmental pressures and to inner emergent needs.

## Process and Goals

Gestaltists believe that individuals seek counseling because their psychological needs are not being met. They expect the counselor to provide environmental support and often attempt to manipulate the counselor into doing so. However, Gestalt therapists seek to assist clients in discovering that they need not be dependent upon others, but that they can become independent beings. This involves helping clients to become responsible for themselves and to work toward achieving integration, in which there is a bringing together of all the parts of themselves that they have disowned. This integration enables one to function as a systemic whole comprised of feelings, attitudes, thoughts, and behaviors. Energy previously directed toward the playing of roles is released for the individual's self-regulating capabilities. All of this is a process, on-going and never completed. As Perls (1969a) points out, "Integration is never completed; maturation is never completed. It's an ongoing process forever and ever . . . There's always something to be integrated; always something to be learned" (p. 64).

Passons (1975) has divided the kinds of problems that individuals experience into six areas: lack of awareness, lack of self-responsibility, a loss of contact with environment, inability to complete Gestalts, disowning of needs, and dichotomizing dimensions of the self.

*Lack of awareness* is usually a problem for people with rigid personalities. The image they have established to maintain the delicate balance between self and self-image causes them to lose contact with the *what* and *how* of their behavior. They simply exist, moving through life from day to day with an uneasy feeling of nonfulfillment.

*Lack of self-responsibility* is related to lack of awareness but takes the form of trying to manipulate the environment instead of manipulating the self. Instead of striving for independence or self-sufficiency, characteristics of maturity, the individual strives to remain in a dependency situation.

*Loss of contact with the environment* is also related to the first problem area, lack of awareness. This problem can take two forms. The first occurs when an individual's behavior has become so rigid that no input from the environment is accepted or incorporated. Such individuals withdraw from contact with the environment, including other people. Such a withdrawal prohibits them from meeting their needs and from moving toward a state of maturity. A second form is manifested by those who need so much approbation that they lose themselves by trying to incorporate everything from the environment, becoming almost totally subsumed by the self-image.

*Inability to complete Gestalt* or to complete unfinished business is another area that accounts for many problems brought to counseling. Unfinished business causes the individual to continue to strive to complete the business, even in her current activities. However, when these unfinished situations within us become powerful enough, they cause difficulties and prevent us from dealing with current situations. "The individual is beset with preoccupation, compulsive behavior, wariness, oppressive energy, and much self-defeating activity" (Polster & Polster, 1973, p. 36).

*Disowning of needs* occurs when someone acts to deny a need. Passons (1975) points out that in our society individuals commonly deny their need to be aggressive;

since this need is generally socially unacceptable, individuals tend not to express it. Instead of moving energy into constructive behavior, people deny the existence of some need and thereby lose the energy it produces.

*Dichotomizing dimensions of the self* takes the form of people perceiving themselves at one end of a possible continuum. An example would be the woman who sees herself only as being weak, who never fully realizes that she has both strengths and weaknesses. The best known split is what Perls called "top dog, underdog." The top dog is that part of the individual characterized as moralistic, perfectionistic, and authoritarian. The top dog strives to get the individual to behave as others expect. The underdog represents the desires of the individual and operates as the defensive and dependent part of the personality. Individuals who listen only to the top dog and fail to recognize and meet their own needs will have an internal conflict.

Each of the six problem areas is related directly to conflicts within the self, conflicts usually resulting from an inability to bring together individual needs and environmental demands. Problems arise when individuals fail to utilize their own capacity for self-regulation and expend their energies in attempting to avoid frustration by depending upon others, by acting helpless, and by manipulating the environment in other ways. Thus one step in the process is for the counselor to frustrate the client's demands for support and help so that the client is forced to rely on his own resources. Of course, the client may resist this transition from external to internal support.

At the point at which the client is unable to manipulate the counselor into solving his problems and is unwilling to move toward self-support, an impasse occurs. The client is stuck, unable to experience his feelings because of the threat involved. For example, the client who is confused, frustrated, or blocked is seen by Perls (1969a) as being in an impasse. At this point the counselor identifies the impasse and provides an accepting situation, a "safe emergency," in which the client can feel safer in working toward self-support. Actually, Perls points out that most clients do *not* want to go beyond the impasse, since it is easier to keep things the way they are. Therefore, the counselor must facilitate the process in an active, propulsive manner so that the client is forced to recognize and deal with his impasse in order to get in touch with, and work through, his frustrations.

Gestalt therapy has several important goals. Certainly the most significant goal is helping individuals assume responsibility for themselves, rather than carrying out duties according to another's expectations. The aim is to challenge the client to move from "environmental support" to "self-support."

A second major goal is achieving integration. An integrated person functions as a systematic whole comprising feelings, perceptions, thoughts, and a physical body whose processes cannot be divorced from the more psychological components. When one's inner state (emotions) and behavior match, little energy is wasted, and one is more capable of responding appropriately to meet one's needs.

As was pointed out earlier, the achievement of self-regulation and integration requires awareness. Awareness is seen as both necessary and sufficient for change. Perls (1969a) emphasized that once one is aware, "the organism can work on the healthy Gestalt principle: that the most important unfinished situation will always emerge and can be dealt with'' (p. 51). Consequently, awareness is always an underlying aim of the counselor.

### Implementation: Techniques and Methods

From the very beginning the Gestalt counselor strives to challenge clients to assume responsibility for their own actions. The counselor quickly attempts to communicate to the client that, although the counselor wants to facilitate the client's growth and self-discovery, the counselor cannot make the changes for the client. In essence, the counselor seeks to force the client into open and honest interaction, refusing to tolerate the games that the client may play with people outside counseling. Such an interaction sets the conditions that will facilitate the client's growth and awareness.

The essential technique at the disposal of the Gestalt counselor is the establishment of what Perls calls a ''continuum of awareness.'' This continuum of awareness is seen as being required for the organism to work on the healthy Gestalt principle that the most important unfinished situation will always emerge and must be dealt with. The counselor does this by integrating the client's attention and awareness, by helping him assimilate into his structure of self the totality of his experiences. A major technique of the Gestalt counselor is deliberately playing provocative games with the client, games intended to force the client to confront and acknowledge feelings that have been so arduously avoided. As Perls (1969b) suggests, individuals who are experiencing difficulty cannot see the obvious. They are full of avoidances and resistances that keep them from full awareness. Perls suggests that clients reach an impasse that they don't want to work through. Such impasses involve unsatisfied needs or unfinished business that clients believe they lack the resources to resolve. The counselor, rather than providing answers to the client's problems, seeks to force the client to work through the impasse—first by structuring the situation so that the impasse comes into the open, then by frustrating the client by refusing to give what is sought. In this situation the counselor's goal is to help the client recognize that the impasse exists in the mind and that the client does have the ability to resolve the impasse. In effect, the counselor is telling the client, ''You can and must be responsible for yourself.''

Gestalt counseling, like client-centered counseling, does not attempt to reconstruct the past or uncover the unconscious motivations of the client. Gestalt counselors focus on the present. They believe that people who tend to intellectualize about the past or future are generally having difficulty with the present and are using these discussions to resist the counselor's attempt to deal with current functioning; therefore, counselors can gain their most important information about clients by what they observe during interaction with the client. Gestalt counselors must be able to pick out discrepancies between verbal and nonverbal expressions and feed these expressions back to clients, making clients more aware of their own behavior and emotions. This here-and-now orientation is further encouraged by the counselor who asks such questions as ''What is your right hand doing now?'' or ''How does your voice sound now?'' The counselor never asks ''why'' because why questions encourage intellectualization, whereas ''how'' and ''what'' questions focus attention on current functioning. In both cases the counselor is seeking to get the client to become more aware of feelings, behaviors, emotions, and sensations in the moment to moment of *now*. At the same time, the counselor is attempting to discover what the client is trying to avoid and in what areas of functioning the client is suffering from internal conflicts.

In addition to the techniques of frustrating the client and fostering here-and-now orientation, Gestalt counselors also use experiential games that increase individuals' self-awareness and awareness of their impasses, then help them reintegrate themselves. This last step is the most crucial, for if individuals are stripped of all their defenses and given no new ways of behavior, they will be even more vulnerable to outside forces than they were prior to counseling. Levitsky and Perls (1970) and Passons (1972) both list a variety of specific techniques. Following are some of those that appear on both lists and seem appropriate for use by counselors.

### Specific Techniques

USE OF PERSONAL PRONOUNS    Clients are encouraged to use *I* instead of words like *it, you,* or *we* when talking about themselves. This helps clients to own their own behavior. For example, the client might say, "I didn't have many dates this year. Next year it will be different." The counselor might respond with *"It* will be different? Who are you talking about?" The client might then respond "Me. *I'll* be different."

CONVERTING QUESTIONS TO STATEMENTS    Clients often use questions to keep the focus off themselves or to hide what they are really thinking. The client who asks "Do you really believe that?" is generally saying, "I don't think you believe that." Forcing clients to make statements makes them declare their own belief systems and forces them to take responsibility.

ASSUMING RESPONSIBILITY    The client is sometimes asked to end all expressions of feelings or beliefs with, "and I take responsibility for it." Sometimes clients are encouraged to assume responsibility by having them change "can't" to "won't," or by changing "but" to "and." For instance, "I want to lose weight, but I just keep eating a lot," sounds different when it is stated "I want to lose weight, and I just keep eating a lot." By changing the *but* to *and* the client is verbalizing the responsibility. This assumption of responsibility helps clients to see themselves as having internal strength, rather than relying on external controls.

PLAYING THE PROJECTION    When a client projects something onto another individual, especially the counselor, the counselor asks the client to play the role of the other person. For instance, when a client says to the counselor, perhaps as the result of the counselor structuring a frustration situation, "I have the feeling you don't really like me," the counselor may ask the client to play the role of the counselor and to express what she believes the counselor is feeling. By doing this the client recognizes that her feelings toward the counselor are being projected in a way that affects what she believes the counselor is feeling toward her.

THE EMPTY CHAIR    In the empty chair technique, clients are given the opportunity to act out the way they would like to behave toward another person, pictured as sitting in the empty chair. This role playing helps clients get in touch with parts of themselves that they were either unaware of or have denied. In addition, the client may also be rehearsing a new role that will be tried outside of counseling. The rehearsal strengthens the client's belief that the new behavior can be carried out. The empty chair technique can also be used when the client is caught between conflicting parts of her personality (top dog, underdog; passive, aggressive). In this situation, the counselor may instruct the client to play both roles, sitting in one chair for one role and sitting in the second chair for the second role. The client carries on a verbal dialogue between the two parts, switching seats to represent the part of the personality being portrayed. Such a dialogue brings the conflict into the open so that the individual can inspect and resolve it.

A variety of other techniques are used by Gestalt counselors. The ones above are frequently used and are representative of many other techniques.

### Contributions and Limitations

Gestalt counseling is particularly effective in avoiding the kind of games clients often play with counselors. Its focus on helping clients to experience all their present feelings more fully avoids allowing clients to use helplessness as an excuse. Gestalt counseling is a confrontive and active approach, stressing the *what* and *how* of behavior and leading to the acceptance of personal responsibility for behavior. Clients are able to work through the barriers that have prevented them from expressing the unfinished business that has interfered with effective contact with themselves and others.

Limitations of Gestalt counseling arise mainly from its failure to develop a solid theory. Perls seemed to discount the value of a systematic discussion of therapy and to discourage research to evaluate the value of Gestalt counseling. As a result, Gestalt therapy often has become a collection of jargon and techniques that the counselor uses *on* the client; the danger is that these techniques may be used to manipulate rather than to release the client.

## EXISTENTIAL THERAPY

Unlike most therapeutic approaches, existential therapy is not closely tied to one person. Primarily the product of European existential philosophers, existential counseling consists of numerous approaches that emphasize the philosophical concerns of what it means to become fully human. Major American exponents of this approach include May, Van Kaam, and Frankl. Their most important works are *Man's Search For Himself* (May, 1953), *Existential Psychology* (May, 1961), *The Art of Existential Counseling* (Van Kaam, 1966), and *Man's Search For Meaning* (Frankl, 1959).

Existential theory focuses on the human condition. Rather than a system of techniques used to influence clients, this approach is primarily an attitude that stresses the understanding of persons. Hence, it is not a school of therapy nor is it a unified and systematic theory.

May (1961) has proposed six essential characteristics which constitute the nature of an existing person.

1. Humans are centered in themselves. Neurosis is only one method the individual uses to protect his own center or existence.
2. Humans have the character of self-affirmation, or the need to preserve their centeredness. The preservation of this centeredness takes will.
3. Humans have the possibility of moving from centeredness to participation with other beings. The moving from centeredness to participation involves risk.
4. Awareness lies on the subjective side of centeredness. Humans are able to be subjectively aware of that with which they are in contact.
5. Humans have a unique form of awareness called self-consciousness. Awareness means knowledge of external dangers and threats, and consciousness has to do with one's experience with oneself as the subject who has a world.
6. Humans have the characteristic of anxiety, the feeling of one in a struggle against that which would destroy one's being.

To these six characteristics Frankl (1959) adds a seventh.

7. The primary force in one's life is one's search for meaning. Each person must have a unique and specific meaning, one that can be fulfilled by that person alone. One's striving toward existence takes will.

Existential theory emphasizes concepts that are more philosophical than those in most therapies. Existentialists see human beings as capable of self-awareness, a unique and distinctive capacity that allows them to think and decide. For the existentialist, the more awareness a person has, the greater the person's possibilites for freedom. Thus, the power to choose among alternatives is an essential aspect of being human. This freedom to choose and to act becomes a responsibility. This, of course, implies that one is responsible for one's existence and one's destiny; they are not the result of deterministic forces of conditioning.

The awareness of freedom and responsibility gives rise to existential anxiety, which is a basic human attribute. The knowledge that one *must* choose, despite an uncertain outcome, results in anxiety. Existential anxiety also results from the awareness of being finite and from facing the inevitable prospect of death. Awareness of death gives the present moment significance, because one realizes one has only a limited time to actualize one's human potential. Existential guilt, then, is the result of failing to become what one is fully able to become. Since no one ever fully fulfills his potential, guilt is universal and is therefore a condition of existence. This existential guilt, however, is a positive force, since it leads to humility, sensitivity in personal relationships, and creative utilization of one's potentialities (May, 1953).

Existential therapists recognize that individuals seek counseling for any of several reasons, but they believe a major reason is that clients seek to expand their psychological world in one way or another. The client's world is unique, and the counselor must understand it to assist the client. The counselor encourages the client to unfold his world in the encounter so that both client and counselor can begin to understand it, and the client can act upon the possibilities inherent in it. Thus the counselor's main task is not only to show the client where, when, and to what extent the client has failed to realize his potential, but also to attempt to help the client *experience* this existence as fully as possible. Technique loses importance, as existential therapists utilize whatever procedure seems appropriate based on their understanding of the client's *being* (May, 1961).

Because honesty is an essential characteristic of an existential encounter, counselors must expose their true selves, and they cannot view the client as an object to be manipulated or exploited. The counselor's ability to be human enables clients to become aware of similar qualities in themselves. Through this process individuals will recognize their potentials and achieve self-growth, because that becomes their responsibility.

In existential counseling knowledge and insight are presumed to follow commitment; this is the direct opposite of most other counseling approaches. Finally, most existentialist counselors do not believe in viewing individuals as divided into conscious and unconscious parts. They hold that what is often called the unconscious is part of the individual's being and that the unconscious is too often used to rationalize behavior and responsibility and thus to avoid the realities of one's existence. The aim of existential counseling is to enable individuals to accept responsibility for themselves.

Basically, the goal of existential therapy, if there is a single goal, is to help the client find and develop meanings in life as a way of reducing the anxiety associated with the threat of *nonbeing*. This is generally accomplished in two stages. In the first stage, the client must recognize his freedom of choice, being capable of choosing both that which is right for him and that which is not. This freedom must be fully recognized, leaving behind various restricting ideas, such as that of believing that only adhering to parental views is acceptable. Once the client accepts this freedom and the resulting variety of possibilities he can explore, the second stage is entered, in which the client learns to accept responsibility for his decisions by recognizing his need to see how the consequences of his choices make a profound impact on his existence.

Existential counseling puts little emphasis on techniques. The emphasis is on flexibility and versatility; what the counselor does depends entirely on the nature of the client's difficulty. The existential counselor recognizes that psychological forces take their meaning from the existential situation of the client's immediate life. Each client's behavior is seen and understood in the light of the client's existence as a human being.

Frankl (1959) did include the technique of paradoxical intention, which requires clients to intend that which they anticipate with fear. For example, the individual who has difficulty sleeping may be asked to practice staying awake. This is a reversal of the client's attitude toward the situation, especially if it is carried out in as humorous a setting as possible. Such a reversal brings out a change of attitude toward the symptom, enabling the client to gain some distance from the symptom, to view the troubling situation with detachment. The goal of the existential counselor, then, is to bring clients to the point where they cease to flee from or to fight their symptoms, and instead exaggerate them. As a result, the symptoms diminish and clients are no longer haunted by them.

## HOLISTIC COUNSELING

Within the past few years, a growing trend has emerged within the fields of both counseling and behavioral medicine that has resulted from individuals "requesting strategies for staying healthy and becoming more healthy" (Stensrud & Stensrud, 1982, p. 378). Holistic health thus developed as "an approach to the well-being of people that includes the prevention of illness, alternative ways of treating illness, and the means by which good health and the full enjoyment of life can be achieved" (Gross, 1980, p. 96).

Within this framework, holistic counseling can be seen as a multidimensional approach that not only utilizes most other counseling approaches, but also goes beyond them to focus on a preventive factor. Holistic counselors thus need to be aware of strategies for preventing stress (Romano, 1984), for encouraging physical fitness, for developing spirituality (Gross, 1980), and for educating about nutrition (Pearson & Long, 1982), in addition to having acquired more conventional counseling skills and knowledge.

Klippel and DeJoy (1984) suggest that holistic concerns are based on educational models, rather than on medical models, as a means of facilitating changes in health behavior. The educational model is emphasized because of the belief that improved physical and mental health results from long-term life-style adjustment that must be preceded by changes in attitudes and self-awareness. Holistic concerns include such issues as factors related to a lack of compliance with health regimens, as well as individual differences in illness and recovery.

By working with the whole person and teaching responsibility for both oneself and one's health, the holistic counselor works to help clients function more fully. Thus the approach relates to one's total life-style to enable one to become healthier and happier (Martin & Martin 1982).

Gross (1980) summarizes the holistic view by stating that his approach involves the following three principles: (1) a focus on the whole person—an integration and interdependence of body, mind, feelings, spirit, and life-style, as well as of the physical and social environment; (2) the goal of counseling is the positive wellness of the person; and (3) the counselor will deliberately work toward clients' assuming self-responsibility for their situations.

Such an approach can be exciting to counselors who accept a "proactive" view that the development of a positive, fully functioning life-style can help prevent the emotional stress and grief which result from problems in day-to-day living.

## SUMMARY

Affective approaches to counseling focus primarily on the way clients feel, particularly about themselves. Counselors with an affective approach believe that if the feelings of clients change, their behavior will also change. This chapter presents three theoretical models, as well as brief summaries of two others.

Client-centered therapy stresses the need for self-acceptance by clients. To facilitate this self-acceptance, the counselor must experience empathic understanding of the client's world and then communicate genuine acceptance of the client's feelings about that world. The relationship between the counselor and the client is of major importance.

Gestalt therapy stresses the importance of clients' gaining awareness of their present experiences and of how they prevent themselves from feeling and experiencing the present. With this awareness clients are able to assume greater responsibility for their own behavior and to work through the barriers that have prevented them from expressing the unfinished business which has interfered with effective contact with themselves and others.

Existential therapy stresses the philosphical concerns of what it means to become fully human. Highly philosophical in its concepts, existential counseling aims at having clients experience their existence as authentic by becoming aware of their own existence and potentials and of how they can act on their potentials.

Holistic counseling has emerged as an approach which emphasizes preventive measures for developing the whole person—physical, emotional, intellectual and spiritual.

## REFERENCES

BOY, A.V., and PINE, G.J. (1982). *Client-centered counseling: A renewal*. Boston: Allyn and Bacon.

FRANKL, V. (1959). *Man's search for meaning*. New York: Washington Square Press.

GROSS, S.J. (1980). The holistic health movement. *Personnel and Guidance Journal, 59,* 96-100.

KLIPPEL, J.A., and DEJOY, D.M. (1984). Counseling psychology in behavioral medicine and health psychology. *Journal of Counseling Psychology, 31,* 219-227.

LEVITSKY, A., and PERLS, F. (1970). The rules and games of Gestalt therapy, In J. Fagan and I. Shepard (Eds.), *Gestalt therapy now.* New York: Harper Colphon.

MARTIN, D., and MARTIN, M. (1982). Nutritional counseling: A humanistic approach to psychological and physical health. *Personnel and Guidance Journal, 61,* 21-24.

MAY, R. (1953). *Man's search for himself.* New York: NAL.

MAY, R., (Ed.). (1961). *Existential psychology.* New York: Random House.

PASSONS, W.R. (1972). Gestalt therapy interventions for group counseling. *Personnel and Guidance Journal, 51,* 183-189.

PASSONS, W.R. (1975). *Gestalt approaches in counseling.* New York: Holt, Rinehart and Winston.

PEARSON, J.E., and LONG, T.J. (1982). Counselors, nutrition, and mental health. *Personnel and Guidance Journal, 60,* 389-392.

PERLS, F. (1969a). *Gestalt therapy verbatim.* Moab, Utah: Real People Press.

PERLS, F. (1969b). *In and out of the garbage pail.* Moab, Utah: Real People Press.

PERLS, F., HEFFERLINE, R., and GOODMAN, P. (1951). *Gestalt therapy: Excitement and growth in the human personality.* New York: Dell.

POLSTER, E., and POLSTER, M. (1973). *Gestalt therapy integrated: Contours of theory and practice.* New York: Bruner/Mazel.

ROGERS, C.R. (1942). *Counseling and psychotherapy.* Boston: Houghton Mifflin.

ROGERS, C.R. (1951). *Client-centered therapy.* Boston: Houghton Mifflin.

ROGERS, C.R. (1959). A theory of therapy, personality, and interpersonal relationships, as developed in the client-centered framework. In S. Koch (Ed.) *Psychology: A study of a science.* New York: McGraw-Hill.

ROGERS, C.R. (1961). *On becoming a person.* Boston: Houghton Mifflin.

ROGERS, C.R. (1970). *On encounter groups.* New York: Harper & Row.

ROMANO, J.L. (1984). Stress management and wellness: Reaching beyond the counselor's office. *Personnel and Guidance Journal, 62,* 533-537.

VAN KAAM, A. (1966). *The art of existential counseling.* Wilkes-Barre, Pa.: Dimension Books.

STENSRUD, R.H., & STENSRUD, K. (1982). Counseling for health empowerment. *Personnel and Guidance Journal, 60,* 377-381.

# 5

# COGNITIVE-BEHAVIORAL APPROACHES TO COUNSELING

RATIONAL-EMOTIVE THERAPY

      **View of Human Nature**

      **Key Concepts**

      **Process and Goals**

      **Implementation: Techniques and Procedures**

      **Contributions and Limitations**

BEHAVIORAL COUNSELING

      **View of Human Nature**

      **Key Concepts**

      **Process and Goals**

      **Implementation: Techniques and Procedures**

      **Contributions and Limitations**

REALITY THERAPY

TRANSACTIONAL ANALYSIS

TRAIT-FACTOR COUNSELING

**NEW TRENDS**

       **Hypnotherapy**

       **Neurolinguistic Programming**

       **Cognitive Therapy**

       **Family Systems Therapy**

**SUMMARY**

This chapter will emphasize the client's thinking process as it relates to behavior and to psychological and emotional difficulties. The synthesis of cognitive and behavioral approaches has occurred as theorists and practitioners have recognized that both approaches were dealing with inner cognitive processes such as thoughts, perceptions, and covert speech as a means of guiding actions that would lead to a more satisfying emotional state. Counselors who subscribe to a cognitive-behavioral approach engage in active, directive teaching as a means of reeducating the client to understand the cognitive input of the emotional disturbance; they seek to change the client's thinking so that he abandons irrational thinking or learns to anticipate possible benefits or aversive consequences to a specific behavior. As such, the counselor places far less emphasis on the relationship itself and takes the role of a teacher-persuader.

## RATIONAL-EMOTIVE THERAPY

Probably the most consistent attempt to introduce logical reasoning and cognitive processes into counseling was that of Albert Ellis, who developed rational-emotive therapy (RET). Ellis stresses thinking, judging, deciding, analyzing, and doing; he puts little emphasis on feeling. Ellis himself has written numerous books and articles about RET; the most important are *Reason and Emotion in Psychotherapy* (1962) and *A Guide to Rational Living* with Robert A. Harper (1961).

**Figure 5-1** Albert Ellis (Institute for Rational Emotive Therapy)

### View of Human Nature

The rational-emotive view of people is dominated by the principle that emotion and reason—thinking and feeling—are intricately entwined in the psyche. RET stresses that all normal humans think, feel, and act, and that they do so simultaneously. Their thoughts affect, and often create, their feelings and behaviors. Their emotions affect their thoughts and actions. Their acts affect their thoughts and feelings. Thus in order to change any one of the three, it is necessary to modify one or both of the other two. Ellis (1974) thus insists that he emphasizes all three: cognitive, emotive, and behavioral. His writings, however, emphasize the thinking process.

In particular, rational-emotive therapy makes certain assumptions about the nature of humanity and about the nature and genesis of the individual's unhappiness or emotional disturbances, among which are the following (Patterson, 1980):

1. The individual is uniquely rational and irrational. When thinking and behaving rationally, the individual is effective, happy, and competent.

2. Emotional or psychological disturbance is the result of irrational and illogical thinking. Emotion accompanies thinking and, in effect, emotion is biased, prejudiced, highly personalized, irrational thinking.

3. Irrational thinking originates in the early illogical learning that the individual is biologically disposed toward and more specifically acquires from parents and culture. In the process of growing up, the child is taught to think and feel certain things about himself and about others. These things that are associated with the idea of "this is good" become positive human emotions—for example, love or joy; those associated with the idea of "this is bad" become negative emotions, painful, angry or depressive feelings.

4. Human beings are verbal animals, and thinking usually occurs through the use of symbols or language. Since thinking accompanies emotion, irrational thinking necessarily persists if the emotional disturbance persists. The disturbed individual perpetuates the disturbance, maintaining illogical behavior by internal verbalization of irrational ideas and thoughts.

5. Continuing states of emotional disturbance, being a result of self-verbalizations, are thus determined not by external circumstances or events but by the perceptions and attitudes toward these events that are incorporated in the internalized sentences about them. Ellis is emphasizing that it is not the situations themselves that create anxiety and unpleasant responses; rather it is the individual's perceptions of those situations that make them unpleasant.

6. Individuals have vast untapped resources for actualizing their potentials and can change their personal and social destinies. Ellis sees individuals as unique and as having the power to understand their limitations, to change basic views and values that the individual uncritically accepted as a child, and to challenge self-defeating tendencies. People have the capacity to confront their value systems and reindoctrinate themselves with different beliefs, ideas and values. As a result, they will behave quite differently from how they behaved in the past. Because they can think and work until they actually make themselves different, they are not passive victims of past conditioning.

7. Negative and self-defeating thoughts and emotions must therefore be attacked by reorganizing perceptions and thinking so that thinking becomes logical and rational, rather than illogical and irrational. The goals of counseling, then, are to demonstrate to the client that the self-verbalizations had been the source of the emotional disturbance, to show that these self-verbalizations are illogical and irrational, and to straighten

out thinking so that the self-verbalizations become more logical and efficient and are not associated with negative emotions and self-defeating behavior.*

## Key Concepts

Rational-emotive therapy emphasizes that "emotions" and "feelings of emotional disturbance" are largely the products of people's thoughts, ideas, or constructs. Ellis (1974) maintained that emotional disturbances are simply the result of an individual's mistaken, illogical ideas about a particular situation. Since almost all individuals do seem to want to be happy in their personal and vocational lives, emotions that interfere with their happiness are usually designated as "inappropriate" or "self-defeating."

Some emotions are "appropriate" in that they help people to get more of what they want and to avoid or eliminate what they do not want. Examples of appropriate emotions include pleasure, joy, love, curiosity, sorrow, regret, frustration, and displeasure. On the other hand, emotions such as rage, mania, depression, anxiety, self-pity, and feelings of worthlessness are inappropriate. These inappropriate emotions typically are not only unpleasant in themselves, but also tend to bring about poor results, such as inertia or alienation of other people (Ellis, 1973). Thus, RET counselors attempt to help people discriminate between "appropriate" and "inappropriate" feelings, as well as to intensify the appropriate while reducing or eliminating the inappropriate. This approach is based on the premise that there are a number of major illogical ideas held and perpetuated by individuals that invariably lead to self-defeat. These eleven ideas (Ellis, 1962) are summarized as follows:

*It is absolutely essential for an individual to be loved or approved by every significant person in his environment.* This is irrational because it is an unattainable goal. If one strives for it, one becomes less self-directing and more insecure and self-defeating.

*It is necessary that each individual be completely competent, adequate, and achieving in all areas if the individual is to be worthwhile.* Again, an impossibility. To strive compulsively for such complete achievement results in a sense of inferiority, an inability to live one's own life, and a constant fear of failure; it also leads one to view every situation in competitive terms and to strive to beat others rather than to simply enjoy the activity.

*Some people are bad, wicked, or villainous, and these people should be blamed and punished.* This idea is irrational because there is no absolute standard of right or wrong and very little free will. Everyone makes mistakes as a result of stupidity, ignorance, or emotional unbalance. Blame and punishment do not usually lead to improved behavior since they do not result in less stupidity, more intelligence, or a better emotional state. Rather, they often lead to worse behavior and greater emotional disturbance.

*It is terrible and catastrophic when things are not the way an individual wants them to be.* The reality of life is that not all situations will be as we would like. To be frustrated is normal, but to be severely and prolongedly upset is illogical. It may be unpleasant or bothersome when things do not work out, but it is not a catastrophe. Treating an event as a catastrophe does not change the situation; it only makes us feel worse. If

*Abridged and adapted selection on 67-68 from Theory of Counseling and Psychotherapy, 3rd ed., by C.H. Patterson. Copyright © 1980 by C.H. Patterson. Reprinted by permission of Harper & Row Publishers, Inc.

we don't like something we can try to change it. If we can't do anything about it, we should accept it.

*Unhappiness is a function of events outside the control of the individual.* Actually most outside events that we perceive as harmful are only psychologically harmful; we cannot be hurt unless we allow ourselves to be affected by our attitudes and reactions. A person disturbs himself by telling himself how horrible it is when someone is unkind, rejecting, or annoying. If he realized that disturbances consist of his own perceptions and internalized verbalizations, he could control or change these disturbances.

*If something may be dangerous or harmful, an individual should constantly be concerned and think about it.* This is irrational because simply thinking about something doesn't change it at all and may, in fact, lead to its occurrence or even make it worse than it actually is.

*It is easier to run away from difficulties and self-responsibility than it is to face them.* This is irrational because running away does not solve the difficulty. Usually the situation remains and must eventually be dealt with.

*Individuals need to be dependent on others and have someone stronger than themselves to lean on.* We are all dependent upon others to some extent, but there is no reason to maximize dependency, for it leads to loss of independence, individualism, and self-expression. Such dependency causes still greater dependency, failure to learn, and insecurity, since one is at the mercy of those on whom one depends.

*Past events in an individual's life determine present behavior and cannot be changed.* Although the past may influence the present, it does not necessarily determine it. Rather, the presumed influence of the past may be used as an excuse to avoid changing one's behavior. It may be difficult to overcome past learnings, but it is not impossible.

*An individual should be very concerned and upset by others' problems.* This is irrational because other people's problems often have nothing to do with us and therefore should not seriously concern us. Even if they do, it is our definition of the implication of the other's behavior that upsets us. Getting upset usually prevents us from helping others do anything about their problems.

*There is always a correct and precise answer to every problem and it is catastrophic if it is not found.* This is irrational because there is no perfect solution to any problem. The search for a perfect solution only produces continued anxiety. The individual is never satisfied and is always searching for the one lost solution.

Ellis formulated the ABC principle of emotional disturbance, which emphasizes the importance of cognitive control over emotional states. It is consistent with the phenomenological position that one's perception of an event determines one's behavioral response to that event. For Ellis, A is the existence of a fact or an event external to the person. B is generally the individual's attitude, beliefs, or interpretation of A. C is the emotional consequence or reaction of the person. In this analysis, A is not the cause of C. Instead, B, the person's belief about A, causes C, the emotional response or reaction. For example, a counselor might explain to a client who is upset and is blaming her parents for it that it is not the behavior of her parents (A) that is upsetting her, but her own *beliefs* (B) about being a failure or being rejected that are upsetting (C) her. Thus the individual herself is responsible for her own emotional reactions and disturbances.

## Process and Goals

The rational-emotive therapist helps clients acknowledge their inappropriate feelings and behavior, assume responsibility for these as self-created and self-perpetuated, accept themselves with their symptoms, and determine the philosophic sources of those symptoms. The first step in this process is to show the clients that they are illogical, to help them understand how and why they became so, and to demonstrate the relationship of their irrational ideas to their unhappiness and emotional disturbance. In doing so, clients become aware of the specific material to be dealt with in order to improve their emotional functioning. In addition, this insight tends to reduce feelings of powerlessness and despair by showing clients that they are not helpless victims of outside forces but have control over themselves. This insight also leads clients to understand the relationship between their values and attitudes and the ''shoulds,'' ''oughts,'' and ''musts'' they have incorporated into their lives.

The second step is to help clients believe that thoughts can be challenged and changed. This allows clients to explore logically their ideas to determine if they are appropriate—those that are pleasurable or that help them change conditions they find objectionable—or inappropriate—those that are unpleasant and do not help them to change obnoxious conditions. This is accompanied by direct disputing of client beliefs by the therapist. This disputing consists of questioning and challenging the validity of the ideas clients hold about themselves, others, and the world. In disputing, the therapist persistently and forcefully repeats this process, using the most direct, persuasive, and logical techniques available. Throughout this process, however, the therapist attempts to teach clients to dispute themselves in such a way that they reach the goal of thinking rationally on their own.

The final step involves helping the client go beyond disputing irrational/inappropriate ideas by encouraging them to continue their efforts toward more rational thinking by rational reindoctrination. This includes dealing with the main general irrational ideas, as well as developing a more rational philosophy of living, so that clients can avoid falling victim to other irrational ideas and beliefs. This rational philosophy of living involves the substitution of rational attitudes and beliefs for irrational ones and leads to the elimination of negative, disturbing emotions as well as self-defeating behaviors.

Although advocates of RET utilize relationship techniques, insight-interpretative techniques, and behavioral techniques, they are used primarily as preliminary strategies to gain the client's trust and confidence and thus increase the possibility of bringing about cognitive change. Ellis (1973) states that the RET counselor

1. Is active-directive with most clients, doing a great deal of talking and explaining, especially in the early stages.
2. Confronts clients directly with their problems so as not to waste unnecessary time.
3. Takes a vigorous approach in getting clients first to think and then to get them to re-educate themselves.
4. Is persistent and repetitive in hammering away at the irrational ideas underlying clients' emotional disturbances.

5. Appeals to clients' reasoning powers, rather than their emotions.
6. Is didactic and philosophical in his approach.
7. Uses humor and shame exercises as a way of confronting the client's irrational thinking.

## Implementation: Techniques and Procedures

RET allows for considerable flexibility. The counselor can be very eclectic in terms of techniques and procedures. Virtually all of the common behavioral techniques discussed in this chapter are mentioned by Ellis and used by various RET counselors. In addition, Ellis utilizes a variety of teaching devices—pamphlets, books, tape recordings, films, and filmstrips—as part of the process through which clients learn to recognize the irrational thoughts which are bringing about the disturbances that are upsetting their lives. Although Ellis recognizes many ways of facilitating change, there is essentially only one technique in RET: active, directive teaching.

Ellis feels that the techniques other counselors use are relatively indirect and inefficient. Techniques such as catharsis, dream analysis, free association, interpretation of resistance, and transference analysis are often successful, at least in bringing the client to recognize her illogical thinking. Even when these techniques are most successful, however, they are wasteful because they do not get at the illogical thinking soon enough and thus time is wasted. The counselor-client relationship and expressive-emotive, supportive, and insight methods, although used in rational-emotive therapy, are simply preliminary techniques to establish rapport, to enable clients to express themselves, and to show them that they are respected.

Soon after the counseling is initiated, the RET counselor assumes an active teaching role to reeducate the client. The counselor demonstrates the illogical origin of the client's disturbances and the self-verbalizations that perpetuate the disturbances in the client's life. Clients are shown that their internalized sentences are quite illogical and unrealistic. The effective counselor continually unmasks the clients' past and, especially, their present illogical thinking or self-defeating verbalizations. The counselor does this by bringing this illogical thinking forcefully to their attention or consciousness, by showing them how it is causing and maintaining their disturbance and unhappiness, by demonstrating exactly what the illogical links in their internalized sentences are, and by teaching them how to rethink, challenge, contradict, and reverbalize these sentences to make their internalized thoughts more logical and efficient.

Ellis has emphasized particularly the use of homework assignments as an essential part of RET. This homework generally involves giving clients specific assignments to ''try out'' behaviors that the clients fear (asking for a date or applying for a job) encouraging them to take risks, or having them intentionally fail at some effort to learn (1) that to fail is not catastrophic and (2) how to cope with feelings of failure. Homework assignments also include a great deal of cognitive work: reading specific materials or, more commonly, utilizing self-help forms to analyze their ABCs and to work toward disputing their irrational beliefs. The RET counselor counters their fear with logic and reason, teaching, suggestion, persuasion, confrontation, deindoctrination, indoctrination, and prescription of behavior to show the client the irrational philosophies, to demonstrate how these lead to emotionally disturbed behavior, to change thinking, and thus to change the client's emotions. As a result, the client is able to replace these irrational philosophies with rational, logical ones. In addition, the counselor instructs the client in the major irrational ideas of our culture and provides more effective rational ones, thus offering protection from future disturbances.

### Contributions and Limitations

Rational-emotive therapy has made an outstanding contribution to counseling through its emphasis on the cognitive process in the development of emotional difficulties. The recognition of the existence and impact, as well as the identification, of commonly held irrational beliefs that are internalized by the individual is particularly worthwhile. Like the behavioral approaches, RET also emphasizes the idea of clients' actually trying out new behaviors and learning the specific desired change in behavior. Thus the stress is on extending change outside the counselor's office and encouraging an active involvement on the part of the counselor.

Probably the major limitation with the use of RET is that, with its emphasis upon persuasion, suggestion, and repetition, those who use this approach are in danger of imparting their own values and philosophies of life on their clients. This danger is particularly present when the counselor assumes the role of expert and acts in an authoritarian manner. At the same time, the almost total emphasis on cognitive and behavioral aspects leaves RET vulnerable to its own criticism—that of ignoring an important dimension of the individual. In this respect, of course, RET tends to shortchange the affective aspects. Also, RET places little emphasis on the need for "timing" when confronting a client, showing little concern for waiting until the client is ready to listen and respond.

## BEHAVIORAL COUNSELING

Although behavioral counseling is a relatively new approach, its focus changed significantly in the late 1970s. Although still primarily concerned with behavior change, behavioral counselors have begun to emphasize processes that are more cognitive in nature, recognizing, for instance, that there is a cognitive element operating whenever behavior changes as the result of its consequences. Thus behavioral counseling has become less significant as a specific counseling approach but continues to make a major impact as its techniques, strategies, and scientific emphasis are integrated into other approaches.

Although not closely identified with any single person, behavioral counseling has several important proponents. Among these are Wolpe, Lazarus, Bandura, Krumboltz, and Thoresen. Important behavioral works include *Revolution in Counseling* (Krumboltz, 1966), *Behavior Therapy Techniques* (Wolpe & Lazarus, 1966), *Behavioral Counseling: Cases and Techniques* (Krumboltz & Thoresen, 1969), and *Action Counseling for Behavior Change* (Dustin & George, 1977).

## View of Human Nature

To behavioral counselors, people are neither good nor bad; they are essentially neutral at birth with equal potential for good or evil. As a result behavioral theorists have not fully defined the basic nature of humanity that supports their theory. However, Dustin and George list four assumptions regarding the nature of humanity and how people change that are central to behavioral counseling:

1. Man is viewed as being neither intrinsically good nor bad, but as an experiencing organism who has potential for all kinds of behavior.
2. Man is able to conceptionalize and control his own behavior.
3. Man is able to acquire new behaviors.
4. Man is able to influence others' behavior as well as to be influenced by others in his own behavior (1977, p. 12).

For the behavioral counselor, the individual is a product of his experience. The behaviorist sees maladaptive behaviors as being learned behaviors; their development and maintenance are the same as that of any other behavior. One implication of this view is that no behaviors are maladaptive in and of themselves; rather a behavior becomes inappropriate because someone deems it so. Certain behaviors that may be considered appropriate at home are not considered appropriate in school and vice versa. A second implication of this view of maladaptive behaviors as learned is the idea that any behavior that brings a pleasant result or that helps to reduce unpleasant results is likely to be increased. Thus the behavioral view suggests that since maladaptive behavior is learned, it can also be unlearned. In dealing with such behaviors in therapy, the behaviorist generally considers the stimulus-response paradigm the basic pattern of all human learning. Each person reacts in a theoretically predictable way to any given stimulus, depending on his previous experiences and reinforcements. In this sense persons are no different from animals, except that their responses to stimuli are more complex and occur on a higher level of organization and conceptualization.

Behavior then is a function of a stimulus. This reduces considerably the complex factors influencing human reactions to situations and allows the behaviorist to focus on a specific problem as a reaction to a given set of stimuli. The key word underlying this behavioral view of humanity is *conditioning*. There are several types of conditioning, but two major parallel forms are usually discussed: *classical* (respondent) *conditioning* and *operant* (instrumental) *conditioning*. Classical conditioning occurs when a stimulus elicits a response; operant conditioning occurs when a response is emitted in order to obtain an outcome that reinforces the individual. Respondent behavior is controlled by its antecedent, whereas operant behavior is controlled by its consequences.

Respondent behavior includes such familiar behaviors as perspiration in response to heat, blinking the eyelids in response to the nearness of a foreign object, and salivation in response to food. A classic example of respondent conditioning is that reported by Watson and Rayner (1960). They elicited an emotional fear response in an infant by showing the infant a rat while a loud noise was produced; after several repetitions the fear response formerly caused by the loud noise was produced simply by presenting the rat.

In operant learning, the consequences that strengthen behavior are called *reinforcers*. A reinforcer is any event that, instead of eliciting a specific class of behaviors, increases the probability of any resulting behavior. For example, a hungry animal may behave in a wide variety of ways; any behaviors immediately followed by food will be strengthened. The activity or event is reinforcing simply because it has an effect on behavior. If a reinforcing stimulus is pleasant—for example, one that provides an individual the opportunity for some novel activity—then the event or stimulus is positive reinforcement; it increases the likelihood that the particular act it is associated with will be repeated. The initial act may have been learned as the result of previous consequences or it may be a random, somewhat spontaneous action. In either case, the action is more likely to recur because of the pleasant consequences that followed.

The process of eliminating an undesirable behavior is referred to as *extinction*. A behavior has been extinguished when it no longer occurs. Counselors must be aware of two important strategies of extinction. The first strategy is that of counterconditioning: A new, desirable behavior is substituted for the undesirable behavior. By way of example, in one of the articles by Jones (1960), originally reported in 1924, this incident is discussed: A three-year-old boy was afraid of rabbits, fur, white rats, and even cotton and wool. Jones treated the boy by desensitizing him to these fears. She introduced a rabbit during a play period, and gradually increased his toleration of the rabbit. At the beginning the rabbit was in a cage twelve feet away; gradually the cage was moved closer until the boy was able to fondle the rabbit affectionately. Jones also associated the rabbit with the presence of a pleasant stimulus (food), which aided in the elimination of the fear. She did this by bringing the rabbit into the room while the boy was eating dinner in his highchair. The rabbit was kept at the far end of the room and the boy was hungry, so the rabbit's presence did not interfere with the boy's pleasure from eating. As the rabbit was moved closer to him over a period of days, the fear response gradually decreased until the boy was able to eat while petting the rabbit.

A second strategy of extinction is that of withdrawing the reinforcement that has previously followed a behavior. For example, many classroom teachers have the problem of students who blurt out questions and interrupt the class. The teacher often reinforces such behavior by answering the student quickly so that the lesson can continue. To extinguish this behavior, the teacher must ignore the student, denying him attention as well as preventing him from getting his question answered. This period of extinction is often difficult. The individual who controls the reinforcing events often fails to wait out the extinction period and gives the student the added attention. If this occurs too often, a partial-reinforcement effect occurs. Reinforcement usually does not occur every time a correct response is made. Partial reinforcement is important not only because it explains resistance to extinction but also because it can be used to increase the permanence of an appropriate or desired behavior. New behaviors are more quickly learned when the behavior is reinforced each time it occurs. However, those behaviors are also easily unlearned. To bring about more permanent learning, the behavior should be reinforced every time it occurs, at the beginning. After the behavior is acquired, partial reinforcement builds a tendency to perform the behavior even when no reinforcement follows. The percentage of behaviors reinforced should be decreased gradually to prevent extinction.

Sometimes it is difficult to create conditions that elicit a desired behavior for the first time so that the behavior can be reinforced. If the probability of the desired behavior occurring is low or if the counselor does not wish to wait for the behavior, then the counselor must shape the response. Shaping is a procedure that reinforces successively closer approximations of the desired behavior. The way most normal children learn to talk illustrates the way shaping works. The first babbling sounds made by infants are certain to cause the parents to smile, speak warmly, and pay attention. Gradually, as the babbling sounds become more and more like words, only those sounds that parents find similar to their language are reinforced. Later, only closer approximations are reinforced, until the child learns to make sounds that are meaningful to adults.

### Key Concepts

Behavior therapy differs from other therapy approaches in that the feelings of clients are secondary to client behaviors. Dustin and George (1977) suggest that while many of the problems brought to the counselor *seem* to be emotional in nature, the problems are actually failures to deal successfully with problems in living. Thus the client who says ''I feel rejected'' or ''I feel lonely'' is actually expressing a need for more successful behaviors that will enable him to relate more satisfactorily with other people.

As a result, behavior therapy is characterized by (1) a focus on specific, overt behavior, (2) very precise therapeutic goals, (3) the development of a specific treatment procedure appropriate to the client's problem, and (4) an objective assessment as to whether the therapeutic goals were accomplished (Corey 1977). As such, behavior therapy is somewhat experimental in approach, concerned primarily with whether or not a desired effect occurs. This emphasis on specific counseling goals that are both observable and measurable means that both the client and the counselor will understand precisely the change that is desired. In addition, the specification of concrete, reachable goals provides greater opportunity for clients to see progress, which is a motivating force in itself.

Basically, then, behavior therapy attempts to help clients (1) alter maladaptive behavior, (2) learn the decision-making process, and (3) prevent problems by strengthening desirable behaviors. This is done by assessing the nature and extent of the problem, specifying counseling goals, choosing the most appropriate counseling strategies, and periodically reevaluating client progress to determine if the counseling has been successful, depending entirely on whether the goals have been accomplished.

### Process and Goals

Behavioral counselors are generally less concerned about process per se than are most counselors. However, they place central importance on specific counseling goals. These goals are chosen by the client with help from the counselor. Once counseling goals are identified, then new conditions for learning are created. The rationale is that all behavior is learned, including maladaptive behavior: If neurosis is learned it can be unlearned, and more effective behaviors can be acquired. Thus behavioral counseling is essentially a process that focuses on changing the client's behavior by helping him to unlearn inappropriate behaviors and replace those with more desirable ones.

To increase the frequency or strength of a desired behavior, six steps are typically employed (Blackham & Silberman, 1975).

1. Identify and state the behavior to be changed in operational terms.
2. Obtain a base line of the desired target behavior.
3. Arrange the situation so that the target behavior will occur.
4. Identify potential reinforcing stimuli and events.
5. Reinforce the desired target behavior or successive approximations of it.
6. Evaluate the effects of the treatment procedure by maintaining records of change in the target behavior.

Although most behavioral counselors believe that counseling goals must be tailored to the individual client, behavioral therapy may be said to have five general goals: (1) altering the maladaptive behavior in the client under therapy, (2) helping the client learn a more efficient decision-making process, (3) preventing future problems, (4) solving the specific behavioral problem requested by the client, and (5) achieving behavioral changes that translate into action in life.

### Implementation: Techniques and Procedures

Behavioral counselors typically use specific techniques, the results of which can be evaluated in terms of the client's progress toward her goals. The techniques are employed in a systematic plan, although many of these same techniques can be used by counselors with other approaches.

*Systematic Desensitization*    A widely used technique in behavioral counseling, systematic desensitization is particularly useful with clients whose problem behavior is associated with a high level of anxiety. Such anxiety may be about dating, taking tests, speaking to groups, or engaging in various sexual activities. The anxiety may cause clients to be overly shy or overly aggressive, suffer from severe headaches or stomach distress, or have difficulty in performing various normal tasks of everyday living.

Desensitization is used to break down certain anxiety-response habits. During desensitization, the anxiety is unlearned or inhibited by an incompatible behavior, usually deep muscle relaxation. The term *desensitization* refers to the process of anxiety reduction. The person becomes desensitized—that is, gradually experiences more comfort in the presence of what formerly caused anxiety. This process of learning an incompatible behavior is sometimes called *counterconditioning* and is carried out on a step-by-step basis.

Counterconditioning became important as a technique after Wolpe (1958) devised a systematic procedure that increased the kinds of problems counterconditioning could deal with. Basically Wolpe contributed the idea of constructing the anxiety hierarchy, a rank list of situations to which the client reacts with increasing degrees of anxiety. By combining this anxiety heirarchy with training in muscular relaxation, the counselor is able to help the client gradually reduce anxiety to the various situations listed. The procedure usually involves three sets of operations: (1) relaxation training, (2) identifying anxiety-producing situations, and (3) working through the anxiety hierarchy.

First, during the initial two or three sessions after desensitization has been decided on, the client is trained in the techniques of progressive muscular relaxation—alternately tensing and relaxing successive gross muscle groups—while the counselor makes verbal suggestions of warmth, calmness, and overall pleasant feelings. At this time the counselor focuses the client's attention on identifying the localized tension and relaxation. The counselor may suggest thoughts and create images of personally relaxing situations, such as lying under a hot sun or drifting on an inner tube on a warm day, to help the client reach a state of peacefulness. The counselor often uses the brief form of Jacobsen's (1938) progressive relaxation training to help the client relax all muscles. This training directs the client's attention to relaxing a particular set of muscles, then working throughout the body in the same way. Ordinarily, the counselor devotes about thirty minutes to relaxation training and then encourages the client to practice between counseling sessions. When the client has learned to relax quickly and completely, the desensitization procedure itself will begin.

During these sessions in relaxation training, time is also spent identifying the anxiety-producing situations which will be part of the client's anxiety hierarchy. The client is first asked to state those situations that make him anxious. Having identified the situations, the client then ranks them from slightly anxiety-producing to highly anxiety-producing. Ideally, the items in the hierarchy form subjectively equal intervals of noticeable differences in the degree of anxiety produced, but this is not always possible. For example, if the client has anxiety related to his fear of failing as a father, the list would begin with a situation that produces relatively little anxiety—perhaps a coworker criticizing fathers who ''work too hard and don't spend time with their kids''—and would work up to a situation that produces high anxiety, such as his wife criticizing him for being too hard on the children. Between might be situations where he is criticized by a coworker, a close friend, and a relative.

When the client has learned relaxation and has constructed his anxiety hierarchy, the third step—simultaneously presenting the relaxation and the anxiety-eliciting stimuli from the hierarchy—begins. The client relaxes himself and then the counselor presents verbal instructions, having the client imagine the least disturbing item on his anxiety list. When the first item no longer evokes any anxiety, the client moves on to the second item on the list. The client progressively works through the entire hierarchy. During this process, the counselor moves slowly so that the feeling of relaxation is always greater than the feeling of anxiety. Whenever the client experiences a reduction in relaxation as he thinks about an item, he signals the counselor, who returns to the imagery of a personally relaxing situation or to a situation that elicits less anxiety. When the client can remain in a relaxed state while imagining the situation that previously produced the most anxiety, he is encouraged to expose himself to the anxiety-producing situations in his daily life.

*Behavior Contract*   The use of the behavior contract in counseling is one behavioral technique that has already been adopted by other counselors. The behavior contract is based on the idea that it is helpful to the client to specify the kind of behavior desired and the reinforcement contingencies. Such a contract enables individuals to anticipate changing their behavior on the basis of a promise or agreement that some positive consequence will be forthcoming.

Basically, a behavior contract is an agreement between at least two people in which the people involved try to change the behavior of at least one of the parties. Dustin and George (1977) suggest that such an approach helps to tell the client "what to do" without nagging. The agreement may be oral or written, but both parties must agree to the basic conditions. One aspect of the contract is the process of negotiating the acceptable terms, which are characterized by (1) reality, (2) specificity, (3) freedom from threat, and (4) flexibility (Dustin & George, 1977). Simply stated, this means that the client and counselor choose realistic goals that they can meet. Such goals are specifically stated, leaving no question as to what is expected of each. Generally, the contract employs positive reinforcement for reaching goals rather than punishment for undesirable behavior, thus eliminating threat. Lastly, the client and counselor agree that the terms of the contract may be changed by mutual consent, providing flexibility to change the goals and conditions whenever such change seems desirable.

*Social Modeling*   Based on the idea that a person will imitate the behavior of others, social modeling is used to help the client progressively modify his behavior toward that of an observed model. Bandura (1965) suggests that modeling procedures may be more effective than positive reinforcement in establishing new response patterns. In addition, behavior patterns acquired through imitation are often maintained without deliberate external reinforcement simply because individuals learn to reinforce themselves for certain behaviors.

Dustin and George (1977) suggest that social modeling can be used both to help the client learn new behaviors and to strengthen or weaken existing behaviors. The counselor uses audio models, filmed models, and live models to enable the client to observe desirable behavior being reinforced and to lead the client to modify his behavior toward that of the model.

*Assertion Training*   A behavioral approach that has gained wide support, assertion training is particularly worthwhile for individuals who have difficulty asserting themselves in particular interpersonal situations. Although used primarily with individuals who are usually nonassertive, assertion training can be appropriate for most people, since almost all have difficulty asserting themselves in certain situations. Corey (1977) points out that assertion training can be particularly helpful for the following people:

1. Those who cannot express anger or irritation

2. Those who are overly polite and who allow others to take advantage of them
3. Those who have difficulty saying "no"
4. Those who find it difficult to express affection and other positive responses
5. Those who feel they don't have a right to have their own feelings or thoughts

Assertion training is ordinarily practiced in a group setting. It emphasizes teaching clients to stand up for their own rights without violating the rights of others. Assertive behavior itself consists of expressing one's thoughts and feelings in direct, honest, and appropriate ways. It involves defending one's rights when one feels that he is being taken advantage of. It means expressing one's needs and wants to others without assuming whether or not the others will help meet those needs. Individuals who have learned to be assertive usually feel good about themselves, recognizing that they have "stood up" for themselves without humiliating or criticizing others. Increased self-respect results.

### Contributions and Limitations

The behavioral counseling approach makes several important contributions to counseling effectiveness. By focusing on the specific behaviors that clients wish to change, the counselor can help clients to better understand what is to be accomplished as part of the counseling process. This focus also gives clients concrete information about their level of progress. Success is apparent and reinforces the whole counseling process. In addition, because the client's behavior changes are likely to be apparent to those around her, she receives positive feedback, further accelerating her progress. Focusing on specific behaviors also provides well-defined criteria for counseling outcomes. The behavioral counselor has the advantage of using a variety of specific counseling techniques that are well-tested in bringing about behavior change.

Major limitations of behavioral counseling include a lack of opportunity for the client to become creatively involved with the whole process of self-fulfillment or self-actualization. A second limitation rests in the possibility that the client may be "depersonalized" in his interaction with the counselor. Further, the whole process does not seem very applicable to clients whose difficulties are not directly related to overt behaviors. Clients who are functioning at relatively high levels but who are searching for meaning and purpose in their lives or who see themselves as failures or who recognize that they are not functioning up to their potential cannot expect much help from behavioral counseling.

## REALITY THERAPY

Reality therapy was developed by William Glasser as a result of his dissatisfaction with the ineffectiveness of standard psychiatric treatment. Glasser changed the focus to present behavior, emphasizing the acceptance of personal responsibility, which he equated with mental health. Reality therapy is behavioral in approach in that the focus is on what the person *does,* not feels. Glasser's important works include *Reality Therapy* (1965), *Schools Without Failure* (1969), and *The Identity Society* (1972).

**Figure 5-2** William Glasser
(Michael Fenster)

The reality therapist, like the behaviorist, views the individual largely in terms of his behavior. But rather than examining behavior in terms of the stimulus-response paradigm, as the behaviorist does, or looking at the individual's behavior phenomenologically, as the client-centered counselor does, the reality therapist measures behavior against an objective standard, which he calls reality. This reality may be a practical reality, a social reality, or a moral reality. The reality therapist sees the individual as functioning in consonance or dissonance with that reality.

Glasser himself believes that all human behavior is motivated by striving to meet basic needs—physiological and psychological—that are the same for all individuals. He suggests that people may label these needs differently but that all people, regardless of location or culture, have the same essential needs. Some of their needs are the traditionally defined physiological needs that maintain the organism. But beyond these basic needs, Glasser states that there are "two basic psychological needs: the need to love and to be loved, and the need to feel that we are worthwhile to ourselves and to others" (1965, p. 9). These two basic psychological needs have been incorporated into one need, which Glasser calls *identity*. Glasser (1969) believes that identity is a person's most important psychological need, built into the biological system from birth. When individuals are frustrated in their attempts to satisfy their need to be loved and to feel worthwhile, they develop a "failure" identity and resort to other avenues such as delinquency and withdrawal. These alternative routes, however, still result in a failure identity. This failure identity can be changed to a success identity, but only when individuals change their behavior in such a way that their needs for love and self-worth are met. The process for bringing about this behavior change involves helping the client to do what is right, responsible, and realistic.

When individuals are frustrated in satisfying their needs, they may lose touch with objective reality, stray from the imposing confines of the real world, and lose their ability to perceive things as they are. Thus Glasser argues that it is in these strivings to satisfy the basic needs that the patterns of our behavior are determined. A person's sense of responsibility for himself helps him change and modify his behavior and to arrive ultimately at more acceptable and satisfactory standards that, in turn, enable him to gratify his needs successfully.

Reality therapy emphasizes the idea of clients' making value judgements about their own behavior. Although Glasser does not suggest a universal code by which all individuals should live, he does believe that certain generally accepted moral principles should be encouraged by the therapist. More importantly, the therapist forces clients to evaluate, or to make value judgements about, their own behavior in terms of whether it is helping or hurting themselves and others.

Once clients are able to make value judgements about their own behavior and to face reality squarely, they are ready to assume personal responsibility for their behavior. Glasser (1965) defines responsibility as "the ability to fulfill one's needs, and to do so in a way that does not deprive others of the ability to fulfill their needs" (p. 13). Glasser insists that change is impossible until individuals stop using conditions in the past, factors in the present, or the behavior of others as excuses for their own actions and start accepting responsibility for their own lives. In particular, Glasser relates responsibility to mental health—the more responsible people are, the healthier they are; the less responsible, the less healthy. Thus, the reality therapist attempts to teach clients an approach to life that involves living responsibly.

Glasser (1972) formulated an eight-step procedure as a guide for the counseling process. Although the order of the steps is sometimes flexible, they present a picture of the typical direction of reality therapy.

1. *Be involved.* Glasser emphasizes the need for the counselor to communicate concern to the client, along with warmth and understanding.
2. *Focus on behavior, not feelings.* The emphasis here is on making clients aware of what they are doing that makes them feel the way they do.
3. *Focus on the present.* The past is important only as it relates to present behavior.
4. *Making value judgements.* Clients must examine the quality of what they are doing and determine whether it is responsible behavior.
5. *Making a plan.* The counselor works with the client to develop a specific course of action that will change irresponsible behavior to responsible behavior.
6. *Getting a commitment.* Glasser believes that a plan was only worthwhile if the client made a specific commitment to carry it out.
7. *Accept no excuses.* Since not all plans succeed, Glasser suggests that the emphasis be on developing a new plan rather than exploring why the old plan failed.
8. *Eliminate punishment.* Plan failures are not to be met with punishment, only with the natural consequence of the future to carry out the plan.

**Figure 5-3**  Eric Berne  (UPI)

## TRANSACTIONAL ANALYSIS

Transactional analysis (TA) was developed by Eric Berne and stresses the interaction between individuals as both a symptom and a cause of psychological difficulties. Although TA can be used in individual counseling, it is particularly effective in group counseling, since the group setting allows the counselor to observe the individual interacting with others and thereby to analyze certain elements of personality structure and interpersonal relationships. Berne's most important books include *Transactional Analysis in Psychotherapy* (1961), *Games People Play* (1964), and *Principles of Group Treatment* (1966).

Transactional analysis focuses on the games people play to avoid intimacy in transactions with others. TA is based on a personality theory utilizing three distinct patterns of behavior or ego states: Parent, Adult, and Child. (Parent, Adult, and Child, capitalized, refer to ego states; whereas parent, adult, and child, written with small initial letters, refer to people.)

The Parent ego state is filled with values, injunctions, shoulds and oughts, and behaviors that the individual has internalized from significant others—parents and parent substitutes—during childhood. This influence leads persons to behave as they believe their parents would want them to behave and includes prohibitions as well as permissions and nurturing messages.

The Adult ego state is focused on data processing, probability estimating, and decision making. It deals with facts, not with feelings. In fact, the Adult state is seen as being devoid of feelings, although it can evaluate the emotional experiences of the Child and Parent ego states. It acts to regulate the activities of the Child and the Parent,

**Figure 5-4**  Playful behavior is a result of the child ego state (Photo Fournier Schlegel, Rapho/Photo Researchers)

mediating between them. The ultimate function of the Adult is to deal with presenting situations in an organized, adaptable, and intelligent way—that is, reality testing.

The Child ego state is conceptualized as the little boy or girl within us. As such, this ego state does not refer to childishness, but childlikeness; it is the fun-loving part of most individuals. The Child is most likely to emerge in response to a communication from a Parent ego state. The Child functions in two distinct forms: the Natural Child and the Adapted Child. The Natural Child strives for total freedom to do what it wants whenever it wants. This includes the natural impulses for love, affection, creativity, aggression, rebellion, and spontaneity. The Adapted Child, however, is influenced by the Parent and has discovered ways, usually compliance or procrastination, to deal with feelings in a way that will prevent Parent reprimand. As a result, the Adapted Child duplicates the original reactions individuals have toward their parents during childhood, including feelings like guilt, fear, anger, and frustration. The emerging adult in the Child is called the Little Professor and is the source of intuition, creativity, and manipulation; it serves as the negotiator between the Natural Child and the Adapted Child.

A central part of TA is learning to analyze one's relationships with others. One step in this is determining the predominant life position one has taken in making certain decisions with regard to compromise in satisfying needs or stimulus hunger. These decisions lead to this position toward self and others, which is ordinarily maintained against influences that question or threaten it. An individual may choose one of four basic life positions: (1) "I'm okay—you're okay"; (2) "I'm okay—you're not okay"; (3) "I'm not okay—you're okay"; (4) "I'm not okay—you're not okay."

TA also emphasizes the human need for emotional and physical strokes. Berne believed that all persons have a basic need for recognition from significant others. This recognition comes in the form of strokes, which can be physical, verbal, or psychological. These strokes can be positive or negative, conditional or unconditional. Berne believed that individuals need to learn how to ask for the strokes they want.

Two kinds of analyses are fundamental to transactional analysis: structural analysis and transactional analysis. Structural analysis involves the analysis and recognition of the influence of the individual's ego states on thinking or behaving. Although the psychologically healthy individual can activate any one of the states whenever it's appropriate, it is possible to diagnose which ego state has the "executive," or controlling, power by observing an individual's overt behavior. By identifying which of her ego states is in power at any given time, the individual is better able to understand the nature of her behavior and the behavior of others within a social context: transactional analysis.

Since transactions are units of social action (Berne 1963), transactional analysis, as process within the theory, is concerned with the diagnosis of the ego states from which a social interchange is emanating for the two persons involved and with the clarification of that exchange. When one person encounters another and speaks, this is called the *transactional stimulus.* The reply is called the *transactional response.*

*Complementary* transactions occur when both parties speak from their Adults, or when the vectors are parallel, as when Parent speaks to Child, and Child responds to Parent. The key to complementary transactions is that the response is appropriate and expected; it follows the natural order of healthy human relationships. Communication can proceed smoothly and indefinitely as long as transactions are complementary.

*Crossed* transactions occur when the vectors are not parallel, and communication is broken off. The most common crossed transaction results from an Adult—Adult stimulus with a Parent—Child or Child—Parent response. Crossed transactions ordinarily end in a deadlock unless the respondent is able to mobilize her Adult to complement the Adult in the other person. Otherwise, the transaction is finished with one or both of the parties feeling hurt, angry, or misunderstood.

*Ulterior* transactions occur when more than two ego states are in operation simultaneously. In ulterior transactions, one message is usually sent on a social level, usually Adult—Adult, and an implied message is sent on a psychological level in another ego state.

One of the most important emphases in TA is the use of the contract, which includes a statement about what the client hopes to achieve in counseling, a statement about what the counselor will do to facilitate that process, and some specific criteria for knowing when the goal has been achieved. This helps to avoid the client's shifting total responsibility to the counselor and establishes positive expectations.

The TA counselor acts very much like a "teacher, trainer, and resource person with heavy emphasis on involvement" (Harris, 1967, p. 239). She explains key concepts such as structural analysis, transactional analysis, script analysis, and game analysis. In addition, the counselor employs various techniques, particularly questioning about the client's earliest memories, to assist the client in understanding the various influences that led to their present life position. By helping clients free themselves from the constraints of those early decisions, TA counselors are attempting to help clients make full and effective use of all three ego states and to live game-free lives with intimate, rewarding relationships.

Thus the basic goal of transactional analysis is to help clients achieve autonomy (Berne 1964). This autonomy is characterized by (1) awareness—a realistic understanding of one's world, (2) spontaneity—the ability to express emotion in an uninhibited, game-free fashion; and (3) intimacy—the capacity to share love and closeness with others. Related to this goal of autonomy is the attempt to enable the client to free his Adult from the influence of the Child and Parent so that the Adult is in control of decision making.

## TRAIT-FACTOR COUNSELING

One other cognitive approach that deserves mention is trait-factor counseling. Developed as a counseling model by E.G. Williamson (1939), the trait-factor approach is the only counseling approach that originated from an essential vocational-counseling base.

A major assumption in the trait-factor approach is that human behavior can be ordered and measured along continua of defined traits or factors (Pepinsky and Pepinsky, 1954). This attempt to apply a scientific approach to counseling by the use of measurement and prediction utilizes a process of gathering data, synthesizing it, forming a diagnosis, and planning a program for the client. The goals of counseling typically include self-understanding, choosing appropriate goals for living, and striving for the "good life." The techniques used by the counselor are establishing rapport, cultivating self-understanding, advising, and checking on the client to see how the client has carried out the advice.

Although the trait-factor approach receives little attention today as a counseling model, almost all counselors who use tests in working with clients are to some degree utilizing trait-factor assumptions in their counseling. While Williamson dealt with the affective aspects of counseling in later writings, the trait-factor approach is essentially a rational, problem-solving approach. As such, it still offers much to the counselor in helping clients deal with problems.

## NEW TRENDS

### Hypnotherapy

Clinical hypnosis has been used to treat various emotional and psychological problems for many decades, but its use has greatly increased in recent years. The work of Milton Erickson in particular has helped make the use of hypnosis acceptable to many counselors. In essence, hypnosis is a state of deep relaxation in which an altered state of consciousness is created. Clients under hypnosis focus their attention on their own functioning, become more aware of their bodies and sensations, their feelings and emotions, and their dreams and fantasies.

During the induction of this trance or altered state, the body and mind interact in such a way that as physical relaxation increases, the awareness of the inner self does also. Most induction methods combine three basic elements: relaxation, suggestion, and repetition. The induction is most effective if the counselor acts as a guide in leading clients in a process they do to themselves. This increases clients' acceptance of responsibility for the whole process and can be enhanced by having clients practice self-induced hypnosis at home through the use of a tape.

Hypnosis is used for many of the same kinds of problems that neurolinguistic programming is used for. It is a particularly effective tool for dealing with symptoms, including pain—real or imagined, tension, smoking, drinking, overeating, or phobias. The client, while in a trance, imagines the undesired situation, and therapeutic suggestions the counselor gives that will alleviate the problem.

Hypnosis is also used in helping clients to relive certain experiences and thus to deepen their awareness of themselves. This is particularly helpful in exploring and understanding feelings and memories that have long been repressed.

### Neurolinguistic Programming (NLP)

Neurolinguistic programming has literally bounded into the field of counseling. The first important book, *The Structure of Magic I* (Bandler & Grinder, 1975), was followed in 1976 by *The Structure of Magic II* (Grinder & Bandler), and the professional enthusiasm for this approach was soon apparent.

Bandler and Grinder state that the following are a *few* of the specific things NLP practioners can do: (1) cure phobias and other unpleasant feeling responses in less than an hour, (2) help children and adults with "learning disabilities" (spelling and reading problems, etc.) overcome these limitations, often in less than an hour, (3) eliminate most unwanted habits—smoking, drinking, overeating, insomnia—in a few sessions, (4) make changes in the interactions of couples, families, and organizations so that they function in ways that are more satisfying and productive, and (5) cure many physical problems—not only most of those recognized as "psychosomatic" but also some that are not—in a few sessions (1979, p. ii).

As might be expected from its name, NLP focuses on a linguistic model as a means to gain access to clients' "deep structure" from the "surface structure" statements they make. Clients are seen as presenting sentences that do not accurately represent their experiences by using *deletions* (leaving out important parts), *distortions* (assigning responsibilities to others that are within the clients' control), and *generalizations* (statements that fail to identify anything specific in their experience). These three elements are key to what is called the *meta-model* (Bandler & Grinder, 1975).

A fourth key element of the meta-model is that of the *representational systems.* The representational systems have to do with the pattern an individual uses in taking in and storing experiences, including seeing, hearing, and feeling. By identifying the client's favored representational system (the one most often used in dealing with stress or in solving problems), the counselor is able to respond out of the same system, which greatly increases trust and rapport. Assessing this system depends on the ability to listen for and identify the process words that are consistent with a particular system. Counselors may also watch eye movements in determining a client's representational system. For instance, NLP counselors believe that when individuals focus their eyes up and to the left, they are using a visual system.

Two major techniques utilized by NLP counselors are *anchoring* and *reframing*. Anchoring is the process by which the counselor attacks a desired emotional state with a specific stimulus, whether a touch, a sound, a facial expression, or a posture change. This process can be utilized to evoke new feelings and behaviors in situations in which the client previously experienced undesirable reactions. This anchoring can be done with or without the client's awareness. The specific steps that are followed in using anchors are outlined by Cameron-Bandler (1978).

Reframing is the process by which the counselor helps the client to see her behavior from a different perspective, thus placing a different valuation on that behavior. This may include learning to discriminate when the behavior is desirable and when it is undesirable, separating intention from behavior so that new behavior becomes desirable, or creating new ways of behaving in situations in which there had previously been only one alternative (Harmon & O'Neill, 1981).

## Cognitive Therapy

Cognitive therapy is based on the idea that psychological problems result primarily from commonplace processes such as faulty learning, making incorrect inferences on the basis of inadequate information, and basing behavior on unreasonable attitudes. Thus the cognitive therapist helps clients sharpen discriminations, correct misconceptions, and learn more adaptive attitudes (Beck, 1976).

The cognitive perspective assumes that a person chooses the alternatives that appear to be in her own best interest, based upon a particular, although subjective, view of the situation. Thus, self-defeating behaviors are not the result of a desire to lose, as Freud might say, but instead result from the individual's inability either to conceive of, or to act upon and carry out, more constructive alternatives.

Various techniques are used to accomplish the following objectives: (1) clients learn to gain insight into the views they take of various events, especially those that are upsetting, (2) clients learn to assess, reality test, and modify these views, so that the meanings they attribute to specific events are more congruent with objective reality, (3) clients learn to identify the conscious thoughts that occur between an external event and a particular emotional response, (4) clients then practice various cognitive and behavioral responses to anticipated and unexpected upsetting situations, and (5) clients generate new assumptions (or thought processes) and apply them to their lives (Rush, 1984).

Although the cognitive counselor acts as a guide, an empathic, objective relationship is stressed. The counselor is expected to think as the client does, to understand both the cognitive and the emotional responses, and to see the world as the client does, while remaining objective and logical about the client's thinking and situation.

Techniques of cognitive therapy include distancing (the ability to view one's thoughts more objectively, to draw a distinction between ''I believe'' and ''I know''), decentering (learning to separate oneself from vicariously experiencing the adversities of others), changing the rules, reality testing, and authenicating the validity of one's thoughts, as well as many of the techniques used in RET. In addition, behavioral methods including activity schedules, graded task assignments, and homework provide a situational context and some behavioral data for testing the validity of the client's assertions, and thus provide a basis for cognitive reappraisal.

### Family Systems Therapy

Although it is not within the scope of this text to deal with the subject of family therapy per se, a brief review of the family systems therapy model is appropriate, because this approach is "among the counseling student's most basic choices for approaching individual as well as group and family counseling" (McKenna, 1984, p. 4). This approach is best understood by reading material by Hoffman (1981), Becvar and Becvar (1982), and Goldenberg and Goldenberg (1982).

Family systems therapy represents a new paradigm, a new comprehensive philosophy which redefines many traditional concepts. Utilizing insights from such theorists as Harry Stack Sullivan (interpersonal psychology) and Kurt Lewin (field theory), systems theory emerged from the coalescing of five seemingly independent developments (Goldenberg & Goldenberg, 1982). These include (1) the extension of psychoanalytic treatment to a full range of emotional problems, including work with families, (2) the introduction of general systems theory, with its emphasis on exploring relationships between parts that compose an interrelated whole; (3) the investigation of the family's role in the development of schizophrenia in one of its members, (4) the evolvement of the fields of child guidance and marital counseling, and (5) the increased interest in the new clinical techniques such as group therapy and milieu therapy.

Of particular importance is the introduction of general systems theory with its emphasis on looking at any part of a whole in terms of its relationship with the other parts. Such a perspective suggests that working with an individual's relationship with other family members is basic, since it focuses the therapist's attention on individuals only in the context of their relationships, consistent with a framework of contextual relativity (Becvar & Becvar, 1982).

As a result, individuals are understood in a relative sense, rather than in terms of diagnostic labels. In fact, family systems therapists tend to see diagnosis as detrimental to achieving therapeutic change, since diagnostic labels may trap people into roles rather than freeing them from role expectations and encouraging them to see themselves as alterable and adaptable.

The process of therapy in this approach is dependent upon the counselor's presenting new information to the system that will help the members of the family to look at themselves and the others differently, thus changing the patterns of interaction. The problem is defined as a family or context problem rather than as an individual's problem; the family system is viewed as consisting of family members but also of the relationships among them.

From a systems perspective, neither intrapsychic labels—such as ego, self-concept, drive, and self-awareness—nor labels assigning internal motivation—such as the concepts of discounting, selfishness, or rescuing—have any importance (Becvar & Becvar, 1982). Rather the emphasis is placed on labels that describe interpersonal processes, or the "observable dynamics which occur when elements of a system interface and when systems (as elements of a larger, supra-system) interface with other systems'' (Becvar & Becvar, 1982, p. 9).

Among the concepts and constructs that have particular importance to systems theory are boundaries, communication/information processing, entropy, homeostatis, open and closed systems, positive and negative feedback, relationship, and wholeness. These concepts have definitions and explanations peculiar to a systems approach and are best understood in relationship with each other (Becvar & Becvar, 1982).

Since the goal of systems therapy is to help the family maintain itself without the use of maladaptive roles, the therapist tries to set the family's own resources into action in a different way. The precise direction this ''different way'' takes is determined by the family's particular style of adapting and maintaining stability.

Becvar and Becvar (1982) suggest one model of the healthy, functioning family. The six characteristics they include are as follows (p. 74):

1. A legitimate source of authority, established and supported over time.
2. A stable rule system established and consistently acted upon.
3. Stable and consistent shares of nurturing behavior.
4. Effective and stable child-rearing and marriage-maintainance practices.
5. A set of goals toward which the family and each individual works.
6. Sufficient flexibility and adaptability to accommodate normal developmental challenges as well as unexpected crises.

Counselors within this framework may employ a variety of styles—behavioral, cognitive, or affective—but do so within a particular understanding of the whole system. Allowing the counselor to use whatever means are deemed appropriate to the context, systems theory provides a unified framework within which techniques and strategies can be used. Some of these techniques are rooted in traditional approaches; some are unique to the individual therapist. Examples of the types of techniques frequently used are paradoxical intention, cognitive restructuring, behavioral reinforcement schedules, and homework assignments.

As a result, although family systems therapy can be viewed as eclectic in terms of techniques and strategies, the approach is unique in its theoretical foundation, which recognizes that as an individual changes, her family or social system changes, thus requiring further change of the individual. When the entire system is worked with, the change within an individual becomes an integrated part of system changes and permits a more ''holistic'' approach to dealing with individual as well as family difficulties.

## SUMMARY

Cognitive-behavioral approaches focus *primarily on* the thinking process as it relates to those behaviors which relate to psychological and emotional difficulties. By helping clients change the way they think about their experiences, counselors induce behavior change, which leads to changes in the way clients feel about themselves.

Behavioral counseling is based on a learning theory called behaviorism. The focus is on overt and specific behavior, with a precise spelling out of goals and the formulation of a specific treatment procedure. The primary techniques include systematic desensitization, behavior contracts, social modeling, and assertion training.

Rational-emotive therapy stresses that what clients think about a particular fact or experience determines how they feel and what they do. Thus the focus is on replacing illogical thinking with logical thinking. In so doing, the counselor assumes an active teaching role.

Other cognitive-behavioral approaches that have contributed much to counseling include reality therapy, transactional analysis, trait-factor counseling, neurolinguistic programming, and hypnotherapy.

## REFERENCES

BANDLER, R., and GRINDER, J. (1975). *The structure of magic I.* Palo Alto, Calif.: Science and Behavior Books.

BANDLER, R., and GRINDER, J. (1979). *Frogs into princes.* Moab, Utah: Real People Press.

BANDURA, A. (1965). Behavior modification through modeling procedures. In L. Krasner and L. Ullmann (Eds.), *Research in behavior modification.* New York: Holt, Rinehart & Winston.

BECVAR, R. J., and BECVAR, D.S. (1982). *Systems theory and family therapy.* Washington: University Press of America.

BECK, A. T. (1976). *Cognitive therapy and the emotional disorders.* New York: Meridian.

BERNE, E. (1961). *Transactional analysis in psychotherapy.* New York: Grove Press.

BERNE, E. (1963). *Structure and dynamics of groups and organizations.* Philadelphia: Lippincott.

BERNE, E. (1964). *Games people play.* New York: Grove Press.

BERNE, E. (1966). *Principles of group treatment.* New York: Oxford University Press.

BLACKHAM, G. J., and SILBERMAN, A. (1975). *Modification of child and adolescent behavior.* (2nd ed.). Belmont, Calif.: Wadsworth.

CAMERON-BANDLER, L. (1978). *They lived happily ever after.* Cupertino, Calif: Meta Publications.

COREY, G. (1977). *Theory and practice of counseling and psychotherapy.* Monterey, CA: Brooks/Cole.

DUSTIN, R., and GEORGE, R. (1977). *Action counseling for behavior change.* (2nd ed.). Cranston, R.I.: Carroll Press.

ELLIS, A. (1962). *Reason and emotion in psychotherapy.* New York: Lyle Stuart.

ELLIS, A. (1973). *Humanistic psychotherapy: The rational-emotive approach.* New York: Julian Press.

ELLIS, A. (1974). Rational-emotive theory. In A. Burton (Ed.), *Operational theories of personality.* New York: Brunner/Mazel.

ELLIS, A., and HARPER, R. (1961). *A guide to rational living.* Hollywood: Wilshire Books.

ERICKSON, M. H. (1983). *Healing in hypnosis.* New York: Irvington Press.

ERICKSON, M. H., ROSSI, E. L., and ROSSI, S. I. (1976). *Hypnotic realities.* New York: Irvington Press.

GLASSER, W. (1965). *Reality therapy.* New York: Harper & Row.

GLASSER, W. (1969). *Schools without failure.* New York: Harper & Row.

GLASSER, W. (1972). *The identity society.* New York: Harper & Row.

GOLDENBERG, I., and GOLDENBERG, H. (1982). *Family therapy: An overview.* Monterey, Calif.: Brooks/Cole.

GRINDER, J., and BANDLER, R. (1976). *The structure of magic II.* Palo Alto, Calif.: Science and Behavior Books.

HARMON, R. L., and O'NEILL, C. (1981). Neuro-linguistic programming for counselors. *Personnel and Guidance Journal, 59,* 449–453.

HARRIS, T. (1967). *I'm OK—You're OK.* New York: Avon.

HOFFMAN, L. (1981). *Foundations of family therapy.* New York: Basic Books.

JACOBSEN, E. (1938). *Progressive relaxation.* Chicago: University of Chicago Press.

JONES, M. C. (1960). A laboratory study of fear: The case of Peter. In H. J. Eyesenck (Ed.), *Behaviour therapy and the neuroses.* London: Pergamon Press.

KRUMBOLTZ, J.D., (Ed.). (1966). *Revolution in counseling.* Boston: Houghton Mifflin.

KRUMBOLTZ, J. D., and THORESEN, C. E. (1969). *Behavioral counseling: Cases and techniques.* New York: Holt, Rinehart & Winston.

LANGE, A. J., and JAKUBOUSKI, P. (1976). *Responsible assertive behavior.* Champaign, Ill.: Research Press.

McKENNA, K. R. (1984). *Family systems therapy: An introduction.* Unpublished manuscript, University of Missouri—St. Louis.

PATTERSON, C. H. (1980). *Theories of counseling and psychotherapy.* (3rd ed.). New York: Harper & Row.

PEPINSKY, H. B., and PEPINSKY, P. N. (1954). *Counseling*

*theory and practice.* New York: Ronald Press.

ROBERTS, A. L. (1975). *Transactional analysis approach to counseling.* Boston: Houghton Mifflin.

RUSH, A. J. (1984). Cognitive therapy. In L. Grinspoon (Ed.), *Psychiatry update.* Vol. III. Washington: American Psychiatric Press.

WATSON, J. B., and RAYNER, R. (1960). Conditioned emotional reactions. In H. J. Eysenck (Ed.), *The hand-book of abnormal psychology.* New York: Basic Books.

WILLIAMSON, E. G. (1939). *How to counsel students: A manual of techniques for clinical counselors.* New York: McGraw-Hill.

WOLPE, J. (1958). *Psychotherapy by reciprocal inhibition.* Stanford, Calif.: Stanford University Press.

WOLPE, J., and LAZARUS, A. (1966). *Behavior therapy techniques.* New York: Pergamon Press.

# 6

# TOWARD A PERSONAL THEORY OF COUNSELING

The preceding chapters have summarized some of the many approaches to counseling. Nisenholz (1983), in fact, has identified over 100 different theories. The picture, at least on the surface, is one of diversity. The various counseling approaches appear to differ considerably, not only in their methods or techniques but also in their goals, their basic concepts, and their philosophical orientations.

These differences in conceptualization of the counseling process have been a source of uncertainty within the counseling profession for some time. Counselor educators seem unsure as to whether such diversity should be seen as cause for despair or whether it is a sign of the healthy growth of the profession. Those who see this diversity as healthy suggest that the diversity has come about because individuals have had different experiences and describe those experiences in different ways. Such a view might be compared to the fable of the blind men attempting to describe an elephant. One, touching the leg of the elephant, saw the elephant as being like a big tree trunk. Another, touching the body of the elephant, described the elephant as being big as a house. A third, touching the elephant's tail, believed that the elephant was something like a long rope. And the fourth, whose experience with the elephant consisted of touching the elephant's trunk, described the elephant as being like a large fire hose.

Many see diversity as a positive direction for counseling: as different views of counseling are clarified and integrated, the counseling profession will gain a more thorough, comprehensive view of the total counseling experience. As recently as 1980 Patterson pointed out that some progress had been made in reaching agreement on some common elements of psychotherapy, although he suggested that this progress had been limited mainly to approaches other than the cognitive-behavioral-therapies. Since 1980, and in some cases prior to that date, some movements within the cognitive-behavioral therapies indicate that they too are looking at these common elements of psychotherapy and counseling.

## CHARACTERISTICS OF THEORIES

If each of us possessed total recall of the past, we would probably have little need for theories. To solve a problem, we would only need to recall some facts from the past. But both our memories and the limitations of our previous experiences deny us a full comprehension of the problems and experiences we face in the present. As a result, we need theories to help us solve problems that we have not encountered before or that we do not recall. A theory provides a systematic approach to dealing with a problem.

Theories, by definition, are formulations of the relationships or the underlying principles of phenomena that have been observed and verified to some degree. Theories deal with principles rather than practice; however, they cannot be viewed as something removed from practice, as impractical formulations of ideas and principles with no relation to day-to-day reality. Rather, theory is an essential underpinning of effective practice.

When the counselor is baffled by a problem, he turns to theory to enlarge his perspective about the various alternatives. Since a theory's ability to explain what we are doing suggests the value of that theory, it follows that a theory would also suggest what needs to be done when we are faced with a problem.

This book takes the position that prospective counselors should familiarize themselves with the major approaches to counseling practice today to acquire a basis for developing their own personal style of counseling. Brammer and Shostrum (1977) point out that a counselor who lacks a solid foundation in the current thinking and research and who also lacks a solid set of assumptions on which to base counseling is doing nothing more than applying techniques to help clients solve their problems. Ford and Urban (1963) concur when they suggest that a counselor who lacks a systematic point of view is not only likely to be extremely inefficient in working with clients but may also do more harm than good. This tends to happen when a counselor works from some implicit rather than explicit theory. Such counselors are never really sure from which assumptions they are currently working. When a theory is made explicit, however, a counselor has a better opportunity to test and evolve his own theory based on his experiences and perhaps some of his own research efforts. Certainly a counseling theory is most useful when it has been tested to some degree by controlled evidence.

Theory has four major functions: first, it summarizes a body of information and draws appropriate generalizations; second, it makes complex phenomena more easily understood; third, it predicts the probable outcome of various sets of circumstances; and finally, it stimulates further fact finding to verify and expand its base.

These functions are directly applicable to the counselor confronted with a client. The counselor attempts to apply her own theoretical approach by giving meaning and life to whatever she does in that situation. The counselor must somehow summarize the data provided by the client. Sometimes the data are both complex and confusing, forcing the counselor to make comparisons between the unique data suppplied by the client and the larger body of generalizations that the counselor has made about human behavior.

All counselors stress understanding as fundamental to the counseling process; however, this understanding must go beyond merely comprehending the data to encompass a larger view of the client's whole life situation. A counselor's efforts and success at understanding this whole array of information—a client's self-perceptions, current feelings, past feelings, self-descriptive statements—are largely based on the particular theory that guides the counselor's behavior.

Although prediction does not seem on the surface to be a functional behavior on the part of the counselor, counselors do predict. The approach they decide to take is based on prediction of probable success. So too are the responses they choose to make to clients. Such predictions cannot be wild guesses, but must result from a systematic view (theory) about human behavior and about the effect of counseling on a client.

Counselors need to continually check out their effectiveness, as defined by their theory of counseling. To do so requires a theory that is explicit enough to enable the counselor to develop appropriate hypotheses.

## STEPS IN BUILDING A PERSONAL THEORY

Developing one's own view of the counseling process is a highly demanding, never-ending task. A personal theory must be continually reviewed and revised to include new experiences and insights that a counselor acquires during years of experience. At the beginning, however, new counselors must follow some particular steps to develop initial personal views. First they must familiarize themselves with the current major approaches to counseling practice. Although Corey (1977) recommends eclecticism as a framework for the professional education of counselors, he also points out the danger in an undisciplined and unsystematic approach—it can be an excuse either for failing to develop a sound rationale or for systematically adhering to certain concepts. Certainly there is the danger that counselors will pick and choose only those fragments from various counseling approaches that support their own biases and preconceived ideas.

This book takes the position that although beginning counselors need a firm understanding of all the major approaches, they must gain this familiarization after first grounding themselves in one theoretical approach to counseling. With experience, they can then judiciously integrate and assimilate techniques from other approaches that fit well within their theory and style; they will not be tempted to adopt every new and dramatic ''in thing'' just because everyone else seems to be doing so.

As a second step in developing a personal view of counseling, counselors must know their own assumptions about the nature of people. It is essential for the counselor to attain a high level of awareness of her philosophical beliefs, values, needs, and attitudes regarding her expectations about what clients are like and what people should be. Shoben (1962) suggests that it is not what the actual research tells us but rather our own psychological need structure that dictates what theory we will adopt as our primary approach. As a result, counselors who are about to develop their own theoretical approaches should look very closely at their own need structures to determine their real reasons for choosing one theory over another.

As a third step, new counselors must identify their own accepted models of the mature, well-functioning individual (see Chapter 1 for review). They can then relate such understandings to their goals for counseling, which they can in turn match with strategies and techniques to reach those goals most effectively. Every counselor borrows from other theorists in the sense that he stands on their shoulders to reach higher levels of understanding and effectiveness in practice. He then puts these pieces together in a unified system that he finds comfortable and effective in a particular setting. Finally, he tests this theory in practice and formulates new hypotheses that can be tested experimentally. He then incorporates the results of these tests into his own system.

## COMPARISON OF THE MAJOR COUNSELING APPROACHES

The various counseling viewpoints summarized in the preceding three chapters have both similarities and differences. The following discussion will compare these theories on a point-by-point basis.

**Figure 6-1** Different theorists emphasize various traits and characteristics as being common to all new-born infants (Color Image Inc., Jim Trotter)

## View of Human Nature

Some approaches emphasize human nature considerably more than others. The existentialists, for example, seem to write much more about human nature than the cognitive-behaviorists. Moreover, in each approach the concepts relating to human nature vary considerably. A view of human nature that sees the individual as determined by the environment or by internal needs and drives would seem to have little in common with a view of the individual as capable of making choices and being free to do so.

Nevertheless, there are similarities. As a beginning, we can state that all agree that the individual is capable of changing or at least of being changed (Patterson, 1980). The individual is not hopelessly predetermined, either by heredity or by early learning experiences, and may still change at any stage in life. Even the behaviorists base their approach on the belief that the individual is infinitely susceptible to change. The theories vary, of course, in their degree of optimism about the changeability of the individual, but all approaches assume change is possible. Otherwise, counseling would be pointless.

Patterson (1980) points out two other common elements among the various counseling approaches. All recognize that a disturbance or conflict or unsolved problem is undesirable and warrants attempts to change it. And all recognize the influence of the future—whether of anticipations, hopes, or expectations related to the future—on present behavior. This idea appears to tie together approaches as different as behavioral counseling and existential counseling, in that both accept the idea that behavior is not entirely caused by the past but is also influenced by future consequences or expectations of those consequences.

Certainly the affective approaches outlined in Chapter 4 tend to take a more positive view of human nature than the other approaches. Rogers, in particular, conceives of the individual as basically good, rational, and self-actualizing. In contrast, Freud viewed human nature as highly deterministic, with individuals being controlled by their biological drives and instincts. Though the behaviorists accept human nature as neither good nor bad, they see the individual's behavior not as self-actualizing but rather as resulting from reinforcements from the environment acting upon the individual. Ellis attempts to avoid the whole idea of potential for good or evil by suggesting that this premise has no empirical basis. Still, Ellis does see humans as being born with potentials for rational thinking, despite their tendencies toward crooked thinking. His view of human nature is somewhat less optimistic than that of either the affective or the behavioral approaches.

**Figure 6-2**   Children at play often reveal some of the most basic emotions and needs of humanity (Color Image Inc., Jim Trotter)

### Key Concepts

*Psychoanalytic Approaches*   A major emphasis of the psychoanalytic approach is the interplay of the three systems of the personality—the id, ego, and superego—with the relative development of each of these as a major factor in the individual's emotional well-being.

Adler emphasized the social nature of humans, especially the need to feel a part of significant social groups, and suggested that an individual's life-style resulted from what the individual learned about behaviors necessary for becoming accepted by the group.

Horney and Sullivan also emphasized the social nature of humans, with Horney pointing out that children who are insecure in their primary social relationships handle these feelings by developing irrational solutions. Sullivan, on the other hand, believed that the self responds to anxiety resulting from one's interactions with others and acts to protect from anxiety and thus guard security.

*Affective Approaches*   In general, the affective approaches emphasize the internal focus of the individual—what is going on inside the individual, and particularly what feelings the individual is either experiencing or forcing out of the conscious.

Client-centered therapy views individuals as positive and emphasizes a counseling relationship in which certain "necessary and sufficient" conditions exist. These conditions apply to the counselor, the client, and the relationship.

Gestalt therapy emphasizes the need for clients to reach present awareness of what they are experiencing. Such awareness leads to increased responsibility and growth. The process is an active, confrontive one and results in clients gaining greater recognition of the strength they have and of how to use that strength in daily living.

*Cognitive-Behavioral Approaches*   The cognitive-behavioral processes emphasize thinking and doing rather than feeling and experiencing. Rational-emotive therapy emphasizes that emotions are the products of human thinking. Thus Ellis maintains that emotional disturbances are simply the result of an individual's mistakes—illogical ideas about a particular situation.

The behavioral approaches to therapy, on the other hand, place their major emphasis on the whole social-cultural conditioning process. In particular, behavioral counseling is characterized by (1) a focus on overt and specific behavior, (2) a precise delineation of treatment goals, (3) a formulation of a specific treatment procedure appropriate to the particular problem, and (4) an objective assessment of the outcome of therapy.

### Process and Goals

In comparing the goals of the various counseling approaches, one finds a diverse group of objectives—finding meaning in life, curing an emotional disturbance, adjusting to society, attaining self-actualization, reducing anxiety, and unlearning maladaptive behavior and learning adaptive patterns. As diverse as these goals seem, they can be placed in perspective by viewing them as existing on a continuum from general, long-term objectives to specific, short-term objectives. The affective counseling approaches tend to stress the general, long-term objectives; the cognitive-behavioral approaches emphasize the specific, short-term objectives.

*Psychoanalytic Approaches*    The psychoanalytic view places a major focus on developing a transference relationship between the client and the counselor so that the client can relive unresolved conflicts, feelings, and experiences that have previously been denied or distorted. Thus the major therapeutic goal for Freudians is to enable clients to gain insight into their problems by uncovering material that was previously unconscious.

Adler suggested that the therapeutic process should include the establishment of a collaborative relationship, an assessment of the client's life-style, the development of the client's problems, and the orientation of the client toward action.

*Affective Approaches*    In the client-centered view, the counseling process consists primarily of the counselor's establishing a therapeutic relationship with the client in which the counselor communicates minimally facilitative conditions, such as respect, congruence, and empathic understanding. The goals center around the individual's becoming more mature and reinstituting the process towards actualization by removing obstacles. Thus, from the client-centered standpoint, counseling is simply a process of releasing an already existing force in a potentially adequate individual.

Gestalt therapy, with its focus on the client's feelings, awareness of the moment, body messages, and blocks to awareness, emphasizes a process in which the counselor's role is to challenge clients to use all their senses fully. By encouraging clients to fully experience being stuck at an impasse, the counselor attempts to help clients through the impasse so that growth becomes possible, and clients move from external to internal support, discovering that they can do themselves what they have been manipulating others to do for them.

*Cognitive-Behavioral Approaches*    For the rational-emotive counselor, the process of counseling is the curing of unreason by reason; that is, of helping clients avoid or eliminate most emotional disturbances by learning to think rationally, and of helping them to get rid of illogical, irrational ideas and attitudes and to substitute logical, rational ideas and attitudes. The process results in the client's attaining rational behavior, happiness, and self-actualization. Although behavioral counselors are generally less concerned about process than most counselors, specific counseling goals occupy a place of central importance. Recent behaviorists have focused on the counselor-client relationship as simply a means of facilitating greater understanding of the client's view of the problem, which enables the counselor to develop a more successful behavioral plan for bringing about change in the client.

## Counseling Techniques

*Psychoanalytic Approaches*   Therapists who subscribe to a psychoanalytic approach utilize several techniques in uncovering unconscious material. Interpretation involves the therapist's explaining to the client the meanings of the newly uncovered material, thus leading to further insight. Dream interpretation permits the therapist to gain access to the unconscious, as does free association, in which clients are asked to share spontaneously whatever thoughts, words, expressions, or feelings come to mind, without censorship.

Adler used various techniques to clarify the client's life-style and facilitate insight. He observed very carefully the client's position in birth order, associating characteristics with that position. He also used the adult's earliest memories to help in the understanding. In addition, he used confrontation, interpretation, and encouragement to help clients to take responsibility for their lives and to make new decisions that would enable them to reach their goals more effectively.

*Affective Approaches*   Client-centered therapy places little stress on technique; it emphasizes the counselor's person, beliefs, and attitudes, and the counseling relationship itself. The relationship is the critical variable, not what the counselor says or does. Thus, the ''techniques'' are expressing and communicating acceptance, respect, and understanding, with an emphasis on the here and now of the individual's existence.

Counselors operating within a Gestalt therapy framework utilize confrontation techniques, establishing situations that will cause clients to experience their frustrations. The Gestalt counselor deliberately plays provocative games that are intended to force clients to confront and acknowledge the feelings that they have been so arduously trying to avoid. The Gestalt counselor also fosters a here-and-now orientation and utilizes a variety of experiential games with clients to increase their awareness of themselves and their impasses and then tries to help them reintegrate themselves.

*Cognitive-Behavioral Approaches*   The major technique of rational-emotive therapy is directive teaching. The counselor assumes an active teaching role to reeducate clients, enabling them to recognize that their internalized sentences are in many ways quite illogical and unrealistic. The effective RET counselor continually unmasks the past and especially the present illogical thinking and self-defeating verbalizations of the client. The counselor brings illogical thinking forcefully to the client's attention, shows him how it is maintaining his unhappiness, demonstrates exactly the illogical links in his internalized sentences, and teaches him how to rethink and reverbalize these sentences to make them more logical and efficient. RET counselors also utilize homework assignments as an integral part of their practice.

Probably more than any other counselors, behavioral counselors use very specific techniques based on learning theory. Techniques utilized by behavioral counselors include systematic desensitization, behavior contracts, social modeling, and assertion training.

Desensitization is particularly useful with clients who are experiencing a high level of anxiety associated with a specific problem behavior, while behavior contracts permit the counselor and client to work together in gaining the client's commitment to specific behavior change. Social modeling is particularly useful in helping clients learn new behaviors and is often utilized in assertion training with individuals who have difficulty asserting themselves in interpersonal situations.

## BUILDING A PERSONAL THEORY OF COUNSELING

### Self-analysis

Those who wish to develop a personal theory of counseling should begin by thoroughly examining their own views of human nature. Such an analysis should include a thorough examination of ideas about what people are like and what their inherent tendencies are. The analysis should also include questions about choice making—Does each individual have freedom to make choices? Or are choices determined by previous events in the individual's life?—and about the trustworthiness of people, about their truthfulness, honesty, helpfulness, and selfishness. Those who wish to develop their own theory must consider how people are motivated to change and how such change can occur. Lastly, they must examine their views regarding the relationship between doing, feeling, and thinking in order to help clarify their philosophical orientation, which in turn will lead to a particular counseling approach.

### Self-clarification

Along with examining views about the inherent nature of people, prospective counselors must develop a clear picture of *themselves* as people. They must achieve a thorough understanding of themselves since their own experiences, personality characteristics, and view of inherent human nature will influence their theoretical approach, which in turn will determine their behavior as counselors. One who attempts to accept and practice something that is incongruent with one's own personal makeup cannot function effectively as a counselor. This underlies the need to examine one's own values, beliefs, and ideas, realizing that only when one is clear about who one is can one be effective in facilitating growth in clients.

### Integrating the Various Approaches

After they have clarified who they are, counselors in training need to examine the ideas regarding counseling process, roles, and techniques that are most congruent with their ideas about people. Few individuals are likely to accept all aspects of any one theory. As we said early in this chapter, the prospective counselor must be able to commit himself to the fundamental tenets of one theoretical approach even while disagreeing with some of the specifics. This commitment to a counseling approach in the first few years of training is a highly tentative decision and subject to considerable modification. With experience and further study, the counselor can then examine the ideas and techniques of other theoretical approaches that seem congruent with the chosen approach. The integration of these techniques and goals within one's own counseling approach will lead to a systematic applicability in practice.

Counseling goals from various approaches can be integrated by recognizing that the behavorial and cognitive approaches have goals that stress specific, immediate change, and the affective approaches tend to stress broader or ultimate long-term goals. The counselor can employ specific short-term goals to deal with client problems that call for immediate change. These short-term, specific goals can also be intermediate steps toward achieving the long-term goals that may be the ultimate purpose of the total counseling process.

Bruce (1984) recommends the development of a framework in which several models can be utilized, depending on the needs and expectations of a particular client. He goes on to present one such framework, similar in concept to Maslow's hierarchy of needs in that more basic goals (such as self-preservation) take precedence over more abstract goals (like self-actualization). Likewise, Ward (1983) recommends the use of an affective-cognitive-behavioral, three-domain approach.

Dustin and George (1977) point out that when a client's problem is the lack of positive self-concept, the action counselor might choose to change the behaviors that cause others to respond to the client negatively. For example, one school counselor was working with a third-grade boy whose teacher was upset about the boy's excessive talking and physical activity in class. Behavioral goals for changing the boy's behavior were developed and reinforcements were used. The child became quiet and less active in the classroom and the teacher reported that she could respond more affectionately and genuinely to the child when she could see that he was trying to change (Jakubowski, 1969). Although the major goal throughout counseling may be to help the client move toward self-insight and self-understanding, and toward growth and self-management, setting specific behavioral goals may aid in this overall process.

### View of the Counselor's Role

Those who would be counselors also need to examine their views of the counselor's role in facilitating therapeutic change. Is the counselor simply a good listener? an advice-giver? Should the counselor clarify, confront, provide alternatives, give information, or make decisions for the client? Does the counselor assume all these roles at various times? If so, what is the counselor's basic role in the overall helping process?

Frequently, beginning counselors see themselves as expert advice-givers, expected to have answers for whatever problems clients bring to them. Such an attitude has built-in problems, suggesting as it does that counselors have expert knowledge about all fields. More important, however, even if counselors had such extraordinary overall knowledge, their providing all the answers would most likely reinforce the client's dependency rather than encourage the clients to learn to make their own decisions, to find their own information, and to solve their own problems.

A second role problem encountered by beginning counselors is deciding whether or not to give a client honest and direct feedback. Is the counselor's role one of an impartial observer who listens to the facts and the subjective feelings in the circumstance and then either provides answers or teaches the client how to find his own answers? Counseling theory for most counselors is not static; rather it is a dynamic, ever-changing process. As counselors function and interact with their clients they learn more about those counseling behaviors that are effective with particular clients in particular settings. As counselors integrate these insights into their counseling practice, their counseling theory is expanded and modified to more accurately reflect what they have come to believe to be the essential factors of their own counseling effectiveness. In the long run that is the purpose of counseling theory—to promote effective individual counseling on the part of every practicing counselor.

## SUMMARY

All counselors interact with clients on the basis of a set of beliefs they have about people and how people change; therefore, the importance of counselors' clarifying those beliefs and developing them into a theoretical foundation is emphasized. To facilitate the development of a personal theory of counseling, the following points are emphasized:

In developing an initial personal appoach, counselors must become familiar with the current major approaches to counseling practice. They must develop a full understanding of their own assumptions about the nature of people and identify their own accepted models of the mature, well-functioning individual. They must clarify their goals and strategies in counseling and test their theory in practice, formulating new ideas based on their own experiences.

A comparison of the major counseling approaches with regard to their respective positions regarding view of human nature, key concepts in counseling, process and goals of counseling, and counseling techniques is presented to help identify similarities and differences among the various theories.

## REFERENCES

BRAMMER, L.M., and SHOSTROM, E.L. (1982). *Therapeutic psychology* (4th ed.). Englewood Cliffs, N.J.: Prentice-Hall.

BRUCE, P. (1984). Continuum of counseling goals: A framework for differentiating counseling strategies. *Personnel and Guidance Journal, 62,* 259–263.

COREY, G. (1977). *Theory and practice of counseling and psychotherapy.* Monterey, Calif.: Brooks/Cole.

DUSTIN, R., and GEORGE, R. (1977). *Action counseling for behavior change (2nd ed.).* Cranston, R.I.: Carroll Press.

FORD, D.H., and URBAN, H.B., (1963). *Systems of Psychotherapy: A Comparative Study.* New York: John Wiley.

HARMAN, R.L., (1977). Beyond techniques. *Counselor Education and Supervision, 17,* 157–158.

JAKUBOWSKI, P. (1969). The behavioral approach: The new eclecticism. Unpublished manuscript.

NISENHOLZ, B. (1983). Solving the psychotherapy glut. *Personnel and Guidance Journal, 61,* 535–536.

PATTERSON, C.H. (1980). *Theories of Counseling and Psychotherapy.* (3rd ed.). New York: Harper & Row.

SHOBEN, E.J., JR. (1962). The counselor's theory as a personal trait. *Personnel and Guidance Journal, 40,* 617–621.

WARD, D.E. (1983). The trend toward eclecticism and the development of comprehensive models to guide counseling and psychotherapy. *Personnel and Guidance Journal, 62,* 154–157.

# 7

# CHARACTERISTICS OF A HELPING RELATIONSHIP

THE HELPING RELATIONSHIP: AN OVERVIEW

      Definition

      Characteristics

      Therapeutic Value

THE THERAPEUTIC CLIMATE

      Trust

      Acceptance

      Barriers to Communication

CHARACTERISTICS OF AN EFFECTIVE COUNSELING RELATIONSHIP

      Core Dimensions

      Measurement of the Core Conditions

SUMMARY

118

The relationship established between the counselor and client is fundamental to the therapeutic process of counseling and psychotherapy. Through this relationship clients learn to examine their thoughts, feelings, attitudes, values, and behaviors, and as a result of this exploration they are able to grow and change. This exploration process is made possible because of the therapeutic climate established at the outset of the counseling experience. In this chapter we will explore the qualities and characteristics of a helping relationship; we will discuss the significance of trust and acceptance in the development of the therapeutic climate; we will review several responses that are barriers to the communication process; and we will examine the core conditions of effective counseling, including genuineness, empathy, positive regard, and concreteness.

## THE HELPING RELATIONSHIP: AN OVERVIEW

The helping relationship has been discussed at length in the literature and has been defined by several authors and theorists.

### Definition

Pepinsky and Pepinsky have defined the relationship ''as a hypothetical construct to designate the inferred character of the observable interaction between two individuals'' (1954, p. 171). Shertzer and Stone (1980) have described the helping relationship as ''the endeavor, by interaction with others, to contribute in a facilitating, positive way to their improvement'' (p. 5). Rogers defines the helping relationship as one ''in which at least one of the parties has the intent of promoting the growth, development, maturity, improved functioning, improved coping with life of the other'' (1961, p. 40).

From these definitions we glean that the helping relationship is a unique and dynamic process through which one individual assists another to use his or her inner resources to grow in a positive direction, actualizing the individual's potential for a meaningful life.

### Characteristics

The above definition might describe various interpersonal relationships, including that between parent and child or teacher and student, but the helping relationship established between client and counselor is unique. A number of specific characteristics contribute to its uniqueness.

*Affectiveness* The relationship established between counselor and client is more affective than cognitive. It involves the exploration of subjective feelings and perceptions. Because of the highly personal content of the discussions, the relationship can be comforting and anxiety producing, intense and humorous, frightening and exhilarating.

*Intensity*   Because it is based on open, direct, and honest communication, the relationship can be intense. Counselor and client are expected to share openly their perceptions and reactions to each other and to the process. This can result in intense communication.

*Growth and Change*   The relationship is *dynamic;* it is constantly changing as the counselor and client interact. As the client grows and changes, so does the relationship.

*Privacy*   All client disclosures are confidential, and counselors are obligated not to share what transpires in the interviews with others unless the client has given permission to do so. This protective aspect of the relationship is unique and frequently encourages client self-disclosure.

*Support*   Counselors, through the relationship, offer clients a system of support that often provides the necessary stability for taking risks and changing behavior.

*Honesty*   The helping relationship is based on honesty and open, direct communication between counselor and client.

The above list of characteristics of the helping relationship is not exhaustive. Many others could be added. These, however, should expand the reader's understanding of the relationship and help distinguish this relationship between counselor and client from other helping relationships.

### Therapeutic Value

The above characteristics clarify what is meant by *helping relationship*, but they do not explain its therapeutic value. The effectiveness of the helping relationship in the remediation of emotional and psychological problems and in the growth, maturation, and self-actualization of individuals can be attributed to many factors.

One important factor is that the relationship established between the client and counselor is a microcosm of the client's world; it mirrors the client's patterns of relating to others. The relationship enables the counselor to observe the client's interpersonal style and also provides a vehicle for changing ineffective communication patterns. From this perspective the relationship is therapeutic, since the client and counselor encounter each other as two individuals working out the complexities of an intimate relationship.

Another factor in the effectiveness of the helping relationship is the establishment of a therapeutic climate based on trust and acceptance as well as the core conditions of genuineness, empathic understanding, positive regard, and specificity of expression.

# THE THERAPEUTIC CLIMATE

## Trust

A prerequisite for establishing a therapeutic climate is trust. Clients entering the counseling relationship are often anxious and afraid. Their expectations for counseling may be unclear. They are seeking help with personal concerns and hope the counselor will respond with understanding. If, in the initial contact, they perceive the counselor as trustworthy, they will take increasingly greater emotional risks, sharing thoughts, feelings, anxieties, and fears that are difficult to discuss and that have sometimes been denied. As clients realize that the counselor is not finding fault with those aspects of themselves they dislike, they will become more accepting of themselves. As trust grows, so does the potential for growth and change. From the initial contact then, the counselor must be perceived as trustworthy.

Rogers emphasizes the importance of trust in establishing a helping relationship. In the following questions he not only clarifies the conditions that must be present, he also provides a challenge to counselors for their personal growth and development.

Can I *be* in some way which will be perceived by the other person as trustworthy, as dependable or consistent in some deep sense?

Can I be expressive enough as a person that what I am will be communicated unambiguously?

Can I let myself experience positive attitudes towrd this other person—attitudes of warmth, caring, liking, interest, respect?

Can I be strong enough as a person to be separate from the other?

Am I secure enough within myself to permit him his separateness?

Can I let myself enter fully into the world of his feelings and personal meanings and see those as he does?

Can I receive him as he is? Can I communicate this attitude?

Can I act with sufficient sensitivity in the relationship that my behavior will not be perceived as a threat?

Can I free him from the threat of external evaluation?

Can I meet this other individual as a person who is in the process of becoming, or will I be bound by his past and by my past? (Rogers 1961, pp. 50–55)*

The core dimensions of genuineness, empathy, and positive regard are also fundamental in establishing trust. These are explored later in the chapter.

## Acceptance

The relationship between trust and acceptance has been alluded to in the above discussion of trust. An accepting attitude implies that the counselor can listen to the client's concerns without making judgments and can appreciate the client as a person

*From *On Becoming a Person* by Carl R. Rogers. Copyright © 1961 by Carl R. Rogers. Reprinted by permission of Houghton Mifflin Co.

regardless of the client's views, attitudes, and values. This accepting attitude communicates respect for the client as a person of dignity and worth. The client feels understood and valued in a very real sense.

Rogers discusses the impact of acceptance on client growth in the "if-then" hypothesis:

> If I can create a relationship characterized on my part:
> by a genuineness and transparency, in which I am my real feelings;
> by a warm acceptance of and prizing of the other person as a separate individual;
> by a sensitive ability to see his work and himself as he sees them;
>
> Then the other individual in the relationship:
> will experience and understand aspects of himself which previously he has repressed;
> will find himself becoming better integrated, more able to function effectively;
> will become more similar to the person he would like to be;
> will be more self-directing and self-confident;
> will become more of a person, more unique and more self-expressive;
> will be more understanding, more acceptant of others;
> will be more able to cope with the problems of life more adequately and more comfortably.
>
> (1961, p. 37–38)*

As summarized in the above hypothesis, the accepting attitude expressed by the counselor in the helping relationship frees the client to acknowledge those aspects of himself that have previously been denied awareness. It is paradoxical that the client must accept himself completely before he is free to move in the direction of positive growth and change (Rogers, 1961).

### Barriers to Communication

As discussed above, acceptance is communicated through the counselor's responses to the client's expressed concerns. Unfortunately, counselors often confuse the communication of acceptance with responses that actually block communication and that say to the client that he or she is not understood, is not valued and respected. The response patterns that communicate a lack of acceptance have been identified and explored by Gordon (1974) as they apply to parenting and teaching relationships. The impact of these barriers to communication on the counseling interview will now be discussed.

*Giving Advice*    Some novice counselors are anxious to help their clients by offering advice. They assume that it is their responsibility to guide clients in the right direction and to solve their problems. Because of their expertise in the areas of human development and behavior, they expect to help clients by instructing them regarding the right course of action. True, many clients want the counselor to give them advice,

---

*From *On Becoming a Person* by Carl R. Rogers. Copyright © 1961 by Carl R. Rogers. Reprinted by permission of Houghton Mifflin Co.

but this response places the counselor in the position of assuming responsibility for the client's life choices. For example, a client experiencing marriage difficulties is questioning whether to end the marriage. If the counselor recommends that the client ask for a divorce and the client acts on this advice, the client may later feel that divorce was a mistake and is likely to resent and blame the counselor for her role in the decision-making process. Offering clients advice only maintains their dependence on others and does not facilitate their movement to an internal locus of evaluation and control.

---

***Box 7-1***  *Some Barriers to Communication*

1. Giving advice
2. Offering solutions
3. Moralizing and preaching
4. Analyzing and diagnosing
5. Judging or criticizing
6. Praising and agreeing; Giving positive evaluations
7. Reassuring

---

**Offering Solutions**    The difficulties with counselors offering solutions to client problems are several. First, the problems clients present in the initial interview may not be the concerns for which they need counseling. If the counselor begins solving these, the more basic problem may never surface. It is unrealistic and pretentious for counselors to assume they have solutions to the myriad concerns that clients face. This problem-solving approach reduces the complexities of living to simple problems that have solutions. Rogers (1961) suggests that once the counselor is willing to listen carefully to the client, he will become more respectful of life's complexities and much less willing to rush in and "fix" things. Rushing in with solutions communicates a lack of trust in the client as a human being who, with some support and understanding, is able to solve his own problems.

**Moralizing and Preaching**    When counselors moralize or preach, they evaluate the client's behavior and indicate what the client "ought" to do or how the client "should" feel. This type of response induces guilt, is judgmental, and attempts to change the client's behavior in the direction of the counselor's value system. Such counselors do not attempt to understand the client's world from the client's perspective. Examples of this type of response include: "You should not hate your mother." "You should not treat your sister that way." "I cannot believe you are smoking dope; don't you know it is illegal!" "You ought to be more assertive with your boss." "Abortions are murder!" "You shouldn't have gotten pregnant to begin with."

**Analyzing and Diagnosing**    Analyzing and diagnosing a client's problem is an example of ineffective and unaccepting communication because it puts the counselor in the position of viewing the client's problem from an external frame of reference. In other words, the counselor is removed and objective, seeking to identify the basic maladaptive behaviors and to put them into a clinical framework. An example would be, "Your basic problem seems to be that you have an inferiority complex that prevents you from relating effectively to others."

*Judging or Criticizing* When a counselor judges or criticizes a client's response, the client typically withdraws and withholds further information or feelings. Like moralizing or preaching, this response does not facilitate client self-disclosure but instead induces guilt. For example, a teacher refers a student to a counselor because the student consistently fails to complete homework assignments. If the counselor is judgmental and assumes that the student is irresponsible, playing after school rather than studying, the student may never feel comfortable enough to disclose the real source of the problem—poor concentration because she is worried about her parents' pending divorce.

*Praising and Agreeing; Giving Positive Evaluations* The two responses of praising and agreeing and giving positive evaluations are somewhat more difficult to view in terms of their negative impact on the client. Acceptance implies a *neutral* stance toward the client's attitudes, values, and behaviors. At times it is appropriate for the counselor to respond to the client's growth or behavior change with genuine enthusiasm; however, the counselor must be careful that the seemingly positive response does not communicate a superficial attempt to make the client feel better, make the problem disappear, or to deny that the client really has a problem. An example of misused praise would be, "You're such a go-getter, I'm sure you can handle the pressures of next week without any problem."

*Reassuring* Reassurance helps the client only on a superficial level. It stops interaction between the counselor and client and communicates to the client that many others have felt the same way. This type of statement prevents further discussion of the client's fears, anxieties, or concerns about particular issues. It says to the client, "Your feelings are not valid; don't feel the way you do." Rather than communicating understanding and acceptance of the client's world as he sees it, the reassuring response attempts to gloss over problems.

## CHARACTERISTICS OF AN EFFECTIVE COUNSELING RELATIONSHIP

We have explored the importance of trust and acceptance in establishing a helping relationship and have discussed those counselor responses that serve as communication barriers. Next we will examine the core dimensions of effective counseling and their impact on the helping relationship.

## Core Dimensions

As discussed in Chapter 1, extensive research efforts have sought to isolate those qualities or characteristics of the counselor that may be associated with positive outcomes in counseling and psychotherapy. Investigators have sought the answers to such questions as: What are the characteristics of an effective counseling relationship? Are there characteristics of counselors that can be associated with positive outcomes in counseling? Do these qualities transcend the theoretical orientation of the counselor? Some researchers have sought to identify lists of adjectives that describe effective counselors. These have included the following: empathic, sincere, warm, spontaneous, understanding, patient, friendly, calm, and stable. Many of the qualities that we intuitively associate with persons who are helpful in relationships with others have been objectively proven effective through extensive investigations (Belkin, 1975).

Various studies have demonstrated that a variety of qualities are associated with effective counseling, and a set of characteristics that consistently plays a central role in establishing and maintaining an effective therapeutic relationship has emerged. These characteristics have been delineated through various studies with a broad spectrum of clients:

> An effective counselor
> (1) is not phony or defensive and comes across as an *authentic* and *genuine* person in the therapeutic relationship;
> (2) is able to provide a nonthreatening, safe, trusting and secure atmosphere, through his acceptance, *positive regard,* or *nonpossessive* warmth for the clients; and,
> (3) is able to understand, and have a high degree of *accurate empathic understanding* of, the client on a moment by moment basis. (Truax & Mitchell, 1971)

Although these qualities have come to be closely associated with the client-centered approach, the research indicates that effective therapists, regardless of their theoretical orientation or training, exhibit high levels of the core conditions (Berenson and Carkhuff 1967; Carkhuff 1969a, 1969b; Rogers, Gendlin, Kiessler, and Truax 1967; Traux and Carkhuff 1967; Truax and Mitchell 1971). Rogers (1957) called these qualities of empathy, genuineness, and positive regard the necessary and sufficient conditions for therapeutic personality change.

These qualities of empathy, genuineness, and nonpossessive warmth seem to be present in most helping relationships and are not new to psychologists. Most of the phenomenologically oriented psychoanalysts, including Freud, Fromm-Reichmann, Otto Rank, and Alfred Adler as well as current behaviorally oriented psychologists, have agreed on the importance of these qualities (Truax and Mitchell 1971). Each of these qualities will be explored and their therapeutic value in developing the helping relationship will be discussed.

***Genuineness, or Congruence***    Perhaps the most fundamental element in the development of the therapeutic climate is the counselor's genuineness, or congruence.

Congruence refers to the ability of counselors to be themselves, without needing to present a professional front or facade. Counselors who are genuine do not hide behind a mask or play a role. They can communicate a ''realness'' in relationships because they are sensitively aware of their feelings and reactions as they are experiencing them and are honest and direct in their communication with their clients. Their verbal responses match their internal reactions and nonverbal communication and are characterized by their spontaneity. This type of interaction facilitates trust; the client does not have to wade through layers of defenses and facades to relate to the counselor. Counselors who are secure with themselves and open with their feelings, reactions, thoughts, and attitudes allow the client to feel safe and secure.

The counselor's genuineness can play an important part in the therapeutic process. As the counselor listens and responds to the content of what the client is saying, on another level the counselor is responding to the client as a person. The counselor who can be sensitively tuned into these internal reactions can promote client growth. For example, if a therapist is genuinely moved by the client's pain and struggle to find his own way, she can share these feelings. Likewise, if a counselor realizes that she is having difficulty listening and is, in fact, feeling very uninvolved and bored, she might try to identify the client behaviors to which she is reacting and share these feelings in a positive confrontation. This type of risk taking by the counselor can be highly facilitative, enabling the client to explore personal issues and behaviors that may be hindering other relationships. This risk taking can also promote intimacy and take communication to a new level. By disclosing reactions to a client as they are occurring, the counselor decreases distance in the relationship. Johnson has illustrated this process (Figure 7–1), which occurs in the therapeutic relationship as both counselor and client learn to trust themselves and each other and allow themselves to be authentic and transparent in the encounter.

**Figure 7-1** (Johnson 1972, p. 88)

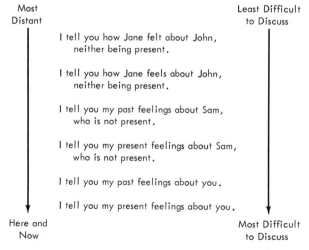

Most Distant / Least Difficult to Discuss

I tell you how Jane felt about John, neither being present.

I tell you how Jane feels about John, neither being present.

I tell you my past feelings about Sam, who is not present.

I tell you my present feelings about Sam, who is not present.

I tell you my past feelings about you.

I tell you my present feelings about you.

Here and Now / Most Difficult to Discuss

*Empathic Understanding*    The ability to be empathic in a relationship requires that the counselor respond sensitively and accurately to the client's feelings and experiences as if they were his own. Empathy is the ability to adopt the client's internal frame of reference so that the client's private world and meanings are accurately understood and clearly communicated back to her. This process, called "trial identification," resembles the relationship a reader establishes with the main character of a novel. Truax and Mitchell have described this identification process:

> As we come to know some of *his* wants, some of *his* needs, some of *his* achievements, and some of *his* failures, and some of *his* values, we find ourselves living with the other person much as we do the hero or heroine of a novel. . . . we come to know the person from his own internal viewpoint and thus gain some understanding and flavor of his moment by moment experiences. (1971, p. 315)

For counselors to respond empathically to the client's verbalizations, they must be sensitive to the client's communications, both verbal and nonverbal, and perceptive. Sensitivity in this context means an increased awareness of the other; perceptivity connotes the ability to understand. Sensitivity is an affective skill that allows the counselor to identify the client's feelings, and perceptivity is a cognitive skill that enables the counselor to identify the stimulus for the feeling. It is a combination of these two interpersonal skills that produces the advanced empathic response. The advanced empathic response is discussed in Chapter 9.

Empathy allows the therapist to hear and respond to the client's feelings—the client's anger, resentment, fear, hostility, depression, and joy. When the therapist can carefully listen to the client's world and accurately identify the feelings the client is experiencing, the client is more capable of listening to himself. Empathy allows counselors to transcend themselves while maintaining their separateness and individuality.

Empathic understanding also involves the therapist's adopting the client's frame of reference. It implies listening to clients without making judgments. As clients share their thoughts, feelings, values, attitudes, hopes, and aspirations, the counselor listens without labeling right or wrong, good or bad. This nonevaluative attitude lets clients become more accepting of themselves.

Some risk is involved in allowing oneself to fully enter another's world. Rogers has described this risk:

> If I am truly open to the way life is experienced by another person—if I can take his world into mine—then I run the risk of seeing life in his way, of being changed myself, and we all resist change. So we tend to view this other person's world only in our terms, not in his. We analyze and evaluate it. We do not understand it. But when someone understands how it feels and seems to be me, without wanting to analyze or judge me, then I can blossom and grow in that climate. (1961, p. 90)*

Rogers adds that when the counselor can grasp the client's inner world without losing his own identity in the process, then change is likely to occur.

*From *On Becoming a Person* by Carl R. Rogers. Copyright © 1961 by Carl R. Rogers. Reprinted by permission of Houghton Mifflin Co.

***Positive Regard or Respect*** The literature refers to positive regard as the therapist's nonpossessive warmth or respect for the client. Rogers (1957) referred to this quality as "unconditionality of regard." By this, Rogers is suggesting the importance of the counselor's being able to genuinely prize the client as a person of worth and dignity. The counselor can reach out in a warm and caring way and accept the client unconditionally. In other words, the therapist does not pass judgment but accepts the client's attitudes, values, and behaviors in a nonevaluative fashion.

Carkhuff and Berenson (1977) have noted that positive regard or respect for others originates in self-respect. Counselors who do not respect their own experiences, thoughts, and feelings will have difficulty respecting other's thoughts and feelings. In many ways, communicating an attitude of caring, warmth, and regard for the client lays the foundation for empathy.

Positive regard is fundamental to the counseling process, and frequently leads counselors in training to wonder if they must like everyone who seeks counseling. Many counselors are able to respond positively to a variety of clients because the helping relationship allows them to move beyond behaviors, defenses, and facades that others find offensive. The counselor who cannot do this should refer the client to another counselor.

Respect or positive regard is somewhat related to the therapist's genuineness or congruence in the relationship. The therapist who does not respect the client's ability to cope with her life, feelings, and reactions will find it difficult to share thoughts, feelings, and reactions to the client's behavior—a sharing that may be essential for client growth. In other words, without respect for the client, the therapist will have difficulty confronting the client in the relationship. Thus, the respect the counselor has for the client enables the counselor to be honest and congruent in the relationship.

Nonpossessive warmth and positive feeling for the client is communicated verbally and nonverbally. Verbal expressions of warmth include statements about the positive relationship: "I like you," "I care about you," "I am concerned about you," "I feel close to you," "I'm worried about you." Essentially these statements convey the speaker's feelings to the other person in a very direct and open manner. To be effective the content of the statement must be congruent with the voice and manner of the therapist. Such statements result in positive attitudes toward the person making them and are related to the trust, acceptance, and understanding that the receiver perceives in the sender (Johnson, 1971).

Warmth toward another person is also communicated nonverbally through eye contact, voice tone, facial expressions, physical position, and touch. Counselors should become aware of the nonverbal messages they send to clients; they should learn to communicate their warmth and regard nonverbally. Johnson (1981) has identified the nonverbal cues that express warmth and coldness. They are listed in Box 7-2. The counselor can learn to act in ways that may be perceived as warm by the client, but these must be real and genuine.

***Concreteness, or Specificity of Expression*** In addition to the core conditions of genuineness, empathy, and positive regard, Carkhuff and his associates have added the dimension of concreteness, or specificity of expression. According to Carkhuff and Berenson concreteness "involves the fluent, direct, and complete expression of specific feelings and experiences, regardless of their emotional content. . ." (1977, p. 13). They further describe the function of the dimension as follows:

1.  Concreteness ensures that the counselor's response is close to the client's feelings and experiences.
2.  Concreteness promotes accuracy and understanding of the client. Misunderstandings can be clarified when experiences and feelings are stated in specific terms.
3.  Concreteness forces the client to deal very specifically with problem areas and emotional conflicts. (1977, p. 13).

---

**BOX 7-2**  *Nonverbal Cues of Warmth and Coldness*

| *Nonverbal Cue* | *Warmth* | *Coldness* |
|---|---|---|
| 1. Tone of Voice | soft | hard |
| 2. Facial Expression | smiling, interested | poker-faced, frowning, disinterested |
| 3. Posture | lean toward other; relaxed | lean away from other; tense |
| 4. Eye Contact | look into other's eyes | avoid looking into other's eyes |
| 5. Touching | touch other softly | avoid touching other |
| 6. Gestures | open, welcoming | closed, guarding oneself and keeping other away |
| 7. Spatial Distance | close | distant |

*From Reaching Out: Interpersonal effectiveness and self-actualization,* by D. W. Johnson, Copyright 1981 by Prentice-Hall, Inc.

---

The importance of concreteness in the counseling relationship cannot be overstated. This dimension, perhaps more than empathy, genuineness, and positive regard, moves the client through the helping process by encouraging the client to explore the problematic areas of his life and his relationship to others. As Egan has stated, "The logic of the counseling process applies to concreteness: if the counselor is as concrete as possible in his responses to the client, the client will learn to be concrete in the exploration of his behavior" (1975, p. 101).

Quite frequently, clients are unable to express their feelings in concrete and specific terms. The counselor has the responsibility to help clients become more in touch with their feelings. The counselor does this by responding to the affect and the underlying stimulus for the feeling. If a client claims to be confused or frustrated, the counselor tries to identify more specifically the feeling the client is experiencing and also tries to identify a stimulus for the feeling.

### Measurement of the Core Conditions

It can be argued that these core qualities of genuineness, empathy, positive regard, and concreteness are more than personality characteristics or qualities; rather they are skills that can be taught or composite responses that can be acquired through training. Research on the core conditions has been extensive and the accumulated evidence has been summarized in various volumes. These include: Rogers et al. (1967), Truax and Carkhuff (1967), Carkhuff and Berenson (1977), Berenson and Carkhuff (1967), Carkhuff (1969a, 1969b), Carkhuff (1971), Truax and Mitchell (1971), and Berenson and Mitchell (1974).

Carkhuff and his associates have expanded the list of core conditions to include several process dimensions. Much of the evidence accumulated has been developed into a systematic model for human relations training. This model has been used to train lay persons and those in the helping professions. Much of the research by Carkhuff and his associates has focused on the development of five-point rating scales used to assess the counselor's level of functioning on each of the core dimensions. Rating scales have been developed for all four core dimensions.

Gazda and his associates (1977) have revised the Carkhuff rating scales, moving from the five-point structure to a four-point scale and have also collapsed the scales for the core dimensions into a global rating scale of counselor effectiveness. Two of the rating scales as revised (Gazda et al, 1977) are presented here as examples (see Tables 7-1, 7-2). On both the Carkhuff and Gazda scales a level of three is considered to be minimally facilitative. The Carkhuff rating scales have been widely used in counselor education to enable counselors in training to discriminate among levels of facilitative responses. Frequently the trainees are asked to rate tapes of their own counseling sessions using the Carkhuff system.

**TABLE 7-1** Empathy Scale

| 1.0 | 1.5 | 2.0 | 2.5 | 3.0 | 3.5 | 4.0 |
|---|---|---|---|---|---|---|

| | | | |
|---|---|---|---|
| An irrelevant or hurtful response that does not appropriately attend to the surface feelings of the helpee. However, in instances where content is communicated accurately, it may raise the level of the response. | A response that only partially communicates an awareness of the surface feelings of the helpee. When content is communicated accurately it may raise the level of the response; conversely it may lower the level of the response when communicated inaccurately. | A response that conveys the helpee is understood at the level he is expressing himself; surface feelings are accurately reflected. Content is not essential, but when included it must be accurate. If it is inaccurate, the level of the response may be lowered. | A response that conveys the helpee is understood beyond his level of immediate awareness; underlying feelings are identified. Content is used to complement affect in adding deeper meaning. If content is inaccurate, the level of the response may be lowered. |

> *KEY WORDS*
>
> Level 4—underlying feelings; additive
> Level 3—surface feelings reflected
> Level 2—subtractive
> Level 1—irrelevant, hurtful

**TABLE 7-2** Global Scale

| 1.0 | 1.5 | 2.0 | 2.5 | 3.0 | 3.5 | 4.0 |
|---|---|---|---|---|---|---|

| | | | |
|---|---|---|---|
| A response in which the helper attends to neither the content nor the surface feelings of the helpee; discredits, devalues, ridicules, or scolds the helpee; shows a lack of caring for, or belief in the helpee; is vague or deals with the helpee in general terms; tries to hide his feelings or uses them to punish the helpee; reveals nothing about himself or discloses himself exclusively to meet his own needs; passively accepts or ignores discrepancies in the helpee's behavior that are self-defeating; ignores all cues from the helpee regarding their immediate relationship. | A response in which the helper only partially attends to the surface feelings of the helpee or distorts what the helpee communicated; withholds himself from involvement with the helpee by declining to help, ignoring the helpee, responding in a casual way, or giving cheap advice before really understanding the situation; behaves in a manner congruent with some preconceived role he is taking, but is incongruent with his true feelings; is neutral in his nonverbal expressions and gestures; is specific in his verbal expressions (e.g., gives advice or own opinion) or solicits specificity from the helpee (e.g., asks questions) but does so prematurely; does not voluntarily reveal, but may briefly answer questions regarding his own feelings, thoughts, or experiences relevant to the helpee's concerns; does not accept discrepancies in the helpee's behavior but does not draw attention to them either; comments superficially on communications from the helpee regarding their relationship. | A response in which the helper reflects the surface feelings of the helpee and does not distort the content; communicates his openness to entering a helping relationship; recognizes the helpee as a person of worth, capable of thinking and expressing himself and acting constructively; communicates his attention and interest through his nonverbal expressions or gestures; shows that he is open to caring for and believing in the helpee; is specific in communicating his understanding but does not point out the directionality emerging for helpee action; shows no signs of phoniness but controls his expression of feeling so as to facilitate the development of the relationship; in a general manner, reveals his own feelings, thoughts, or experiences relevant to the helpee's concerns; makes tentative expressions of discrepancies in the helpee's behavior but does not point out the directions in which these lead; discusses his relationship with the helpee but in a general rather than a personal way. | A response in which the helper goes beyond reflection of the essence of the helpee's communication by identifying underlying feelings and meanings; is committed to the helpee's welfare; is intensely attentive; models and actively solicits specificity from the helpee; shows a genuine congruence between his feelings (whether they are positive or negative) and his overt behavior and communicates these feelings in a way that strengthens the relationship; freely volunteers specific feelings, thoughts, or experiences relevant to the helpee's concerns (these may involve a degree of risk taking for the helper); clearly points out discrepancies in the helpee's behavior and the specific directions in which these discrepancies lead; explicitly discusses their relationship in the immediate moment. |

Note: From *Human Relations Development: A Manual for Educators* (1st ed.) by G. M. Gazda, F. R. Asbury, F. J. Balzer, W. C. Childers, R. P. Walters. Copyright 1977 by Allyn & Bacon, Inc., Boston. Reprinted with permission.

## SUMMARY

The helping relationship established between the counselor and client lies at the core of the helping process. Theoretical orientations may vary in the amount of emphasis placed on the relationship, but its significance in the therapeutic process has been widely acknowledged.

The helping relationship provides the opportunity for clients to examine patterns of relating under controlled conditions and with a person (counselor) who is skillful in interpersonal communication.

The qualities of trust and acceptance are fundamental to the therapeutic climate since they provide an atmosphere in which clients feel safe enough to examine those facets of themselves that have not previously been explored.

Several common response patterns inhibit therapeutic communications. These barriers to communication include giving advice, offering solutions, moralizing and preaching, analyzing and diagnosing, judging or criticizing, praising and agreeing, giving positive evaluations, and offering reassurance.

Research has isolated four core conditions of effective counseling that must be present if the relationship is to be therapeutic. These core conditions include genuineness, empathy, positive regard, and concreteness. Each plays a critical role in the establishment and maintenance of the therapeutic climate and must be exhibited by effective counselors. Counselors can be trained in response skills that will facilitate the communication of the core conditions. Persons who lack these basic qualities must seek personal counseling to grow in these areas if they are to be helpful to others.

## REFERENCES

BELKIN, G. S. (1975). *Practical counseling in the schools.* Dubuque, Iowa: Wm. C. Brown.

BENJAMIN, A. (1969). *The helping interview* (2nd ed.). Boston: Houghton Mifflin.

BERENSON, B. G., and CARKHUFF, R. R. (1967). *Sources of gain in counseling and psychotherapy.* New York: Holt, Rinehart & Winston.

BERENSON, B. G., and MITCHELL, K. M. (1974). *Confrontation: For better or worse!* Amherst, Mass.: Human Resources Development Press.

BRAMMER, L., and SHOSTROM E. (1982). *Therapeutic psychology: Fundamentals of counseling and psychotherapy* (4th ed.). Englewood Cliffs, N.J.: Prentice-Hall.

CARKHUFF, R. R. (1969a). *Helping and human relations: A primer for lay and professional helpers. Vol. 1: selection and training.* New York: Holt, Rinehart & Winston.

CARKHUFF, R. R. (1969b). *Helping and human relations: A primer for lay and professional helpers. Vol. 2: practice and research.* New York: Holt, Rinehart & Winston.

CARKHUFF, R. R. (1971). *The development of human resources: Education, psychology, and social change.* New York: Holt, Rinehart & Winston.

CARKHUFF, R. R. and BERENSON, B. G. (1977). *Beyond counseling and therapy* (2nd ed.). New York: Holt, Rinehart & Winston.

EGAN, G. (1975). *The skilled helper: A model for systematic helping and interpersonal relating.* Monterey, Calif.: Brooks/Cole.

GAZDA, G. M., ASBURY, F. R., BALZER, F. J., CHILDERS, W. C., and WALTERS, R. P. (1977). *Human relations development: A manual for educators* (2nd ed.). Boston: Allyn & Bacon.

GORDON, T. (1974). *T.E.T.: Teacher effectiveness training.* New York: McKay.

JOHNSON, D. W. (1971). The effects of expressing warmth and anger upon the actor and listener. *Journal of Counseling Psychology, 18,* 571–578.

JOHNSON, D. W. (1981). *Reaching out: Interpersonal effectiveness and self-actualization.* Englewood Cliffs, N.J.: Prentice-Hall.

PEPINSKY, H. B., and PEPINSKY, P. N. (1954). *Counseling Theory and Practice.* New York: Ronald Press.

ROGERS, C. R. (1957). The necessary and sufficient conditions of therapeutic personality change. *Journal of Consulting Psychology, 22,* 95–103.

ROGERS, C. R. (1961). *On becoming a person.* Boston:

Houghton Mifflin.

ROGERS, C. R., GENDLIN, E. T., KIESSLER, D., and TRUAX, C. B. (1967). *The therapeutic relationship and its impact: A study of psychotherapy with schizophrenics.* Madison: University of Wisconsin Press.

ROGERS, C. R., and STEVENS, B. (1971). *Person to person: The problem of being human.* New York: Pocket Books.

SHERTZER, B., and STONE, S. C. (1980). *Fundamentals of counseling* (3rd, ed.). Boston: Houghton Mifflin.

TRUAX, C. B., and CARKHUFF, R. R. (1967). *Toward effective counseling and psychotherapy.* Chicago: Aldine.

TRUAX, C. B., and MITCHELL, K. M. (1971). Research on certain therapist interpersonal skills in relation to process and outcome. In A. E. Bergin and S. L. Garfield (eds.), *Handbook of psychotherapy and behavior change: An empirical analysis.* New York: John Wiley.

# 8

# COUNSELING PROCEDURES/SKILLS:I

In this chapter, we will explore the counseling environment and the initial interview and review skills that are basic to the beginning stages of the counseling process. At the outset of the counseling experience, attention must be given to the specifics of organizing the first interview. Seating arrangements, intake procedures, opening the first session, structuring the interview, setting goals for the process, termination, and referral are all fairly simple procedures that must be dealt with regardless of the theoretical orientation of the counselor.

As counseling begins, the counselor's primary goal is to establish rapport with the client so that the therapeutic climate described in Chapter 7 will develop. In large measure, the establishment of the therapeutic climate will depend on the personality of the counselor and the extent to which the core conditions are communicated. There are some basic skills, however, such as observing nonverbal behaviors, and using attending behaviors, open-ended leads, silent listening, and summarization, that facilitate the initial stages of communication.

## INITIAL PROCEDURES

### The Counseling Environment

Several investigations have focused on the importance of the setting and the relationship of such factors as chair arrangements and room size to the client's response to counseling. Haase and DiMattia (1976) studied room size, and furniture arrangements to ascertain the degree to which these factors effected changes in the verbal behavior of the client. Their most significant finding was that room size does, in fact, affect the counseling process. In this particular investigation, a small room diminished the number of positive self-referent statements made by the client. In another study, Chaikin, Derlega, and Miller (1976) found that client self-disclosure is significantly more intimate in a soft room environment than in a hard one. Client preference for seating arrangements was investigated by Brockmann and Moller (1973). They reported that subjects who were submissive and dependent tended to prefer greater distance between chairs; subjects who were dominant, self-assured, and independent preferred the closer seating arrangements.

While these investigations lend support to the theory that the environment does affect the counseling interview, the counselor cannot always control environmental conditions. Some schools, for example, may not provide the counselor with an office, and interviews may have to be conducted wherever space is available.

In arranging an environment conducive to counseling, the privacy and soundproofness of the room are possibly the most significant factors to consider. Counseling interviews can be anxiety producing, the clients should be able to discuss their concerns without fear that their personal self-disclosures will be heard by people walking by. Frequently, counselors prefer a casual environment as conducive to relaxation. Comfortable chairs, indirect lighting, and warm colors help develop a relaxed mood. Seating should be arranged so that the client is not threatened by the counselor's physical proximity. The counselor's freedom of movement toward the client is also important. Some counselors have found swivel chairs useful for keeping spatial distance directly under their control. Clients with high levels of anxiety may prefer the security of a desk between themselves and the counselor, but generally a desk is felt to be a barrier to communication.

The secretary plays a significant role in the counseling environment. Often the first person to greet the client, the secretary sets the tone and therefore should be a warm and friendly individual who relates well to others. The secretary needs to be hospitable, but should not assume the role of therapist by becoming emotionally involved in the clients' lives. Likewise, a secretary who has access to client records and files must understand that these are strictly confidential. The secretary can also insure that the counselor is not interrupted during the session.

### Intake Procedures

In private settings or community agencies the intake procedure includes clients filling out personal data sheets and often also taking a battery of psychological tests. In some settings an intake interview may be required. These interviews are conducted either by the counselor assigned to the case or by a paraprofessional who acts as an intake worker. Counselors in the public school setting may not follow formal intake procedures.

The purpose of the intake interview is to obtain a case history on the client. This case history is a collection of facts about the client's current and past life and may take many forms depending upon the style and preference of the counselor or therapist and the type of problem situation (Brammer & Shostrom, 1982). A career counselor, for example, would focus on factors influencing career choices; a psychoanalytically oriented therapist would want a detailed description of the client's early childhood experiences and affective development.

### Confidentiality and Counselor Dependability

All that transpires in an interview is private, and counselors are obligated not to discuss client relationships with outside parties unless the client has given the counselor written permission to do so. The counseling relationship may be the only relationship in which the client can freely share the anxieties, fears, and feelings that have been harbored in many instances for a lifetime. As the client becomes confident that the counselor respects the privacy of the relationship, trust in the counselor grows. Because of the relationship between trust and confidentiality, counselors must respect at all times the client's right not to have information divulged to parties outside the relationship unless the client has given permission. The legal and ethical considerations involved here will be further explored in Chapter 15.

The dependability of the counselor affects the client's perception of trust in the relationship. As Benjamin has noted, it is more than a matter of courtesy for the counselor to meet scheduled appointments and to be on time. Counselors who are late or miss appointments can cause clients to wonder ''whether we have forgotten him, whether he is of importance to us, whether we are keeping him waiting for some dark purpose unknown to him, whether we are being fair with him'' (Benjamin, 1974, p. 16).

## THE INITIAL COUNSELING INTERVIEW

Counseling is a process that moves through predictable phases and stages. The process has a beginning, a middle, and an end, and counselors must be familiar with the appropriate procedures for opening the interview, for continuing the interview, and for terminating it.

### How to Open the Session

After the client has been introduced to the counselor by name, the counselor may want to spend a few minutes in social conversation to relieve the tension and anxiety the client is probably experiencing; however, the counselor must be careful not to spend too much time in this fashion . Whether the client is self-referred or has been referred to counseling by another party will influence how the counselor opens the session. With a self-referred client, the counselor could begin the session by saying to the client any of the following: ''We have about a half hour to talk and I'm wondering what brings you to counseling.'' ''We have an hour and I'd be interested in listening to anything you would like to share.'' ''I thought we might begin today by your telling me about your expectations for counseling. We have an hour to talk.'' ''How would you like to spend our time today? We have about forty-five minutes.''

In the above examples, note that some structure is given in terms of time limits. Also, each statement communicates that the responsibility for the interview is the client's and that the client is to use the time in the most meaningful way.

Some clients come to counseling at the insistence of a third party. Teachers, parents, and the courts often require an individual to see a therapist for psychological counseling. Clients referred under such circumstances are frequently more anxious and resistant to the process. This situation requires careful thought and planning on the counselor's part. Regardless of the reason for the referral, the counselor must come across as warm and accepting. The counselor may want to discuss the reasons for the referral, but the client should not feel judged and the client should be allowed to choose the topic for the interview. Although the client may have been referred to the counselor for fighting on the school grounds, the client may need to discuss other personal concerns, such as his parents' divorce. Counselors must be careful not to allow their preconceived notions of the problems to interfere with their response to the client's immediate needs.

### Structuring the Session

The counselor must give attention both to structuring the initial session and to establishing the long-term counseling relationship. Structuring the interview is essential because it clarifies for the client what can be expected of the counseling process.

Clients frequently come to counseling with misconceptions. Some perceive counseling as a magical cure, as quick help, as problem solving or advice giving. Others often assume that the responsibility for success lies on the counselor's shoulders. These unrealistic expectations need to be clarified at the outset of the counseling process.

The counselor should open the first session by addressing the specific issues of client and counselor roles, client goals, and the confidentiality of the relationship. Such a statement should be as brief as possible. As noted above, the counselor could choose to begin by asking the client what brought her to counseling and what is expected of the process. After listening carefully to the client, the counselor reacts to the expectations expressed. Time permitting, the interview can then proceed with a topic of the client's choosing.

In this initial interview, the counselor must also deal with time limits as part of the structuring process. The length of the interview will vary, depending on the age of the client and the setting. An interview with a child between five and seven years old would be approximately twenty minutes long; between eight and twelve, approximately a half hour long; and for twelve and above, approximately an hour. Obviously, these are guidelines and cannot always be strictly adhered to. In the school setting, for example, the length of the interview will probably depend on the length of a class period.

The counselor should state at the beginning of the session how long the interview will be. This is important; clients need to understand how much time is available so that they can pace themselves accordingly and can bring up personally relevant material early enough in the session to allow discussion. Counselors who do not specify time limits frequently find that clients will hold on to a particularly painful concern until just before the end of the interview. This behavior can be very manipulative. To help prevent this situation, the counselor tells the client toward the end of the session how much time is left, giving the client an opportunity to raise any unfinished business before time runs out. A typical counselor statement might be, ''John, we have about ten minutes left today; is there anything else you would like to discuss?'' Clients are often so involved in their concern that they often lose track of the time and need a reminder from the counselor.

The duration of the counseling relationship can also be discussed in the initial interview, although the counselor will probably want one or two sessions with the client before estimating the duration. Most counseling will continue for at least a month and not longer than a year; the duration will depend on the severity of the problem and the effectiveness of the counseling.

### Goals for the First Session

The initial counseling interview is in some ways the most important. The client begins to build trust in the counselor during this session, and many of the counselor's behaviors are being carefully scrutinized. The primary goal of the first session is establishing rapport. Eisenberg and Delaney have listed the following as appropriate process goals for the first session:

1. Stimulate open, honest, and full communication about the concerns needing to be discussed and the factors and background related to those concerns.
2. Work toward progressively deeper levels of understanding, respect, and trust between self and client.
3. Provide the client with the view that something useful can be gained from the counseling sessions.
4. Identify a problem or concern for subsequent attention and work.
5. Establish the "Gestalt" that counseling is a process in which both parties must work hard at exploring and understanding the client and his or her concerns.
6. Acquire information about the client that relates to his or her concerns and effective problem resolution. (1977, p. 75)

## Termination of the Initial Interview

At the close of the initial counseling session, the client and counselor must make a decision regarding the continuation of their relationship. If the client and counselor both agree that another session is in order, then the next appointment must be scheduled. It should be reiterated that the client should be notified that the session is drawing to a close before the time period ends. The counselor may do this or may instruct the secretary to knock on the door or buzz the intercom at the appropriate time.

At the end of the initial interview, the counselor must decide whether or not to refer the client to another counselor or agency. The referral procedure requires some skill.

## Referral Procedures

In many instances counselors cannot provide the counseling service needed by the client and must send the client elsewhere. Although referring a client may be viewed as a sign of inadequacy by some, a great deal of competency is needed to identify situations that require specialized services. It is unrealistic for counselors to assume that they can be of service to every person seeking assistance.

*When to Refer*   To make a good referral, the counselor must have information about the client and the nature of the client's concern. A brief interview may be conducted to gather this information, or as noted above, the referral can be made at the close of the initial interview.

It is appropriate to refer a client when

1. the client presents a concern that is beyond your level of competency.
2. you feel that personality differences between you and the client cannot be resolved and will interfere with the counseling process.
3. the client is a personal friend or relative, and the concern is going to require an ongoing relationship. Because of their basic skills in human relations, counselors are often the first persons sought out by friends and relatives in need of assistance, and it would be inhumane not to respond. However, it is difficult and in fact undesirable to maintain a counseling relationship over a period of time with a friend or relative. When

it becomes obvious that the concern requires an ongoing therapeutic relationship, the individual should be referred to another counselor.

4. the client is reluctant to discuss his problem with you for some reason.

5. after several sessions, you do not feel your relationship with the client is effective.

### *How to Refer*

1. Rather than referring a client to an agency, whenever possible you should refer the client to a specific person in the agency. Become familiar with the services provided by local agencies and with the staff of each agency, so that you can match the client's needs with a specific counselor's competencies.

2. Provide the client with accurate and specific information, including the names, addresses, and phone numbers of the persons or agencies to whom you are referring him. The client may wish to place a call for an appointment from your office, but you should not make the appointment for the client. The client must assume responsibility for getting further help, and making the appointment reflects some commitment to the process.

3. The client may ask you to share information about his concern with the person to whom he has been referred. It is recommended that this information not be given in front of the client. Often this kind of contact relieves some of the client's anxiety about seeing a new counselor. It is preferable to get written permission from the client for this consultation.

4. Do not expect to be informed regarding the confidence shared by the client with the next counselor without the client's permission. If you continue to have a working relationship of a different nature with the client, you can request information regarding how to relate to the client in future interactions if such information is necessary.

5. Whenever possible, follow up the referral by checking with the client to see if the new relationship is satisfactorily meeting the client's needs. But avoid pressuring the client for information and accept whatever the client wishes to share.

Like the counseling process, referral procedures must be based on trust and respect for the individual seeking assistance. Counselors can only make clients aware of the alternatives that will provide the best means of assistance on the client's terms. The client may choose to ignore or accept the help available. The counselor's role is to create an awareness of the alternatives and to see that the client has the maximum opportunities to utilize them. Counselors should be aware of the legal issues surrounding the referral process and should be careful to take appropriate steps to prevent the possibility of legal action.

## COUNSELING SKILLS

The following section will focus on specific counselor skills that are basic to the therapeutic process and are used by most counselors and therapists regardless of their particular theoretical orientation. We will define each skill, explore how it is performed, and attempt to assess the impact of the skill on the client.

### Nonverbal Behavior

Mehrabian (1972) has stated that individuals are continuously transmitting information about themselves through their facial expressions, body movements, and proxemic behavior. In many ways, we cannot avoid communication. We send many messages about how we feel, what we think, and how we react to people and situations without uttering a word. Hence, nonverbal behavior plays a significant role in the communication process, and nonverbal channels are frequently less distorted (Haase, 1970; Hall, 1966).

The importance of nonverbal behavior in the counseling process has been acknowledged by counseling theorists and practitioners who assert that the complex interplay of verbal and nonverbal messages is an integral part of the counseling process. Counselors must be skillful at observing and responding to the nonverbal messages of clients, and they must be aware of the impact of their nonverbal behavior on the client during the counseling interview.

*Modalities of Nonverbal Communication*   This section will begin by examining nonverbal communication and its modalities in general terms, and then explore specific client and counselor nonverbal behavior and its impact on the counseling interview.

Gazda, Asbury, Balzer, Childers, and Walters (1984) have categorized nonverbal behaviors into four modalities, presented below as an aid in developing awareness and observation of nonverbal behaviors. It should be emphasized that nonverbal behaviors are highly idiosyncratic; interpretation of these clues must be tentative and based on the context in which they are sent.

1. NONVERBAL COMMUNICATION BEHAVIORS USING TIME
   *Recognition*
       Promptness or delay in recognizing the presence of another or in responding to his/her communication
   *Priorities*
       Amount of time another is willing to spend communicating with a person
       Relative amounts of time spent on various topics.

2. NONVERBAL COMMUNICATION BEHAVIORS USING THE BODY
   *Eye contact* (important in regulating the relationship)
       Looking at a specific object
       Looking down
       Steady to helper
       Defiantly at helper (''hard'' eyes), glaring
       Shifting eyes from object to object
       Looking at helper but looking away when looked at
       Covering eyes with hand(s)
       Frequency of looking at another
   *Eyes*
       ''Sparkling''
       Tears
       ''Wide-eyed''
       Position of eyelids

*Skin*
   Pallor
   Perspiration
   Blushing
   "Goose bumps"
*Posture* (often indicative of physical alertness or tiredness)
   "Eager," as if ready for activity
   Slouching, slovenly, tired looking, slumping
   Arms crossed in front as if to protect self
   Crossing legs
   Sits facing the other person rather than sideways or away from
   Hanging head, looking at floor, head down
   Body positioned to exclude others from joining a group or dyad
*Facial expression* (primary site for display of affects; thought by researchers
        to be subject to involuntary responses)
   No change
   Wrinkled forehead (lines of worry), frown
   Wrinkled nose
   Smiling, laughing
   "Sad" mouth
   Biting lip
*Hand and arm gestures*
   Symbolic hand and arm gestures
   Literal hand and arm gestures to indicate size or shape
   Demonstration of how something happened or how to do something
*Self-inflicting behaviors*
   Nail biting
   Scratching
   Cracking knuckles
   Tugging at hair
   Rubbing or stroking
*Repetitive behaviors* (often interpreted as signs of nervousness or restlessness
        but may be organic in origin)
   Tapping foot, drumming or thumping with fingers
   Fidgeting, squirming
   Trembling
   Playing with button, hair, or clothing
*Signals or commands*
   Snapping fingers
   Holding finger to lips for silence
   Pointing
   Staring directly to indicate disapproval
   Shrugging shoulders
   Waving
   Nodding in recognition
   Winking
   Nodding in agreement, shaking head in disagreement
*Touching*
   To get attention, such as tapping on shoulder
   Affectionate, tender
   Sexual
   Challenging, such as poking finger into chest

Symbols of camaraderie, such as slapping on back
Belittling, such as a pat on top of head

3.  NONVERBAL COMMUNICATION BEHAVIORS USING VOCAL
        MEDIA
    *Tone of voice*
        Flat, monotone, absence of feelings
        Bright, vivid changes of inflection
        Strong, confident, firm
        Weak, hesitant, shaky
        Broken, faltering
    *Rate of speech*
        Fast
        Medium
        Slow
    *Loudness of voice*
        Loud
        Medium
        Soft
    *Diction*
        Precise versus careless
        Regional (colloquial) differences
        Consistency of diction

4.  NONVERBAL COMMUNICATION BEHAVIORS USING THE
        ENVIRONMENT
    *Distance*
        Moves away when the other moves toward
        Moves toward when the other moves away
        Takes initiative in moving toward or away from
        Distance widens gradually
        Distance narrows gradually
    *Arrangement of the physical setting*
        Neat, well-ordered, organized
        Untidy, haphazard, careless
        Casual versus formal
        Warm versus cold colors
        Soft versus hard materials
        Slick versus varied textures
        Cheerful and lively versus dull and drab
        "Discriminating" taste versus tawdry
        Expensive or luxurious versus shabby or spartan
    *Clothing* (often used to tell others what a person wants them to believe
            about him/her)
        Bold versus unobtrusive
        Stylish versus nondescript
    *Position in the room*
        Protects or fortifies self in position by having objects such as desk or table
            between self and other person.
        Takes an open or vulnerable position, such as in the center of the room,
            side by side on a sofa, or in a simple chair. Nothing between self and
            other person.
        Takes an attacking or dominating position. May block exit from area or

may maneuver other person into boxed-in position.

Moves about the room.

Moves in and out of other person's territory.

Stands when other people sits, or gets in higher position than other person.

(Gazda et al., 1984, pp. 62–66)*

*Interpretation of Nonverbal Behavior*     As Gazda and his associates (1984) have noted, nonverbal behaviors must be viewed simply as clues to the individual's underlying feelings and motives rather than as proof of them. The counselor must interpret nonverbal messages tentatively and must realize that a given behavior may have opposite meanings for two individuals or even for the same person on two different occasions (Gazda et al., 1984). The meaning of nonverbal behaviors also varies among societies and cultures, and counselors should be sensitive to these differences.

The client's nonverbal behavior within the counseling interview is obviously important. It provides the counselor with additional information about the client's thoughts and feelings. Often an individual will communicate one message verbally and an entirely different message through voice tone, facial expression, or body posture. Such an interaction might sound like this:

COUNSELOR:  "How are you feeling today?"

CLIENT:  "Oh, fine. Everything's just fine."

COUNSELOR:  "You didn't look as though you felt good as you walked into the office. You were holding your head down and staring at the floor and now you seem to be avoiding my eye contact."

CLIENT:  "Well, I guess it's difficult for me to talk about how depressed I feel."

A common goal of the counseling process is to help the client openly express emotion (Loesch 1975); therefore, the counselor must be sensitive to nonverbal cues and, as illustrated in the above example, skillful at responding to discrepancies between the client's underlying feelings and verbal expressions of those feelings. The counselor's ability to be empathic is directly related to her ability to observe and respond to nonverbal communication.

In many instances it is sufficient for the counselor to bring the client's attention to the nonverbal behavior. For example:

COUNSELOR:  "Are you aware that you break out in a rash each time we discuss your relationship with your husband?"

CLIENT:  "I suppose I just get terribly anxious when we discuss my marriage because I feel guilty that I have been wanting a relationship with another man."

By bringing the nonverbal behavior to the client's awareness, the counselor encouraged the client to share more important and personally relevant unspoken feelings.

*From George M. Gazda et al., *Human Relations Development: A Manual for Educators,* 3rd ed. Copyright © 1984 by Allyn and Bacon, Inc., Boston. Reprinted by permission.

Frequently the ability to observe nonverbal behavior and to respond on some level to the message being sent, enables the counselor to project an unusual warmth, sensitivity, and perceptiveness that enhances the intimacy of the relationship. Responding to a client's frown before the concern has been verbalized makes the client feel that the counselor is tuned in to her at a level that perhaps she is not yet aware of experiencing. This type of interaction is possibly the source of the idea that counselors have a sixth sense and an almost mystical perceptiveness.

### Counselor Nonverbal Behavior

The nonverbal behavior of the counselor also communicates unspoken feelings and thus has an impact on the client's perception of the relationship.

*Attending Behaviors*    The nonverbal behaviors of counselors that have received the most attention in the literature are referred to as *physical* attending behaviors. The physical presence of the counselor helps communicate to the client that the counselor is involved in what the client is sharing. The concept of physical attending may seem basic, yet in daily interactions we often fail to exhibit or experience basic attending.

How many times has someone said to you,

"You're not even listening to what I'm saying!" Or someone reads a magazine while you are talking to him, or it becomes obvious that the person at the other end of the telephone conversation is eating lunch, reading, or engaging in some clandestine activity that prevents him from giving his complete attention to you. (Egan, 1975, p. 61)*

These examples from daily interactions illustrate that, simple though the principles of basic attending are, we frequently find it difficult to apply them.

Among the physical attending behaviors, Egan (1975) lists eye contact, adopting an open posture, facing the person squarely, leaning slightly forward, and assuming a natural and relaxed position.

EYE CONTACT    It is important that the counselor maintain good eye contact with the client. This does not imply that the eye contact should be uninterrupted. Rather, it should be as natural as possible.

ADOPTING AN OPEN POSTURE    As discussed previously, nonverbal behaviors are idiosyncratic. The same behavior by an individual can mean different things at different times. Crossed legs and arms are generally interpreted as signs of withdrawal. Although such an interpretation may not always be valid, the counselor should avoid communicating a lack of involvement through crossed leg and arm positions.

FACING THE PERSON SQUARELY    The physical environment should allow counselor and client to face each other without a table or desk between them. A posture directly facing the client promotes involvement.

*From *The Skilled Helper: A Model for Systematic Helping and Interpersonal Relating* by G. Egan. Copyright © 1975 by Wadsworth. Reprinted by permission of the publisher, Brooks/Cole, Monterey, Calif.

LEANING SLIGHTLY FORWARD   Physical proximity to the client is an important indicator of involvement. Some counselors begin an interview leaning back on their chairs, then lean forward as the level of interaction becomes more intense.

ASSUMING A NATURAL AND RELAXED POSITION   Since many clients are anxious as they enter a counseling session, it is important that the counselor act as normal and relaxed as possible. As the counselor becomes more and more comfortable with the basic attending posture, it will seem more natural without losing the sense of involvement.

## Basic Communication Skills

*Open-Ended Leads*   An open-ended lead essentially says to the client, "tell me about it." Unlike a closed question, the open-ended lead requires more than a yes or no; typically, it opens the door to a discussion of feelings rather than facts. Some examples of open and closed questions are as follows:

OPEN:   "Where would you like to begin today?"
"How are you feeling about that?"
"What kinds of things make you feel sad?"
CLOSED:   "What time did you leave the room?"
"Where did you go after that?"
"Which way did you go?"
"How many times did that happen?"

Open-ended leads encourage clients to share their concerns with the counselor. They place the responsibility for the interview on the client and allow the client to explore attitudes, feelings, values, and behaviors without being forced into the counselor's frame of reference. Closed questions, by comparison, elicit factual information that rarely has actual relevance to the client's concern and are asked out of the counselor's curiosity (Ivey, 1971).

Ivey (1971) has noted that open-ended leads can be used in several different counseling situations.

1. They help begin an interview.
   (What would you like to talk about today? How have things been since the last time we talked together?)
2. They help get the interviewee to elaborate on a point.
   (Could you tell me more about that? How did you feel when that happened?)
3. They help elicit examples of specific behavior so that the interviewer is better able to understand what the interviewee is describing.
   (Will you give me a specific example? What do you do when you get "depressed"? What do you mean when you say your father is out of his mind?)
4. They help focus the client's attention on his feelings.
   (What are you feeling as you're telling me this? How did you feel then?) (p. 151–152)

Despite the value of good, open questions in the counseling process, most beginning counselor trainees rely too heavily on questions simply because they have not mastered other, more productive responses. Excessive reliance on questions may lead to the following problems: (1) the interview digresses to a question-and-answer interrogation in which the client waits for the counselor to come up with the next topic; (2) the responsibility for the interview and the material to be discussed reverts to the counselor; (3) the discussion moves from affectively oriented topics to cognitively oriented topics; and (4) the interview loses a sense of flow and movement. For these reasons beginning counseling trainees are often instructed to avoid questions except as a way to open the counseling session.

**Silence or Passive Listening**   Possibly the most basic of all skills is using silence within the counseling interview. Clients need opportunities to explore their feelings, attitudes, values, and behaviors; initially they need someone to listen, even passively, to what they wish to share. New counselors are typically uncomfortable with time lapses during the interview, but if the counselor can become sensitive to the various meanings of silence and skillful at handling these pauses, these silences can prove very useful. First, silence lets clients know that the responsibility for the interview lies on their shoulders. Too often counselors rush in to fill up the space, thus assuming inappropriate responsibility for the session. Second, silence allows clients to delve further into thoughts and feelings and to ponder the implications of what has transpired during the session. Clients need this time to reflect and process without feeling pressured to verbalize every thought and feeling.

As Brammer and Shostrom (1982) have noted, silence during the interview can have other meanings. It can mean that the client feels uncomfortable and is anxious or embarrassed at having been sent to the counselor. It may also indicate client resistance to the process. In this instance the client may attempt to use it to manipulate the counselor. Silence can mean that the counselor and client have reached an impasse in the session and both are searching for direction. In each of these instances the question raised is whether or not the counselor should interrupt the pause. Counselors must learn to trust their own feelings in particular situations, which requires great sensitivity to the client's nonverbal communication. Often the most appropriate response a counselor can make to client-initiated silence is an accurate empathic statement such as, "You look very thoughtful; would you like to share what you're feeling?" or "You seem pretty quiet, and I'm wondering if you really are angry that you are here." As a rule of thumb it is wise to let the client assume responsibility for breaking the silence when the silence is client-initiated.

In summary, the therapeutic value of silence cannot be overstated. Silence communicates to the client a sincere and deep acceptance. It demonstrates the counselor's deep concern and willingness to let the client experience the relationship without sensing pressure to be verbal. Rogers has cited an excellent example of the therapeutic value of silence:

> I have just completed the strangest counseling case I've ever had. I think you might be interested in it.

Joan was one of my very first clients when I started counseling one half-day each week at the local high school. She told the girls' adviser, ''I feel so shy I couldn't even tell her what my problem is. Will you tell her for me?'' So the adviser told me before I saw Joan that she worried about having no friends. The adviser added that she had noticed that Joan seemed always to be so alone.

The first time I saw Joan she talked a little about her problem and quite a bit about her parents, of whom she seemed to be quite fond. There were, however, long pauses. The next four interviews could be recorded verbatim on this small piece of paper. By the middle of November Joan remarked that ''things are going pretty good.'' No elaboration on that. Meanwhile, the adviser commented that the teachers had noticed that Joan was now smiling a friendly greeting when they met her in the halls. This was unheard of before. However, the adviser had seen little of Joan and could say nothing of her contacts with other students. In December there was one interview during which Joan talked freely; the others were characterized by silence while she sat, apparently in deep thought, occasionally looking up with a grin. More silence through the next two and one-half months. Then I received word that she had been elected ''woman of the month'' by the girls of the high school! The basis for that election is always sportsmanship and popularity with other girls. At the same time I got a message from Joan, ''I don't think I need to see you any more.'' No, apparently she doesn't, but why? What happened in those hours of silence? My faith in the capacity of the client was sorely tested. I'm glad it did not waver. (1951, pp. 158–59).*

This example demonstrates Rogers's unfailing trust in clients' ability to help themselves if the therapeutic relationship is available.

*Listening*    The process of tuning in carefully to the client's messages and responding accurately to the meaning behind the message has been referred to simply as listening. Yet this type of listening moves a social conversation to different levels of communication, and it is the core of effective counseling. Listening at its simplest level calls on the counselor to feed back the content and feelings that the client has expressed. On another level, listening requires that the counselor decode the client's message. This decoding process is necessary because human communication is often indirect. When we speak, we have a tendency to encode our messages rather than communicating clearly and directly what we are thinking and feeling. This process is illustrated in Figure 8–1.

**Figure 8-1**    Process of Decoding.

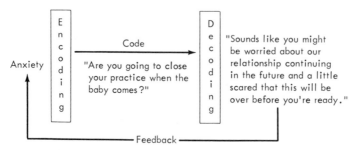

*From *Client-Centered Therapy* by Carl R. Rogers. Copyright © 1951, renewed 1979 by Houghton Mifflin Co. Reprinted by permission.

Listening, then, is a synthesis of the skills of restatement of content and reflection of feeling. It promotes within the client the feeling of being understood. It must be emphasized, however, that listening, as critical as it is to the counseling process, is not sufficient to produce the desired client growth and change. It must be implemented in conjunction with other counseling skills, described in detail in Chapter 9.

Rogers has spoken of the therapeutic value of listening in many of his writings. In the following excerpt Rogers describes the impact of being listened to.

> A number of times in my life I have felt myself bursting with insoluble problems, or going round and round in tormented circles or, during one period, overcome by feelings of worthlessness and despair, sure I was sinking into psychosis. I think I have been more lucky than most in finding at these times individuals who have been able to hear me and thus to rescue me from the chaos of my feelings. I have been fortunate in finding individuals who have been able to hear my meanings a little more deeply than I have known them. These individuals have heard me without judging me, diagnosing me, appraising me, evaluating me. They have just listened and clarified and responded to me at all the levels at which I was communicating. I can testify that when you are in psychological distress and someone really hears you without passing judgment on you, without trying to take responsibility for you, without trying to mold you, it feels *damn* good. At these times, it has relaxed the tension in me. It has permitted me to bring out the frightening feelings, the guilts, the despair, the confusions that have been a part of my experience. When I have been listened to and when I have been heard, I am able to reperceive my world in a new way and to go on. It is amazing that feelings which were completely awful become bearable when someone listens. It is astonishing how elements which seem insoluble become soluble when someone hears, how confusions which seem irremediable turn into relatively clear flowing streams when one is understood. I have deeply appreciated the times that I have experienced this sensitivity, empathic, concentrated listening. (1969, pp. 225–226)

As is evident from the above description, this kind of listening differs dramatically from the type of social interaction that typifies most of our daily experiences. Listening in on social conversations reveals that people rarely take the time or energy to be genuinely and sensitively involved in what someone else is sharing. Rather, they pretend to listen long enough to gain the floor so that they have the opportunity to share what is of importance to them. Perhaps this explains why listening, as described above, has such a powerful impact on clients—they rarely experience someone who is genuinely interested in understanding their world.

*Restatement of Content*     The ability to restate the content of the client's message or to paraphrase a client's statement is a beginning in the process of learning to listen. In restating the content of the client's message, the counselor feeds back to the client the content of the statement using different words. Restatement of content serves three purposes:

> (a) to convey to the client that you are with him, that you are trying to understand what he is saying; (b) to crystallize a client's comments by repeating what he has said in a more concise manner; (c) to check the interviewer's own perception to make sure she/he really does understand what the client is describing. (Ivey, 1971, p. 156)

In paraphrasing a client's statement, the counselor may respond to a feeling, but the focus of the restatement is on content. Some examples of paraphrasing are as follows:

CLIENT:    "I am so sick of school I can hardly get up in the morning to go to class."

COUNSELOR: "You've just about reached your limits as far as school is concerned."

CLIENT:    "I don't know what to do with my life. Sometimes I think I should just go out and get a job for the experience, and then again sometimes I think I should just go on to graduate school, but I'm not sure what to major in."

COUNSELOR: "You're struggling with a big decision about where to go from here with your life, and you're not sure which of the two choices makes the most sense."

In each of the above examples, the counselor responds to the content of the client's statement by paraphrasing the message in different words.

Paraphrasing is appropriate at the beginning of a counseling interview because it encourages the client to open up and elaborate upon the concern. However, paraphrasing does not lead to in-depth exploration and can result in circular discussion if the counselor does not bring in other skills as the interview proceeds.

*Reflection of Feeling*    The basic difference between restatement of content and reflection of feeling is one of emphasis. In reflecting a client's feeling, the counselor listens carefully to the client's statement and responds by paraphrasing the content of the message, but she places the emphasis on the feeling the client expressed. By responding to the client's feelings, the counselor is telling the client that she is trying to perceive and understand the client accurately from the client's internal frame of reference. The counselor tries to identify the feeling accurately by listening not only to what the client says but also to how the client says it. Some examples:

CLIENT:    "I was happy to hear I've been selected for a scholarship to the university I want to attend."

COUNSELOR: "What a thrill for you. You must be very excited and proud to know that you were selected for such an honor."

CLIENT:    "My mom and dad fight constantly. I never know what to expect when dad comes home from work."

COUNSELOR: "It must be pretty scary for you to live with such uncertainty."

In both instances, the counselor's response reflects the basic feeling state of the client and thus communicates to the client the counselor's acceptance of her world.

*Summarization of Content*    Summarization enables the counselor to condense and crystallize the essence of the client's statements. It can further client exploration and can also serve as a perception check for the counselor. The summary of content differs from paraphrasing in that the summary typically responds to a greater amount of material. A paraphrase normally responds to the client's preceding statement; a summary can cover an entire phase of the session or even a total interview (Ivey, 1971).

Ivey has noted that a summarization of content is most frequently used in the following situations:

1. When the interviewer wishes to structure the beginning of a session by recalling the high points of a previous interview.
2. When the interviewee's presentation of a topic has been either very confusing or just plain lengthy and rambling.
3. When an interviewee has seemingly expressed everything of importance to him on a particular topic.
4. When plans for the next steps to be taken require mutual assessment and agreement on what has been learned so far.
5. When, at the end of a session, the interviewer wishes to emphasize what has been learned within it, perhaps in order to give an assignment for the interval until the next session. (1971, p. 159)

*Summarization of Feeling*    In a summarization of feeling the counselor attempts to identify and respond to the overriding feelings of the client, not only the expressed feelings but also the general feeling tone of the phase of the interview being summarized. Summarizing a client's feelings forces the counselor to synthesize the emotional aspects of the client's experience; as such it requires that the counselor respond in a deep and perceptive way to the emotional component of the client's experience (Ivey, 1971).

Ivey has suggested that the counselor

1. Use reflections of feeling to indicate to the client that you are with him. Selective attention to feelings will assist him in exploring his emotional states.
2. Note consistent patterns of emotion as he (she) progresses through the interview. Also note his inconsistencies or polarities of feelings. Most clients have mixed feelings toward important love objects or situations and showing the client how he has expressed his mixed feelings may be especially valuable to him.
3. At two or three points during the session and at the close of the session restate in your own words the feelings and perceptions that the client has been communicating. (1971, p. 158)

## SUMMARY

In this chapter we have explored the practical considerations involved in conducting a counseling interview and have discussed some basic skills that can facilitate initial communication.

Counselors should give special attention to the counseling environment. Room size, seating arrangements, privacy, lighting, and decor all have been found to have some impact on the counseling process and seem to affect the establishment of rapport.

The confidentiality of the counseling relationship enhances the growth of trust between counselor and client. Counselors should communicate in specific terms any circumstances under which a client disclosure will be shared with other parties.

The counseling process moves through somewhat predictable stages or phases. There are procedures and skills appropriate for each of the phases. Thus, counselors must be prepared to open the interview and establish rapport; to structure the session with reference to counselor and client roles, client goals, confidentiality, and time factors; to terminate the session; and to refer clients to other counselors or agencies when appropriate.

Nonverbal behavior plays an important role in the communication process. Counselors must be sensitive to the client's nonverbal behavior and must be aware of the impact of their nonverbal behavior on the client.

The counselor's primary goal during the initial stage of counseling is to establish rapport with the client. The development of the therapeutic climate will depend primarily on the personality of the therapist and the extent to which the core conditions are communicated; however, basic skills such as attending behaviors, open-ended leads, silence, listening, and summarization facilitate the initial stages of the process.

## REFERENCES

BENJAMIN A. (1974). *The helping interview* (2nd ed.). Boston: Houghton Mifflin.

BRAMMER, L., and SHOSTROM, E. (1982). *Therapeutic psychology: Fundamentals of counseling and psychotherapy*, (4th ed.) Englewood Cliffs, N.J.: Prentice-Hall.

BROCKMANN, N. C., and MOLLER, A. T. (1973). Preferred seating position and distance in various situations. *Journal of Counseling Psychology, 20,* (6), 504–508.

CHAIKIN, A. L., DERLEGA, V. J., and MILLER, S. J. (1976). Effects of room environment on self-disclosure in a counseling analogue. *Journal of Counseling Psychology, 23,* (5), 479–481.

EGAN, G. (1975). *The Skilled Helper: A model for systematic helping and interpersonal relating.* Monterey, Calif.: Brooks/Cole.

EISENBERG, D., and DELANEY, S. (1977). *The counseling process.* Chicago: Rand McNally.

GAZDA, G. M. ASBURY, F. R., BALZER, F. J., CHILDERS, W. C., and WALTERS, R. P. (1984). *Human relations development: A manual for educators.* Boston: Allyn & Bacon.

HAASE, R. F. (1970). The relationship of sex and instructional set to the regulation of interpersonal interaction distance in a counseling analogue. *Journal of Counseling Psychology. 17,* 233–236.

HAASE, R.F., and DiMATTIA, D. J. (1976). Spatial environments and verbal conditioning in a quasi-counseling interview. *Journal of Counseling Psychology, 23,* (5), 414–421.

HALL, E. T. (1966). *The hidden dimension.* New York: Doubleday.

IVEY, A. (1971). *Microcounseling: Innovations in interviewing training.* Springfield, Ill.: Chas C. Thomas.

LOESCH, L. C. (1975). Non-verbalized feelings and perceptions of the counseling relationship. *Counselor Education and Supervision, 15,* (2), 105–113.

MEHRABIAN, A. (1972). *Non-verbal communication.* Chicago: Aldine Publishing Co.

ROGERS, C. R. (1951). *Client-centered therapy.* Boston: Houghton Mifflin.

ROGERS, C. R. (1969). *Freedom to learn.* Columbus, Ohio: Chas. E. Merrill.

# 9

# COUNSELING PROCEDURES/SKILLS: II

**ADVANCED EMPATHY**

**THEME IDENTIFICATION**

**SELF-DISCLOSURE**

**PERCEPTION CHECK**

**INTERPRETATION**

> **Clarification**
> **Confrontation**
> **Immediacy**

**ACTION STRATEGIES**

> **Behavioral Techniques**
> **Decision-Making Methodologies**
> **Problem-Solving Strategies**

**GOAL SETTING**

**TERMINATION AND FOLLOW-UP**

**SUMMARY**

Once the counseling process has begun and the therapeutic climate has been established, the counselor's task is to facilitate client self-exploration and to increase the level of client self-understanding so that effective and desired changes in behavior can occur. The counselor must employ more advanced skills to help clients reach this level of self-exploration and self-understanding. Such skills include advanced empathy, theme identification, self-disclosure, perception checks, interpretation, clarification, confrontation, and immediacy; they are discussed in this chapter. While these advanced skills will facilitate action in terms of behavior change in some clients, it is necessary for counselors to be prepared to implement action programs in the advanced stages of the counseling process with those clients who need specific help. The underlying principles of behavior change, which are grounded in learning theory, are discussed in Chapter 5. This chapter will briefly explore the issue of facilitating action to achieve behavior change.

## ADVANCED EMPATHY

The relationship of empathy to the helping process was discussed at some length in Chapter 7. Empathy was defined as the ability to tune in to the client's feelings and to be able to see the client's world as it truly seems to the client. Empathy, then, can be viewed as a skill as well as an attitude, and it can be employed at different levels. At its primary level, an empathic response communicates an understanding of the client's frame of reference and accurately identifies the client's feelings. In contrast, advanced empathy takes the client a step further into self-exploration by adding deeper feeling and meaning to the client's expression. Egan has illustrated the difference between primary and advanced accurate empathy in the following example:

CLIENT: "I don't know what's going on. I study hard, but I just don't get good marks. I think I study as hard as anyone else, but all of my efforts seem to go down the drain. I don't know what else I can do."

COUNSELOR A: "You feel frustrated because even when you try hard, you fail."

COUNSELOR B: "It's depressing to put in as much effort as those who pass and still fail. It gets you down and maybe even makes you feel a little sorry for yourself."

> Counselor A tries to understand the client from the client's frame of reference. He deals with the client's feelings and the experience underlying these feelings. Counselor B, however, probes a bit further. From the context, from past interchanges, from the client's manner and tone of voice, he picks up something that the client does not express overtly, that the client feels sorry for himself. The client is looking at himself as a victim, as the one who has failed, as the one who is depressed. This is "his" frame of reference, but in reality he is also beginning to say, "Poor me, I feel sorry for myself." This is a "different" perspective, but one that is also based on the data of the self-exploration process. (1975, p. 135)

In the above example, the advanced empathy of counselor B takes the client to a new level of self-understanding. Because this counselor sees the situation from the client's perspective, but sees it more clearly and more fully, he can share the implications of the client's perspective for effective or ineffective living (Egan, 1975).

## THEME IDENTIFICATION

The advanced empathic response also helps the counselor identify themes in the counseling session. Typically, clients express a variety of concerns during a session. At the outset these concerns may seem unrelated. The counselor who listens carefully and with a trained ear can begin to hear the relationship among various incidents, situations, problems, and feelings. For example, a client may bring up a concern such as his wife making most of the household decisions and then may express a concern that he doesn't feel very competent at work. As the session develops, the counselor may respond with the following statement: "It sounds to me like your inability to make decisions is beginning to have an impact on how you see yourself both at home and at the office."

Themes that might arise in a counseling situation could include the following:

The client's self-concept—a poor self-image
The client as a dependent person
The client's need for approval
The client's need to be loved and accepted by everyone
The client's lack of assertiveness
The client's need for control
The client's rebellion against authority
The client's insecurity with women (men)
The client's manipulative nature
The client's need for security
The client's inability to experience feelings in the here and now

As Egan (1975) has noted, by identifying themes the counselor takes clients beyond their expressed concerns and facilitates the self-exploration process by helping clients confront their interpersonal style. A counseling session may consist of several themes, but the central theme underlying the client's interpersonal style will be repeated throughout the interview. Often a theme will be signaled by what might be called a "red flag"—a word or phrase that stands out from the rest either through the voice tone used or the significance the word or phrase seems to have in the context of the discussion. Themes that are repeated throughout the session appear and reappear like a red thread woven into a cloth.

> Consider the client who begins the session complaining about her teacher who caught her cheating, and progresses to talking of her difficulty relating to her father, and ends by complaining about how you confront her about the inconsistencies she has stated. The red thread is the client's difficulty relating to authority figures in her world. (Pietrofesa et al., 1978, pp. 289–290)

This example illustrates the importance of theme identification in helping clients come to new awareness regarding their interpersonal style. In this sense the identification of a central theme communicates an understanding of the client's frame of reference beyond the present level of self-awareness and thus is related to the advanced accurate empathic response.

A helpful description of how to make an advanced accurate empathic response is given by Means (1973).

## SELF-DISCLOSURE

Self-disclosure involves revealing your feelings and reactions to events and people as they occur. Within the counseling relationship, the counselor may choose to reveal himself to the client to facilitate the client's openness. In one method of self-disclosure, the counselor might use immediacy to share his reactions to the client or to their relationship openly in the here and now. In another method the counselor might respond to a client statement that is closely related to the counselor's own experience by sharing the similar experience in feeling terms. This, however, can be difficult, for two reasons: first, the counselor's experience must in fact closely resemble that of the client; and second, the counselor must make the self-disclosure long enough to draw the similarity and brief enough so as not to take the focus of the session off the client.

Self-disclosure, when properly implemented, can promote a client's feeling of being understood. It can also enable the counselor to identify client feelings at a deeper level than might otherwise be achieved. In this respect, self-disclosure can facilitate an advanced empathic response. The following example illustrates how this skill might be used in the counseling session:

CLIENT: "I'm having difficulty with my father. He's getting older and he's very lonely. He comes over and stays all day and I feel like I have to entertain him. I get behind on all of my chores and my children are neglected. I want to be helpful to him, but it's becoming more and more difficult."

COUNSELOR: "I think I can understand how angry and resentful and yet guilty you must feel. My mother-in-law is widowed and is lonely and bored. She keeps showing up at the most inconvenient times and stays for hours. I can hardly be pleasant anymore, and I feel guilty for being so selfish."

In this statement the counselor bridges the gap between herself and the client first by letting the client know something about her personal life and second by communicating an accepting and understanding attitude toward the client's guilt. In essence, such a self-disclosure communicates to the client that the counselor is a real person with problems and concerns too.

Timing is very important in the success of self-disclosure. It cannot be overemphasized that the self-disclosure must be brief so as not to take the focus off the client.

Several investigators have examined the impact of counselor self-disclosure on the client. Studies by Jourard (1971), Powell (1968), and Truax and Carkhuff (1965) lend supporting evidence to the contention that therapist disclosures can facilitate client self-disclosures (Simonson, 1976).

Giannandrea and Murphy (1973) conducted an investigation using college males as subjects. They found that when the counselor employed an intermediate number of self-disclosures, significantly more students returned for a second interview than when the counselor used fewer or more self-disclosures. Thus, they surmised that an intermediate number of self-disclosures may increase the counselor's attractiveness as well as encourage the client to respond to the counselor.

Jourard and Jaffee (1970) found that when counselors increased the length of their self-disclosures before discussing a topic, the client responded with lengthier self-disclosures.

Drag (1969) found that counselors who themselves use self-disclosure elicit more self-disclosures from their clients and are also perceived as more trustworthy.

## PERCEPTION CHECK

Counselor statements made in response to a client's feelings should be stated tentatively. Counselors must avoid coming across in an "I *know* how you feel" manner that will alienate the client. One alternative is, "I think I understand how you feel." Another alternative is for the counselor to use a perception check, which is an interpretation of the other's feelings stated in a tentative form. A perception check communicates to the client the counselor's interest in understanding exactly what the client is experiencing, especially when the client may not be expressing feelings directly. A counselor could check his or her perception with a tentative statement: "You seem to be really irritated with me for being late," or "Peggy, you seem rather removed from the discussion today, and I'm not sure if you're feeling bored or just tired." Still another example might be, "Diane, if I were you I might be feeling hurt that my feelings were not responded to. Is that what you're experiencing?"

## INTERPRETATION

Interpretive statements cover a broad range of counselor responses; their purpose is to add meaning to client's attitudes, feelings, and behavior. Interpretive responses draw causal relationships among these three areas. Because interpretations are a process of imposing meaning on behaviors, the interpretation will vary depending on one's theoretical orientation (Brammer & Shostrom, 1982).

Timing is important in making interpretive responses. In the early stages of the relationship, the counselor typically stays with the client and responds to the client's concerns from the client's frame of reference. As the relationship progresses, the counselor gains increasingly greater insight into the client's dynamics and is more able to suggest or infer relationships, perceive patterns of behavior and motives, and help the client integrate these understandings. It is of utmost importance that the client is at a point of readiness that will allow the counselor's response to facilitate growth and behavior change. If inappropriately timed, an interpretive response can cause the client to become defensive and resist the process. Because of the nature of the interpretive response, it should always be phrased tentatively, allowing the client to reject the comment if it is inaccurate or if the client is not ready to hear it.

How the counselor uses interpretive techniques will depend on his or her theoretical orientation. Traditionally, client-centered counselors have cautioned against the use of interpretive responses (Rogers, 1942). However, the classic client-centered technique, reflection of feeling, can be viewed as an interpretation.

Below we discuss three interpretive techniques: clarification, confrontation, and immediacy.

## Clarification

In clarification, the counselor's response attempts to make a client's verbalization clearer to both the counselor and the client. A clarification can focus on cognitive information, or it can seek to highlight client meanings that are not initially clear. Clarification is related to both skill of interpretation and the core condition of concreteness. Some examples of clarification are: "I'm not sure if you got into a fight before or after you got to the school playground"; "Are you feeling angry or resentful?" and "Is the issue whether or not you can afford to quit your job or are you concerned about how others might respond to your unemployment?"

## Confrontation

Confrontation holds the potential for promoting growth and change or for devastating the client. Because it is so powerful, counselors must implement a confrontive response with great skill. Here we will examine the various uses of confrontation, some guidelines in practicing the skill, and some cautions.

Confronting another's behavior is a delicate procedure requiring both a sense of timing and a sensitivity and awareness of the client's receptivity. When properly done, confrontation can help clients become more integrated and consistent in their behavior and in their relationships with others. A confrontive response should only be made in the context of trust and caring for the client and should not be used as a means of venting anger and frustration.

A confrontation may take several forms. It can be used to point to discrepancies

"between what we think and feel, and what we say and what we do, our views of ourselves and others' views of us, what we are and what we wish to be, what we really are and what we experience ourselves to be, our verbal and nonverbal expressions of ourselves." (Egan, 1975, pp. 159–160)

Some specific examples of these discrepancies adapted from Egan would be the following:

"I'm depressed and lonely, but I say that everything's okay."

"I believe that people need to make their own decisions, but I constantly give my children advice about their lives."

"I see myself as witty and others perceive me to be sarcastic."

"I would like to be a good student, but I'm a slow learner; yet I party every night and don't study."

"I experience myself as overweight when in fact others see me as having a good build."

"I say 'yes' with my behavior and dress, and yet hold others at a distance and am fearful of physical intimacy."

"I say that I want to listen and be helpful to others, but I consistently dominate conversations."

Confrontation can also be used to help clients see things as they are rather than perceiving situations on the basis of their needs. In other words, counselors can help clients attain an alternative frame of reference, enabling them to clear up distortions in experience. An example of a distorted perception would be, "My husband has taken a job that requires him to travel because he doesn't love me." In a marriage counseling situation, the counselor could confront this message by responding to observations that indicate that the husband does love her, but that their financial situation requires that he take this better paying position, although it will require him to be away from home.

Still another use of confrontation is to help clients understand when they may be evading issues or ignoring feedback from others. When a client is evading an issue, the counselor might confront him with a statement such as this: "We've been meeting for two sessions, and you haven't raised the one issue you mentioned as a major concern—your sexual relationship with your wife. Every time we get close to the topic, you change the subject. I'm wondering what's going on."

When a client is ignoring feedback, the counselor might say: "I heard Joan saying that she has difficulty feeling close to you because you speak so cognitively about your experience, yet I haven't heard you even acknowledge her comment. What is your reaction to her statement?"

Because the question of when to confront so often arises, the following guidelines are offered: Confront when

1. you are willing to become more involved with the client;
2. the relationship has been built and the client's level of trust in you is high;
3. the confrontation can be done out of a genuine caring for the client's growth and change. Confrontation should not be used as a way to meet the counselor's needs.

Little research has been done on confrontation. Kaul, Kaul, and Bedner (1973) examined the relationship between client self-exploration and counselor confrontation. They found that confrontive counselors did not elicit more client self-exploration than speculative counselors, whether judged by raters or clients. When Berenson and Mitchell (1974) investigated confrontation they found it to be useful and concluded that confrontations help clients to see and experience problems rather than just understanding them. The research on confrontation is rather inconclusive, and it is recommended that confrontation be used discreetly and with care rather than as a *modus operandi*.

### Immediacy

Of the myriad difficulties clients bring to counselors, most involve interpersonal relationships. The counselor-client relationship mirrors the client's behavior in the outside world, which makes it an ideal situation in which to explore the client's interpersonal skills. If counselors can be sensitive to the dynamics of their relationships with clients, they can help their clients explore interpersonal issues ranging from trust and dependency to manipulation. The skill of immediacy involves counselors' being sensitively turned in to their interactions with and reactions to clients as they occur. They can respond to these feelings about either the client or the relationship in the here and now. Immediacy is closely related to the skills of self-disclosure and confrontation, as well as to counselor genuineness.

Immediacy requires that counselors trust their gut-level reactions and that they respect the client. The following example may help to illustrate this point.

COUNSELOR: "I'm having difficulty staying tuned in today. It seems that we're rehashing old stuff, and I suppose that I'm getting tired of hearing the same things over again. How are you feeling about being here and what's transpired between us?"

CLIENT: "Well, I suppose I'm avoiding talking about some issues that are very painful and that I'd like to ignore."

In this dialogue the counselor was able to share quite candidly her lack of involvement in the process, and this exchange led the client to explore more personally relevant material.

## ACTION STRATEGIES

Since the purpose of all counseling is to facilitate client change, counselors should be familiar with the basic principles underlying behavior change. As noted in the discussion on goal setting, internal processes and behavior are not viewed as separate entities; rather, they are intimately related to each other. Many clients are able to act on the insights and new understandings they gain through the therapeutic climate and through the various advanced skills employed by the counselor. However, at times counselors must facilitate the behavior change process by implementing specific action strategies or programs. The timing for implementation of these programs will depend on the theoretical orientation of the counselor and on the nature of the client's concern. In this section we will briefly review the behavioral techniques based on learning theory, which are discussed at length in Chapter 5. We will then consider two approaches that facilitate action in counseling.

### Behavioral Techniques

Based on the principles of learning theory described in Chapter 5, behavioral techniques are designed to alter maladaptive behaviors and to strengthen desirable ones.

These techniques are the basis of behavior therapy and are often used as part of an action strategy by counselors who operate from other theoretical orientations.

*Systematic Desensitization*    Desensitization is appropriate when the client has a high level of anxiety associated with a problem behavior. Examples of such problems would include anxiety about test taking, fear of heights, fear of speaking to groups, and so on. Counterconditioning coupled with muscle relaxation procedures are used to desensitize the client to anxiety-producing situations. These procedures are discussed in detail in Chapter 5.

*Behavior Contracts*    A behavior contract is an agreement between two parties aimed at changing the behavior of one of the persons involved. The agreement specifies the reinforcement contingent on reaching the goal. The behavior contract obviously has many applications in facilitating client action and has been used with behaviors ranging from smoking and weight reduction to disruptive behavior and speech problems. An example of a behavior contract follows:

---

*Behavioral Contract between (Son) and (Mother)*

Son agrees to:
    Speak distinctly when talking, with no reminder

Mother agrees to:
    Give 1 cent to son each time he speaks distinctly

Both parties agree to the following conditions:
    1. Penalty for failing to speak distinctly will be reduction of 1 cent for each failure.
    2. Amount of payment or penalty will not exceed 45 cents per day.
    3. Account will be balanced at end of each day; payment will be each Friday.
    4. Mother must be present to hear speech.
    5. Reevaluation after a trial period of one week.

Signed: _____
                            Mother

Signed: _____
                            Son

Date:    _____ June 26, 1972 _____

---

(Dustin & George, 1977, p. 77)

*Social Modeling*    When the presenting concern of the client involves a problematic relationship with another, it is often useful for the client to practice new ways of relating to the other party with the counselor. The counselor is given instructions regarding how to act so that the situation will resemble real life, and then the client and counselor act out the situation. This gives the client the opportunity to get feedback from the counselor regarding the effectiveness of the client's behavior. This technique is similar to the "empty chair" technique from the Gestalt approach.

*Assertion Training*   Used in conjunction with a therapeutic relationship, assertion training may supplement client growth and change when clients have difficulty saying no or expressing both their positive and negative feelings.

The above behavioral techniques, though typically associated with behavioral counseling, may be used in conjunction with the therapeutic relationship to facilitate client action.

In addition to the behavioral techniques described above, counselors should be familiar with two other approaches that facilitate client action: decision-making methodologies and problem-solving strategies.

### Decision-Making Methodologies

The ability to make good decisions is an integral part of healthy personal functioning. We are constantly faced with situations that require effective decision-making skills. Many problems clients bring to counselors involve the inability to make good decisions. As discussed in the section on barriers to communication in Chapter 7, counselors are not interested in solving clients' concerns for them; rather, they aim to give clients the skills to solve their own problems. This approach facilitates client independence.

Many authors have proposed that the decision-making process involves sequential steps. Stewart, Winborn, Johnson, Burks, and Engelkes (1978) list the following steps in their decision-making model:

1. *Identify the problem.* This step should include answers to problems such as: What is the problem? What prevents a solution? When and under what circumstances does the problem occur? and so on.
2. *Identification of values and goals.* During this phase the clients' values are examined so that the solution will be consistent with the clients' values and long range goals.
3. *Identify alternatives.* A list of possible alternatives is formulated.
4. *Examine alternatives.* At this stage the advantages and disadvantages of each proposal are weighed, based on factual information such as amount of time and money involved.
5. *Make a tentative decision.*
6. *Take action on the decision.* If the decision is critical and the client is unsure about the choice, the decision may be tested at this stage, then further information can be gained and fed back into the decision-making process.
7. *Evaluate outcomes.* Evaluation should be a continual part of the process.

It should again be emphasized that the role of the counselor is not to make clients' decisions for them but to give them the skills not only to deal with the present concern but also to deal effectively with future problems. Krumboltz's (1966) model emphasizes this important point by adding the step of generalizing the decision-making process to future problems. This model is presented below:

1. Generating a list of all possible courses of action
2. Gathering relevant information about each feasible alternative course of action
3. Estimating the probability of success in each alternative on the basis of the experience of others and projections of current trends
4. Considering the personal values which may be enhanced or diminished under each course of action
5. Deliberating and weighing the facts, probable outcomes and values for each alternative
6. Eliminating from consideration the least favorable courses of action
7. Formulating a tentative plan of action subject to new developments and opportunities
8. Generalizing the decision-making process to future problems (1966, p. 153–159)

### Problem-Solving Strategies

Egan (1975) proposes a systematic problem-solving methodology that includes his approach to the decision-making process and incorporates force-field analysis. The steps of the model are briefly summarized here.

1. *Identify and clarify the problem.* Clients often present counselors with rather vague problems that, as stated, are insolvable. Therefore, as a first step the problem must be stated in a solvable manner. Instead of accepting vague descriptions of feelings, such as "I'm so depressed," the counselor seeks the stimulus for the client's feelings: "I'm feeling sad and lonely because I've just moved into this new city and I don't have any friends." The counselor emphasizes that problems cannot be solved when stated vaguely, when they are not dealing with the present, and when they are attributed to outside forces.
2. *Establish priorities in choosing problems for attention.* After clients have a grasp of their problems as well as their resources, they must decide which problems to tackle first. Some criteria would include (a) problems directly under clients' control; (b) crisis situations; (c) a problem that is easily handled; (d) a problem that, when solved, will bring about some improvement; (e) move from lesser to greater severity (other than crises).
3. *Establish workable goals.* Problems reflect the way things are, and goals represent the future. In other words, problems equal "restraining" forces; goals equal "facilitating" forces. Goals should be workable and concrete and should be "owned" by the client.
4. *Take a census of available means for reaching the goal.* List restraining and facilitating forces related to goal achievement. List action steps that could reduce restraining forces and enhance facilitating forces.
5. *Choose the means that will most effectively achieve established goals.* The means must be consistent with client values, should have a high probability for success, and should help the client move systematically toward the goal.
6. *Establish criteria for the effectiveness of action programs.*
7. *Implementation:* Use chosen means to achieve the established goals.

Those who are interested in learning more about the model presented above are referred to Egan (1975) for an excellent discussion of the process with examples of each phase.

## GOAL SETTING

Whether or not to set goals for the counseling process and the type of goals considered acceptable will largely be determined by the counselor's theoretical orientation. Traditionally, behaviorists have been concerned with identification of specific counseling goals, stated as behaviors, that can be easily identified and measured. Counselors with a humanistic orientation, on the other hand, would be inclined to identify a few broad goals, such as improved self-concept or increased self-understanding, rather than to focus on behaviors. The difference here may be attributed to the value placed on observable behaviors, which can be measured, versus the value of unobservable feelings, attitudes, and values, which can only be inferred from clients' behavior and clients' self-report of their internal experiencing.

The broad goal of all counseling is one of change, whether in attitudes, values, beliefs, feelings, or behavior. Since internal processes and behavior walk hand in hand, many counselors feel it is appropriate to focus on both areas, if at different points in the process. Behavioral goals give the humanistic counselor a focus for action either during the session or between sessions. These action goals can be formulated throughout the process as they coincide with changes in the client's awareness. The basic difference between these approaches, then, becomes one of emphasis and the formality of the goal-setting procedure.

Most counselors find it useful to formulate both process and outcome goals for each client for each counseling session. Process goals refer to the goals that counselors set for their own behavior in the relationship. These goals will obviously change throughout the duration of the relationship. Examples of appropriate goals for a counseling session midway through the process would be: to confront the client's unwillingness to be assertive with his or her boss; to disclose instances when the counselor has experienced a similar difficulty; and to use advanced accurate emphatic responses. Some outcome goals might be to work on assertive responses through behavior rehearsal and to work on having the client become more direct and honest in the session.

## TERMINATION AND FOLLOW-UP

A counselor must learn how to bring a counseling session to a close effectively; he must also be familiar with issues and skills involved in terminating a counseling relationship.

In closing an individual session, the counselor must be aware of time and should let the client know when the session is near ending. These timing considerations were explored in Chapter 8. As the session draws to a close, the counselor may ask the client to summarize the main themes, feelings, or issues of the session. This helps clients crystallize in their own minds the important things that took place during the session. The counselor may prefer to do the summary as a means of tying themes, issues, and feelings together into a synthesized framework. A summary by the counselor is particularly useful since it recapitulates the entire session and serves as a stimulus to the formulation of goals for the client to work on between sessions.

Termination of the counseling relationship in most cases is a natural process in which both counselor and client decide that the relationship should draw to a close. In some instances, however, the counselor may feel that it is time to terminate, but the client may not feel ready. Then the counselor must explore and weigh the client's needs to continue against his feelings about ending the relationship. In other instances the client may wish to terminate the relationship, but the counselor may think that this is premature. When this happens the counselor can only confront the client's needs to terminate and express reservations about severing the relationship at that particular time. The counselor cannot, however, force a client to continue against her wishes.

Once the relationship has been terminated, the counselor will want to keep in touch with the client to see how things are progressing. This communicates the counselor's genuine concern for the client's further growth and development.

## SUMMARY

Once the counseling process has been initiated and rapport between client and counselor has developed, the counselor begins to promote and facilitate client self-exploration and self-understanding.

To facilitate client self-exploration and self-understanding, advanced counseling skills are required. These skills include advanced empathy, theme identification, self-disclosure, perception checks, interpretation, clarification, confrontation, and immediacy.

The goal of all counseling is client change. Thus, counselors should be familiar with the learning principles that underlie changes in behavior.

Internal processes and behavior are viewed as interacting rather than as separate entities. Some clients are capable of translating new insights and perceptions into changes in their behavior with minimal help from the counselor. Other clients must be worked with more directly if behavior change is to occur. Thus, counselors should develop action strategies to help clients translate insight into behavior change.

Behavioral techniques such as desensitization, behavior contracts, social modeling, and assertion training may be implemented as action strategies by counselors from a variety of theoretical orientations as an adjunct to the therapeutic process.

Decision-making and problem-solving methodologies are particularly useful in working out action programs for clients.

## REFERENCES

BERENSON, B. G., and MITCHELL, K. M. (1974). *Confrontation: For better or worse!* Amherst: Human Resource Development Press.

BRAMMER, L., and SHOSTROM, E. (1982). *Therapeutic psychology: Fundamentals of counseling and psychotherapy* (4th ed.). Englewood Cliffs, N.J.: Prentice-Hall.

DRAG, R. M. (1969). Self-disclosure as a function of group size and experimenter behavior. *Dissertation Abstracts International, 30*(5–B), 2416.

DUSTIN, R., and GEORGE, R. (1977). *Action counseling for behavior change* (2nd ed.). Cranston, R. I.: Carroll Press, p. 77.

EGAN, G. (1975). *The Skilled Helper: A model for systematic helping and interpersonal relating.* Monterey, Calif.: Brooks/Cole.

EGAN, G., and COWAN M. (1979). *People in systems: A model for development in the human-service professions and education.* Monterey, Calif.: Brooks/Cole.

GIANNANDREA, V., and MURPHY, K. C. (1973). Similarity self-disclosure and return for a second interview. *Journal of Counseling Psychology, 20*(6), 545–548.

JOURARD, S. (1971). *Self-disclosure: An experimental analysis of the transparent self.* New York: Wiley Interscience.

JOURARD, S. M., and JAFFEE, P. E. (1970). Influence of an interviewer's self-disclosure on the self-disclosing behavior of interviewees. *Journal of Counseling Psychology, 17,* 252–257.

KAUL, T. T., KAUL, M.A., and BEDNAR, R. L. (1973). Counselor confrontation and client depth of self-exploration. *Journal of Counseling Psychology, 20*(2), 132–136.

KRUMBOLTZ, J. (1966). Behavioral goals for counseling. *Journal of Counseling Psychology, 13* 153–159.

MEANS, R. (1973). Levels of empathic response. *Personnel and Guidance Journal. 52*(1), 23–28.

PIETROFESA, T. J., HOFFMAN, A., SPLETE, H. H., and PINTO, D. V. (1978). *Counseling: Theory, research, and practice.* Chicago: Rand McNally.

POWELL, W. J. (1968). Differential effectiveness of interviewer interventions in an experimenter interview. *Journal of Counseling and Clinical Psychology. 32,* 210–215.

ROGERS, C. R. (1942). *Counseling and psychotherapy.* Boston: Houghton Mifflin.

SIMONSON, N. R. (1976). The impact of therapist disclosure on patient disclosure. *Journal of Counseling Psychology, 23* (1) 3–6.

STEWART, N., WINBORN, B., JOHNSON, R., BURKS, H., and ENGELKES, J. (1978). *Systematic counseling.* Englewood Cliffs, N.J.: Prentice-Hall.

TRUAX, C. B., and CARKHUFF, R. R. (1965). Client and therapist transparency in the psychotherapeutic encounter. *Journal of Counseling Psychology. 12,* 3–9.

# 10

# COUNSELING
# SPECIAL POPULATIONS

This chapter will introduce the reader to the issues involved in providing counseling services to various subgroups within the general population: the culturally different, women, individuals with disabilities, and older adults.

## THE CULTURALLY DIFFERENT

Many practitioners in the helping professions have concluded that racial and ethnic factors frequently impede the counseling process (Attneave, 1972; Ruiz & Padilla, 1977; Sue, 1975; Vontress, 1971). These barriers often prevent counselors from establishing an effective relationship with clients from different populations (Sue, 1977).

Research studies (Padilla, Ruiz, & Alvarez, 1975; Sue & Kirk, 1975) indicate that culturally different clients frequently do not take advantage of counseling services, and that when they do, they frequently terminate the relationship prematurely (Sue, 1977). In fact, Sue and associates (Sue & McKinney, 1975; Sue, McKinney, Allen & Hall, 1974), found that the termination rate for Asian-Americans, blacks, Chicanos, and Indians was fifty percent after the first interview; this compares with a thirty percent termination rate for Anglo clients (Sue, 1977). It is evident from these findings that counselors must be specifically prepared to work with the culturally different.

For many years authors who were concerned with culturally different clients focused on specific minority groups within the population. This approach to counseling the culturally different client was fragmented and often resulted in stereotypic representations of clients from different subgroups.

Recently, research efforts have attempted to develop a broad framework that is applicable across cultures for working with these clients. These researchers are concerned with cultural, class, and language differences, as well as differences in cognitive style, identity issues, and acculturation of subgroups (Copeland, 1983).

Sue has led research efforts in the cross-culture counseling area. He defines cross-cultural counseling (1981) as a relationship in which the client and counselor do not share the same cultural background, values, norms, roles, life-style, and methods of communicating. He also lists the following characteristics which he feels distinguish culturally effective counselors (Sue, 1978):

### Effective Counselor Characteristics

1. Counselors who are culturally effective are aware of their own values and assumptions regarding human behavior. They can understand and accept those whose values differ from their own and can translate this understanding into words and actions.
2. Culturally effective counselors are aware of the generic characteristics of counseling that cut across various schools of thought. They also aware of what Sue has described as culture-bound and class-bound values.
3. Culturally effective counselors understand the influence of racism and oppression on the culturally different, and they consider the environment as well as the individual when searching for an explanation.

4. Culturally effective counselors do not engage in cultural oppression.
5. Culturally effective counselors are eclectic and draw from a variety of counseling techniques as they determine those which are most appropriate for the life-style of the client (1978, p. 451).

## Counseling Goals

Pederson (1978a) has identified several appropriate goals for counselors who are interested in working with clients from other cultures. These goals include the following:

1. Increase the counselor's awareness of the ways that cultural differences affect the counseling process.
2. Identify advantages and disadvantages of working with clients who are culturally different.
3. Anticipate the adjustment process for a client moving from one culture to another.
4. Estimate the client's own cultural bias.
5. Understand how value affiliations derived from socioeconomic status and sex role can be described as cultures.
6. Estimate how cultural values influence test interpretation.

## Implications for Training

If the above list truly reflects a profile of a culturally effective counselor, how might such a counselor be trained?

There should be four basic components to training programs for culturally effective counselors. The components should include (1) consciousness raising, (2) cognitive understanding, (3) an affective component, and (4) a skills component (Copeland, 1982; Henderson, 1979; Sue, 1981). Consciousness raising involves the trainee's becoming familiar with a specific culture's history and present environmental conditions. Cognitive understanding might include knowledge of factors such as geography, socioeconomic status, family structure and socialization patterns, rates of unemployment, and literacy level. (Henderson, 1979).

Pederson (1977) has proposed a triad model for the training of cross-cultural counselors. In the triad model, a third person from the client's culture role-plays a client concern in a simulated counseling session involving a counselor from one culture and a client from the same culture. Pederson chooses to call the third person the "anticounselor" and describes the anticounselor role as being similar to that of the alter ego as used in Gestalt or psychodrama. The counselor and anticounselor vie for an alliance with the client. The anticounselor has the advantage of cultural similarity and is not constrained by logical consistency. Thus, the anticounselor is subversive in his attempt to disrupt the interview (Pederson, 1977). The cross-cultural counseling model as presented in the literature by Pederson (1977, 1978b) seems to be an effective training paradigm for preparing counselors to work with the culturally different. This model (1) enables the counselor to perceive the problem from the cultural viewpoint of the client, (2) prepares the counselor to deal more effectively with resistance to counseling, and (3) discusses the counselor's defensiveness when working with culturally different clients (Pederson, 1977).

Copeland (1982) has proposed four basic approaches to incorporate the above components into graduate training. These include teaching a separate course, interdisciplinary courses, integration and an area of concentration. Regardless of whether the approach in the training program involves any or a combination of the above, Sue (1981) feels that skill building is an area of weakness and deserves more focused attention (Copeland, 1983).

Counselors who plan to work with the culturally different should avoid stereotyping clients from any given subgroup of the general population. In working with these groups counselors will find that the basic qualities of empathy, respect, genuineness, and understanding are as fundamental to establishing a relationship with a culturally different client as they are in any counseling relationship. However, counselors must be cognizant of the differences that exist in working with culturally different clients. There are factors present in these relationships that are not operative in other counseling relationships; to be effective, counselors must recognize these factors and learn how to deal with them.

## WOMEN

The issues related to counseling women are many, ranging from sex discrimination and sex role stereotyping to career choice and support services for women combining a profession and a family and for those reentering the work force. Research investigations into all facets of counseling women are expanding in an attempt to enable counselors to assist women with the new personal and vocational choices they are making. For our purposes, we will briefly examine some of the above issues, as well as the implications for training.

During the past twenty years our society has become increasingly aware of the extent to which women have been victims of discrimination. Sexist attitudes have permeated our social, religious, and educational institutions. The work place has been structured in such a way that it has been highly discriminatory and, in fact, has negatively impacted most women entering the work force. Federal legislation (Title IX of the Education Amendments of 1972) has sought to reduce sex discrimination, but discriminatory practices persist. In the fight against discriminatory practices toward women, we have become acutely aware of the negative impact of sex role stereotyping. Women throughout history have been socialized to relate in traditionally feminine ways. This socialization has presented difficulties for women as they enter the work force and has seriously limited the opportunities available to them. Recent research has investigated all aspects of women and career choice. Chusmir (1983) has summarized the research related to the characteristics and predictive dimensions of nontraditional career choices. He concludes in summary that research findings show that the woman who chooses a career in a male-dominated occu- pation is likely to possess many of the same personality and motivation characteristics commonly attributed to men. She may have internalized these psychologically mascu- line attitudes from an environment in which she had close contact as an only or first child with both a father and a mother who treated her as a person as well as a female. Although she is comfortable with these characteristics and prefers being with men or other nontraditional women, research results indicate she is at the same time probably pro-feminist and desirous of maintaining her femininity and identity as a woman. (p. 46)

Expandinng career options for women into nontraditional, male-dominated occupations have important implications for counselors. As stated above, women choos- ing nontraditional careers have been significantly influenced by their home environ- ments and appear to possess androgynous personality characteristics. Since career decisions are made by many women during high school, interventions must begin in the early years (Chusmir, 1983). Counselors must become involved in career explora- tion activities with elementary-school-age girls. Additionally, they must design inter- ventions that help young girls develop positive self-concepts. While a preventive approach is obviously preferable, we must continue to expand sex role definitions through inter- ventions that are designed to make women feel more powerful and capable of handling the demands of the multiple roles they face. Counselors can be trained using either a behavioral skills approach (Beamish & Marinelli, 1983) or a simulation methods ap- proach, which promotes self-discovery (Kahn & Greenberg, 1980).

An important issue in counseling women is related to sex discrimination prac- tices by counselors. Counselors have been brought up through the same institutions that have promoted sex bias and sex role stereotyping; hence many of these attitudes have become part of their value structure and surface in the helping relationship. We should, then, examine the contention that counselors are biased in their attitudes and behavior, especially when counseling women clients on career development. Below we examine some of the research that has explored sexist attitudes of counselors in the help- ing relationship.

### Review of Research

In what is now considered a classic study, Broverman, Broverman, Clarkson, Rosenkrantz, and Vogel (1970) used a sex role stereotyping questionnaire to determine whether therapists would judge a client's mental health on the basis of the sex of the client. The investigators found that all of the therapists in the sample applied a dif- ferent standard of mental health for men than for women.

In 1970 Neulinger, Schillinger, Stein, and Welkowitz used a personality ques- tionnaire to examine 114 therapists' responses to questions regarding the optimally in- tegrated person. Results of the study indicated that female therapists viewed achievement as more necessary for males than for females, and male therapists rated abasement as necessary for women. Characteristics ascribed to mentally healthy males included achievement, aggression, dominance, and counteraction; those attributed to mentally healthy females included nurturance, patience, play, deference, succorance, and abasement.

Naffziger (1972) studied attitudes toward women's roles and found that women counselors, counselor educators, and teachers placed more value on work-oriented women than men did. Women saw their ideal woman as more responsible for the success of a marriage. The male subjects viewed career women as less attractive to men.

In an interesting study with counseling trainees, Schlossberg and Pietrofesa (1973) had their subjects interview a female client who was struggling with a career decision between a traditionally masculine occupation (engineering) and a traditionally feminine (teaching) occupation. All subjects discouraged the female client from making engineering her career choice.

The above studies lend support to the contention that many counselors are sex biased in their counseling practice. Such biases must be eliminated if counselors are to relate to women in a way that will promote positive self-concept development and occupational choices that reflect the wide range of skills and abilities women bring to the job market.

Counselors must also be prepared to help women cope with the issues accompanying their personal and vocational choices. For example, many women are choosing to combine a career with a family. This choice results in "career restrictions resulting from factors such as limited time, the oft-assumed primacy of the husband's career, geographical limitations, and, in the case of the woman professor, nepotism rules" (Gray, 1980, p. 43). Gaining emotional support from significant others, dealing with conflicting societal demands, and resolving the conflicts between roles are other psychological problems experienced by women who attempt to combine a family with a career (Gray, 1980). Counselors must be free from any bias regarding women's roles if they are to assist with this problem. They must also be knowledgeable about the kinds of problems experienced by women and be able to assist in the development of coping strategies; some important skills would include time management, realistic goal setting, and assertiveness. Additionally, because of the time demands of combining a career and a family, many women need assistance with building support systems and developing and maintaining intimate friendships.

The process of building and maintaining supportive intimate friendships seems to be crucial. As women meet the demands of marriage, parenting, and career, the time for friends decreases as the need for these relationships increases. Rather than choosing to maintain one or two intimate friendships, many women withdraw from intense and committed friendships and instead choose to maintain several social relationships in which there is no commitment. This kind of relationship, while saving time and reducing obligations, reduces the intimacy which feeds the self, so that there is less self to give to family and career. Thus, women need support for meeting their own needs and encouragement for choosing satisfying relationships in which they can get the emotional and psychological support they need to survive daily stressors. Women must learn how to choose friends carefully so that the time they spend with friends replenishes them. Counselors can facilitate this process not only by supporting women's taking care of their own needs, but also by giving women the interpersonal skills that build intimate relationships, such as self-disclosure and confrontation.

Women also may need assistance with divorce and reentry into college or the work force. Counselors should be familiar with the particular problems each of these poses so that they can adequately understand their clients' experiences.

### Implications for Training

Counselors must be aware of their own sexist attitudes and should be encouraged during training to examine these biases and their impact on women clients. Westervelt (1963) suggests that including more content from social psychology, anthropology, sociology, and economics in counselor education programs would provide additional exposure to issues such as psychosocial sex differences and changing sex roles. Westervelt goes on to suggest that counselors in training should have as many opportunities as possible to counsel females of all ages so that they can observe the patterns of continuity and discontinuity at all levels of female development.

From a preventive viewpoint, counselors should be trained to implement career exploration activities at the elementary level to help young girls become aware of all their aptitudes, skills, and abilities. Counselors at all levels should be prepared to become involved in the evaluation of textbooks and the identification of sex-biased classroom practices.

Schlossberg and Pietrofesa suggest a model for counselor training to deal with sex bias. Their model includes

1. Expanding participants' cognitive understanding regarding the role of women through lectures and readings.
2. Raising the consciousness of participants regarding sexual bias through group techniques.
3. Promoting the acquisition of nonbiased helping skills through audio-video taping and role playing.
4. Fostering skill development in program planning and implementation through tutorial projects (1978, p. 70).

## INDIVIDUALS WITH DISABILITIES

With the implementation of Public Law 94–142, which provided for the reintegration of students with disabilities into the mainstream of education, counselors are increasingly providing services to disabled students in the educational setting (Cristiani & Sommers, 1978; Fagan & Wallace, 1979; Sproles, Panther, & Lanier, 1978). This section will explore the particular problems that persons with disabilities face and the issues that counselors must be prepared to deal with as they provide direct and indirect services to these students.

Like the culturally different, persons with disabilities have been isolated from the general population, in this instance because of their particular physical, emotional, or cognitive disabilities. This isolation has resulted in labeling, stereotyping, and limited services—partially because counselors in the school setting have assumed that they lack the necessary skills or training to provide services to this special population. True, counselors do need some information regarding handicapping conditions in order to develop sensitivity to the compounding factors with which most of these children live. However, the basic skills and procedures that form the core of any helping relationship are integral to the counseling relationship with these persons (Cristiani & Sommers, 1978; Hosie, 1979; Vandergriff & Hosie, 1979). They need warmth, empathy, genuineness, and understanding. In this sense, they are no different from the general population.

### Problems

As noted above, persons with disabilities have both greater need for and more restricted access to counseling services. The need and access variables differ from one disability group to another and from one individual to another in the same disability group; however, they share the common problem of management of their disability. The disability experience results from their having to function in a nondisabled world in which they are perceived in distorted terms that are at variance with the reality of their situation. Thus, any exception, no matter how limited, tends to become generalized in the minds of others to include the whole person; such generalizations tend to induce others to consider the disabled person as more limited than she really is, and to build barriers between environmental resources and the disabled individual. In this psychosocial view of the disability experience, the disabled individual is confronted by not one, but three interrelated disabilities: (1) the condition that renders her exceptional in the first place, (2) the unreal perceptions that others have of her because she is disabled, and (3) the impact of these interpersonal responses on her self-perceptions. The combined influence of these three forces exposes the exceptional person to social and self attitudes and resultant behaviors that can render her even less capable of solving her own problems than would be anticipated on the basis of the original disability (Rusalem & Cohen, 1975, p. 616).

Counselors must be aware of the complexity of the above forces and must be prepared to relate effectively to students with disabilities in the educational setting. Again, this does not mean that counselors must acquire a new set of therapeutic skills to work with this population. As previously emphasized, they are more similar to the general population than they are different; they require the basic qualities and characteristics that render any helping relationship effective. What, then, would be essential in training counselors to work with persons with disabilities?

### Implications for Training

Counselors in training should be exposed to a variety of experiences that will enable them to relate effectively to students with disabilities. This training is essential, because recent surveys indicate that counselors are spending disproportionate amounts of time with students with disabilities (Lombana, 1980) and are ill-prepared to provide services to these students (Lebsock & DeBlassie, 1975; Lombana & Clawson, 1978; Lombana, 1980; Filer, 1982).

Hosie suggests that counselors should be familiar with the following list of skills and facts:

1. Federal and state legislation, guidelines, and local policies relating to programs and services for the handicapped.
2. Rights of handicapped children and their parents, and the skills necessary to advise parents and enable them to exercise their rights.
3. State guidelines for classification, diagnostic tools and their limitations, and the skills necessary to relate these to learning characteristics and the common elements of correction.
4. Informal assessment procedures, and the skills necessary to relate these to the special learning strategies of the handicapped.
5. Growth and development process, characteristics, and impediments of the handicapped, and the skills necessary to relate this knowledge to developmental learning tasks and strategies.
6. Characteristics and development of the learning disabled, and the skills necessary to diagnose why the individual is failing tasks and to change methods and objectives when necessary.
7. Sensory impairments, speech disorders, and communication deficits, their effect on diagnosis and remediation, and the skills necessary to overcome or lessen their effect in learning and counseling settings.
8. Input, structure, and potential outcomes of the Individual Educational Program (IEP), and the skills necessary to consult and assist in their construction for the mainstreamed student.
9. Ability, learning rates, and modes of learning of the handicapped, and the skills necessary to utilize these factors in recommending educational placements and environments.
10. Attitudinal biases of teachers and others, and the skills necessary to teach and consult with regular and special educators to produce a facilitative learning environment.
11. Learning disorders, the social and emotional behavior problems of handicapped students, and the skills necessary to instruct and consult with teachers, using behavior modification and management principles to enhance academic learning and social behavior.
12. Potential growth and development of the handicapped child; fears, concerns, and needs of the parents; and the skills necessary to consult, counsel, and teach parents regarding methods to facilitate their child's academic and social development.
13. Characteristics of the handicapped related to employment skills, training programs, and potential occupational and educational opportunities, and the skills necessary to assist the individual in career decision making and development.
14. Roles and skills of other personnel within and outside the institution, and the skills necessary to refer them or work with them to enhance the learning and development of the handicapped individual. (Hosie, 1979, pp. 271–272)

In addition, counselors in the educational setting must be prepared to incorporate into their counseling programs specific activities designed to facilitate the integration of students with disabilities into the regular classroom.

*Interdisciplinary Staffings* Counselors can organize interdisciplinary staffings, which bring all support personnel in the school together to share information from their disciplines and to develop future plans for providing services to the child under consideration.

*Consultation with Teachers* When students with disabilities are integrated into the regular classroom, they frequently are physically integrated but remain socially and emotionally isolated. Counselors must be prepared to work with teachers to develop activities that will improve the self-concepts and social acceptance of integrated students with disabilities.

*Consultation with Parents* Counselors can help parents of children with disabilities through a variety of activities. Raising a handicapped child can be a devastating experience, often presenting situations and problems that very few parents are prepared to handle (Prescott & Hulnick, 1979). Many parents find counseling groups very supportive. Effective models for group counseling with this population have been developed and often include use of the Kübler-Ross (1969) loss model, which has been described by Huber (1979).

Counselors may also offer parents accurate resource and referral information. McIlroy and Zeller (1979) present a comprehensive list of community resources that may be available at the local level.

### Direct Services

Filer (1982) and Lofaro (1982) provide specific suggestions for training counselors to more effectively meet the needs of students with disabilities. Counselors who will be providing direct services to persons with disabilities should experience a variety of training activities. First, they should be encouraged to examine their biases, prejudices, and values regarding handicapping conditions, since these have a profound effect on the counseling relationship (Nathanson, 1979).

Second, counselors should have personal contact with persons with disabilities either as part of regular classroom presentations and discussions or as components in practice and internships. For example, parents of handicapped children could be invited to share their experiences and to explain the impact of handicapping conditions on the family to counselors in training.

Counselors should also be familiar with the psychosocial needs of disabled individuals and should be informed of specific counseling strategies to deal with such special needs as self-concept, body image, frustration and anger, and dependency and motivation (McDowell, Coven, & Eash, 1979). Counselors who are working with persons with a specific disability should acquire whatever additional skills they will need; for example, counselors who are working with the deaf should learn to use a wide range of communicative modes including expressive and receptive sign language (Zieziula, 1979).

With mainstreaming, most school counselors are being expected to provide counseling services to students with disabilities. Additionally, counselors are beginning to seek job opportunities outside of the school setting which require that they possess the skills needed to work with disabled individuals. While rehabilitation counselors have traditionally provided services to persons at the postsecondary level, their counseling activities have focused primarily in the vocational area. Today, counselors who work outside of the school system are increasingly specializing in counseling persons with disabilities. Counselor training programs should be responsive to the training needs of students and should better prepare them for their future roles.

## OLDER ADULTS

The number of adults in this country age sixty-five and older is rapidly increasing. In 1975 an estimated twenty million persons, approximately ten percent of the population, were over age sixty-five (Butler, 1975; Lombana, 1976). The reasons for this increase are several: Medical advances have been made in the prevention and treatment of major fatal diseases. Our health care delivery system has improved, and our birth rate is declining. Thus, the average life expectancy has risen from 47 years at the turn of the century to the current 66.8 years for males and 74.3 years for females (Butler, 1975). With the increasing number of persons in the sixty-five-and-over age bracket, it is important that counselors direct their attention to this frequently neglected age group.

The transitions and role losses in old age affect the vulnerability of the older adult (Glass & Grant, 1983). Some of these transitions merely precipitate the need for counseling; typical transitional difficulties include reentering school or the work force, relocation, employers' ageist attitudes toward older workers, terminal illness, sexuality, aging parents, widowhood, isolation and chronic health problems. The four later-life transitions considered to require the most significant adjustments include late-life career changes, death, dying and grief, and institutionalization (Glass & Grant, 1983).

Other problems confronting the aging are primarily associated with finances and health. As difficult as these problems are in themselves, they are compounded by the feelings associated with the social isolation often experienced by the aging—feelings of loneliness, depression, and despondence (Lombana, 1976). Lombana has outlined the remedial and preventive services that should be provided for the elderly. These services are presented and briefly discussed below.

### Remedial Services

Mental health counseling services should be provided to enable the aging to deal with the severe depression frequently associated with late life crises. Depression most often results from loneliness, loss of loved ones, isolation, and forced institutionalization.

Supportive counseling services should be available to help the aging cope with a wide range of physical difficulties, especially since persons in this age group frequently have no family members to function as a support system. Adjustment counseling can enable older adults who have been in residential institutions to make the transition from these temporary care units to life outside the residential facility. Counseling for avocational and leisure activity could facilitate the adjustment to forced early retirement.

### Preventive Services

Many of the problems associated with aging can be prevented or ameliorated through counseling. Preretirement counseling can help the retiree plan for all areas of retirement—from health and insurance needs to avocational and leisure interests. Health education over the life span can supply information on all aspects of good physical and mental health, including nutrition, exercise, and the need for regular medical checkups. Information about community resources would make existing services more accessible to the older adult.

Counselors can educate the general public about the myths surrounding the senior citizen. Stereotypical views can be dispelled in an attempt to create a more useful and helpful view of the aging adult. Family counseling services can enable better communication among family members, thus promoting empathy and acceptance of the adjustment required by the aging process for all involved (Lombana, 1976).

In providing counseling services to the aging, the counselor must consider several factors. First, the counselor must be prepared to broaden the scope of "appropriate" counseling activity. As noted in the discussion on preventive and remedial services, the counselor, in addition to providing therapeutic counseling, should be able to respond to a variety of the senior citizen's concerns—legal and financial matters, community resources, and medical and health services. The counselor need not be an expert on all of these matters, but he must possess some basic information.

Second, the counselor must give special attention to establishing a helping relationship with an older adult. The older adult's values may differ from the counselor's in some basic areas. The older adult client may be more hesitant to discuss such matters as sexual concerns and financial problems. Thus, the counselor must be certain to take enough time to establish a warm, trusting, and open relationship and must make clear the confidential nature of the relationship, recognizing that the client may be concerned about involvement of family members in such personal matters.

Counselors in recent years have begun emphasizing a developmental approach to counseling. The older adult, from a developmental perspective, is simply at a later stage in the life span. Due the difficult life adjustments that accompany aging, the senior citizen should receive increasingly sophisticated counseling services. Thus training programs must prepare counselors to respond to the wide range of issues these clients face.

In a recent survey of counselor education programs, Meyers (1983) found that the number of programs that offer courses to train counselors to work with older people is increasing. It is hoped that this trend will continue.

### SUMMARY

In this chapter we have considered some of the specific issues involved in working with the following subgroups within the general population: the culturally different, women, individuals with disabilities, and older adults. In each section specific issues impacting the subgroup were explored. Counselors who are interested in specializing in work with clients from a specific population are encouraged to familiarize themselves with the particular dynamics that may be present. It is emphasized, however, that counseling skills do not change from one client to the next; rather, the core conditions of empathy, genuineness, positive regard, and respect form the basis of any helping relationship.

# REFERENCES

## The Culturally Different

ATTNEAVE, C. (1972). Mental health of American Indians: Problems, perspectives, and challenge for the decade ahead. Paper presented at the 80th Annual Convention of the American Psychological Association, Honolulu, Hawaii, August.

COPELAND, E. (1983). Cross-cultural counseling and psychotherapy: A historical perspective; implications for research and training. *Personnel and Guidance Journal, 62,* 10–15.

COPELAND, E. (1982). Minority populations and traditional counseling programs: Some alternatives. *Counselor Education and Supervision, 21*(3), 187–193.

HENDERSON, G. (1979). *Understanding and counseling ethnic minorities.* Springfield, Ill.: Charles Thomas.

PADILLA, A. M., RUIZ, R. A., and ALVAREZ, R. (1975). Community mental health services for the Spanish-speaking/surnamed population. *American Psychologist, 30,* 892–905.

PEDERSON, P. (1977). The triad model of cross-cultural counselor training. *Personnel and Guidance Journal, 56*(2), 94–100.

PEDERSON, P. (1978a). Introduction to special issue. *Personnel and Guidance Journal, 56*(8), 457.

PEDERSON, P. (1978b). Four dimensions of cross-cultural skill in counselor training. *Personnel and Guidance Journal, 56*(8), 480–484.

RUIZ, R. A., and PADILLA, A. M. (1977). Counseling Latinos. *Personnel and Guidance Journal, 55*(7), 401–408.

SUE, D. W. (1975). Asian Americans: Social-psychological forces affecting their life-styles. In S. Picou and R. Campbell (Eds.), *Career behavior of special groups.* Columbus, Ohio: Chas. E. Merrill.

SUE, D. W. (1977). Counseling the culturally different: A conceptual analysis. *Personnel and Guidance Journal, 55*(7), 422–425.

SUE, D. W. (1981). *Counseling the culturally different: Theory and practice.* New York: John Wiley.

SUE, D. W. (1978). Counseling across cultures. *Personnel and Guidance Journal, 56*(8), 451–462.

SUE, D. W., and KIRK, B. A. (1975). Asian-Americans: Use of counseling and psychiatric services on a college campus. *Journal of Counseling Psychology, 22,* 84–86.

SUE, S., MCKINNEY, H., ALLEN, D., and HALL, J. (1974). Delivery of community mental health services to black and white clients. *Journal of Consulting and Clinical Psychology, 42,* 794–801.

SUE, S., and MCKINNEY, H. (1975). Asian Americans in the community mental health care system. *American Journal of Orthopsychiatry, 45,* 111–118.

VONTRESS, C. E. (1971). Racial differences: Impediments to rapport. *Journal of Counseling Psychology, 18,* 7–13.


## Women

BEAMISH, P., and MARINELLI, R. (1983). A power-base training model for women. *Personnel and Guidance Journal, 61*(9), 542–544.

BROVERMAN, I. K., BROVERMAN, D. M., CLARKSON, F. E., ROSENKRANTZ, P., and VOGEL, S. R. (1970). Sex role stereotypes and clinical judgments of mental health. *Journal of Consulting and Clinical Psychology, 34,* 1–7.

CHUSMIR, L. (1983). Characteristics and predictive dimensions of women who make non-traditional vocational choices. *Personnel and Guidance Journal, 62*(1), 43–47.

GRAY, J. (1980). Counseling women who want both a profession and a family. *Personnel and Guidance Journal, 59*(1), 43–45.

KAHN, S., and GREENBERG, L. (1980). Expanding Sex-Role Definitions By Self Discovery. *Personnel and Guidance Journal, 59*(4), 220–225.

NAFFZIGER, K. G. (1972). A survey of counselor-educators' and other selected professionals' attitudes toward women's roles. (Doctoral dissertation, University of Oregon) Ann Arbor, Mich.: University Microfilms, No. 72-956.

NEULINGER, J., SCHILLINGER, K., STEIN, M. I., and WELKOWITZ, J. (1970). Perceptions of the optimally integrated person as a function of therapists' characteristics. *Perceptual and Motor Skills, 30,* 375–384.

SCHLOSSBERG, N. K., and PIETROFESA, J. J. (1978). Perspectives on counseling bias: Implications for counselor education. *Counseling Psychologist, 1973, 4*(1), 44–54. Appeared in *Counseling Women,* Hermon, L., Birk, J., Fitzgerald, L., and Tanney, M. (eds.), Monterey, Calif.: Brooks/Cole.

WESTERVELT, E. (1963). The recruitment and training of educational/vocational counselors for girls and women. Background paper for Sub-Committee on

Counseling, President's Commission on the Status of Women.

## Individuals with Disabilities

CRISTIANI, T., and SOMMERS, P. (1978).   The counselor's role in mainstreaming the handicapped. *Viewpoints in Teaching and Learning, 54*(1), 20–28.

FAGAN, T., and WALLACE, A. (1979).   Who are the handicapped? *Personnel and Guidance Journal, 58*(4), 215–220.

FILER, P. (1982).   Counselor trainees' attitudes toward mainstreaming the handicapped. *Counselor Education and Supervision, 22*(1), 61–69.

HOSIE, T. (1979).   Preparing counselors to meet the needs of the handicapped. *Personnel and Guidance Journal, 58*(4), 271–275.

HUBER, C. (1979).   Parents of the handicapped child: Facilitating acceptance through group counseling. *Personnel and Guidance Journal, 57*(5), 267–269.

KUBLER-ROSS, E. (1969).   On death and dying. New York: Macmillan.

LEBSOCK, M., and DEBLASSIE, R. (1975).   The school counselor's role in special education. *Counselor Education and Supervision, 15,* 128–134.

LOFARO, G. (1982).   Disability and counselor education. *Counselor Education and Supervision, 21*(3), 200–207.

LOMBANA, J. (1980).   Guidance of handicapped students: Counselor in-service needs. *Personnel and Guidance Journal, 19*(4) 269–275.

LOMBANA, J., and CLAWSON, T. (1978).   School counselors and P.L. 94–142. Report prepared for the APGA Board of Directors. Washington, D.C.: American Personnel and Guidance Association.

MCDOWELL, W., COVEN, A., and EASH, U. (1979).   The handicapped: Special needs and strategies for counseling. *Personnel and Guidance Journal, 58*(4), 228–232.

MCILROY, J., and ZELLER, R. (1979).   Agency and organizational help for the handicapped. *Personnel and Guidance Journal, 58*(4), 276–283.

NATHANSON, R. (1979).   Counseling parents with disabilities: Are the feelings, thoughts, and behaviors of helping professionals helpful? *Personnel and Guidance Journal, 58*(4), 233–237.

PRESCOTT, M., and HULNICK, H. R. (1979).   Counseling parents of handicapped children: An empathic approach. *Personnel and Guidance Journal, 58*(4), 263–270.

RUSALEM, H., and COHEN, J. (1975).   Guidance of the exceptional student. In William M. Cruickshank and G. Orville Johnson (Eds.), *Education of Exceptional Children and Youth,* Englewood Cliffs, N.J.: Prentice-Hall, 613–622.

SPROLES, H., PANTHER, E., and LANIER, J. (1978).   PL 94–142 and its impact on the counselor's role. *Personnel and Guidance Journal, 57*(4), 210–212.

VANDERGRIFF, A., and HOSIE, T. (1979).   PL 94–142: A role change for counselors or just an extension of present role? *Journal of Counseling Services, 3*(1), 6–11.

ZIEZIULA, F. (1979).   Counseling deaf children: A new art. *Personnel and Guidance Journal, 58*(4), 287–289.

## Older Adults

BUTLER, R. N. (1975).   *Why survive? Being old in America.* New York: Harper & Row.

GLASS, J., and GRANT, K. (1983).   Counseling in the later years: A growing need. *Personnel and Guidance Journal, 62*(4), 210–213.

LOMBANA, J. H. (1976).   Counseling the elderly: Remediation plus prevention. *Personnel and Guidance Journal, 55*(3), 143–144.

MEYERS, J. (1983).   Gerontological counseling training: The state of the art. *Personnel and Guidance Journal, 67*(7), 398–400.

# 11

# SPECIAL CONCERNS IN COUNSELING

In this chapter we will consider several special counseling situations which require either additional knowledge of the particular issues involved—such as sexuality, loss and separation, and substance abuse—or additional skills—such as group counseling and crisis intervention.

## SPECIAL CLIENT CONCERNS

This section addresses several concerns that clients are increasingly presenting to counselors, specifically, concerns involving human sexuality, loss and separation, and substance abuse. It is not our purpose to enable counselors to be experts in working with these concerns. Rather, we hope that through exposure to some of the issues involved, counselors will develop increased awareness, understanding, and sensitivity to clients who have these problems, and will know when to seek further training and information.

### Sexuality

Our society has become increasingly open in its attitudes and values about sexuality and sexual behavior. We are currently more aware of the probable relationship between our sexual attitudes and values and the problems existing in marriage and many of our other interpersonal relationships. As sex and sexual issues are discussed with greater openness, counselors are more frequently involved in helping clients resolve sexual issues. These issues range from birth control, abortion, and sexual dysfunction to sexual preference. Counselors must broaden their awareness of and responses to these problems. What, then, is the counselor's role in matters of sexuality?

The counselor's role must include both prevention and remediation. Preventive activities involve the creation and implementation of sex education programs; remedial activities include sexual counseling and sex therapy.

What is the difference between sex education, sex counseling, and sex therapy? Calderone has offered these distinctions.

> Education is the process by which factual information about sexuality is offered and assimilated so that attitudes about the information undergo modification and internalization by individuals to fit their needs. Counseling is the art of helping individuals transmute their sexual education into fulfilling and socially responsible sexual behavior. Therapy is highly specialized in-depth treatment by which impediments to an individual's satisfactory sexual evaluation and fulfillment can be brought to consciousness and dealt with. (1976, p. 350)

With these guidelines in mind, we will discuss each of these areas.

***Sex Education For Youth***   Mitchell (1973), in a useful resource on counseling and sexuality, emphasizes that a successful program for sex education must have a sound philosophical base that stresses the relationship between sexuality and the individual's total development. From this perspective, sex education promotes the development of a positive self-concept. Mitchell offers the following as an example of philosophically based goals for a sex education program at the secondary level:

Students will

1. demonstrate understanding of thier sexual development;
2. accept their sexual development as part of their total development;
3. acquire more positive self-concepts;
4. increase interpersonal relationship skills with members of their own sex, the opposite sex, their peers, adults, and younger age groups;
5. acquire attitudes which respect the rights, viewpoints, and attitudes of others towards human sexuality;
6. develop a sense of responsibility in their heterosexual relationships;
7. be able to distinguish between facts and fictions regarding sexual development, activities, and values. (1973, p. 57)

School counselors must, of course, be sensitive to the values of the school and community in which they are working; yet it is part of the counselor's role to help develop and implement programs for sex education. An emphasis on the prevention of pregnancy and abortion may help counselors gain administrative and parental support for sex education programs. It is essential for counselors to lay the appropriate groundwork for establishing a sex education program; often they must begin by educating the parents and the entire school staff.

*Sexual Counseling*   Counselors must be prepared to respond to the sexual concerns of clients of all ages. Kirkpatrick (1975) has formulated nine guidelines for sexual counseling;

1. Counselors working with sexual problems of clients must be comfortable with their own sexuality. Sex issues of the client can be transferred onto the counselor-client relationship, and counselors must be relaxed enough with their own sexuality so that the client's expression can be viewed as part of the client's sexuality.
2. Counselors should be able to discuss matters of human sexuality with candor and openness. This means that the counselor should avoid using slang expressions and should help the client enter into a frank discussion by using the appropriate terms for genitals or sexual acts.
3. In working with adolescent or college-aged clients, counselors must not assume that these clients are knowledgeable in matters of human sexuality. There are numerous examples of clients who have assumed that they became pregnant after drinking from the same glass as someone else; many others misunderstood the use of contraceptive devices.
4. Counselors should be knowledgeable in matters of human sexuality so as to be a resource to clients in the areas of anatomy and pharmacology, contraception, etc.
5. Counselors should recognize their limitations in working with clients with sexual concerns. They should not try to provide sex therapy if they are not trained in the treatment of sexual dysfunction.

6. Counselors should know when to refer a client and should be familiar with appropriate referral resources. This is particularly important in sexual matters because crucial decisions must often be made in a short time.

7. In counseling clients with sexual concerns, counselors must be particularly skillful at deciphering disguised messages of distress since clients may be more hesitant to discuss sexual matters openly.

8. Counselors must be direct and comfortable in introducing sexual matters in the interview. Often clients will talk around a sexual concern, hoping that the counselor will raise the sexual issue directly.

9. It is critical in counseling for human sexuality, as in other matters, that counselors not be judgmental regarding the values and behaviors of their clients.

Tegtmeyer (1980) supports many of the above points.

***Sex Therapy*** Sex therapy is a specific field of counseling begun by Masters and Johnson (1970) that focuses on the treatment of sexual dysfunction. Most sex therapy focuses on couples, but in recent years more reports have appeared in the literature of individual and group treatment programs. Sex therapy is based on several underlying principles: responsibility for self; permission to be sexual; reeducation regarding sexual functioning; increased awareness of feelings, fantasies, and communication; and structured behavior change (Maddock and Chilgren, 1976). Among the specific problems dealt with in sex therapy are impotence (primary and secondary), premature ejaculation, delayed ejaculation, orgasmic dysfunction, and vaginismus. As previously noted, counselors should be prepared to identify sexual dysfunction and to make an appropriate referral when the client's concern indicates the need for sex therapy.

***Homosexuality*** The unique needs of gay clients have received more attention in recent counseling literature, and counselors must be informed of and sensitive to some of the issues facing this population. Winkelpleck and Westfield (1982), in a recent survey of gay couples, sought information regarding the strengths of these couples. Respondents identified commitment, emotional strength and understanding, and freedom of individual choice as strengths unique to these couples. The major issues faced by gay couples were identified as discrimination, and inadequate communications about and information on sexuality. Special counseling needs included communication skill development, pride in the relationship, and help with families, friends, jobs, health, legal issues, investments, and property.

Groves and Ventura (1983) and Sophie (1982) have discussed the therapeutic needs of lesbians. A major therapeutic issue revolves around denial of sexual orientation. Denial may be used as a defense, but it may also have a negative influence on the client's interpersonal relationships. Counselors should be familiar with the complexity of issues around acceptance of one's sexual identity. Most importantly, counselors must be secure with their own sexuality and sensitive to and accepting of others' choices.

***Implications for Training*** The American Association for Sex Educators and Counselors (AASEC) is now certifying competent individuals as "AASEC-certified Sex Therapists." (Schiller, 1976). Schiller lists the skills required for certification. These include basic knowledge and understanding of the psychological principles that form the basis of the counseling process, including personality theory, communication theory, ego defense systems, the function in counseling of catharsis, insight, and support, and transference and countertransference. The counselor must also have an understanding of counseling methodologies from the basic schools of thought. Counselors should be prepared through workshop activities to take a sex history. They should be skillful in such interviewing techniques as listening and reflection of feeling. They should acquire referral techniques and the consultation skills needed to work with other professionals. They should also be trained in counseling management, including matters such as making appointments, keeping case records, confidentiality, fee structure, and ethical behavior. These guidelines are documented in *The Professional Training and Preparation of Sex Counselors* (1973).

From the preceding discussion, and from a nationwide survey conducted by Kirkpatrick (1980), it is obvious that all counselors need some preparation in working with the sexual concerns of clients. This preparation or sex education for counselors can and should be offered as part of the counselor education curriculum. Kelly (1976) suggests that a course for prospective counselors include desensitization; information on the biology, psychology, and sociology of sex; interviews in which participants role play clients with sexual concerns; and activities that focus on self-awareness and understanding.

### Loss and Separation

In 1969, Kubler-Ross published her pioneer research on the psychological processes associated with death and dying. Since that time the profession has begun to explore in more depth the processes associated with loss and separation, and theoretical models are being developed to help us understand this core human experience. As Headington (1981) states, "An understanding of the nature of loss, its interrelatedness to other emotions and experiences, its developmental history in personality, and its role as a change agent is critical to the counselor (p. 338)." It is important to realize that death and separation in interpersonal relationships are not the only losses we experience. We experience loss of the tangible as well as the intangible in our lives. And every loss, whether tangible—such as loss of property or personal belongings—or intangible—such as friendship or divorce—involves a grieving process (Cheikin, 1981). The external and internal dimensions of loss are summarized in Table 11-1. Thus, as Frears and Schneider have stated,

> Loss touches all of our lives, throughout our lifetimes. Yet we frequently fail to recognize its existence except in extreme cases of change, such as death, war, or natural disasters. We rarely reflect on the potential for loss in getting promoted, graduating, moving to a new community, or having a baby. Instead, only the positive is seen as the capacities to adapt are the focus. Later, we wonder why our joy was not so joyful, why we feel sad, tired, guilty—just when everything seemed to be going our way. (p. 341)

It seems that change in any aspect of life—vacation, promotion, birth, and marriage included—involves both loss and potential for growth. However, "unless the loss aspect

**TABLE 11-1**  Dimensions of Loss - Examples

| | EXTERNAL | | | INTERNAL | |
|---|---|---|---|---|---|
| Ease of Recognition | Relationships | External Objects | Environment | Self | Natural |
| Apparent losses | Death of loved one Permanent involuntary separation Incest | Theft Destruction Disappearance | Natural disasters (Floods, tornados, etc.) | Failure Being fired Rape Arrest Chronic illness | Illness Injury/disability Miscarriage |
| Loss as a part of change | Divorce Role reversals Intense involvement Separation | Moving Buying/selling New Job | Change in pace, rhythm, space noise level, "environmental press" | Changing roles Leaving home Retirement | Weaning Puberty Mid-life Aging |
| Unnoticed loss: growth or competence related | Marriage Birth of a child Terminating therapy | Being able to buy anything desired Achieving long sought after prize | Living in "ideal" environment Homogeneous environment | Promotion Graduation Success Creativity | Maturation Insight |

is recognized and acknowledged, and unless support is received, any significant change will become and probably remain a source of stress'' (p. 341).

Many authors have sought to analyze the loss process and have developed theoretical models to facilitate understanding of the loss and separation experience. The February, 1981 Special Issue of the *Personnel and Guidance Journal* is devoted to the issue of loss and is an important resource on this topic. Here we have chosen to present one loss model, while acknowledging that others have much to offer. While this model provides a framework for understanding loss in a general sense, we will separately explore the problems related to divorce and the uncoupling process and examine the effect of divorce on children.

***Schneider's Loss Model***  Schneider's loss model (1980a, 1980b) differs from those proposed by others such as Kubler-Ross because

a) it is applicable to a broader range of life circumstances,
b) it is wholistic and includes how grief effects biological, attitudinal, and spiritual processes, as well as physical and emotional ones,
c) it incorporates growth potential from the grief process. (Frears & Schneider, 1981)

Schneider's model includes six phases for the resolution of grief: initial awareness, strategies to overcome loss, awareness of loss, compilations, empowering of self, and transcending the loss. The model is presented in Figure 11-1 (1981, p. 343). This model is comprehensive and should be very useful to counselors.

### Divorce and the Uncoupling Process

With the rising divorce rate, counselors find themselves dealing more frequently with the separation and divorce of married couples. The "uncoupling" process, as it has been called, is painful. Those going through it need counselors who are prepared to respond to their wide range of feelings and experiences. The uncoupling process in-

**Figure 11-1** Beginning from the Center of Model and Radiating Outwards are the Successive Phases of Loss.

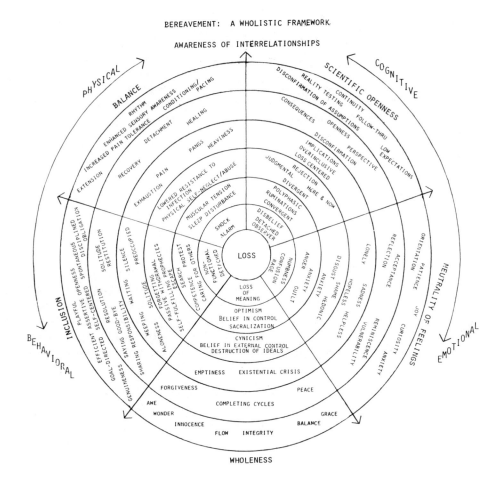

volves the death of a relationship, and the separation and grieving process proceeds through various stages. We will first explore the dynamics of divorce and will then examine some useful treatment models for working with those experiencing divorce; last, we will examine the impact of divorce on children.

### Dynamics of Divorce

Divorce, like death, involves a complex emotional response to the loss of a relationship. Because of the similarities involved, Froiland and Hozman (1977) have adapted the stages of the Kubler-Ross loss model to the separation process experienced in divorce. The basic stages of the Kubler-Ross model include denial, anger, bargaining, depression, and acceptance. The stages as applied to divorce by Froiland and Hozman (1977, pp. 525–529) are briefly summarized.

DENIAL   The initial reaction of one of the partners is often a refusal to accept the reality of the situation. The individual has invested much time, energy, and feeling in the relationship, and finds it extremely difficult in the initial stages to deal rationally with the separation. Clients in this phase typically defend the relationship and need help to realistically evaluate the strengths and weaknesses of the marriage.

ANGER   Clients defend themselves against feeling hurt by expressing hostile and negative feelings toward the other partner. Children are frequently involved during this stage as parents vent their anger by trying to influence the children's perception of the situation.

BARGAINING   The bargaining stage of divorce is perhaps the most complex. A great deal of manipulation occurs during this phase. As partners attempt to negotiate the disintegrating marriage, other people often attempt to put pressure on one of the partners. Sexual bargaining frequently occurs and often includes pregnancy and threat of pregnancy. Attempts at reconciliation are common, but unless the underlying problem has been dealt with, they do not last.

DEPRESSION   As clients begin to realize that denial, anger, and bargaining have been unsuccessful, they are usually overcome with depression. During this serious phase, the client often experiences a sense of failure, which can have a negative impact on the client's self-concept. The client may begin to withdraw from and distrust others. Because of the extreme sense of hurt and rejection frequently experienced during divorce, clients may have difficulty establishing intimate relationships with others for a long time.

ACCEPTANCE   As clients work through the stages of denial, bargaining, and depression, the counselor's goal becomes one of moving the client into a genuine acceptance of the loss of the relationship. At this stage the client is able to begin adjusting to all of the changes of a new single life-style and must learn the skills to continue to cope with the changes.

*The Readjustment Process*    As clients successfully complete the stages of their emotional response to divorce, they must develop the skills to function effectively as single, divorced individuals. The necessary skills may range from handling financial responsibilities to single parenting. In a world that is geared toward couples, possibly the biggest readjustment is growing into a single life-style. As Edwards (1977) has noted, our society is structured for pairs. Singles face discrimination ranging from higher income taxes to inability to obtain loans and credit. But the problems of being single do not end here. Counselors must be prepared to help clients cope with multiple social issues. The first difficulty new singles face is going out alone to movies, restaurants, parties, concerts, or bars. Not only must they overcome loneliness, but they are also faced with concern about what others might think of them because they are alone. Another major social adjustment is that of meeting sexual needs in ways that are healthy, productive, and acceptable to the individual. The sex life of a single person can be extremely unpredictable and erratic, if not nonexistent (Edwards, 1977).

How can counselors respond to their clients' needs to adjust to a single life-style? Some counselors offer divorce adjustment groups. Many counselors (Kessler, 1976; Carter, 1977) feel that the divorce adjustment process can best be facilitated through the supportive atmosphere of a group; clients adjusting to divorce are helped by a support system composed of others who are experiencing similar problems. Many of these groups are structured for women, yet men need the same kind of help. Edwards (1977) has conducted workshops across the country on the "challenge of being single." She recommends group counseling for the divorce adjustment process during which she emphasizes the advantages of being single. She helps singles distinguish between being alone and being lonely, and encourages them to explore their feelings, attitudes, and values about sex in order to enable them to make more effective decisions regarding their own sexual behavior.

*The Effects of Divorce on Children*    Many counselors who will never work with divorcing couples will come into contact with children or adolescents who are deeply experiencing the effects of a divorce. As the divorce rate rises, the number of children caught up in the process increases at a frightening rate. In fact, it has been estimated that each year over one million children under the age of eighteen are affected by divorce.

Wallerstein and Kelly have conducted extensive research investigations (1975, 1976a, 1976b) examining the effects of divorce on children according to the developmental stage. These studies have contributed greatly to our understanding of the impact of divorce on children. The effects of divorce on the child depend on many factors, including the child's age, self-concept, emotional maturity, sensitivity, and ability to cope. The relationship and communication between the child and the parents also greatly affect the child's adjustment. Regardless of the child's coping skills, the child needs to openly vent all feelings related to the divorce. A skillful counselor can facilitate the child's emotional and psychological adjustment.

What approach should be used in working with children facing divorce? Hozman and Froiland (1977) have found that children tend to experience the same basic stages in their emotional reponse to divorce as their parents do: denial, anger, bargain-

ing, depression, and acceptance. Understanding these phases helps the counselor formulate hypotheses regarding the child's behavior. As in all counseling relationships,
a hypothesis enables the counselor to check out perceptions regarding the client's feelings, experiences, and behavior and also helps the counselor determine which specific
counseling procedure will be most effective at a given time in the relationship.

A variety of approaches can be used with children facing divorce. The
appropriateness of the approach must be determined by the counselor and will depend
on which stage the child is experiencing. Play therapy or the use of play media can
be particularly facilitative in enabling the child to verbalize his perceptions and feelings about the divorce. Doll houses with puppets have been found to be very useful.
Role-playing techniques enable the child to recreate situations and to share previously
unexpressed perceptions of patterns in relationships. Both of these techniques can help
the child share her "private logic" as related to the emotional and psychological crisis
she is experiencing.

Hozman and Froiland (1977) and Magid (1977) acknowledge the value of
counseling groups in working with these children. These groups can be unstructured
or can be structured around certain topics. Magid (1977) has suggested using an adapted
version of the "magic circle" (Bessell & Palomares, 1967).

At various stages in the counseling relationship, it will be useful to treat the
family as a unit. The child may need individual counseling, but the parents should
be included in the process whenever possible.

Divorce has a tremendous emotional and psychological impact on everyone
involved. With the rapidly rising divorce rate, counselors must be prepared to respond
to the growing number of affected persons who will seek counseling each year. Much
more research is needed on the effects of divorce on both adults and children so that
effective counseling models can be developed.

### Substance Abuse

The use and abuse of drugs has spread at a remarkable rate throughout our
society and has become a national concern. Drug use is not limited to any socioeconomic
or racial group or to any age group.

Due to the extent of the drug problem, a number of new programs and approaches have been established, including drop-in centers, hot lines, peer-counseling
programs, crisis intervention programs, programs using former addicts, rap sessions,
and the development of new curricula and visual materials for comprehensive drug
education programs. Counselors may be involved in any or all of these approaches from
either a remedial or a preventive perspective. Before counselors can become involved
in drug-related concerns, they must have information regarding drug abuse.

***What Is Drug Abuse?***   The counselor should understand the following terminology associated with drugs and the drug culture: drug use, drug misuse, drug abuse,
drug addiction, drug dependence (both physical and psychological), and habituation.

*Drug use* refers to the consumption of a drug. *Drug misuse* involves the improper use of a drug. *Drug abuse* refers to drug usage that interferes with the individual's health or adjustment.

The following have been defined by the World Health Organization Expert Committee on Addiction-Producing Drugs:

| | |
|---|---|
| *addiction* | A state of periodic or chronic intoxication produced by the repeated consumption of a drug and involving tolerance, psychological dependence, usually physical dependence, an overwhelming compulsion to continue using the drug, and detrimental effects on both the individual and society. Its characteristics include (1) an overpowering desire or need (compulsion to continue taking the drug and to obtain it by any means); (2) a tendency to increase the dose; (3) a psychic (psychological) and generally a physical dependence on the effects of the drug; and (4) detrimental effects on the individual and society. |
| *drug dependence* | A state arising from repeated administration of a drug on a periodic or continuous basis. |
| *physical dependence* | A condition in which the body has adjusted to the presence of a drug, and when forced to function without the drug, reacts with a characteristic illness, called "abstinence syndrome," or "withdrawal illness." |
| *psychic dependence* | The individual who receives satisfaction from his first use of a drug tends to make repeated use of the drug. Through continued repetition he may find it necessary to utilize the drug as an instrument in his adjustment to life, relying upon it for fulfillment which others achieve without the help of drugs. |
| *habituation* | A condition, resulting from the repeated consumption of a drug, which involves little or no evidence of tolerance, some psychological dependence, no physical dependence, and a desire (but not a compulsion) to continue taking the drug for the feeling of well-being that it engenders. Its characteristics include (1) a desire (but not a compulsion) to continue taking the drug for the sense of improved well-being which it engenders; (2) little or no tendency to increase the dose; (3) some degree of psychic dependency on the effect of the drug, but absence of physical dependence and hence of an abstinence syndrome; and (4) detrimental effects, if any, primarily in the individual. (Cornacchia et al., 1973, p. 34). |

In determining the impact of a drug on an individual, one must also consider the harmfulness of the particular drug in use. For example, an individual who is regularly using marijuana is risking much less than the regular heroin user.

**The Counselor's Role**   Counselors work with drug-related problems in both educational and community settings. Depending on the particular setting and role responsibilities, counselors should be prepared to offer services with three primary thrusts. The first thrust, organizing a drug education program, is preventive. The counselor must be informed regarding all aspects of drug use and abuse and should be prepared to present accurate information about drug usage. Many new drug-related curricula and instructional media are available. As part of a drug education program counselors may choose to organize peer group activities in which older students talk with students in the primary grades. Drop-in, "rap," or informational centers are also possibilities. These centers can be staffed by the counselor or by trained students.

The second major thrust of the counselor's service should be therapeutic. It is essential that the counselor who is providing counseling for individuals with drug-related problems have a grasp on the pharmacology involved. Drug abuse is often accompanied by other personal, psychological, and emotional problems, however, and the counselor's therapeutic skills are essential in establishing a climate that allows all aspects of the client's functioning to be discussed. Frykman (1971) has emphasized the importance of confidentiality, patience, acceptance, support, and trust in counseling youth about drugs.

A third major thrust is for the counselor to become sensitive to the impact of alcohol and drug abuse on the day-to-day functioning of individuals. School counselors, career counselors, marriage and family counselors, and counselors in various other roles need to become aware of the characteristics of the drug abuser so that they can more readily identify those who are in need of specialized treatment. Related to this is the need for counselors to be aware of the treatment programs available in their communities, so that appropriate referrals can be made.

In conclusion, the rapidly increasing use of drugs in this country is a national concern that requires innovative programs, both preventive and therapeutic. Counselors working in both educational and community settings should be prepared to respond to drug-related problems with sensitivity, understanding, and valid information if they are to play a primary role in fighting the drug problem in our society.

### Summary

In this section we have introduced special client concerns in counseling including sexuality, loss and separation, divorce, and substance abuse. While we have attempted to identify issues that are currently receiving attention in the literature, the importance of these topics changes rather quickly, and it is impossible to cover all of the special problems being brought to counselor's today. For example, we have not devoted a section to exploring child abuse, neglect, and incest. These problems have typically been dealt with by social workers who specialize in family interventions. Today, however, counselors are increasingly dealing with these important and seemingly rampant concerns, both because of mandated reporting required of school counselors and because an increasing number of counselors are becoming trained in family therapy. Counselors should be aware of the laws in their state regarding child abuse and incest and should familiarize themselves with the crucial dynamics of this pressing family problem. It is hoped that the information provided in this chapter and in the reference lists will assist counselors in researching their particular areas of clinical interest.

## GROUP COUNSELING

Group therapy has been recognized as a therapeutic procedure for many years, but only recently have group methods gained popularity. Groups of all varieties are now available to those seeking help for serious psychological problems, to those experiencing a situational crisis such as divorce, and to healthy individuals who wish to expand their self-awareness and increase their level of interpersonal functioning. There are rehabilitation groups for alcoholics and those with other drug-related problems; there are women's groups, divorce adjustment groups, conjoint family therapy groups, children's groups, and assertiveness training groups. There are also groups characterized by the theoretical orientation of the leader—transactional analysis groups, Gestalt groups, bioenergetics groups, and so on. In this chapter we will introduce group counseling by examining (1) the terminology associated with the group movement; (2) the advantages and goals of working in groups; (3) the limitations of group work.

### Terminology of the Group Movement

The group movement has generated its own terminology. Such terms as group guidance, group counseling, group therapy, T-groups, sensitivity groups, and so on have been misused in the literature and by practitioners. To help eliminate this confusion over terminology, we will attempt here to distinguish among the various types of groups and to define such group terminology as group process, norms, and cohesion. Our discussion will be restricted to those groups in which the focus and content are primarily personal and psychological as contrasted with groups organized to reach a goal or to complete a task, such as committees.

#### Types of Groups

GUIDANCE GROUPS    Guidance groups are group discussion sessions in which the content of the discussion is affective or psychological. These groups may also be used to distribute information relevant to the student's personal needs and interests, such as educational, vocational, or social information. Guidance groups are most often found in the educational setting and are typically conducted with a class. They range in size from twelve to forty participants. One characteristic that distinguishes a guidance group from a counseling or therapeutic group is that a guidance group is relatively structured and the topic to be discussed is generally chosen by the group leader. Another distinguishing feature is that a guidance group is concerned with preventing problems rather than remediating psychological difficulties.

There is disagreement in the literature about what constitutes a guidance group. Perhaps the term *guidance* has become outdated and a broader term such as *psychological education* should be substituted. The new psychological education or affective education curricula typically rely on group process within the classroom setting and meet other criteria of guidance groups.

COUNSELING GROUPS Counseling groups, as contrasted with guidance groups, focus on the individual rather than on the topic (Mahler, 1969). A counseling group is smaller (five to ten participants), and less structure is provided by the counselor. The counselor's role is to create a safe and secure environment where group members feel comfortable sharing personal concerns related to their families, interpersonal relationships, self-concepts, or other personal, social or educational difficulties. The content of the discussions is affective and personal; each member has the opportunity to discuss developmental and interpersonal concerns, and these concerns are ultimately related to desired behavior change.

THERAPY GROUPS Therapy groups were the first groups to be used for therapeutic purposes. Group therapy procedures were developed during World War II in response to the high rate of psychiatric problems and the concurrent shortage of personnel to provide individual therapy (Lifton, 1972; Corey & Corey, 1977). Unlike those in counseling groups, the participants in therapy groups need intensive psychological help. Their problems are typically deep-seated and involve personality disorganization. Group therapy, then, most often involves persons who are unable to function "normally." Therapy groups would be of longer duration than counseling groups and would require a leader with more training and expertise.

ENCOUNTER OR SENSITIVITY GROUPS Encounter groups, sensitivity groups, or personal growth groups are part of the larger human potential movement, which focuses on expanding personal self-awareness and developing individual potential. These groups are at the opposite end of the continuum from therapy groups and obviously serve an entirely different population. The purpose of an encounter group is to provide the opportunity for healthy, well-functioning individuals to explore and to actualize their potential in the areas of self-awareness and interpersonal relationships.

Encounter groups typically provide participants with an intense, very personal, and intimate experience that grows out of trust, openness, sharing, and risk-taking. Nonverbal exercises emphasizing touch and other sensory awareness experiences are frequently used to facilitate this intimacy (Corey & Corey, 1977).

An encounter group can be highly structured, with the leader guiding the participants through a series of structured exercises. These experiences are often referred to as *microlabs*. Encounter groups are sometimes conducted over a weekend. In essence, participants go on a retreat for an intensive group experience. These weekend growth groups are frequently referred to as *marathons*. The group meets for unusually long periods of time and capitalizes on fatigue to facilitate letting go of roles and facades to promote directness and honesty in communication.

T-GROUPS Human relations training began in the 1950s with the development of the first training center at Bethel, Maine. The National Training Laboratories, or NTL, were founded by Leland Bradford, Ronald Lippitt, and Kenneth Benne. The "T-Group," or Training Group, first gained acceptance in industry as a method for studying the process by which a group functions in an attempt to improve the efficiency and effectiveness of the team. T-groups emphasize member roles within the group and focus on the relationship of each group member to what is going on in the group at the time (Lifton, 1972). As contrasted with guidance, counseling, therapy, or encounter groups, the T-group is more task-oriented and concerned with how the group functions and with educating participants to become better group members.

### Group Terminology

GROUP PROCESS  *Group process* can be distinguished from *group content* in that *content* refers to what the group is discussing, whereas *process* refers to how the discussion is being conducted (Johnson & Johnson, 1982). To be an effective group leader or member, one must be able to both participate in the discussion and observe what is going on. In a counseling group, the counselor must be able not only to listen carefully and intently to each speaker but also to observe patterns in communication, roles assumed by each member, nonverbal communication, and so on.

GROUP COHESION  *Group cohesion* refers to the interacting forces that keep the group together. A group is cohesive to the extent that the positive aspects of group membership outweigh the negative ones. However, since group cohesion is dependent on the attractiveness of the group for each member at any given time, the cohesiveness of the groups is always changing (Johnson & Johnson, 1982).

A cohesive group is dependent on group members' sharing similar goals for group membership. Group cohesiveness can be evaluated by such factors as whether or not members attend regularly, whether the participants arrive promptly, and the level of affection, trust, and mutual support that members express toward each other (Johnson & Johnson, 1982).

GROUP NORMS  Group norms are closely related to group cohesiveness. *Group norms* refer to the formal and informal rules that govern what is considered to be appropriate behavior within the group (Corey & Corey, 1977). For example, an important norm when working with children in groups would be that only one person talks at a time. Another common group norm is that of maintaining the confidentiality of what is discussed in the group. Giving and accepting feedback and sharing personally relevant and meaningful material might also be appropriate group norms. It is important that groups establish their formal norms at the outset of the group experience. The informal norms arise as members try out various behaviors and experience the positive and negative consequences of their actions.

## Why Counsel in Groups?

Group counseling has many advantages, but it is not appropriate as an intervention strategy for all clients. What are the advantages of counseling clients in groups? When is group counseling the most effective therapeutic approach with a client? What limitations are associated with group counseling? When should one recommend group as opposed to individual counseling? These questions have been addressed by many practitioners and theoreticians. This section will summarize their opinions and offer some guidelines regarding the use of group counseling as a therapeutic intervention.

*Advantages*   In citing the advantages of counseling in groups, the first and most obvious is its practicality. Counselors in most settings are overloaded with clients. Group counseling is viewed as a preferred mode of treatment not only because it is efficient but also because it is more effective than individual counseling with certain client concerns. When working in groups, counselors can meet with as many as eight clients in the same amount of time that they spend with a single client in individual counseling. Group counseling offers other distinct advantages and is based on a sound theoretical rationale.

One argument for counseling individuals in groups is that many psychological problems are of an interpersonal nature, and group counseling provides the individual with the opportunity to work through these interpersonal problems in a social context. For example, feedback about behavior is much more influential in group therapy since it comes from the client's peers rather than from the counselor. Clients in the group setting, then, have the opportunity to grow through the process of receiving honest feedback from members of their own peer group.

Clients also have the opportunity to practice new behaviors and to receive support for and feedback on their experimentation. Personal growth, change, and exploration can thus take place in a safe, secure environment before new and risky behaviors are tried out in the world in which the client lives.

Group counseling enables clients to explore their problems and also exposes them to the feelings, concerns, and experiences of others. Clients are often experiencing their difficulties in isolation; they find it hard to put their problems in perspective. The group setting gives clients the opportunity to learn that others also have problems. As clients share themselves in the group, a level of trust develops that results in close, intimate contact among the group members. The group experience develops into a support system and as such becomes an important source of security and strength to the participants.

While clients in groups are focusing on resolving their own interpersonal or intrapersonal difficulties, they are also exposed to interpersonal relationship skills being modeled by both the group leader and the other group members. As such skills as empathy, active listening, feedback, and confrontation are modeled within the group, group members observe and have the opportunity to practice them within the group. Learning these skills and behaviors, which are essential to effective interpersonal relationships, enables clients to improve their interpersonal functioning.

A final benefit of group counseling is that clients have not only the opportunity to receive help from the counselor and other group members but also the opportunity to give help to others. Responding in a helpful way to others redirects the client's attention outside himself and helps build a more positive self-concept as the helping behavior is reinforced by other group participants.

*Limitations*   Despite its many advantages, as with any therapeutic approach group counseling has its limitations. Shertzer and Stone (1974) have identified the following:

1.  Some clients need individual help before they can function in a group. The client may be insecure and incapable of entering the group environment without first experiencing the counseling process on a one-to-one basis. After working through some basic issues, however, many clients are able to enter a group smoothly, if the nature of their concerns fits the goals of the group process.

2.  The counselor's role in group counseling tends to be much more diffused and therefore more complex. The counselor must be simultaneously able to focus on the concerns of each client, respond to the interaction among group members, and observe the dynamics of the group.

3.  The group can become bogged down in ''group process'' issues that are time-consuming and may detract from individual concerns of group members.

4.  Some clients may find it difficult to develop trust with a group of individuals; therefore, feelings, attitudes, values, and behaviors that are considered unacceptable may not be brought out for discussion.

5.  There is still some disagreement and lack of information about which client concerns can better be dealt with in a group than on a one-to-one basis.

Corey and Corey (1977) add the following limitations of groups:

1.  Some counselors and clients expect too much from the group experience and view group therapy as a ''cure-all.''

2.  Pressure to conform to group norms can cause clients to inappropriately substitute the group's norms for their own.

3.  For some clients the group experience becomes an end in itself rather than an experience that is used to improve their functioning in daily interactions.

4.  Some clients misuse the understanding and acceptance of the group experience. They vent their problems to the group and do not attempt to change their behavior.

5.  There is a danger of inadequate leadership in groups as persons with no training other than involvement in a group experience decide to organize and lead groups.

6.  The potential for psychological destruction is as great as the potential for psychological growth. Group participants can make themselves very vulnerable and can experience extreme pain when confronted by group members. Because of the number of group participants, the leader can lose control of the situation, resulting in psychological harm to the group members.

---

**Box 11-1**   *Advantages of Counseling in Groups*

1.  It is efficient. Counselors can provide services to many more clients.
2.  Group counseling provides a social interpersonal context in which to work on interpersonal problems.
3.  Clients have the opportunity to practice new behaviors.
4.  It enables clients to put their problems in perspective and to understand how they are similar to and different from others.
5.  Clients form a support system for each other.
6.  Clients learn interpersonal communication skills.
7.  Clients are given the opportunity to give as well as to receive help.

### Group Goals

Closely related to the advantages and limitations of group counseling as outlined above are the appropriate goals for clients entering a group counseling experience. These goals, which have been identified by Corey and Corey (1977), are illustrated in Box 11-2.

---

**Box 11-2**

1. To become more open and honest with selected others
2. To decrease game-playing and manipulating, which prevent intimacy
3. To learn how to trust oneself and others
4. To move toward authenticity and genuineness
5. To become freer and less bound by external "shoulds," "oughts," and "musts"
6. To grow in self-acceptance and learn not to demand perfection of oneself
7. To recognize and accept certain polarities within oneself
8. To lessen one's fears of intimacy and to learn to reach out to those one would like to be closer to
9. To move away from merely meeting others' expectations and decide for oneself the standards that will guide one
10. To learn how to confront others with care, concern, honesty, and directness
11. To learn how to ask directly for what one wants
12. To increase self-awareness and thereby increase the possibilities for choice and action
13. To learn the distinction between having feelings and acting on them
14. To free oneself from the inappropriate early decisions that keep one less than the person one could or would like to be
15. To recognize that others struggle too
16. To clarify the values one has and to decide whether and how to modify them
17. To be able to tolerate more ambiguity—to learn to make choices in a world where nothing is guaranteed
18. To find ways of resolving personal problems
19. To explore hidden potentials and creativity
20. To increase one's capacity to care for others
21. To learn how to give to others
22. To become more sensitive to the needs and feelings of others*

---

The goals outlined by Corey and Corey in Box 11-2 are related to self-concept development. The group counseling experience is possibly most beneficial to clients when the major issues or concerns to be dealt with reside in the client's feeling about self. In other words, the group experience seems to be of particular value in helping the client find answers to questions such as "Who am I?" "Am I lovable and capable?" "How do others respond to me?" "How am I similar to and yet different from my peers?"

*From *Groups: Process and Practice,* by G. Corey and M. S. Corey. Copyright © 1977 by Wadsworth, Inc. Reprinted by permission of the publisher, Brooks/Cole Pub. Co., Monterey, Calif.

*When to Recommend Group Counseling*   Since group counseling is very effective in self-concept development, clients with poor self-concepts, with a lack of self-confidence and self-esteem, should be carefully considered as participants in group counseling. The goals of group counseling as listed in Box 11–2 should serve as a guideline in determining whether group counseling should be recommended. When is group counseling unwise? Mahler (1969) has suggested that one-to-one counseling is indicated in the following situations:

1. When the client is in a state of crisis
2. When confidentiality is essential to protect the client
3. When interpreting tests related to self-concept
4. When the client has an unusual fear of speaking
5. When the client is grossly ineffective in the area of interpersonal relationship skills
6. When the client has very limited awareness or his or her own feelings, motivations, and behaviors
7. When deviant sexual behavior is involved
8. When the client's need for attention is too great to be managed in a group.

# CRISIS INTERVENTION COUNSELING

## Overview of the Crisis Situation

Counselors in all settings, as well as those engaged in a wide variety of helping professions, encounter crisis situations as an incidental development in their work. These situations are frequently explosive in nature and often involve a threat to the survival of the individual or to the family unit to which the individual belongs.

Puryear (1979) indicates that a crisis state is characterized by (1) symptoms of stress, primarily psychological and physiological, always with extreme discomfort, (2) an attitude of panic or defeat, wherein the individual feels overwhelmed, inadequate, and helpless, but may exhibit either agitation or withdrawal, (3) a focus on relief, with little interest in the initial problem, (4) lowered efficiency, and (5) limited duration.

Crisis intervention is an approach to helping people in crisis. As such, it consists of intensive work over a short period of time, with emphasis on the concrete facts of the current situation and on the client's own efforts at changing it. While crisis intervention is clearly a ''helping'' strategy, it is not counseling; it has a narrower and more superficial focus, more modest goals, and briefer duration.

Since most of counselor training focuses on therapeutic intervention over a period of time, crisis situations typically create an intense sense of frustration and inadequacy for the counselor who is unsure of exactly which direction should be taken. Resorting to normal counseling strategies may be inadequate since the crisis could be ended by disaster—suicide, homicide, chronic psychosis, or a permanent disintegration of the family unit—before the next counseling session can take place.

Thus the primary goal of crisis intervention is to avoid catastrophe. In addition, one must distinguish the unresolved initial problem from the coping efforts, the stress symptoms, and the relief efforts. The individual or family must be prevented from dangerous action until a state of equilibrium can be reached, creating a situation in which therapeutic intervention can be effective.

## A Model for Crisis Intervention

There are three stages in crisis intervention which are similar to the counseling process, but which recognize the nature of the crisis situation. Emphasis in each stage is given to the special needs of the individual in crisis. During the first stage, the counselor is particularly concerned about establishing that she genuinely understands what the individual is going through—the fears, dangers, feelings, and hopelessness. This involves getting into the client's world. By doing so, the counselor establishes that she is not only a professional who *may* be able to help, but one who *can* help, since the individual knows that the counselor recognizes the desperateness of the situation. The three important processes of the first stage are establishing rapport, assessing the situation, and clarifying the problem.

To establish rapport, the counselor creates an environment that allows the client to discuss his crisis. Roadblocks may occur here, preventing the intervention to continue. The client may test the helper with questions like, "Are you married? Divorced? How old are you? What are your qualifications?" It is important to remember that the client is really asking "Can you help me?" Also, clients often communicate a problem that is only an introduction to the underlying problem as the reason for seeing the counselor. Counselors must remain sensitive to the possibility that the presenting problem may just be a way of mustering enough courage to discuss a more serious problem. Thus, as in typical counseling situations, the counselor's emphasis should be on communicating genuine warmth and empathic understanding.

Once a crisis situation has been identified, the counselor should immediately assess the urgency of the situation. If there is no reason to believe that an immediate emergency exists—if, for example, the client has already taken steps that would be of severe danger to self or others—the counselor may begin assessing the overall problem, including some judgment as to the severity of the crisis, a formulation of the series of events that led up to the crisis, and an identification of the problem that lies behind the crisis. At this point, counselor behaviors that may lead to further problem clarification can be utilized.

The transition from the first stage to the second stage of crisis intervention can be made most smoothly if the counselor, believing that the problem has been sufficiently explored for the moment, summarizes and reviews her perceptions with the client. This serves two functions: First, it reassures the client and the counselor that the counselor has a reasonably clear perception of the crisis as the client perceives it, and second, it helps in determining whether the client is ready to move into the second stage. During the second stage, the counselor and the client agree on the possibility and direction of change. This can be initiated by either, but both must be in agreement to ensure the best possibility of crisis resolution.

Once the client and counselor agree on the possibility and direction of change, they are ready to enter the third stage of the process, in which possible alternatives are considered and a plan of action is eventually determined. The first set of variables to explore during this stage are the resources and support immediately available to the client. Information to discuss at this point includes prior methods of coping with crisis situations, the client's ability to help himself, related support groups (both from within the client's immediate world and from social agencies), and facts needed to locate an appropriate agency or private practitioner who might provide the kind of services necessary to resolve the current crisis; these facts include age, sex, religious affiliation, finances, insurance coverage, location, and occupation. After alternatives have been discussed and the client seems in agreement, the alternatives should be reviewed and the client should commit himself to following through. The task to which the client agrees should be simple and clear. If many tasks are necessary, it may be helpful to focus on those that are immediately necessary, making additional agreements during follow-up sessions. During the follow-up sessions, once the crisis has been resolved, the counselor may return to her usual methods of counseling.

Cavanagh (1982) identifies five factors that are particularly relevant for the counselor to be aware of in dealing with a crisis situation: (1) *dealing with reality,* thus helping the individual to broaden her perspective and see beyond the negative aspects; (2) *emphasizing beneficial effects,* allowing the person to utilize crisis reactions as a healing process until effective steps can be taken to counteract that situation; (3) *attempting to help,* which may lead to frustration and withdrawal for the counselor and the significant others within the client's life and thus leaving the client feeling even more alone, alienated, and hopeless; (4) *avoiding further anxiety,* recognizing that the crisis reaction may create a new set of anxieties or a new, separate crisis; and (5) *anticipating delayed reactions,* which may occur weeks or even months after the precipitating event.

While crisis counseling is usually anxiety producing for the counselor, it is potentially highly rewarding, since even a minimal amount of intervention can often bring relief for the client. The satisfaction resulting from being there when needed and from helping someone through what is often a life-saving process makes the counselor's fear and anxiety worthwhile. In addition, a crisis frequently presents an excellent opportunity for change, because individuals are usually more willing and more motivated to change during crisis than they are at other times.

## SUMMARY

This chapter has focused on several counseling situations that require the counselor to either possess or to acquire additional knowledge or skills.

In the section on special client concerns, we introduced information relevant to working with clients around such topics as sexuality, loss and separation, and substance abuse.

Because counselors often work with clients in groups, we reviewed the terminology associated with the group movement and examined the advantages and limitations of group work.

Crisis intervention counseling was presented, and a specific model for crisis counseling was discussed.

# REFERENCES

## Sexuality

AMERICAN ASSOCIATION OF SEX EDUCATORS AND COUNSELORS. (1973). The Professional Training and Preparation of Sex Counselors. Washington, D.C.

CALDERONE, M.S. (1976). Introduction: The issues at hand. *Personnel and Guidance Journal, 54* (7), 350–351.

GROVES, P.A., and VENTURA, L.A. (1983). The lesbian coming-out process: Therapeutic considerations. *Personnel and Guidance Journal, 62,* (3), 146–149.

KELLY, G.F. (1976). Sex education for counselors. *Personnel and Guidance Journal, 54* (7), 354–357.

KIRKPATRICK, J. (1980). Human sexuality: A survey of what counselors need to know. *Counselor Education and Supervision, 19* (4), 276–282.

KIRKPATRICK, J.S. (1975). Guidelines for counseling young people with sexual concerns. *Personnel and Guidance Journal, 54* (3), 145–148.

MADDOCK, J.E., and CHILGREN, R.A. (1976). The emergence of sex therapy. *Personnel and Guidance Journal, 54* (7), 371–374.

MASTERS, W.H., and JOHNSON, V.E. (1970). *Human sexual inadequacy.* Boston: Little, Brown.

MITCHELL, M.H. (1973). *The counselor and sexuality.* Boston: Houghton Mifflin.

SCHILLER, P. (1976). The sex counselor and therapist. *Personnel and Guidance Journal, 54* (7), 369–370.

SOPHIE, J. (1982). Counseling lesbians. *Personnel and Guidance Journal, 60* (6), 341–344.

TEGTMEYER, U. (1980). The role of the school counselor in facilitating sexual development. *Personnel and Guidance Journal, 58* (6), 430–433.

WINKELPLECK, J.M., and WESTFIELD, J.S. (1982). Counseling considerations with gay couples. *Personnel and Guidance Journal, 60* (5), 294–296.

## Loss and Separation

BESSELL, H., and PALOMARES, U. (1967). *Methods in human development.* San Diego: Human Development Training Institute.

CARTER, D.K. (1977). Counseling divorced women. *Personnel and Guidance Journal, 55* (9), 537–541.

CHEIKIN, M.L. (1981). Loss and reality. *Personnel and Guidance Journal, 59* (6), 335–338.

EDWARDS, M. (1977). Coupling and recoupling vs. the challenge of being single. *Personnel and Guidance Journal, 55* (9), 542–545.

FREARS, L.H., and SCHNEIDER, J.M. (1981). Exploring loss and grief within a wholistic framework. *Personnel and Guidance Journal, 59* (6), 341–345.

FROILAND, D.J., and HOZMAN, T.L. (1977). Counseling for constructive divorce. *Personnel and Guidance Journal, 55* (9), 525–529.

HEADINGTON, B.J. (1981). Understanding a core experience: Loss. *Personnel and Guidance Journal, 59* (6), 338–341.

HOZMAN, T.L., and FROILAND, D.J. (1977). Children:

Forgotten in divorce. *Personnel and Guidance Journal, 55* (9), 530–533.

KESSLER, S. (1976). Divorce adjustment groups. *Personnel and Guidance Journal, 54* (5), 250–255.

KUBLER-ROSS, E. (1969). *On death and dying.* New York: Macmillan.

MAGID, K.M. (1977). Children facing divorce: A treatment program. *Personnel and Guidance Journal, 55* (9), 534–536.

SCHNEIDER, J. (1980a). Growth from bereavement. In *Proceeding of the 1980 International Congress on Death and Dying.* London: Pittman Medical Publishers.

SCHNEIDER, J. (1980b). Loss and grief: A wholistic approach. Unpublished manuscript.

WALLERSTEIN, J. and KELLY, J. (1975). The effects of parental divorce: Experiences of the preschool child. *Journal of American Academy of Child Psychiatry, 14* (4), 600–616.

WALLERSTEIN, J. and KELLY, J. (1976a). The effects of parental divorce: Experiences of the child in early latency. *American Journal of Orthopsychiatry, 46* (1), 20–32.

WALLERSTEIN, J. and KELLY, J. (1976b). The effects of parental divorce: Experiences of the child in later latency. *American Journal of Orthopsychiatry, 46* (2), 256–269.

## Substance Abuse

BELKIN, G.S. (1975). *Practical counseling in the schools.* Dubuque, Iowa: Wm. C. Brown.

CORNACCHIA, H.J., BENTEL, D.J., and SMITH, D.E. (1973). *Drugs in the classroom: A conceptual model for school programs.* St. Louis, Mo.: C. V. Mosby.

FRYKMAN, J.H. (1971). *A new connection: An approach to persons involved in compulsive drug use.* San Francisco, Calif.: Scrimshaw Press.

## Group Counseling

COREY, G., and COREY, M.S. (1977). *Groups: Process and practice.* Monterey, Calif.: Brooks/Cole.

JOHNSON, D.W., and JOHNSON, F.P. (1982). *Joining together: Group theory and group skills* (2nd ed.), Englewood Cliffs, N.J.: Prentice-Hall.

LIFTON, W.M. (1972). *Groups: Facilitating individual growth and societal change.* New York: John Wiley.

MAHLER, C.A. (1969). *Group counseling in the schools.* Boston: Houghton Mifflin.

SHERTZER, B., and STONE, S. (1974). *Fundamentals of counseling.* Boston: Houghton Mifflin.

## Crisis Intervention

CAVANAUGH, M.E. (1982). *The counseling experience.* Monterey, Calif. Brooks/Cole.

PURYEAR, D.A. (1979) *Helping people in crisis.* San Francisco: Jossey-Bass.

# 12

# CAREER COUNSELING

In the late twentieth century, as during most of history, work is still one of our most important life activities, occupying almost half of our adult lives. When enjoyed, work can be a source of need satisfaction, self-esteem, and healthy adjustment. When disliked or dreaded, it can cause worry, stress, frustration—even physical illness and psychological and social maladjustment. To a large extent, work determines our social status, level of income, and standard of living. Work influences our self-concept and feelings of value, worth, and personal identity.

Most individuals can fulfill their need to work and be happy at any of several jobs. They may have no great desire for career assistance from a counselor. Most people view getting and holding a job as a simple procedure, never recognizing that they might be able to find a more meaningful and relevant job with counseling assistance.

The need for guidance in career development has long been an accepted function of counseling. The whole counseling movement, as outlined in Chapter 1, sprung largely from the career guidance movements. Yet there is a rising awareness that this one aspect of counseling services—career planning and related elements—is not being provided as effectively as the current circumstances facing youth and adults require. Too often the client has not understood the need for assistance or the potential value of seeking help from a counselor.

Hansen, Stevic, and Warner (1977) have pointed out four potential benefits of counseling. First, the client improves her prospects for job placement, since counselors may have information about potential employment opportunities. Second, the counselor can aid the client in the process of job adjustment, which may well make the difference between job advancement or stagnation. Third, the counselor can provide assistance in the area of job satisfaction by helping the client understand the good and bad aspects of the job prior to job entry. Finally, the counselor can help the individual who either is forced to or decides to change his current position. In short, the skilled career counselor can provide assistance to individuals as they develop vocationally, seek and choose a job, advance in a job, and change or leave employment.

In a nationwide study of student career development involving over 28,000 students, Prediger, Roth, and Noeth (1973) found that three-fourths of the eleventh-grade students in the study wanted help with career planning. The proportion of eighth graders wanting such help was almost as high. Still, although eighty-four percent of the eleventh-grade students indicated that they could almost always see a counselor when they wanted to, only thirteen percent felt that they had received "a lot of help" with career planning from this school; another thirty-seven percent felt they had received "some help." In addition, approximately forty percent were uncertain whether their educational plans were appropriate for the occupations they were considering, and approximately one-fourth were not sure if they would be able to complete the steps necessary for entering those occupations.

The results of this study are consistent with those of other studies that have indicated that students want help with career planning yet receive far less help than they wish. The students' apparent lack of knowledge about work options and the career-planning process suggest that much time and energy is lost through floundering and indecision and that this loss has a direct impact on society itself in terms of work loss, diminished productivity, and individual alienation.

Few comprehensive surveys of adult needs for career counseling are available, but there is every reason to believe that the career-counseling needs of this group are also very high. The services provided by our vocational rehabilitation agencies and our employment services have made a major impact on the careers of those who have sought help. But these agencies typically deal with very visible or very severe problems of career choice or adjustment, and as a result such agencies frequently have little time or assistance for the individual experiencing job alienation in subtle, agonizing ways—the woman who has been out of the labor force for many years, or the veteran who simply cannot find a satisfying role in the work world.

## THE CHANGING WORLD OF WORK

One of the most profound changes in the past few decades has been in the area of attitudes toward work. An increasing number of people no longer view work as toil and drudgery; rather, they see it as a means of personal expression, of growing and of building self-esteem, and of satisfying personal needs. In the past individuals typically remained in a particular occupation throughout most of their lives. Today more are changing their occupations many times in their lives. In addition, more and more people are questioning the validity of yearly income as the sole criterion of occupational success and are changing from higher-paying jobs to lower-paying jobs simply because they find the lower-paying jobs more desirable in other respects. Such individuals have determined that such criteria as personal need fulfillment, living where they want to, and having time to spend with their family are more important indicators of success to them than high income. And as the drastically increased earning power of blue-collar workers continues to undermine the idea that only people with college degrees can find suitable, well-paying jobs, attitudes about the importance of college are also changing.

Several striking changes have also occurred in the American occupational structure during the past quarter century. The number of workers involved in industries providing services has dramatically increased, while the number of workers in goods-producing industries has remained relatively constant. The number of employees in blue-collar occupations has increased relatively little, while the number in white-collar occupations has grown markedly. The average educational attainment of those in the labor force has also risen appreciably; more than 75 percent of workers now have at least a high school education. The proportion of American women in the labor force has increased significantly.

These trends in the work world are readily apparent. Determining what will happen in the future is a much more complex problem. Many of today's occupations did not exist fifteen years ago; still more new occupations will surface in the next fifteen years, making it difficult to project specific occupational categories that will be in demand in the future.

Career counseling parallels other kinds of counseling, but it focuses on planning and making decisions about occupations and education. As in all counseling, the personal relationship between the counselor and the client is critical. Values and attitudes are explored in career counseling, but more information and factual data are required than in personal counseling. Career counselors also recognize that they cannot help someone with a career problem while ignoring such other aspects of the person's life as needs, conflicts, and relations with others.

Morrill and Forrest (1970) have identified four types of vocational counseling events in terms of the width of focus that the counseling situation has on the kinds of situations for which the counseling has relevance. Type 1 is counseling that aids the client with a specific decision by providing information and clarifying issues. Type 2 is counseling that aids the client with a specific decision by focusing on decision-making skills rather than on only the decision at hand, applying these skills to the specific situation as well as later choice points. Type 3 counseling views the career as a process rather than an end-point toward which all decisions lead; thus, it changes the focus from the objective of making a correct ultimate choice and a once-and-for-all pronouncement of identity to a process of making a continual series of choices. Type 4 counseling focuses on giving individuals the ability to utilize their personal attributes to achieve self-determined objectives and to influence the nature of future choices rather than merely adapting to external pressures.

A number of considerations determine the level or focus of counseling. First are the expectations of the client, the immediacy of the client's needs, and the client's level of development. Career counseling involves counseling the whole person; an effort must be made to avoid compartmentalizing personal and vocational counseling. The developmental nature of career counseling is recognized today and is placed in perspective as an aspect of the growth of the whole person. A career-counseling process that provides individuals with only the information and self-knowledge to select a single vocational direction or job does little to provide them with the developmental skills and abilities necessary to make continual progress and to shape their own destiny.

## THEORIES OF CAREER DEVELOPMENT

Professional interest in the process of how an individual selects an occupation is relatively new. With industrialization and urbanization, vocational choices were no longer limited to what a person's father or mother did or to the types of work that existed within a particular community. The every-increasing range of occupational alternatives and the accompanying uncertainties and confusion created the need for professional assistance in selecting a career. As the field of career counseling has attempted to meet the need, various theoretical rationales have been developed to provide a framework for the practice of career counseling.

A theory of career development must account for the fluid, changing process of vocational awareness and feelings. The value of any particular theory to counselors lies in its ability to help them organize and integrate client data simply, logically, and usefully. A theory should provide a counselor with the expertise necessary to help a client make decisions that will lead to personal growth and attainment of specific objectives. A theory should also allow a counselor to predict client behavior more successfully, thus helping clients accurately anticipate the consequences of their decision. Most of all, career development is intimately related to the factors that motivate or impede decisions.

Just as the way in which the counselor proceeds with a counseling session depends to a large degree on that counselor's personal counseling theory, so the career counselor's conduct during a career-counseling session depends on the counselor's career-counseling theory. The numerous theories of career development postulated over the past few decades can be classified into four areas: trait-factor theories, structural theories, developmental theories, and decision-making theories.

### Trait-factor Theory of Williamson

From a historical standpoint, the first theory that attempted to explain the process of occupational choice was the trait-factor theory. This approach, evolving out of the testing movement, is essentially a theory of individual differences (Williamson, 1965). The trait-factor theory is based on the assumption that each person possesses a uniquely organized pattern of personal traits (interests, abilities, and personality characteristics) that are fairly stable and seldom change after late adolescence. These traits can be identified through objective means, usually psychological tests or inventories, and then profiled to represent the individual's potential. Occupations can also be profiled by analyzing them in terms of the amounts of the various individual traits they require. When one profile is matched to the other, the probable degree of fit between person and job can be identified.

Essentially, then, the trait-factor approach is a rigorous, scientific, and highly personalized method of matching individuals with occupations. Without assistance, a person may or may not choose an occupation that will agree with her profile of abilities, interests, and personality. If an inappropriate choice is made, the individual may waste much time and energy before eventually gravitating toward a more satisfying occupation. A major task of the career counselor who is oriented toward trait-factor theory is to assist people in making better career decisions by helping them become more knowledgeable about their own traits, learn more about job requirements, and match those personal characteristics with the job requirements. Such a process is highly cognitive in nature.

### Structural Theories

The first structural theory to be examined is the one proposed by Roe (1956). She theorized and researched the concept that there are definite personality differences between members of various occupations and that these differences are attributable to early parent-child relationships. Basing her theory upon Maslow's ideas of the integrated unity of the individual as a bond of interacting levels of needs, Roe specifically postulates three psychological climates in the home that are a function of parent-child relations: (1) emotional concentration on the child—either over-protecting or over-demanding climate; (2) avoidance of the child—either neglecting or rejecting climate; and (3) acceptance of the child—either casual or loving climate.

Deficiencies during childhood can be compensated for, by, and through work. Thus, individuals who did not receive sufficient praise and respect from their parents may attempt to elicit these through their work and, consequently, may seek jobs that can bring them praise and respect. The same holds true for other needs that were unmet at earlier stages of development: the individual turns to work to gratify these needs.

Roe's concerns with specific child-rearing practices, the manner in which the parents interact with the child, the resulting need structure, and the ensuing orientation toward or away from persons were then translated into a useful classification of occupations by field and level, including the following (Roe, 1956):

| FIELDS | LEVELS |
|---|---|
| I. Service | 1. Professional and Managerial (1) |
| II. Business Contact | 2. Professional and Managerial (2) |
| III. Organizations | |
| IV. Technology | 3. Semiprofessional, Small Business |
| V. Outdoor | 4. Skilled |
| VI. Science | 5. Semiskilled |
| VII. General Culture | 6. Unskilled |
| VIII. Arts and Entertainment | |

Although Roe's system has received a number of valid criticisms, it does have a number of strong points. Her theory allows an integrative role to the job function and relates occupational choice to the entire structure of the personality. From a counseling point of view, Roe's insights help the counselor to better understand the variety of factors that play a part in the individual's decision to pursue or avoid certain jobs, as well as to understand why a job does or does not meet an individual's needs.

Hoppock (1976) has developed a composite view of personality approaches to career development. His theory is basically a summary of other theories. Hoppock proposes a series of straightforward points about career choice that give prominence to need satisfaction:

1. Occupations are chosen to meet needs.
2. The occupation that we choose is the one that we believe would best meet the needs that most concern us.
3. Needs may be intellectually perceived, or they may be only vaguely felt as attractions that draw us in certain directions. In either case, they may influence choices.
4. Occupational choice begins when we first become aware that an occupation can help to meet our personal needs.
5. Career choice improves as we become better able to anticipate how well a prospective career will meet our needs. Our capacity to anticipate depends on our knowledge about ourselves, our knowledge about occupations, and our ability to think clearly.
6. Information about ourselves affects career choice by helping us to discover the careers

that may meet our needs and by helping us to anticipate how well satisfied we may hope to be in one career as compared with another.

7. Information about occupations affects career choice by helping us to discover the occupation that may meet our needs.

8. Job satisfaction depends on the extent to which the job we hold meets the needs we feel it should meet. The degree of satisfaction is determined by the ratio between what we have and what we want.

9. Satisfaction can result from a job that meets our needs today or from a job that promises to meet those needs in the future.

10. Career choice is always subject to change when we believe that a change will better meet our needs.

The last structural theory to be examined in this chapter is the one proposed by Holland (1985). He has stated that his theory is a theory of personality structure as well as of vocational choice. It focuses primarily upon vocational choice, but it is also concerned with emotional functioning, creativity, and personal development.

Four assumptions constitute the heart of Holland's theory: First, in our culture most persons can be categorized as one of six types—realistic, investigative, artistic, social, enterprising, or conventional. Second, most environments can also be categorized as realistic, investigative, artistic, social, enterprising, or conventional. Third, people search for environments that will let them exercise their skills and abilities, express their attitudes and values, and take on agreeable problems and roles. And finally, a person's behavior is determined by an interaction between his personality and the characteristics of his environment.

To emphasize this person-situation correspondence, Holland has classified work environments into the six categories analogous to the six personal orientations. By do-

**Figure 12-1** John Holland

ing so, Holland makes explicit that occupations are ways of life, helping to define social status, life-style, and standard of living. He postulates that stereotypes of occupations have important psychological and sociological significance. Thus, he suggests that a person's occupational choice can have limited but useful value as a projective device in revealing motivations, insight, and self-understanding (Holland, 1985).

Since a person's behavior is determined by the interaction between his personality and the characteristics of the environment, Holland believes that vocational satisfaction, stability, and mobility are a function of the extent to which a person's personality and occupational environment are congruent. Such congruent interactions of people and their environments lead to more stable vocational choice, higher vocational achievement, higher academic achievement, better maintenance of personal stability, and greater satisfaction.

Since the theories of Roe, Hoppock, and Holland all stress the importance of need satisfaction in choosing an occupation, it becomes highly important for a structurally oriented counselor to assess clients' cognitive, affective, and social needs. Counselors are then able to provide clients with enough career information to allow them to choose a career that will satisfy their needs and be congruent with their personality structure.

### Developmental Theories

Developmental theories of career behavior and decision making differ from the trait-factor and the structural theories in that they are typically more inclusive, more concerned with longitudinal expressions of career behavior, and more inclined to highlight the importance of the self-concept (Herr & Cramer, 1979).

Ginzberg and his associates (1951) were early leaders in theorizing about career development as a process that culminates in an occupational choice in one's early twenties. In their early work they stressed that occupational choice is an irreversible development process involving a series of decisions that extend over many years. That is, as each occupationally relevant decision is made, other choices are eliminated. They identified four sets of factors that interact to influence the ultimate career choice: individual values, emotional factors, amount and kind of education, and impact of reality through environmental pressures.

Ginzberg and his associates also identified three phases in the period of career choice development: fantasy (from birth to age eleven), tentative (from ages eleven to seventeen), and realistic (between ages seventeen and early twenties). With the exception of the fantasy stage, each period is broken into subaspects. The tentative period is divided into stages of interest, capacity, value, and transition. The realistic period is broken into exploration and crystallization stages. During these life stages individuals are faced with certain tasks. As they confront these tasks, they make compromises between wishes and possibilities, and each compromise contributes to the irreversibility of the unfolding process.

In his reformulation of the theory, Ginzberg (1971) suggested some modifications. First, he believes that the process of career choice making is not limited to the

**Figure 12-2** Donald E. Super

period up to and including young adulthood but is likely to occur throughout the individual's working life. Second, he has reduced his emphasis on the irreversibility of occupational choice, emphasizing the cumulative effect on occupational prospects of the educational and occupational decisions that the young person makes between childhood and the twenty-first or twenty-fifth year. Third, he has substituted the word *optimization* for the earlier term *compromise*. This change suggests that rather than emphasizing the compromises individuals make between wishes and possibilities, he is emphasizing the individual's search to find the best occupational fit between changing desires and changing circumstances, a continuing search.

Probably the theoretical approach that has received the most continuous attention and is most widely used in career development is the one proposed by Super (1953). His theory of career choice is based on the idea that individuals' self-concepts influence their occupational choice and their ultimate satisfaction or dissatisfaction with their choice. This vocational choice is the result of a developmental process that puts the individual's self-concept into practice. Although his initial statement of theory was a response to the theory proposed by Ginzberg and associates, Super attempted to integrate several approaches to career development theory, including aspects of differential, social, developmental, and phenomenological psychology. His position, however, is primarily developmental.

Super has made some refinements to his original proposal, but his theory remains substantially the same as originally proposed. The original ten propositions that characterize his theory include the following:

1. People differ in their abilities, interests, and personalities.
2. They are qualified, by virtue of these characteristics, each for a number of occupations.
3. Each of these occupations requires a characteristic pattern of abilities, interests, and

personality traits, with tolerances wide enough, however, to allow both some variety of occupations for each individual and some variety of individuals in each occupation.

4. Vocational preferences and competencies, the situations in which people live and work, and hence their self-concepts, change with time and experience (although self-concepts are generally fairly stable from late adolescence until late maturity), making choice and adjustment a continuous process.

5. This process may be summed up in a series of life stages characterized as those of growth, exploration, establishment, maintenance, and decline, and these stages may in turn be subdivided into (a) the fantasy, tentative, and realistic phases of the exploratory stage, and (b) the trial and stable phases of the establishment stage.

6. The nature of the career pattern (that is, the occupational level attained and the sequence, frequency, and duration of trial and stable jobs) is determined by the individual's parental socioeconomic level, mental ability, and personality characteristics, and by the opportunities to which he is exposed.

7. Development through the life stages can be guided, partly by facilitating the process of maturation of abilities and interests and partly by aiding in reality testing and in the development of the self-concept.

8. The process of vocational development is essentially that of developing and implementing a self-concept: it is a compromise process in which the self-concept is a product of the interaction of inherited aptitudes, neural and endocrine make-up, opportunity to play various roles, and evaluations of the extent to which the results of role playing meet with the approval of superiors and fellows.

9. The process of compromise between individual and social factors, between self-concept and reality, is one of role playing, whether the role is played in fantasy, in the counseling interview, or in real life activities such as school classes, clubs, part-time work, and entry jobs.

10. Work satisfactions and life satisfactions depend upon the extent to which the individual finds adequate outlets for his abilities, interests, personality traits, and values; they depend upon his establishment in a type of work, a work situation, and a way of life in which he can play the kind of role which his growth and exploratory experiences have led him to consider congenial and appropriate. (1953, pp. 189–190)

As these ten propositions clearly point out, Super's developmental approach is comprehensive. It is a theory of career development rather than of occupational choice. His attempts to synthesize various approaches seem apparent as he emphasizes the various factors that contribute to a career pattern. The jobs individuals hold over a lifetime represent the development of their self-concepts as expressed in the world of work. For Super, then, work is a way of life as well as an expression of selfhood and a means of support.

### Decision-making Theories

The most recent trend in career development theory has resulted from attempts to theorize about educational and occupational choice through the use of decision models. The major concept in decision-making theory is that each individual has several possible alternatives from which to choose. Each alternative has identifiable results or consequences. Each of the anticipated results has a specific value for the individual, a value that can be estimated through some method of psychological scaling. Therefore, if the resulting values of the alternatives can be determined and arranged in a hierarchy, the probable occurrence of each outcome can also be determined. Then the value of each event can be multiplied by the probability of its occurrence to determine the sound decision for the particular individual (Hills, 1964).

Bergland (1974) has identified a sequence of events that occur in decision making, including the following steps:

1. Defining the problem
2. Generating alternatives
3. Gathering information
4. Processing information
5. Making plans and selecting goals
6. Implementing and evaluating plans

A somewhat different labeling of the decision-making process has been suggested by Clarke, Gelatt, and Levine (1965). This model suggests four stages, and at each stage the person doing the choosing requires certain information: at the first stage, information about alternative actions; at the second, information about possible outcomes; at the third, information about probabilities linking actions to outcomes; and at the fourth, information about preferences for the various outcomes.

Together, these emphases in decision making suggest that the individual needs both a prediction system and a value system that permit decisions to be made among preferences and expectancies for action within a climate of uncertainty.

Gelatt's (1962) decision-making framework assumes a decision maker who requires information as ''fuel'' and who produces a recommended course of action, which may be terminal or investigatory (that is, instrumental in both acquiring and requiring more information) depending upon how it relates to the decision maker's purposes. In Gelatt's process, information is organized into three systems: (1) a predictive system, which includes information about alternative actions, possible outcomes, and probabilities linking actions to outcomes; (2) a value system, which determines relative preferences among outcomes; and (3) a decision system, which provides rules for evaluation.

Gelatt's model emphasizes that the better the decision maker's information, the clearer the risks in implementing different actions. In effect, this model prescribes the characteristics of adequate informational inputs and suggests an organization to be imposed on it.

Kalder and Zytowski (1969) take still another approach to the application of decision-making theory to career choice. In their model, the elements consist of inputs (personal resources such as intellectual and physical characteristics), alternatives, and outputs. Again, the inputs are priced in terms of what the decision maker forgoes in using them in a particular occupational alternative. The alternative to be chosen is the one offering the greatest net value—the highest value in input costs are balanced against output gains. Implicit in such a model is the asssumption that the decision maker has sufficient information about personal characteristics and the alternatives available to rank the values, utilities, and sacrifices associated with each possible action.

More recently, Krumboltz (1979) has proposed a social learning theory of career decision making. His theory attempts to explain how educational and career preferences and skills are acquired and how selections of courses and careers are made. It identifies the interactions of genetic factors, environmental conditions, learning experiences, cognitive and emotional responses, and performance skills that produce movement along one career path or another. Krumboltz points out that combinations of these factors interact in different ways to produce different decisions.

Three types of influence and their interactions lead to several types of outcomes:

1. Self-observation generalizations (SOGs), which include overt or covert statements evaluating one's own actual or vicarious performance in relation to learned standards.
2. Task approach skills (TASs), which are cognitive and performance abilities and emotional predispositions for coping with the environment, interpreting it in relation to SOGs, and making covert or overt predictions about future events.
3. Actions, which include entry behaviors that indicate overt steps in career progression.

The Krumboltz model accents the importance of learning experiences as well as task approach skills as instrumental in producing preferences for activities. Such a model, however, suggests that becoming a particular kind of worker is not a simple function of preference or choice but is the result of complex environmental factors, many beyond the control of any single individual. These factors, however, can be recognized by the individual, and career decision-making skills can be systematically learned.

## THE CAREER-COUNSELING PROCESS

In the several approaches covered in this chapter, career development has been described as a process shaped by an interaction of self-references, self-knowledge, knowledge about training and occupations, educational and occupational opportunities, genetic and early childhood influences, personality styles, and patterns of traits that individuals express in their choice of behavior and career identity. This suggests that career development is no different from all human behavior in that it is complex and part of the total fabric of personality development.

Herr and Cramer (1979) have suggested a number of career development implications that provide a conceptual base for those planning career-counseling activities. First is the recognition that work provides a means for meeting needs of social interaction, dignity, self-esteem, self-identification, and other forms of psychological gratification. Each individual's personal, educational, occupational, or career maturation is reached through a complex of learning processes that began in early childhood and continue throughout life. The actual choice occurs not at a particular point in time but in relation to antecedent experiences and future alternatives. It is a continuous, tentative, and often more psychological than logical process of decision making. Value systems, both individual and cultural, are important in shaping career development.

Herr and Cramer also include the need for adequate information. Career information must include not only the objective facts, such as earning possibilities, training requirements, and numbers of positions available, but also the social and psychological aspects of careers. Moreover, since occupational and career choices are methods of implementing an individual's self-concept, information about self-characteristics—attitudes, aptitudes, and values—is as necessary as career or occupational information.

Career development theory indicates that decision making involves action. Therefore, another implication is that ways must be found to help persons take responsibility for their own learning and for their own direction. They need to be helped to develop a conscious awareness that they do have choices, to determine at any given time what kind of decision is involved, and to recognize the factors inherent in the decision that make a personal difference.

Occupational choices and career patterns are basic to one's life-style and reflect developmental experiences, personality, goals, and so on. As Herr and Cramer state, career choice can be an essentially rational process if the person knows how to select and obtain appropriate information and then apply the decision-making process to it.

During the past few decades career counseling had been in the somewhat paradoxical position of being seen as less exciting and meaningful than personal counseling. Yet career counseling remains a major area of need for those individuals who seek help from a counselor. Career counseling is not a totally unique version or variety of counseling. It requires many of the skills necessary to conduct any form of counseling dealing with the individual's intellectual and emotional being. Still, there are some notable differences. Leigh (1977) has identified three differences between career counseling and other counseling specialties. First, the prime focus of career counseling is to assist a person in choosing and adjusting to the world of work. Second, career counseling requires that a counselor be familiar with current occupational information and is, therefore, more concrete than other counseling specialties. Last, career problems are often seen by clients as a safe and socially acceptable way into psychotherapy. Thus, a career counselor must be able to determine the actual nature of the client's complaint in the early stages of counseling by conducting a thorough assessment during the initial counseling contacts.

Career counseling generally follows an orderly process, beginning with the development of the relationship and ending with follow-up and potential change of plans. Between these two steps the counselor helps clients to develop an understanding of their problems or concerns. Data from several sources are presented to clients so that they better understand themselves and their vocational decisions and alternatives. The counselor and client then work to synthesize the appraisal process and individual client profile into a plan of action or choice.

In particular, the counselor should be aware of six factors in career counseling: appraisal of the client's characteristics, introduction of outside information, exploration of alternatives, clarification of occupational possibilities, integration of the factual material with the personal information, and decision making (Brammer & Shostrom, 1982).

A counselor should help the client examine her personal characteristics. A counselor should determine a client's level of intelligence, interests, special abilities,

**Figure 12-3**   A counselor provides feedback regarding personal data related to a career decision   (Color Image Inc., Jim Trotter)

aspirations, needs, and values, among other qualities. Various methods—including checklists, inventories, tests, previous records, and interview data—can aid the counselor in assessing this information. Counselors may wish to focus the attention of the client on such areas as special aptitudes, personality traits, and educational attainment.

While clients are learning more about themselves, they must also learn about the environment in which they will eventually be seeking employment. The environment includes all the facets within which the individual functions. Such information can be gathered from a number of sources, including publications, audiovisual aids, programmed instruction materials, computer-based systems, interviews with experts, and direct observation of work experiences. Obviously, such information should be accurate, current, usable, and thorough.

Once clients have had adequate opportunity to explore career possibilities, they need to thoroughly understand the various possibilities available. Thus the counselor participates in the clarification and integration phases, by helping clients gain factual information which promotes full understanding and integrates this material into career decisions. By this point, clients have accumulated a great deal of data about themselves and have information about various occupations. Clients need to understand that this is not the end point and should be invited back for further discussions regarding the actual job chosen. As clients then begin to act on their choices, the counselor provides supportive assistance in implementing the choice. If the client is not ready to make the decision, the counselor may have to spend more time helping the client understand what has occurred, perhaps even dealing with the client's inability to make such a decision.

## CAREER-COUNSELING TOOLS

Almost all of the career counseling theorists assume that the greater the degree of accurate self-understanding one has, the more likely one is to make realistic, satisfying educational and career choices. Certainly, accurate self-understanding does not *guarantee* good decision making, but good decisions only rarely occur without a realistic picture of one's abilities and interests. Thus, career counselors typically utilize assessment devices as a vehicle for helping the client gain greater self-understanding.

Individuals facing educational and career decisions also require accurate information about their choices. Individuals must possess and be able to use information about occupational outlook, entry, education and training required, social and psychological factors, and salary. Career counselors must be able to identify and utilize sources of this information.

### Career Testing

Assessment in career counseling usually involves the use of aptitude tests and interest inventories, which measure abilities and interests. Since no one aptitude test provides enough information for most individuals, career counselors usually employ a test battery to provide a multiscore summary of the various strengths and weaknesses. Some of the most widely used aptitude test batteries include:

> *The Differential Aptitude Tests* (DAT).Published by the Psychological Corporation, the DAT requires approximately four hours to complete and provides scores in eight areas: verbal reasoning, numerical reasoning, abstract reasoning, space relations, mechanical reasoning, clerical speed and accuracy, spelling, and language usage. The DAT also provides a verbal score and a numerical score, which combine for a general intelligence measure.
>
> *The General Aptitude Test Battery* (GATB). Published by the United States Employment Service, the GATB requires two and one-half hours to complete and provides nine scores: intelligence, verbal aptitude, numerical aptitude, spatial aptitude, form perception, clerical perception, motor coordination, finger dexterity, and manual dexterity.
>
> *Flanagan Aptitude Classification Tests* (FACT). Published by Science Research Associates, the FACT requires approximately five to six hours to complete and provides fourteen scores related to thirty occupations.

Interest inventories attempt to measure an individual's interest in various careers by determining the pattern of interest from his responses to lists of occupations and activities. Some of the widely used interest inventories include the following:

> *Strong-Campbell Interest Inventory* (SCII). Published by Stanford University Press, the SCII requires about thirty to forty-five minutes to complete and provides scores for the six theme areas of Holland, as well as for twenty-three basic interests and one hundred twenty-four occupations.
>
> *Kuder Preference Records and Interest Surveys.* Published by Science Research Associates, these include a total of five instruments which can be used for different age groups and

different purposes. The information provided range from scores on ten interest scales (Form E) to scores on seventy-seven occupational scales and twenty-nine college major scales (Form DD).

*Ohio Vocational Interest Inventory* (OVII). Published by Harcourt Brace Jovanovich, the OVII requires about one and one-half hours to complete and provides scores for twenty-four interest scales.

*Occupational Interests Inventory* (OII). Published by the California Test Bureau, the OII requires approximately forty minutes to complete and provides scores in six fields of interest: personal-social, natural, mechanical, business, arts, and sciences, and in three types of interest: verbal, maniuplative, and computational.

One other instrument which is in wide use is the *Self-Directed Search* (SDS), Form E. Broader in scope than interest inventories, the SDS utilizes self-reports and estimates regarding occupational daydreams, preference for activities, competencies, preferences for kinds of occupations, and abilities in various occupational areas. This information then provides for summary codes according to Holland's career scales.

### Career Information

Most counselors have in-depth information on only a few occupations. Thus, career counseling typically requires the use of career information sources that will give clients a complete, accurate picture of various occupations. Certainly, the two best known of the published materials are the *Dictionary of Occupational Titles* (DOT) and the *Occupational Outlook Handbook* (OOH).

The DOT is published periodically (most recent was the fourth edition, published in 1978) by the U.S. Department of Labor. Information relating to approximately twenty thousand jobs is provided alphabetically by occupational categories, by worker traits, and by industries. Each job entry includes alternate job titles, summary of the occupation, and the specific tasks performed.

The OOH is also published periodically by the U.S. Department of Labor. Used with the Occupational Outlook Quarterly, the OOH provides information regarding trends and outlook for eight hundred occupations and industries.

There are a number of other sources of career systems (for example, Occupational Library, Careerdex, Career Information Kit, and Mini-briefs). There are also various printed series of occupational booklets as well as career guidance media that use audio and visual means of disseminating information. In addition, a number of career guidance simulations and games have been developed to give individuals the opportunity to explore careers vicariously.

## SUMMARY

A major function of counseling is that of helping clients develop vocationally as they choose, seek, advance in, and change jobs. This vocational guidance function, an early emphasis of counseling, is frequently undervalued today by counselors, but it is still highly important to individuals who seek help in planning and making decisions about their jobs and education.

Career counseling is based on a positive, personal relationship between client and counselor; it includes exploration of values and attitudes as well as gathering and assessment of information and factual data. The major career development theories include trait-factor theories, structural theories, developmental theories, and decision-making theories.

Generally, career counselors help clients explore, clarify, and integrate various vocational possibilities to enable them to choose among the available alternatives. In doing so career counselors use a number of career-counseling tools, including career-testing materials and career information sources.

## REFERENCES

BERGLAND, B. (1974). Career planning: The use of sequential evaluated experience. In E. L. Herr (Ed.), *Vocational Guidance and Human Development*, Boston: Houghton Mifflin.

BRAMMER, L. M., and SHOSTROM, E. L. (1982). *Therapeutic psychology* (4th ed.). Englewood Cliffs, N.J.: Prentice-Hall.

CLARKE, R., GELATT, H. B., and LEVINE, L. (1965). A decision-making paradigm for local guidance research, *Personnel and Guidance Journal, 44,* 40–51.

GELATT, H. B. (1962). Decision-making: A conceptual frame of reference for counseling. *Journal of Counseling Psychology, 9,* 240–245.

GINZBERG, E. (1972). Restatement of the theory of occupational choice. *Vocational Guidance Quarterly, 20,* 169–176.

GINZBERG, E., GINZBERG, S. W., AXELRAD, S., and HERMA, J. R. (1951). *Occupational choice: An approach to a general theory.* New York: Columbia University Press.

HANSEN, J. C., STEVIC, R. R., and WARNER, R. W., JR., (1977). *Counseling: Theory and process* (2nd ed.). Boston: Allyn & Bacon.

HERR, E. L., and CRAMER, S. H. (1979). *Career guidance through life span.* Boston: Little, Brown.

HILLS, J. R. (1964). Decision theory and college choice. *Personnel and Guidance Journal, 43,* 17–22.

HOLLAND, J. L. (1985). *Making vocational choices* (2nd ed.). Englewood Cliffs, N.J.: Prentice-Hall.

HOPPOCK, R. (1976). *Occupational information* (4th ed.). New York: McGraw-Hill.

KALDER, D. R., and ZYTOWSKI, D. G. (1969). A maximizing model of occupational decision-making. *Personnel and Guidance Journal, 47,* 781–788.

KRUMBOLTZ, J. D. (1979). A social learning theory of career decision making. In A. M. Mitchell, G. B. Jones, and J. D. Krumboltz (Eds.), *Social learning and career decision making.* Cranston, R.I.: Carroll Press.

LEIGH, K. B. (1977). Career counseling. In G. J. Blackham, *Counseling: Theory, process, and practice.* Belmont, Calif.: Wadsworth.

MORRILL, W. H., and FORREST, D. J. (1970). Dimensions of counseling for career development. *Personnel and Guidance Journal, 49,* 299–305.

PREDIGER, D. J., ROTH, J. D., and NOETH, R. J. (1973). *Nationwide study of student career development.* Iowa City, Iowa: The American College Testing Program.

ROE, A. (1956). *The psychology of occupations.* New York: John Wiley.

SUPER, D. E. (1953). A theory of vocational development. *American Psychologist, 8,* 185–190.

WILLIAMSON, E. G. (1965). *Vocational counseling: Some historical, philosophical, and theoretical perspectives.* New York: McGraw-Hill.

# 13

# DIAGNOSIS AND ASSESSMENT

JAMES T. HURLEY, ED.D., AABM

$T$his chapter focuses on two significant issues in the field of counseling—diagnosis and assessment. Diagnosis is a new issue which may face practitioners in the counseling profession. With more states licensing counselors, and with the potential for third-party reimbursement to counselors, these professionals will find themselves in a new role—that of diagnosing their clients.

Assessment, to many counselors, is not new. Many techniques and strategies have changed, however, making assessment a viable tool for counselors and other mental health professionals.

## DIAGNOSIS

Although few counselors go through the formal process of making diagnostic decisions, most informally diagnose in order to formulate a plan of treatment for a client. Hansen, Stevic, and Warner, Jr. (1982) indicate that the concept of diagnosis was brought into counseling via psychiatry, which, as a branch of medicine, was already accustomed to diagnosing. The art of diagnosing is alien to most counseling professionals, however, since most graduate curricula do not teach counselors to diagnose.

### Purposes

What are the uses of diagnosis in counseling? With the trend toward employment of counselors in nonschool settings such as mental health centers, hospitals, and drug and alcohol abuse programs, many counselors have encountered new responsibilities, one of which is the need to diagnose emotional difficulties (Seligman, 1983). Seligman also points out that the growing trend toward licensure for counselors has brought along the potential to establish private practices and to receive health insurance reimbursement. She also concludes that diagnosis had become a vehicle for human service agencies to classify the clients they serve in order to demonstrate accountability and to justify their role in the community.

Hansen et al. (1982) explains that the purpose of diagnosis is to identify the client's life-style of functioning, or the disruption of the life-style. Diagnosis can help to identify the problem area, label it, and establish goals for the client.

Hersen, Kazdin, and Bellack (1983) suggest that establishing a diagnosis enables the counselor to predict the symptoms that are likely to be seen. Thus, in reviewing a file on a client diagnosed as having a generalized anxiety disorder, we would expect this client to have a certain group of symptoms based on the diagnostic category.

Weiner (1959) suggests that diagnosis

1) allows the counselor to make a prediction about the client's behavior.
2) allows the counselor to determine whether he will be able to provide appropriate treatment for the client.
3) aids the counselor in determining what the client needs most.

As suggested by Weiner and others, there seem to be plausible reasons for diagnosing clients; this is probably more true today than ever before. Most likely, diagnosing will become a routine practice for counselors out of necessity, dictated by the demands of others, rather than out of what counselors themselves see as necessary.

### Classification

Today there are basically two systems of diagnostic classification used by mental health professionals. One is the third edition of the *Diagnostic and Statistical Manual of Mental Disorders* (DSM-III), published in 1980; the other is the *Manual of the International Statistical Classification of Diseases, Injuries, and Causes of Death*, Volume I (1977), also known as the *ICD-9*.

The DSM-III is the current standard nosology for the United States (Hersen et al., 1983). It was preceded by the DSM in 1952, and the DSM-II in 1958. A major innovation of the DSM-III is the use of a multiaxial system of diagnosis.

According to the DSM-III (1980), a multiaxial evaluation requires that every case be assessed on several "axes," each of which refers to a different class of information. In order for the system to have maximal clinical usefulness, there must be a limited number of axes; there are five in the DSM-III multiaxial classification system. The first three axes constitute the official diagnostic assessment.

| | |
|---|---|
| AXIS I | Clinical Syndromes |
| | Conditions Not Attributable to a Mental Disorder |
| | That Are a Focus of Attention or Treatment (V. |
| | Codes) Additional Codes |
| AXIS II | Personality Disorders |
| | Specific Developmental Disorders |
| AXIS III | Physical Disorders and Conditions |

Axes IV and V are available for use in special clinical and research settings and provide information supplementing the official DSM-III diagnoses (Axes I, II, and III) that may be useful for planning treatment and predicting outcome:

| | |
|---|---|
| AXIS IV | Severity of Psychosocial Stressors |
| AXIS V | Highest Level of Adaptive Functioning Past Year. |
| | (1980, p. 23) |

The following example of a multiaxial diagnosis illustrates how this system works (Seligman, 1983):

> AXIS I—296.22; Major depression, single episode, without melancholia
> 305.91; other substance abuse, continuous
> AXIS II—301.60; Dependent personality disorder
> AXIS III—Headaches

AXIS IV—Psychosocial stressor: marital separation.
        Severity: 5—severe
AXIS V—Highest level of adaptive functioning in past year: 4—fair.

The DSM-III is longer and includes 265 categories, compared to 108 in the DSM-I and 182 in the DSM-II (Hersen, et al., 1983). For each of the 265 categories of disorders, the DSM-III provides a description of each illness including the diagnostic criteria required. Seligman (1983) reports that for each disorder, the diagnostic description generally contains the following:

1. A list of its essential features and a clinical sketch
2. A summary of characteristics usually associated with the disorder
3. Information on the typical onset and course of the disorder, the impairment caused and potential complications
4. Information on known predisposing factors and frequency of occurrence of the disorder
5. Information on similar disorders, to facilitate differential diagnosis
6. Diagnostic criteria.

To many, the DSM-III classification system is overwhelming at first glance. Like any other system, proficiency in using it comes with practice. Some additional sources of help in understanding and using the DSM-III are *The New Language of Psychiatry* (Levy, 1982), *DSM-III Casebook* (Spitzer et al., 1981), and the *DSM-III Training Guide* (Webb et al., 1981). Additionally, there are workshops offered through the American Psychological Association's group of approved continuing education programs and through independent groups throughout the country. Today, the DSM-III is accepted as an approved diagnostic model by most insurance companies for third-party reimbursement.

### Cautions

While there are advantages for using diagnosis, there are those who oppose its use. Sundberg, Taplin, and Tyler (1983) point out that many notable professionals, including Carl Rogers, argue that categorizing people dehumanizes and deindividualizes them and prevents proper attention to therapy. Attaching a label may stereotype an individual and may bias others toward him.

Sundberg further indicates that one of the most significant problems with diagnosing is the reliability of agreement between diagnosticians. The most common examples are the multitude of professional opinions expressed in evaluating individuals who are on trial for various crimes, and the studies of individuals who are readmitted to hospitals for various mental conditions and are seen by different psychiatrists or psychologists. The diagnostic reliability among professionals in these cases seems to be lacking.

Another consideration is that the individual's ability to change may be affected by the diagnostic labeling process. Clients may be too eager to accept a label as proof of limitations in their psychological structure. Monahan (1977) did an interesting study on the effects of labels on expectations for clients' change and recovery. The use of preliminary labels, such as in a hospital or clinic, may affect the way staff members behave with clients. Monahan used thirty-nine staff members who were given a description of a client and asked to predict (1) the length of stay in the hospital, (2) the chance of readmission, (3) the chances of leading a normal life, and (4) the overall prognosis. The results showed the the staff members who worked in acute treatment areas were significantly negatively affected by the diagnosis when rendering a prognosis. This evidences one of the hazards in using diagnostic labels and should serve as a caution to those who diagnose.

Some further cautions in diagnosing have been brought about by the modern age of technology. Hersen et al. (1983) indicate that by the beginning of the twenty-first century, many mental health professionals will have computers in their offices to perform billing, record keeping, communication, and other functions—including diagnosing. This modern technology already exists. More and more mental health professionals are using computers for assessment and for record keeping. Some programs already exist to help the professional to make diagnostic decisions based on the DSM-III.

Hersen explains that the major advantage to using a computer for diagnosis is that computers are almost perfectly consistent; when given the same information, the computer program will always formulate the same diagnosis. Human decision makers, on the other hand, lack consistency. The hazard is that computers are not flexible and lack the skills of the trained clinician to make exceptions based upon data that may not be in the computer program. As is the case with computer assessment, the trained mental health professional cannot accept on face value the diagnostic decision made by a computer. It should only be used to help the professional make the decision.

## ASSESSMENT

Assessment has long been a function in the mental health professions. However, there has been a long-running debate among these professionals about its value. Specifically, assessment is more widely used among those in the practice of psychology than among counseling professionals. Many counseling professionals feel that assessment relies too heavily on complex concepts, overlooking a true understanding of the individual. Despite these criticisms, assessment does have a role in the practice of counseling as it exists today, and the following information is provided as an aid in understanding the uses of this tool.

### Purposes

Why do we use assessment as a counseling tool? Assessment can be a positive factor in counseling. Of course, there are specific reasons for assessment—it is not done just for fun or to occupy time. A. D'Augelli, J. D'Augelli, and Danish (1981) suggest that assessment helps address two questions: (1) What is the problem? and (2) Why did the problem occur and what causes the problem to continue?

Certainly few could argue that many clients enter a counseling situation not knowing specifically what the problem is that brought them to counseling. General statements dealing with feelings of anxiety, confused thoughts, or a general depressed mood do not specifically define the problem area. Thus, assessment may help to further clarify for the client the specific nature of the problem.

Hansen et al. (1982) suggest four basic functions of assessment: (1) *Prediction*—Tests can help predict an individual's success or degree of success in a course of study, job, or career; (2) *Diagnosis*—Tests can help both the client and the professional gain insight into strengths and weaknesses; (3) *Monitoring*—Tests can serve a useful function of monitoring the progress, or lack of progress, the client is making; and (4) *Evaluation*—Tests can be used to evaluate the client's growth, the counselor's success, or the achievement of certain goals.

Sundberg et al. (1983) discuss three important functions of assessment. The first is decision making, which usually takes place during the initial contacts with the client. Decisions have to be made regarding whether the counselor can work with the client, or whether an appropriate referral should be made.

The second function of assessment in this framework is image forming. The counselor and all who are involved with the client need a working image of the person seeking assistance. As Sundberg points out, dangers exist here, and the clinician must always attempt to keep the working image tentative and open to modification.

The third factor, that of hypothesis checking, basically refers to the checking and rechecking by the clinician of tentative informed guesses or diagnoses in an attempt to confirm or disconfirm them. Checking also keeps the other two functions in perspective so that quick decisions and distorted images are prevented.

Assessment has distinct purposes and functions. It is not an all-inclusive tool, but is merely one aid in the professional's repertoire of skills. A look now at specific types of assessment should prove useful to further understanding the benefits of assessment.

### Types

There are basically two categories of assessment—testing and nontesting. Within each are many techniques, and all can be useful to the professional in counseling. The relative value of one technique or test over another depends in part on the situation, the specific client and her needs, and the training and skill level of the professional.

*Nontesting*    This type of testing refers to the use of techniques that do not involve standard psychological tests. Most of these techniques have been used for years by counselors and other mental health professionals; in most cases, they have preceded the development of standardized formal testing.

Belkin (1981) discusses the use of some nontest forms of assessment. *Observation*, he reports, is the basis of all science. From the psychologist's studying animals in the laboratory to the counselor's observing a student's behavior in the classroom, observation has long been one of the most useful clinical techniques. The problem with observation is the potential for subjective biases and poor insight, which may prevent an accurate evaluation.

Belkin further lists *anecdotal records*—the recording of observations—as a form of nontest assessment. He sees the anecdotal record as playing a positive role in the counseling process by providing the counselor with a developmental and longitudinal portrait of the client.

The *cumulative record* is another technique Belkin discusses. He describes it as a progressive, coordinated record. Certainly this information can be valuable to the counselor not only as factual data but also for predictive purposes.

Other techniques described by Belkin are the *autobiography*, which gives the counselor insight into the clients' self-perceptions, and *rating scales*, which are used to quantify and categorize the client according to the rating categories.

Perhaps the most important nontest assessment technique is the *diagnostic interview*. The diagnostic interview is the first and most important skill that the new clinician must learn (Sundberg et al., 1983). Hersen et al. (1983) describe the diagnostic interview as the cornerstone of psychodiagnosis. Methods of conducting the interview vary widely from informal to formal structured situations. The diagnostic interview relies heavily on the skill of the professional. A skilled professional can obtain essential information from this technique. The *Psychiatric Diagnostic Interview (PDI)* (1981) published by Western Psychological Services is an excellent example of a structured diagnostic interview.

***Testing***   The majority of assessment techniques fall into the category of testing. Sundberg et al. (1983) define a test as a method for acquiring a sample of a person's behavior in a standard situation.

There are many types of tests, some of which will be discussed shortly. In fact, the *Eighth Mental Measurements Yearbook* (Buros, 1978) reviews some 1184 tests. It is somewhat overwhelming to look at the number of tests available to mental health professionals. Deciding which test or tests to use requires an assessment of validity and reliability, two important constructs in the field of test development.

VALIDITY   Validity refers to whether the test accurately measures what it purports to measure. To what extent does a personality test really measure personality? Sundberg et al. (1983) lists four kinds of validity.

1) Concurrent Validity—correlating scores with outcomes on other tests or current real life conditions
2) Predictive Validity—correlating scores with outcomes on later achievements
3) Content Validity—Analyzing the nature and sampling of items in the test
4) Construct Validity—Ascertaining how scores link up with many variables that theory suggests should be related to them.

Validity is an important factor to consider in choosing a test and having faith in the ability to relate valid results to the client.

RELIABILITY    Reliability refers to the ability of the test to produce the same or similar results again and again. Correlations help determine whether tests are reliable. Tests can be given to subjects on two separate occasions and a correlation run to check for reliability.

It is important to choose a test with a high degree of reliability to be certain that the test is measuring the same concept each time. The higher the correlation coefficient in reliability, the better the test.

## TYPES OF TESTS

There are many tests available to counseling professionals. These tests measure different concepts and therefore can be divided into several categories. Belkin (1981) divides tests into the following categories:

1. Achievement Tests—basically measure what a person has learned
2. Aptitude Tests—are used to measure a person's potential in a particular area
3. Interest Inventories—are used to help individuals make career decisions
4. Intelligence Tests—are used to measure the general aptitude for intellectual performance, known as IQ
5. Personality Tests—are used to formulate the absence or presence of psychopathology and to determine personality characteristics.

Most authors seem to agree with this classification of tests. Within these categories there are many individual and group instruments to measure a specific construct. A closer look at some of the more popular test instruments may give the reader insight into what is available and what is currently being used by practitioners.

### Intelligence Tests

Intelligence tests can be administered to individuals or to groups. By far, group testing has been used most commonly by the school systems. In terms of individual instruments, the two most widely used are the Stanford-Binet, which was adapted by Dr. Lewis Terman in 1916 from a version developed in France by Alfred Binet and Theodore Simon, and the Wechsler series of tests, developed by David Wechsler. This series consists of the Wechsler Pre-School and Primary Scale of Intelligence (WPPSI), the Wechsler Intelligence Scale for Children-Revised (WISC-R), and the Wechsler Adult Intelligence Scale-Revised (WAIS-R). The different versions are available for different age groups. The Wechsler series of tests has been more widely used in recent years and are considered to be the most sophisticated measure of intelligence available today. Unlike the Stanford-Binet, the Wechsler series gives scores of intelligence in verbal, performance, and full-scale measures.

Group intelligence testing is not regarded as an equal to individual testing because valuable clinical information is lost in group administration. With an individual-

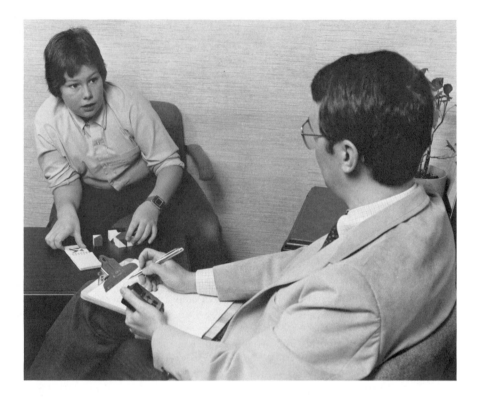

**Figure 13-1** Individualized intelligence testing provides essential clinical data
(Color Image, Inc., Jim Trotter)

ly administered intelligence test, the clinician gains valuable information from observing how the individual performs while taking the test.

Group testing today is mostly confined to large organizations such as schools. Two frequently used group tests are the Otis-Lennon Mental Ability Test and the California Test of Mental Maturity.

### Achievement Tests

Achievement tests have been widely used by our educational systems for years. Even the advanced sections of the Graduate Record Examination (GRE) are measures of what one has learned. Some popular achievement tests include the Iowa Tests of Basic Skills and the Wide Range Achievement Test. Achievement testing may be seen as more the function of a counselor in a school setting than the function of one in a mental-health setting, although many professionals in private practice do include some type of achievement test in a standard battery of psychological tests. Today many school psychologists compare achievement test scores to intelligence test scores as a tool in assessing learning disabilities.

## Aptitude Tests

The focus of aptitude tests is on potential, not on what has been learned. Aptitude tests are used to predict potential success. The verbal and quantitative parts of the Graduate Record Examination are one such type of aptitude test. Another type of aptitude test that is used by many counselors and psychologists is the Differential Aptitude Test (DAT).

## Interest Inventories

Interest inventories, such as the Career Assessment Inventory, the Strong-Campbell Interest Inventory, and the Kuder Preference Record, usually are designed to put the client in a position of having to make a formal choice of items. The way the client responds, and the pattern of responses, gives an indication of the type of occupation in which the client would be successful. Of course, as with many psychological tests, the data obtained is only as good as the client's honesty in answering the questions.

## Personality Tests

Personality testing seems more identified with the mental health profession than any other type of testing. There are a wide variety and a large volume of personality tests from which to choose. We can categorize personality tests into two subcategories, objective and projective.

The most widely used objective measure of personality assessment is the Minnesota Multiphasic Personality Inventory (MMPI). The MMPI was developed in the late 1930s by Hathaway and McKinley, who were working on a set of personality scales. The current version of the MMPI consists of 550 true or false items which reveal scores based on the following scales: L (Lie Scale), F (Fake Bad Scale), K (Subtle Defensiveness), Hs (Hypochrondriasis), D (Depression), Hy (Hysteria), Pd (Psychopathic Deviate), MF (Masculinity-Feminity), Pa (Paranoia), Pt (Psychasthenia), Sc (Schizophrenia), Ma (Mania), and Si (Social Introversion-Extroversion). Years of research and work have been done on and with the MMPI, yielding many additional scoring scales. This, combined with the ease of administration and scoring, makes the MMPI one of the most significant and respected objective measures of personality.

Of course there are many other objective measures of personality; they are too numerous to mention here. Two of the most widely used are the California Psychological Inventory (CPI) and the Sixteen Personality Factors Questionnaire (16PF). New tests are always being developed and must undergo rigid clinical trials before being accepted.

The other type of personality testing is projective assessment. These types of assessment usually require that the clinician have more formal training and experience in order to derive clinical judgments from them. Projective techniques require a client to project his own perceptions onto stimuli that are ambiguous, such as inkblots or making up stories from pictures.

The most commonly used projective techniques are the Rorschach, the Thematic Apperception Test (TAT), the Draw-A-Person or House-Tree-Person tests, and the various forms of sentence completion tests (Sundberg et al., 1983).

The Rorschach technique was developed by Hermann Rorschach, a Swiss psychiatrist, in 1921 (Klopfer & Davidson, 1962). Probably more than any other projective technique, the Rorschach has been used both by researchers and practitioners, and today there are a variety of scoring systems and interpretation systems available for use.

Levitt (1980) describes the widespread use of the Rorschach as following the trend of most projective techniques—it has had its ups and downs. He describes the period from 1960 to 1970 as one of disenchantment with psychological testing, and particularly with the projective techniques, including the Rorschach. Today, however, the Rorschach and other projective techniques have regained a high degree of use in clinical practice. Numerous workshops are offered around the country on the administration, scoring, and interpretation of the Rorschach and other instruments.

The TAT, another popular projective instrument, was developed around 1935 by Morgan and Murray. Today much research and many articles have been written about the TAT. The basic premise is that the client is given a series of pictures to look at and is asked to formulate a story based upon what is happening in the picture, who the characters are, and what the outcome of the situation will be. The individual must rely on her own perceptions and personality structure to formulate a story based on an ambiguous picture.

There are many other forms of projective techniques that utilize such activities as drawing and sentence completion. There are also many critics of projective techniques who base their criticisms on the vagueness and complexity of interpretation of these instruments. The question of lack of reliability and validity of the instruments also presents problems for some clinicians. Taken in conjunction with other measures of personality and with clinical observation, projective techniques can offer the clinician additional information to use in assessment.

### Computerized Testing

With the availability and decline in price of the small office computer, there has been a rapid growth in the use of computers among mental health professionals. Office management systems, billing systems, and word processing are just a few of the popular uses that clinicians find for their computers. But perhaps most importantly, the computer for the counselor, psychologist, and psychiatrist can serve the function of administering, scoring, and interpreting the many clinical instruments that are now available for the office microcomputer and that once required processing by larger computer test-scoring services.

Turkington (1984) discusses some advantages and disadvantages of computerized assessment. For example, test scores are available faster—within minutes rather

**Figure 13-2**   Computerized testing is expedient for the counselor and fun for the client
(Color Image Inc., Jim Trotter)

than within the days or weeks needed for the scores to return from a test-scoring service. Other advantages are that computerized testing in the office can be less expensive, and clients seem to like it better because they feel less intimidated by the computer than traditional testing procedures.

There are both simple and sophisticated systems. Several companies sell complete programs including the computer terminals and testing software. Or the practitioner can purchase a microcomputer and then choose various kinds of programs that best suit his needs. Most software companies that sell psychological test programs for computers have standardized the programs for the most popular computers, such as the Apple and the IBM PC. Such programs may include WISC-R and WAIS-R interpretations, MMPI scoring and interpretations, Beck Depression Inventory, Bender-Gestalt interpretations, vocational assessment techniques, and many others. Even Rorschach interpretive programs are available.

Of course in many cases, such as with the WISC-R, the WAIS-R, and the Rorschach, the computer does not actually administer the test. Administration still requires a skilled examiner. But it can provide some consistency in interpretation, especially if the examiner gives a large number of tests.

There are disadvantages and dangers to be considered with computerized assessment. Many psychologists question the accuracy of the interpretations made by computerized assessment. If the tests are carried out by a well-trained clinician, the results can be useful. But there seems to be a fear that many of these instruments may be used by individuals who are not well trained, especially since there are so many companies now selling these products. Most reputable testing companies will only sell to qualified individuals. Usually only licensed psychologists or those showing evidence of advanced training in testing courses at the graduate level are considered qualified. Many companies require the potential purchaser to complete a qualifications form. Not all companies require this, however, and there is no law mandating it.

Turkington further points out that as the use of computerized assessment grows, guidelines will need to be developed to protect the public from inadequate users of this form of testing. The Colorado Psychological Association in 1982 developed such guidelines, and two committees of the American Psychological Association are currently working on similar guidelines for their membership.

In the hands of a well-qualified mental health professional, computerized assessment can be a valuable tool. However, the clinician should not accept and feed back the results verbatim from the computer. Skilled judgment in reviewing the results should always be the rule.

## COMMUNICATING RESULTS

Perhaps as important as obtaining test data is interpreting or presenting the findings of such data to various individuals. Whether the results are reported to the client, teachers, other counselors, or psychologists and other professionals, the responsibility of presenting accurate and understandable information is crucial.

As Hansen et al. (1982) indicate, counselors sometimes face a dilemma when presenting test results. The task can be a pleasant one if the client has scored well and has shown no significant problem areas, but counselors must avoid displaying a negative reaction to the test results if they are not pleasant, since this attitude can easily be detected by the client. Objectivity is the key element to maintain.

Some types of test information are easier to interpret to clients than others. Achievement, aptitude, and interest tests are less threatening than intelligence and personality tests. Many clinicians would argue that there are inherent dangers in giving clients too much information, especially if there are severe psychopathological problems present. Sometimes these interpretations are best left among professionals; they may be too complex for the client to comprehend.

Keeping the information to be communicated simple and free of technical jargon appears to be a rule agreed upon by many professionals. Parents sitting in on a conference during which test results concerning their child or adolescent are presented are sometimes overwhelmed by the technical nature of the discussion. They often leave such a conference wondering if they really understood what had taken place. It is the responsibility of the examiner to be able to convey the results to persons with any and all levels of expertise. The counselor or clinician faces a great responsibility in providing not only an expertise in assessing but also an expertise in interpreting and communicating assessment results.

## SUMMARY

This chapter has focused on two issues of vital importance in counseling today. Diagnosis, although not a new tool in the mental health professions, will be a new and challenging tool for many counseling professionals. Although many counselors have used informal diagnosis, the trend is toward using more specific and detailed approaches that will be required as counselors take on new roles outside the school environment.

Assessment, the other issue featured in this chapter, is more familiar to counselors. Counselors have used assessment for years, but modern trends and concepts have brought new importance to this area. The need for better and more accurate assessment is indicated, and new advances with the use of computers have made assessment easier, more accurate, and more useful.

## REFERENCES

AMERICAN PSYCHIATRIC ASSOCIATION. (1980). *Diagnostic and statistical manual of mental disorders* (3rd ed.). Washington, D.C.: Author.

BELKIN, G.S. (1981). *Practical counseling in the schools.* Dubuque, Iowa: Wm. C. Brown.

BUROS, O.K. (1978). *Eighth mental measurements yearbook.* New Jersey: Gryphon Press.

D'AUGELLI, A.R., D'AUGELLI, J.F., and DANISH, S.J. (1981). *Helping others.* California: Brooks/Cole.

HANSEN, J.C., STEVIC, R.R., and WARNER, R.W., Jr. (1982). *Counseling: Theory and process* (3rd ed.). Boston: Allyn & Bacon.

HERSEN, M., KAZDIN, A., and BELLACK, A.S. (1983). *The clinical psychology handbook.* New York: Pergamon Press.

KLOPFER, B., and DAVIDSON, H.H. (1962). *The Rorschach technique: An introductory manual.* New York: Harcourt Brace Jovanovich, Inc.

LEVITT, E.E. (1980). *Primer on the Rorschach technique: A method of administration, scoring, and interpretation.* Springfield, Ill.: Charles C. Thomas.

LEVY, R. (1982). *The new language of psychiatry: Learning and using DSM-III.* Boston: Little, Brown.

MONAHAN, L. (1977). Diagnosis and expectations for change: An inverse relationship? *Journal of Nervous and Mental Disease, 164,* 214–217.

SELIGMAN, L. (1983). An introduction to the new DSM-III. *The Personnel and Guidance Journal, 61,* 601–605.

SPITZER, R.L., SKODOL, A.E., GIBBON, M., and WILLIAMS, J.B.W., *DSM-III Case Book*, 1981, American Psychiatric Assoc. Washington, D.C.

SUNDBERG, N.D., TAPLIN, J.R., and TYLER, L.E. (1983). *Introduction to clinical psychology.* Englewood Cliffs, N.J.: Prentice-Hall.

TURKINGTON, C. (1984). The growing use, and abuse of computer testing. *APA Monitor, 15,* 7 & 26.

WEBB, L.J., DICLEMENTE, C.C., JOHNSTONE, E.E., SANDERS, J.L., and PERLEY, R.A. (1981). *DSM-III Training Guide.* New York, N.Y.: Brunner-Mazel.

WEINER, I. B. (1959). The role of diagnosis in a university counseling center. *Journal of Counseling Psychology, 6,* 110–115.

# 14

# CHANGING ROLE OF THE COUNSELOR: COUNSELOR AS CONSULTANT

234

How can the role of the counselor change to meet the needs of the population he serves? Can counseling survive as a profession? Are there new, untapped settings in which counseling skills will be applicable? These are important questions which have no simple answers.

Counselors have defined their major role responsibility as counseling with individuals and in groups. In other words, counselors have been primarily concerned with remediation of personal, emotional, and psychological problems. This remedial approach to helping has been criticized as dealing primarily with the casualties of our society rather than attempting to change those institutions, organizations, systems, and communities that contribute to individual problems. Thus, counselors have encouraged clients to adjust and adapt to their environments rather than to work systematically to change them.

A more broadly defined role seems essential for counselors of the future. The remedial approach is receiving much criticism in the literature (Bradley, 1978; Egan & Cowan, 1979). Strong arguments are being made for counselors to define their roles with greater emphasis on the prevention of problems. Counselors are being encouraged to get out of their offices and assume a more active role in influencing environments. This emphasis on prevention and outreach is appropriate for counselors in settings ranging from mental health centers to schools. In this chapter we will explore the need for counselors to maximize the services they provide by expanding their consulting function. The consultant role gives counselors an opportunity to influence environments and work toward prevention of problems.

## COUNSELOR AS CONSULTANT

The counselor's role as a consultant to organizations and individuals has been widely discussed in literature during the past ten years (Aubrey, 1978; Berdie, 1972; Blocher, Dustin, & Dugan, 1971; Carkhuff, 1972; Dinkmeyer & Carlson, 1977; Egan & Cowan, 1979; Fullmer & Bernard, 1972; Kurpius, 1978; Kurpius & Brubaker, 1976; Kurpius & Robinson, 1978; and Walz & Benjamin, 1978). These authors and many others (Lewis & Lewis, 1977) have asserted that the effective counselors of the future will be prepared to expand their expertise and provide service as consultants so that they can effect institutional change as well as individual client growth. In fact, Gibson (1978) in his report of the results of a comprehensive study on guidance programs predicts that the school counselors of the future will function more as consultants and less in an administrative role. Fundamental to this emphasis on a consulting role is an assumption that clients must not continuously be expected to adjust to their environments but rather that the environment should be changed to facilitate client growth.

## Consultation Defined

Lippitt (1959) has defined consultation to be

a voluntary relationship between a professional helper (consultant) and a help-needing system (client) in which the consultant is attempting to give help to the client in the solving of some current or potential problem, and the relationship is perceived as temporary by both parties. Also, the consultant is an "outsider," i.e., is not a part of any hierarchial power system in which the client is located. (p. 5)

In the above definition *client* refers to any functioning social unit such as a "family, industrial organization, individual, committee, staff, membership association, governmental department, delinquent gang, or hospital staff" (p. 5). The *professional helper* would typically include persons functioning in such occupations as marriage counselors, management consultants, ministers, social workers, psychiatrists, and psychologists. It is possible for the "outsider" role to be performed by someone inside the system (Lippitt, 1959). A counselor in a school, for example, might take on the consultant role. Dinkmeyer and Carlson (1973) describe the consultant's role in the school as a collaborative relationship through which significant others in the child's life, including administrators, teachers and parents, communicate about the student.

As noted by Lippitt, the consulting relationship is appropriate in a variety of settings, with the stipulation that the client is a functioning social unit. Thus, counselors might seek consultation work not only in the schools but also in community agencies and in business and industry. The applicability of the counseling/consulting relationship in these other settings broadens the scope of employment opportunities for counselors and also points to the necessity for training in consultation skills in graduate counselor education programs.

## Consultant Roles

Kurpius and Robinson (1978) note that consultants may assume a variety of roles because of the variety of purposes of consulting activity. Consultant roles are frequently delineated according to the particular model of consultation followed. Four broad consultant roles have been identified (Kurpius & Robinson, 1978) and are briefly outlined here.

*Trainer/Educator*   Under some circumstances the consultant may be hired to teach the staff a set of skills. For example, a school district might employ a counselor-educator to train its teachers in basic communication skills; a corporation might hire a consultant to teach its managers performance appraisal skills.

*Expert/Prescriptive*   In this approach to consultation the consultee buys the expertise of the consultant. The relationship resembles that of the medical model in that the consultant diagnoses the problem and prescribes a solution.

*Negotiator*    When a client system is experiencing difficulty, a consultant may be hired to mediate the conflict between parties. In this instance, the consultant works as a facilitator of communication and gives the system objective feedback regarding the processes that are blocking change.

*Collaborator*    The consultant may choose to form egalitarian relationships with consultees, resulting in joint diagnosis with the consultant working as a facilitator in the problem-solving process. This collaborative relationship has the advantage of teaching clients methods for solving their own problems. In the collaborative model the consultant must possess good relationship skills.

## Consultant Skills

Many writers have discussed the skills and qualities that characterize an effective consultant. Dinkmeyer and Carlson have suggested the following counselor competencies:

1.  He must be empathic and be able to understand how others feel and experience their world.
2.  He must be able to relate to children and adults in a purposeful manner. While he should be effective in developing rapport and working relationships, he must be judicious in the use of this time. This necessitates the capacity to establish relationships with his clientele which are in line with the purposes of this program.
3.  He must be sensitive to human needs. He would understand Maslow's hierarchy of needs, but more than that, it is vital that he be able to perceive a need and be available as a facilitator to help the person meet that need.
4.  He must be aware of psychological dynamics, motivations, and purpose of human behavior. His training qualifies him not only to talk about psychological dynamics, but actually to deal with them in the here and now.
5.  He must be perceptive of group dynamics and its significance for the educational establishment. This suggests that he is aware of the impact of group forces upon the teacher, that he sees the teacher in the context of forces from *without* (such as administration and parents) and forces from *within* (such as his own goals and purposes).
6.  He must be capable of establishing relationships which are characterized by mutual trust and mutual respect. His appearance as a consultant to either a group or an individual should inspire confidence. His personal approach to people should make it apparent that they are collaborators with him.
7.  He must be personally free from anxiety to the extent that he is capable of taking a risk on an important issue. He must be able to take a stand on significant issues that affect human development. The consultant's role requires a courageous approach to life. He has the courage to be imperfect, recognizing that he will make mistakes, but realizing mistakes are learning experiences and he must not be immobilized by the fear of making one. This courage is developed through group experiences and in the supervised practical experience.
8.  Perhaps the most important of all, assuming he is able to establish the necessary and sufficient conditions for a helping relationship, the consultant should be creative, spontaneous, and imaginative. The consultant position, by its very nature, demands flexibility and the ability to deal with a variety of expectations—on one hand, the principal's

need for order and structure; on the other, the child's need for participation, care, and concern. Thus, the consultant will find his creativity continuously challenged.

9. He should be capable of inspiring leadership at a number of levels from educational administrators who look to him as a specialist in understanding human relations and human behavior to parents who see him as a specialist in child psychology. Teachers would see him as a resource in connection with pupil personnel problems. He would be available to children who see him as a resource in helping them to understand self and others. (1973, pp. 24–25)

The above competencies, while written for use in an educational environment, are appropriate for consultants in all settings. These nine competencies emphasize relationship building and counseling/communication skills which are essential to the consultant role.

Problem assessment skills are also fundamental in the counseling/consulting role. Consultants should be able to identify the focal issue in a given situation. Blake and Mouton (1978) state that the focal issue is that aspect of a situation which is causing the client difficulty. Blake and Mouton further suggest four basic focal issues: (1) the exercise of power and authority, (2) morale and cohesion, (3) problems that arise from standards or norms of conduct, and (4) issues in the area of goals and objectives. In assessing the consultee's problem, the consultant may discover that any one of the above issues or a combination of them could be the source of the problem. The ability to accurately assess the client problem and prescribe an appropriate intervention may be the determinant of consultant effectiveness (Blake & Mouton, 1978).

Bargaining, negotiating, and mediating abilities are basic consulting skills since the consulting role may require the consultant to negotiate conflicts or to use problem-solving methods in a small-group situation (Kurpius & Robinson, 1978).

As a trainer/educator the consultant must possess effective human relations skills. She should be able to teach communication skills and organize and plan workshop activities. Perhaps most important, the trainer/educator should understand group dynamics and small-group process. The consultant/trainer must not only understand a wide range of skills but must also be able to teach these skills to others. The literature has emphasized the necessity for counselors to "give away" their skills. The trainer role is therefore essential in the consultant's skill development process.

### The Consulting Process

As a consultant enters into a relationship with a client, group, or institution, the consulting process should be organized around recognizable stages or phases. All consultants will not organize their work in an identical fashion; however, their approaches will have some similarities. Here we will examine some approaches that describe the phases and stages of the consulting process.

In a comparative study of approaches used by consultants, Lippitt, Watson, and Westley (1958) identified a seven-phase process that consultants used with some consistency.

1. A need for change is developed.
2. A consulting relationship is established.
3. The problem of the consultee is clarified.
4. Alternative goals and solutions are examined.
5. Intentions are translated into actual change efforts.
6. A new level of functioning or group structure is generalized and stabilized.
7. A terminal relationship with the consultant is achieved as is some continuity of change-ability.

Kurpius (1978) suggests the following nine-stage consulting process: (1) pre-entry, (2) entry, (3) information gathering, (4) problem definition, (5) identifying and selecting alternative solutions, (6) stating objectives, (7) implementation, (8) evaluation, and (9) termination (p. 337).

PREENTRY   Prior to engaging in a consulting relationship, consultants must make a careful self-assessment to determine their beliefs, values, needs, assumptions, practices, and skills that are related to the problem-solving process for clients and organizations. Questions consultants should ask themselves at this stage include the following:

(a) What assumptions do I hold for people, e.g., their worth, position, authority, power, competencies?
(b) What assumptions do I hold about organizations, e.g., purpose, structure, operational methods, and usage of reward and punishment?
(c) What conceptual definition do I operate from when doing consultation . . .? (Kurpius, 1978, p. 337)

ENTRY   As the consultant enters the relationship the roles and ground rules must be defined and established; a contract that includes a statement of the presenting problem should be signed.

GATHERING INFORMATION   The consultant gathers additional information as an aid to clarifying the presenting problem. As it becomes more clearly defined, the presenting problem often turns out to be a symptom of the real problem. Consultants should take the necessary steps to insure that the information gathered is objective. Information-gathering methods include: "listening, observing, questionnaires, standardized records, interviews, or group meetings" (p. 337).

PROBLEM DEFINITION   At this stage information is assessed and the problem statement is translated into a goal statement, which should be presented in writing and agreed upon by both the consultant and the consultee.

IDENTIFYING AND SELECTING ALTERNATIVE SOLUTIONS   A solution to the problem is sought based on an analysis and synthesis of the information. The process of problem solving may be facilitated through brainstorming and the ordering of priorities.

STATING OBJECTIVES Objectives that can be accomplished and measured within a stated period of time under a given set of conditions must often be clearly stated when the problem is complex and involves many people.

IMPLEMENTATION This stage is based on all of the preceding steps and is the first direct action that is initiated in the problem-solving process.

EVALUATION This includes both the monitoring of the activities undertaken to solve the problem and a measurement of the final outcome.

TERMINATION At this stage the consultant and consultee agree to discontinue direct contact. Decisions at this stage include a determination of whether or not the objectives have been met and to what degree and then what action is to follow—redesign and reimplement or completely terminate.

## PRIMARY PREVENTION

The need for preventive approaches in mental health has received attention in counseling literature. Two special issues of the *Personnel and Guidance Journal* (April and May, 1984) were devoted to primary prevention in settings ranging from college counseling centers and community agencies to schools. Here we will define primary prevention, examine community- and campus-based prevention models, and outline the counselor's role as a consultant with a primary preventive approach in the educational setting.

### Definition

Primary prevention involves lowering the incidence of psychological/emotional problems of a targeted population while promoting mental health among others not assumed to have any specific problems. It can be contrasted with secondary prevention, or the early identification and treatment of problems, and with tertiary prevention, which attempts to decrease the long-term effects of disabilities (Lewis & Lewis, 1984). Primary prevention may be operationally defined as follows:

1. It must be group—or mass—rather than individually oriented, even though some of its activities may involve individual contacts.
2. It must have a before-the-fact quality, that is, be targeted to groups not yet experiencing significant maladjustment (even though they may, because of their life situations or recent experiences, be at risk for such outcomes).
3. It must be intentional, that is, rest on a solid knowledge base suggesting that the program holds potential either for improving psychological health or for preventing maladaption.
4. School learning problems, and behavior problems that contribute to school learning problems, are also appropriate targets for primary preventive activities (Shaw & Goodyear, 1984, p. 444).

Another definition has been offered by the Task Panel on Prevention, of the President's Commission on Mental Health (1978);

1. Most fundamentally, primary prevention is proactive, in that it seeks to build adaptive strengths, coping resources, and health in people; not to reduce or contain already-manifest deficit.
2. Primary prevention is concerned about total populations, especially including groups at high risk; it is less oriented to individuals and to the provision of services on a case-by-case basis.
3. Primary prevention's main tools and models are those of education and social engineering, not therapy or rehabilitation, although some insights for its model and programs grow out of the wisdom derived from clinical experience.
4. Primary prevention assumes that equipping people with personal and environmental resources for coping is the best of all ways to ward off maladaptive problems, not trying to deal (however skillfully) with problems that have already germinated and flowered. (p. 1833)

Strategies recommended by the Task Panel to accomplish the above include (a) educational programs for the community to build interpersonal competencies, (b) an analysis and modification of social systems which influence development, (c) development of programs which aid victims of life crises so that dangers are minimized and learning opportunities maximized (1978).

### College Campus

An excellent example of primary prevention on the college campus is reported by Drum (1984). The program described is theme oriented and is aimed at reducing the risks associated with the accelerating developmental demands resulting from moving to adulthood and independent living. The four theme programs mentioned are the following: Stress Awareness Week; Transitions: The Challenge of Change; Relationships: One Plus One; and Future Forecast: Examining The Life Ahead. One of these programs, Transitions: The Challenge of Change, is reported in detail and appears to be an outstanding prevention model. The preventive programming described by Drum reflects attention to important principles of design and implementation. Several of these key principles are outlined below:

1. Prevention programs must go beyond informing. They must enable the individual to transform information into a change strategy.
2. The consumers motivation, sense of urgency, and readiness for change must be considered or the effort will fail.
3. The program must be carefully designed with attention given to goals, sequence of activities, exercises, etc.
4. The problems to be focused on must be preventable and the intervention must be well timed.
5. The intervention should target people who are at risk.
6. Participants should be given a sense of hope and movement toward the desired outcome.
7. The interaction between the person and the environment must be given attention.

8. The program should reflect a delicate balance between the challenges to the participant and the supports the participant has to cope with the presented challenges.
9. The program should be evaluated. (Drum, 1984)

The above list is a summary of those presented by Drum. The complete list as discussed by the author is most helpful and should be considered by those planning primary prevention efforts specifically for the college campus, but for other settings as well. Other primary prevention programs for the campus include friendship networks for dormitories (Fondacaro, Heller, & Reilly, 1984) and problem-solving training (Heppner, Neal, & Larson, 1984). The importance of primary prevention programs for the college campus, such as the ones mentioned here, cannot be overemphasized. It seems imperative that college counseling centers balance a remedial approach with strong preventive efforts.

## Community

Cowen (1984) has proposed a general model for primary prevention in mental health settings. He states that primary prevention can be accomplished by either ''(a) providing people with skills, competencies, and conditions that facilitate effective adaptation and ward off psychological problems before they occur; and (b) developing interventions designed to short-circuit negative psychological sequelae for those who have experienced risk-augmenting life situations or stressful life events'' (p. 485).

The five steps of the primary prevention cycle include

1. Identifying the program's *generative base,*
2. Translating that base into *guiding program* concepts,
3. Developing *workable program technology* based on those concepts,
4. *Conducting* the program, and
5. *Evaluating* the program. (p. 485)

The cycle is fully represented in Figure 14–1.

Lewis and Lewis (1984) have reported on several community-based preventive programs, ranging from a play about touching which was developed in Kansas to help prevent child abuse, to Project C.A.N. (Community Action Network) which was developed in Atlanta to help prevent mental health problems resulting from the missing and murdered black children. Other community-based programs reported in the special issue of the *Personnel Guidance Journal* on primary prevention include the Family Development Project, which was designed to have a positive effect on young women in their transition to parenthood (D'Andrea, 1984), and a lay home visitor program for families with newborns (Barquest & Martin, 1984).

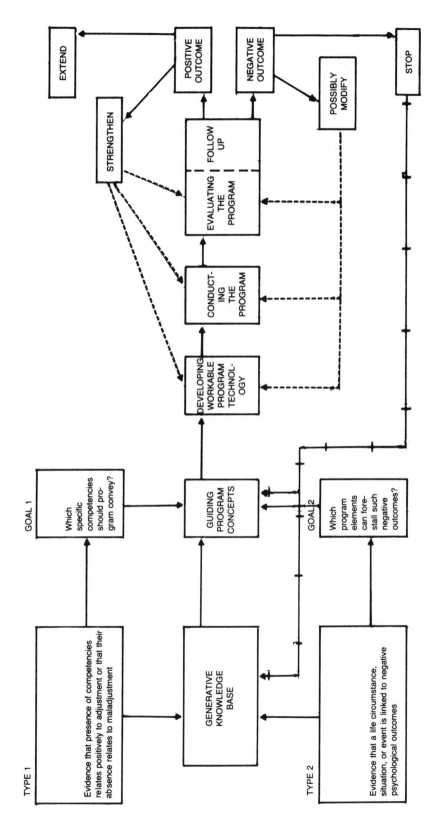

**Figure 14-1** General Structural Model for Primary Prevention Program Development in Mental Health

## CONSULTANT ROLES

The counselor's role as a consultant in the schools was formally acknowledged for the first time in 1966 when the American School Counselor Association (ASCA) and the Association for Counselor Education and Supervision (ACES) specified that counseling, coordination, and consultation should be the three primary role responsibilities of the elementary school counselor (Aubrey, 1972). The consulting role is perhaps more integral to the functioning of the counselor on the elementary level, but it is appropriate for secondary school counselors as well. In this section we will examine specifically the counselor's role as a consultant within the educational setting. First, we will look at methods consultants use in attempting to mobilize change within the school as a system. Second, we will examine the consultant's role with individual teachers and parents. Finally, we will look at methods, or psychological education strategies, that are useful in humanizing classroom environments.

For years, school counselors have spent their time helping students adjust to parents, to teachers, and to the school system itself. Although this approach to school counseling has been useful, in many situations it has fallen short. As noted previously, counselors cannot always expect clients to adjust to unhealthy situations. Counselors must be trained as consultants so that they can function as agents of change. School environments must be improved through changes within the school in general and within the guidance program in particular. This is not a simple task. Counselors are most frequently working for change within their own system, which increases potential roadblocks to their effectiveness. One very difficult roadblock is the counselor's lack of power. Another is the counselor's close identification with existing programs, which makes the image difficult to change (Walz & Benjamin, 1978). However, counselors should develop skills that will allow them to be effective agents of change.

### Change Agent Processes

Walz and Benjamin (1970) have presented a conceptual model of the change agent process that is applicable to the school setting. These steps are presented here as guidelines for counselors who seek to implement change.

ESTABLISH THE NEED FOR CHANGE  This can be done through a needs assessment that communicates the faculty's, parents', or students' reactions to the guidance program. The need for change can also be established by brainstorming ideal programs or by visiting schools with innovative practices.

BUILD INTERACTIVE RELATIONSHIPS  Before the change process can begin, counselors must identify allies in the system who can act as a support group. It is important that the group include people in key positions who have power in the school. Aubrey (1972) recommends that parents be included in the power base.

ASSESS THE SYSTEM  Counselors should assess the system and identify available resources, facilities, and methods of operating. At this stage, the problem must be clearly defined and the desired outcomes for change must be agreed upon.

GENERATE OPTIONS   All possible options for solving the problem should be considered.

DECIDE   Once the possible options have been generated, they must be related to the project goals, and a decision must be made regarding their appropriateness. Factors to be considered in the decision-making process include: goals of the project, comparative costs, accessibility of materials, benefit to the system, amount of training required, and so forth.

FACILITATE ADOPTION AND IMPLEMENTATION   Much work remains once a plan has been put into action. Counselors who have worked as change agents for the plan must monitor the project's acceptance and keep communication lines open so that resistance to the plan can be openly dealt with.

REFINE AND RENEW   Refining a plan is an ongoing activity that helps the plan gain acceptance. The plan is best viewed as an experiment so that people are more patient with any initial rough spots that need additional work.

### Individual Consultation

Another consultant role that counselors in the schools assume is that of individual consultations with significant others in the student's life. Students do not exist in a vacuum; the relationship the counselor establishes with teachers and parents is fundamental to initiating change in the student's functioning (Dinkmeyer, D., Jr. & Dinkmeyer, D., Sr., 1984). This consulting relationship, while similar to the individual counseling relationship, has important differences.

The consulting relationship is perhaps best described as a collaborative relationship in which significant others in the student's life communicate about him. *Collaborative* is a key term; it implies that the counselor and significant others relate to each other as equals. Thus, the counselor does not present herself as an expert who has all of the answers.

The counselor brings to the collaborative consulting relationship all of the components of a helping relationship: empathy, open communication, commitment, and encouragement (Dinkmeyer & Carlson, 1973). Within the context of this relationship the consultant can help consultees explore the dynamics of their relationship with the student in a way that helps ensure that any changes made in the relationship are more than superficial problem solving.

### Consulting with Teachers

As we discuss specifically the counselor's role as a consultant to teachers, the importance of collaboration cannot be overstated. The counselor who assumes the position of expert will eventually run out of solutions to problems and will create more problems as teachers find the ''expert'' advice ineffective. The collaborative relationship circumvents the above difficulties; it utilizes the resources of both parties, and neither individual is expected to have all the answers.

In working with teachers, counselors must first establish who their client is; in most instances, it is the person who presents the problem to the consultant—that is, the teacher (Krumboltz & Thoresen, 1969). Counselors, then, must work with teachers to help them own the problem that they are experiencing with a student and help teachers realize that they can change only their own behavior (Dinkmeyer & Carlson, 1973). This view is, of course, the opposite of that taken by Krumboltz and Thoresen (1969), who would recommend that the teacher work out behavior modification programs to change the students' behavior.

In their discussion of problem ownership, Dinkmeyer and Carlson (1973) emphasize that in stating that the teacher needs to change his behavior, they are not suggesting that the teacher is at fault. They are merely asserting that if the student is to change, the teacher must do some things differently. As the teacher's behavior begins to change, the student's perception of both the teacher and the situation will change. An excerpt from a teacher/consultant interview based on the principles discussed above is presented here.

CONSULTANT: "I'm here to do what I can to help you, Pat. Would you like to tell me about the child you are having a problem with?"

CONSULTEE: "In these past three months I've been doing some observations of him. I'm kind of disappointed because he isn't producing any work that is worthwhile in any way. He is becoming a problem on the playground so that the children are complaining that he always steals their chips."

CONSULTANT: "Could you give me one specific example of misbehavior?"

CONSULTEE: "Well, the children take their snacks out at lunch, and they come in and complain that Douglas stole their Fritos. But it's his paper work that bothers me. He doesn't follow any directions—he just scribbles, and I've mentioned it to him."

CONSULTANT: "Could you give me an example of his paper work?"

CONSULTEE: "It's the regular work we give the children that goes along with the reader. They're supposed to fill in the missing words or do the comprehension and color the pictures. Well, he would just as soon scribble the whole page instead of putting the answers down. They are either incomplete or so poorly printed that I can hardly read it."

CONSULTANT: "How do you feel when this happens? How does it affect you?"

CONSULTEE: "Well, it affects me in that it bothers me that he isn't doing the normal work of a first grader."

CONSULTANT: "When you say it bothers you, could you describe the feeling that you have?"

CONSULTEE: "It's not so much that he as a person bothers me. It bothers me because I feel that he is the loser, not myself."

CONSULTANT: "What do you do in a situation when you feel he is wasting his time?"

CONSULTEE:     "I try to isolate him and put him in a place where I feel he won't have so many distractions. He watches others at their work, and he can tell me what somebody in the back of the room is doing when he is sitting in the front. He is a very lovable child. He just looks at you and you melt; this is how he catches people. His mother says he does only what he wants to do."

CONSULTANT:    "Then, you feel that he gets along socially. He just doesn't act responsible when it comes to performing these certain work tasks that you assign. You mentioned that you have isolated him in certain situations. Has that helped at all?"

CONSULTEE:     "No, not really, because he can divert his own mind even in an isolated situation. He will find someone he can pester in some way."

CONSULTANT:    "Do you feel he is trying to get attention?"

CONSULTEE:     "Oh, definitely. There's no doubt about that at all."

CONSULTANT:    "Have you found other ways to give him attention, or some things that he has done well? Can you think of any situations where you might have given him attention when he wasn't looking for it?"

CONSULTEE:     "I usually praise him for any work he does well."

CONSULTANT:    "I am thinking more of encouraging any positive effort instead of rewarding him for functioning. What about his class participation?"

CONSULTEE:     "He will participate at times, but you always have to initiate his answers. He doesn't volunteer."

CONSULTANT:    "In other words, he finds that he will get more attention from you if he is reticent to speak. This could be another way of attention getting."

CONSULTEE:     "Yes."

CONSULTANT:    "On the playground he does things to get you to notice him so you have to correct him."

CONSULTEE:     "Yes." (Dinkmeyer & Carlson, 1973, p. 181)

## Consulting with Parents

The counselor can counsel individual students about their personal problems and can consult with the student's teacher to improve the classroom environment, but too often all efforts are wasted if a consulting relationship with the student's parents cannot be established. Home environments obviously have a dramatic impact on how students view themselves and their problems.

The relationship a consultant establishes with a parent should resemble the consulting relationship established with a teacher. It should be a collaborative endeavor that mobilizes the resources of both consultant and parent to facilitate the growth and development of the student. Many parents have never had a skillful listener to help them sort through the complex dynamics of parent-child communication; giving them this opportunity can often significantly improve the home situation and thus help the student.

In some schools, counselors have chosen to use group consultation methods with parents. Although it is not always appropriate to deal with parents in groups, the group approach does maximize the use of the counselor's time. Various models for parent consultation in groups have been developed. Tom Gordon's Parent Effectiveness Training (P.E.T., 1970) has been widely used as a communication skills training program for parents. Daniel Fullmer, Virginia Satir, Rudolf Driekurs, and others have developed effective models for working with parents. Because of the importance of family group consultation, counselors are encouraged to become skillful in this area.

### Humanizing Classroom Environments

In an attempt to maximize the service provided to students and to work for the primary prevention of mental health and behavioral difficulties, counselors have expanded their role in the educational setting to include working with teachers to humanize the classroom. Since the overall goal of counseling involves promoting human growth and development (Kohlberg, 1975), this role seems highly appropriate.

The consultant role in this instance requires that counselors give away their skills to teachers. This demystification process has been advocated by many (Ivey & Alschuler, 1973; Miller, 1969; Skovholt, 1977).

The emphasis on dealing with students' feelings within the classroom in an attempt to promote psychological growth and development has been given a variety of labels ranging from confluent education (Brown, 1971) to affective education and deliberate psychological education. Those in the counseling profession have settled on psychological education. In this section we will examine the different methods that counselors functioning in a consultant role to teachers might use to improve classroom environments.

*Psychological Education Strategies*   Several approaches to psychological education are currently in use in the schools.

ADOPTING AN AFFECTIVE CURRICULUM   The first approach, typically used at the elementary level, involves teachers adopting an affective curriculum. These curricula are designed to be used on a daily basis in the classroom. Two widely used curricula are briefly described below.

"Magic Circle" was developed by the Human Development Training Institute (1967). Magic Circle is a relatively structured small-group technique that teachers can use on a daily basis with a class. Magic Circle is based on the three themes of mastery, awareness, and social interaction. Teachers are instructed in methods of running these small-group discussions, which help students become aware of their feelings. Each small-group discussion is based on a topic, and the topics are sequentially introduced.

"Developing Understanding of Self and Others" (DUSO), developed by Dinkmeyer (1970), is a set of multimedia materials designed to help students deal with development problems. With DUSO, puppetry, music, open-ended stories, and problem situations are used by the teacher or counselor in classroom discussions. The curriculum focuses on positive self-concept development (Dinkmeyer & Carlson, 1973).

Counselors can do much to encourage the adoption and implementation of materials such as those listed above. Some counselors initiate the use of affective curriculums by spending time in various classrooms introducing the materials and modeling their effective use for the classroom teacher. This procedure is recommended since it exerts some quality control over the procedures. Counselors may also choose to conduct workshops for teachers wishing to implement an affective curriculum in their class.

TEACHING A CLASS WITH PSYCHOLOGICAL CONTENT    The types of classes taught in this approach may range from psychology courses for students at the high school level to values clarification classes at either the elementary or secondary level. In the Values Clarification approach developed by Simon, Howe, and Kirschenbaum (1972), teachers help students explore their values through a series of activities that are intended to create dissonant situations. These institutions help students to organize and clarify their own values.

BRINGING FEELINGS INTO REGULAR CLASSROOM DISCUSSIONS    Counselors can help teachers explore methods of integrating students' feelings into regular classroom discussions. For example, in a discussion of heart transplants, students could be encouraged to discuss the values involved in transplanting one person's heart into another person's body; in a history lesson on the Pilgrims, students could explore issues regarding prejudice and discrimination and then discuss times when they have been treated unfairly.

HUMAN RELATIONS TRAINING FOR TEACHERS    On a broader level, counselors can conduct in-service training for teachers to teach them basic communication skills that will improve all their interactions with students. Tom Gordon's T.E.T., Teacher Effectiveness Training (1974), is one useful model for examining the teacher-student relationship. As part of the human relations skills training, counselors might also develop in-service training in preventive behavior management, student motivation, and self-concept development.

The counselor's consulting role with teachers to improve and humanize classroom environments cannot be overemphasized. Psychological education brings school counselors out of their offices, gives them visibility with students, demonstrates to teachers that counselors can help them, and thus improves the counselor's image and interaction with teachers. Most important, the counselor's consulting role with teachers in the classroom maximizes the services they are providing to students and emphasizes a preventive/developmental approach to student problems.

## CONSULTANT ROLE IN NEW SETTINGS

Decreased school enrollments and cutbacks in educational financing are forcing many in the field of education to seek new settings in which to apply their skills (Doll, 1980; Corrigan, 1980; Smith, 1980). Counselors looking beyond the traditional avenue of educational employment have typically chosen work settings such as community mental health clinics, child abuse agencies, and other service agencies that are already flooded with social workers and psychologists (Cristiani & Cristiani, 1979). Counselors must seek new, untapped settings in which to apply their skills. In this chapter we have discussed the need for counselors to develop consulting skills that allow them to take an active role in changing environments.

Counselors in community mental health have developed outreach and prevention activities as have counselors in college and university counseling centers, and in public and private K–12 educational institutions. These consulting skills, long a part of many counseling activities in traditional settings, can open the door to a wide range of job opportunities in nontraditional settings. In this section we will examine new skill applications for counseling skills in nontraditional settings, including business and industry and physical health. In so doing, we hope to encourage counselors of the future to define counseling more broadly and to share their skills to improve the quality of life for many more individuals.

### Business and Industry

Cristiani and Cristiani (1979) have suggested that although only a minimal number of counselors are actually employed by business and industry, counselors have many skills that can benefit the business and industrial community. The contention that counseling/consulting skills are applicable in this nontraditional setting has been supported by responses to a 1978 survey conducted by the American Society for Training and Development (ASTD). In tabulating responses from 2,790 ASTD members regarding the most important skill or knowledge requirements for training and development professionals, a majority of members (60.5 percent) indicated human relations skills and communication skills to be the most important skill or knowledge requirements: human relations skills received 35.1 percent and communications skills received 25.4 percent. Knowledge of the training and development field ranked third with 13.9 percent (Clement, Walker, & Pinto, 1979). Many in the business and industrial communities have argued that background and experience in business is essential and is, in fact, the most important prerequisite to a job in training and development. The above statistics would seem to indicate, however, that this traditional view may not necessarily be accurate; it may instead reflect a bias against education. In this section we will examine the application of counseling skills in the business and industrial setting.

*Training and Development* Many counselors are not aware of how much money most companies spend to train their managers and sales people in basic human relations skills. While the training and development function in business and industry includes a wide range of educative functions, management development is a major focus. The intent of management training is to improve the relationship between superiors and subordinates by giving managers training in such counseling or communication skills as open-ended leads, summary statements, and empathic responses. These skills, along with training in performance appraisal and coaching and counseling, are taught through programs employing methodologies familiar to counselors: team building, structured group experiences, behavior rehearsal, modifications of interpersonal process recall (Kagan, Krathwohl, & Farquhar, 1965), and microcounseling (Ivey, 1971; Cristiani & Cristiani, 1979).

The skills that are basic to the job responsibilities in the training and development area in business and industry are skills that counselors possess. Counselors who have developed effective consultation skills and are skillful in the specific trainer/educator role described earlier in this chapter will find a wide range of job opportunities in the training and develoment programs in business and industry if they are tenacious and convincing with their potential employers.

*Direct Counseling Services*    The need for direct counseling and psychological services for employees in business and industry seems to be increasing, though the area still does not offer as many opportunities for employment as the training and development area. The impact of corporate stress on managers is currently receiving a great deal of attention as corporations begin to realize its direct cost in terms of on-the-job performance. The impact of stress on employees creates other problems: alcoholism, drug addiction, marital and family problems, and emotional problems (Smith, Piercy, & Lutz, 1982). Some companies are responding by making gym facilities available to employees during the day to work off tensions; others are offering weekend growth seminars on coping with stress, marriage, and personal crises. Still others are offering direct counseling services. These counseling services are often called Employee Assistance Programs (EAPs). These programs, which initially focused on alcohol treatment, have grown rapidly in the past ten years and have broadened their focus to include employees whose problems range from marital and family problems to depression, stress, anxiety, or even financial management (Forrest, 1983). Due to the rapid growth of these programs, as well as to their expanded focus, ''EAPs should provide a fruitful potential market for counselors over the next ten years'' (Forrest, 1983, p. 106).

Counselors obviously have the skills to provide direct counseling services for corporations. The job market, which currently seems to be monopolized by psychologists, is open to counselors who can market their skills and publicize their expertise to gain credibility with decision makers in the business community (Cristiani & Cristiani, 1979).

In conclusion, business and industry remains a major untapped setting for counselors. Counselors have many essential skills required by the business community and are encouraged to pursue positions in this area.

### Physical Health

As Allen (1977) has suggested, there appear to be numerous opportunities to apply counseling skills in areas related to physical health.

*Direct Counseling Services*    The work of Kubler-Ross (1969) has drawn attention to the emotional and psychological needs of those facing death and has increased interest in this country in the hospice concept for the treatment of the terminally ill. This concept emphasizes all aspects of the patient's functioning, including the physical, psychological, and sociological factors. Counseling for the patient and emotional support services for the family are the integral part of the hospice approach, yet very few professional counselors have been employed. Cheikin (1979) suggests that counselors can provide vital services in this new institution.

The relationship between stress and disease is another area receiving increased attention in the literature (Cohen, 1978; Pusateri-Ulach & Moracco, 1981). If stress is considered part of the epidemiology of disease, then coping is part of the cure. Cohen (1978) suggests that counselors can and should play an important role in providing individuals with the social support necessary for reducing stress and for coping, and hence for reducing physical health problems.

Counseling services for preoperative and postoperative patients have largely been ignored. Most types of surgery cause the patient anxiety and stress; the results of surgery may often require a major adjustment on the patient's part. Heart by-passes, radical mastectomies, and losses of a limb can all result in major emotional and psychological difficulties. Counselors could be employed by either private physicians or major medical complexes to assist patients in adjustment to the results of surgery. Emergency rooms in all hospitals could be staffed by crisis counselors. Patients and their families in emergency situations often find themselves coping with the most difficult of life experiences, and counseling services could provide invaluable assistance. Today, there are support groups for persons living with disease. Counselors could become involved in this important service.

Some private obstetricians are sensitive to the emotional and psychological factors surrounding childbirth and are hiring counselors to work with postpartum depressions.

*Training*   Counselors could also develop and implement training programs in human relations skills for those in the health professions, including nurses, physicians and dentists. These personnel, typically identified as helping professionals, frequently have little or no training in interpersonal skills. Some medical schools, nursing schools, and dental schools have hired counselor/consultants to train their students in communication skills (Jason, Kagan, & Shulman, 1971; Werner & Schneider, 1974; Bartnick & O'Brien, 1980).

In this final section we have identified two relatively new settings in which counseling skills are applicable. There are still roadblocks facing counselor/consultants who seek employment in these settings. However, counselors must be assertive in pursuing jobs in new areas and must give careful consideration to marketing their skills in new settings if counseling as a profession is to expand and grow.

## SUMMARY

Counselors have traditionally defined their role as one of remediation of emotional and psychological problems. As necessary as remedial counseling is, counselors of the future should assume a more active role in the prevention of problems. The consulting function is therefore viewed as essential. This chapter focused on the counselor as consultant. Consultants can assume several roles, including trainer/educator, expert/prescriber, negotiator, and collaborator. Particular skills are essential for each role. The consulting process should be organized around recognizable stages and phases.

As consultants, school counselors must move out of their offices and take an active role in changing school environments. Counselors in the schools can also serve as consultants to teachers and parents. Because counselors are concerned about preventing problems, they should work with teachers to humanize classroom environments through psychological education strategies.

With cutbacks in educational financing, counselors must seek other settings in which to apply their skills. Two relatively untapped settings—business and industry, and physical health—offer new opportunities to the counselor as consultant.

## REFERENCES

ALLEN, T. (1977). Physical health: An expanding horizon for counselors. *Personnel and Guidance Journal, 56* (1), 40-43.

AUBREY, R. (1972). Power bases: The consultant's vehicle for change. *Elementary School Guidance and Counseling, 7* (2), 90-97.

AUBREY, R. (1978). Consultation, school interventions, and the elementary counselor. *Personnel and Guidance Journal, 56* (6), 351-354.

BARQUEST, K., and MARTIN, H. (1984). Use of lay home visitors: A primary prevention strategy for families with a newborn. *Personnel and Guidance Journal, 62* (9), 558-560.

BARTNICK, R. W., and O'BRIEN, C. (1980). Health care and counseling skills. *Personnel and Guidance Journal, 58* (10), 666-667.

BERDIE, R. F. (1972). The 1980 counselor: Applied behavioral scientist. *Personnel and Guidance Journal, 50* (6), 451-456.

BESSELL, H., and PALOMARES, U. (1967). *Methods in human development.* San Diego: Human Development Training Institute.

BLAKE, R., and MOUTON, J. (1978). Toward a general theory of consultation. *Personnel and Guidance Journal, 56* (6), 328-334.

BLOCHER. D., DUSTIN, E. R., and DUGAN, W. (1971). *Guidance systems: An introduction to student personnel work.* New York: Ronald Press.

BRADLEY, M. (1978). Counseling, past and present: Is there a future? *Personnel and Guidance Journal, 57* (1), 42-45.

BROWN, G. (1971). *Human teaching for human learning: An introduction to confluent education.* New York: Viking.

CARKHUFF, R. R. (1972). The credo of a militant humanist. *Personnel and Guidance Journal, 50* (6), 451-456.

CHEIKIN, M. (1979). The counselor in the hospice: A new role. *Personnel and Guidance Journal, 58* (3), 186-189.

CLEMENT, R. W., WALKER, J. W., and PINTO, P. R. (1979). Changing demands on the training professional. *Training and Development Journal, 33* (3), 3-7.

COHEN, J. (1978). Health care, coping, and the counselor. *Personnel and Guidance Journal, 56* (10), 616-620.

CORRIGAN, G. (1980). Corporate training: A career for teachers? *Phi Delta Kappan, 61* (5), 328-331.

COWEN, E. L. (1984). A general structural model for primary prevention program development in mental health. *Personnel and Guidance Journal, 62* (8), 485-490.

CRISTIANI, T., and CRISTIANI, M. (1979). The application of counseling skills in the business and industrial setting. *Personnel and Guidance Journal, 58* (3), 166-169.

D'ANDREA, M. (1984). Primary prevention and high risk populations. *Personnel and Guidance Journal, 62* (9), 554-558.

DINKMEYER, D. (1970). *Developing understanding of self and others (DUSO D-1).* Circle Pines, Minn.: American Guidance Service.

DINKMEYER, D. (1973). *Developing understanding of self and others (DUSO D-2).* Circle Pines, Minn.: American Guidance Service.

DINKMEYER, D., and CARLSON, J. (1973). *Consulting: Facilitating human potential and change processes.* Columbus, Ohio: Chas. E. Merrill.

DINKMEYER, D., and CARLSON, J. (1975). *Consultation: A book of readings.* New York: John Wiley.

DINKMEYER, D., and CARLSON, J. (1977). Consulting: Training counselors to work with teachers, parents, and administrators. *Counselor Education and Supervision, 16* (3), 172-177.

DINKMEYER, D. Jr., and DINKMEYER, D. Sr. (1984). School counselors as consultants in primary prevention programs. *Personnel and Guidance Journal, 62* (8), 464-466.

DOLL, R. (1980). Speculations on the meaning of the trend toward corporate education. *Phi Delta Kappan, 61* (5), 333-337.

DRUM, D. (1984). Implementing theme-focused prevention: Challenge for the 1980s. *Personnel and Guidance Journal, 62* (9), 509–514. (Special issue).

EGAN, G., and COWEN, M. (1979). *People in systems: A model for development in the human-service professions and education.* Monterey, Calif.: Brooks/Cole.

FONDACARO, M., HELLER, K., and REILLY, M. J. (1984). Development of friendship networks as a prevention strategy in a university megadorm. *Personnel and Guidance Journal, 62* (9), 520–523. (Special issue).

FORREST, D. U., (1983). Employee Assistance Programs in the 1980s: Expanding career options for counselors. *Personnel and Guidance Journal, 62* (2), 105–107.

FULLMER, D., and BERNARD, H. (1972). *The school counselor consultant.* Boston: Houghton Mifflin.

GIBSON, R. L. (1978). Future directions for school programs. *Viewpoints in Teaching and Learning* (School of Education, Indiana University), *54* (1), 1–9.

GORDON, T. (1970). *Parent effectiveness training.* New York: Peter H. Wyden.

GORDON, T. (1974). *Teacher effectiveness training.* New York: Peter H. Wyden.

HEPPNER, P., NEAL, G., and LARSON, L. (1984). Problem-solving training as prevention with college students. *Personnel and Guidance Journal, 62* (9), 514–519.

IVEY, A. (1971). *Microcounseling: Innovations in interviewing training.* Springfield, Ill.: Chas. C. Thomas.

IVEY, A., and ALSCHULER, A. (1973). An introduction to the field. *Personnel and Guidance Journal, 51,* 591–597.

JASON, H., KAGAN, N., and SHULMAN, L. (1971). New approaches to teaching basic interview skills to medical students. *American Journal of Psychiatry, 127,* 1404–1407.

KAGAN, N., KRATHWOHL, D., and FARQUHAR, W. (1965). *Interpersonal process recall: Stimulated recall by videotape.* Educational Research Series, No. 24. East Lansing, Mich.: Michigan State University.

KOHLBERG, L. (1975). Counseling and counselor education: A developmental approach. *Counselor Education and Supervision, 14* (4), 250–256.

KRUMBOLTZ, J., AND THORESEN, C. (1969). *Behavioral counseling: Cases and techniques.* New York: Holt, Rinehart & Winston.

KUBLER-ROSS, E. (1969). *On death and dying.* New York: Macmillan.

KURPIUS, D. (1978). Consultation theory and process: An integrated model. *Personnel and Guidance Journal, 56* (6), 335–338.

KURPIUS, D., AND BRUBAKER, J. (1976). *Psychoeducational consultation: Definition = functions = preparation.* LAB for Educational Development. Indiana University.

KURPIUS, D., AND ROBINSON, S. (1978). Overview of consultation. *Personnel and Guidance Journal, 56* (6), 321–323.

LEWIS, J., AND LEWIS, M. (1977). *Community counseling: A human-services approach.* New York: John Wiley.

LEWIS, J. A., AND LEWIS, M. D. (1984). Preventive programs in action. *Personnel and Guidance Journal, 62* (9), 550–553.

LIPPITT, R. (1975). Dimensions of the consultant's job. *The Journal of Social Issues,* 1959, *15,* 5–12. Appeared in D. Dinkmeyer and J. Carlson *Consultation: A book of readings.* New York: John Wiley.

LIPPITT, R., WATSON, J., AND WESTLEY, B. (1958). *The dynamics of planned change.* New York: Harcourt Brace Jovanovich.

MILLER, C. A. (1969). Psychology as a means to promote human welfare. *American Psychologist, 24,* 1063–1075.

PRESIDENT'S COMMISSION ON MENTAL HEALTH. (1978). *Task panel reports.* (Vol. 1) Appendix. Washington, D.C.: U.S. Government Printing Office.

PUSATERI-ULACH, N., AND MORACCO, J. (1981). Counseling intervention in cancer therapy. *Personnel and Guidance Journal, 59* (5), 267–273.

SHAW, M., AND GOODYEAR, R. (1984). Introduction to the special issues on primary prevention. *Personnel and Guidance Journal, 62* (8), 444–445. (Special issue).

SIMON, S. B., HOWE, L. W., AND KIRSCHENBAUM, H. (1972). *Values clarification: A handbook of practical strategies for teachers and students.* New York: Hart.

SKOVHOLT, T. (1977). Issues in psychological education. *Personnel and Guidance Journal, 55* (8), 472–476.

SMITH, N. (1980). Corporate training and the liberal arts. *Phi Delta Kappan, 61* (5), 311–313.

SMITH, R., PIERCY, F., AND LUTZ, P. (1982). Training counselors for human resource development positions in business and industry. *Counselor Education and Supervision, 22* (2), 107–112.

WALZ, G., AND BENJAMIN, L. (1978). A change agent strategy for counselors functioning as consultants. *Personnel and Guidance Journal, 56* (6), 331–334.

WERNER, A., AND SCHNEIDER, J. (1974). Teaching medical students interactional skills. *New England Journal of Medicine, 290,* 1232–1237.

# 15

# PROFESSIONAL ISSUES

Counseling as a profession entails more than facilitative skills and attitudes. Counselors must respond to the complex legal and ethical considerations that have a direct impact on both the delivery of counseling services and the attitude of the public toward those services. Public acceptance of counseling as a valued service and of counselors as respected professionals depends in large measure on an adherence to a high level of ethical and legal behavior. Such acceptance further depends on the profession's demanding respected credentials of its practitioners. In addition, professional behavior calls for a continuing evaluation of the service being provided as a means of improving that service.

In this chapter these issues of ethics, law, credentials, and evaluation as they apply to counselors are reviewed.

## ETHICAL CONSIDERATIONS IN COUNSELING

Counselors, like all professionals, have ethical responsibilities and obligations. The counseling literature contains numerous references to ethics and the legal status of the counselor, but for a number of reasons ethical problems pose particularly difficult situations for people in the various helping professions. First, clear-cut, specific ethical codes that provide adequate guidelines for ethical behavior in the very wide range of situations encountered in counseling relationships have yet to be evolved. Second, most counseling professionals work within the context of institutions such as schools, colleges, hospitals, churches, and private agencies whose institutional value systems may be quite different from those of the counseling profession itself. Finally, counselors are particularly likely to encounter situations where their ethical obligations overlap or conflict. Often a counselor is working simultaneously with several people who are involved in their own close interpersonal relationships, whether in the family, the school, or other institutions. In such situations, ethical obligations become exceedingly complex.

The principal rule supporting ethical obligations is that the counselor must act with full recognition of the importance of client rights, the ethics of the profession, and the relationship of moral standards and values, individual or cultural, in the life of that client.

### The Nature of Ethical Obligations

Ethics are suggested standards of conduct based on a consensus value set. When an aspiring professional group undertakes an activity that involves a considerable element of public trust and confidence, it must translate prevailing values into a set of ethical standards that can serve to structure expectations for the behavior of its members in their relationships with the public and with each other. As the group emerges in its development toward professionalization, ethical standards are generally formalized in terms of a code of ethics. National professional organizations, such as the American Association for Counseling and Development (AACD) and the American Psychological

Association, have developed ethical standards which they have made available to practitioners. In each case members who were directly involved in writing the code reviewed and examined a wide range of ethical behavior and problems of professional practice that were of concern to a broadly based membership. Both codes stress adherence to rigorous professional standards and to exemplary behavior, integrity, and objectivity toward clients.

The AACD ethical code (1981) consists of a preamble and seven sections: general, counseling, testing, research and publication, consulting and private practice, personnel administration, and preparation standards. This code, which is found in Appendix 1, does not contain any classification of misbehavior nor does it attach penalties to the violation of the standards. Rather, the standards focus on guidelines for professional conduct. The fundamental rule is that the human being must be respected and protected at all times, which can be done only by counselors who manifest honesty, integrity, and objectivity in their behavior toward their clients. Talbutt (1981) provides an excellent analysis of these standards. Although the standards state that a counselor is obligated to attempt to remedy those situations in which the counselor observes or possesses information concerning violations of ethical standards by other counselors, little has been done to provide the process by which the professional organization can deal with such behavior.

Unethical behavior usually occurs when the counselor communicates in a way that establishes one set of expectations and then behaves in a way that is inconsistent with those expectations. For example, the counselor structures the counseling situation verbally or nonverbally to imply mutual trust, concern, and confidentiality. The counselor then behaves in a way that upsets these expectations because the counselor then assigns greater value to another societal role. Clients see such inconsistent behavior as unethical, although the inconsistency may stem from the lack of professional identity on the part of the counselor.

### Confidentiality

The greatest single source of ethical dilemma in counseling results from questions of confidentiality. As indicated above, confidentiality brings into sharp focus the issue of the counselor's responsibilities to the profession, to the institution or agency that employs the counselor and, most of all, to the individual seeking help.

*Principles of Confidentiality*    Schneiders (1963) terms the information revealed in counseling an "entrusted secret," information revealed with the condition that it be kept secret. Schneiders suggests seven general principles that govern confidentiality and communication:

1.  The obligation of confidentiality is relative rather than absolute since there are conditions which can alter it.
2.  Confidentiality depends on the nature of the material, so that material which is already public or can easily become so is not bound by confidentiality in the same way as is the entrusted secret.

3. Material that is harmless does not bind the counselor to confidentiality.

4. The material that is necessary for a counselor or an agency to function effectively is often released from the bonds of confidentiality.

5. Confidentiality is always conditioned by the intrinsic right of the counselee to his integrity and reputation, to the secret, and to resist aggression. Such rights can be protected by the counselor even against the law.

6. Confidentiality is limited also by the rights of the counselor to preserve his own reputation and integrity, to resist harm or aggression, and to preserve privileged communication.

7. Confidentiality is determined and limited by the rights of an innocent third party and by the rights of the community. (1963, p. 263)

Schneiders goes on to state that the obligation of secrecy is no longer relevant when (1) the common welfare demands revelation, (2) the secret is invalid, (3) there is unjust aggression, (4) the client gives consent, or (5) there is publication of the secret.

Questions of confidentiality, however, are clearer when they are examined in terms of "levels of confidentiality" (Blocher, 1966). Confidentiality involves a commitment that is always relative rather than absolute. For example, it is hard to conceive of any counselor withholding the information that a client had put a time bomb in a crowded auditorium.

***Levels of Confidentiality***    Three rather distinct levels of confidentiality can be established in counseling. The first level of confidentiality involves the professional *use* of information. Every counselor has the obligation to handle information about clients or potential clients only in professional ways. Such information, no matter how it is acquired or how trivial it may seem, should never be used loosely in social conversation or in nonprofessional settings. This includes not only information obtained in counseling interviews, but also the fact of the client *being a client*. All sources of information should be handled in ways that insure that they do not fall into the hands of persons who might handle the information in nonprofessional ways.

The second level of confidentiality relates to information that arises out of a counseling relationship. In all such situations, clients have a right to expect that information will only be used for their welfare. The very nature of the counseling relationship implies this, whether or not the counselor verbally communicates it. This sharing of information obtained during the counseling session can pose a particularly difficult ethical dilemma when the counselor wishes to share the information with others—for example, other counselors, teachers, social workers, psychologists, parents, or a spouse—who may have a primary concern for the client's welfare. Blocher (1966) points out that the ideal solution to this kind of problem is to clearly communicate to the client this level of confidentiality before confidences are accepted. If clients understand in advance that the counselor will use information only for professional purposes and only in the client's best interest, then many of the resulting decisions will be professional judgments rather than ethical decisions.

A third level of confidentiality occurs when it is obvious that the client will not communicate in complete confidence, except in cases of clear and immediate danger to human life. In such a case the counselor is providing the client with an opportunity for sharing some disturbing and shocking confidences in order to provide that client a helping, confidential relationship. The key to the whole matter rests in the counselor's ability to structure in advance the level of confidentiality at which she operates. Keeping that confidence once it is accepted at a particular level is an ethical matter. The counselor who does not keep confidences in an ethical manner will soon have no confidences to keep.

Denkowski and Denkowski (1982) review the historical rationale for confidentiality and argue for a limited and qualified standard. They analyze the need for balance between the rights of the individual and the safety of society with specific attention to the importance of counselors keeping up-to-date with the legal status of confidentiality in their states. Knapp and Vandecreek (1983) give further clarification to this issue, pointing out that judicial courts do not always interpret privileged communication laws the way counselors would like them to. One particularly important issue is that of the "duty to warn" whenever the counselor has reasonable knowledge that a client's conduct may be harmful to self or to another (Gehring, 1982).

The case of *Tarasoff v. Board of Regents of the University of California*, which occurred in 1969, highlighted this particularly sticky problem. In this instance, the California Supreme Court ruled that the University and its employees acted in an irresponsible manner when they failed to notify an intended victim of a threat, resulting in the victim's murder. Knapp and Vandecreek (1983) point out that differences in state laws make the legal aspects of the "duty to warn" difficult to interpret; however they suggest that if counselors follow reasonable standards in predicting violence and in providing proper warning, the counselors will have acted properly. (As may be seen, the principle of confidentiality is complex and requires continuous updating. Corey et al. (1984), however, provide an excellent overview of the issue.)

## LEGAL CONSIDERATIONS FOR COUNSELORS

Counselors are ordinarily governed by the laws of their particular states with regard to the profession of counseling; there is wide diversity among the states in terms of the specific application of the law to counselors. Actually, relatively few court cases and even fewer pertinent statutes deal directly with the counselor. In most instances the examination of the legal status of the counselor must be based on the law as it applies to everyone. The law is generally supportive or neutral toward codes of ethics and standards such as those discussed in the previous section (Stude and McKelvey, 1979). The law is supportive in that it enforces minimum standards for counselors through licensing requirements and generally protects the confidentiality of statements and records provided by clients during counseling. It is neutral in that it allows the counseling profession to police itself and to govern counselors' relations with their clients and other counselors. The law intervenes and overrides professional codes of ethics only when necessary to protect the public health, safety, and welfare. This happens primarily when the counseling profession's standards of confidentiality require the suppression of information, when the necessity of preventing harm overrides the necessity to insure effective treatment.

### Buckley-Pell Amendment

McGuire and Borowy (1978) have reviewed the issues relating to confidentiality and the Buckley-Pell Amendment of Public Law 93–380 passed in 1974. Although this amendment was seen by some counselors as undermining the confidentiality codes of their ethical standards, McGuire and Borowy suggest that the Buckley-Pell Amendment may be interpreted to be supportive rather than in conflict with these ethical standards. As a result, they recommend that counselors critically examine their own record-keeping practices, limit their use of technical language, diagnostic labels, and such, and maintain only information considered critical to the counseling situation. Information that is accessible only to counselors and to the support personnel who are directly related to the treatment of the client is excluded from the definition of the kind of records that must be made available to students and their parents. However, psychologically relevant materials obtained or utilized for purposes other than counseling treatment, or materials that are maintained in files accessible to other officials or staff at the institution or agency, would be defined as part of the student's educational records and would be available to the student or parent.

### Privileged Communication

The legal support for privileged communication is also unclear. Privileged communication is simply anything said by a client to a counselor in a counseling interview with the understanding that the counselor will not be called upon to divulge the information, regardless of its nature. Privileged communication has long existed for ministers, for lawyers, for spouses, and for medical doctors. It is not always clear whether counselors have privileged communication, since there is little consistency in the law across states.

*Types of Privileged Communication*   There are two types of privileged communication: absolute and qualified. The best that most counselors can expect is qualified, which means that exceptions are possible and in some cases specific. Thus some conditions should be made clear before any exchange of privileged communication. First, there must be an understanding that the communications will not be disclosed. The counselor may need to indicate at times during the interactions that the material being discussed may be outside his or her protected area of privilege.

Second, confidentiality must be deemed necessary to the maintenance of the relationship. This creates difficulties in that the counselor may not know until after some portion of the communication has occurred that confidentiality is essential. Thus the counselor needs to be sensitive to the intensity of the interaction so that any potential problem area can be anticipated and a satisfactory method devised for dealing with it.

Third, the relationship between the privileged parties must have support or

**Figure 15-1**    Attending professional meetings is one way of keeping up-to-date on legal considerations    (Michael Drummond, Picture Atlanta)

be fostered by the community. Although society frequently places enough value in the counseling service to include it in this category, there is often sufficient doubt in people's minds to render this condition ambiguous.

Fourth, there is concern over the extent to which disclosure would harm the individual. The benefit to the client by maintaining confidentiality must be greater than the benefit to society by disposition of the case.

*Counselor Alternatives*    Since privileged communication does not occur in many states, counselors must take action to protect their clients. Counselors should inform clients, at an appropriate time, what the status of privileged communication is as the counselor understands it. This suggests that the counselor is alert to various statements of the client that may need to be discussed later with others. Examples might be statements concerning a client's inclinations toward violence, an abhorrence of what the client has done, and similar statements. The counselor may eventually be asked to repeat, under oath, the statements made by the client.

Since the counselor may have to produce whatever records he may have on the client, he needs to keep very careful records, purging them from time to time to eliminate any material that is no longer relevant. In addition, counselors may wish to keep records that require their interpretation, in this way maintaining some control over interpretations by people who have not interacted with the client. Clearly some method of insuring the highest degree of confidentiality is necessary.

Even with such precautions, a counselor may be called upon to testify in a court case involving the client. In those situations the counselor has several alternatives. The counselor may give testimony, which has the effect of saying that the issue is best settled by due process rather than by an individual decision. Or the counselor may refuse to testify, claiming violation of confidence and conscience. Such counselors may find themselves held in contempt of court and may face a lawsuit. The counselor may feel compelled to refuse to testify despite the potentially damaging consequences.

Other alternatives are sometimes available. The counselor may develop a compromise kind of activity for this court appearance. If the counselor relies on memory, it is usually difficult to remember specifics well enough to be of value in any court of law. Or the material which the court is interested in is frequently hearsay from the counselor's point of view since the counselor did not actually observe the activities reported by the client. The counselor knows only what she was told, and this is usually not admissible evidence. Such suggestions should not be misinterpreted to suggest that counselors play games with client data and the serious problem of courtroom appearance; rather, these ideas are intended to show the difficulty and possibility of conflict in this area. Counselors should check out their rights as established by their own local laws.

## COUNSELOR CREDENTIALING

### Problems in Credentialing Counselors

To a large extent the issue of counselor licensure was forced on counselors by the aggressive action of state psychology licensure boards when they moved to restrict the practice of qualified counseling psychologists and other counselors. Actually, psychologists have been developing legislation for more than twenty years so that to-day forty-nine states have some form of legislation. In recent years, however, the dominant voices among psychologists have called for a restriction on which professionals should be allowed to provide nonmedical mental health services, a restriction that would eliminate all but doctoral trained psychologists. Since such restrictions often limit counseling to those who have been trained in a department of psychology, individuals trained as counselors in counselor education departments in colleges of education would be ineligible for licensure, regardless of the educational level attained.

In addition, such licensure regulations would eliminate all subdoctoral persons. Leaders of the American Association for Counseling and Development have taken a position of supporting licensure/certification for counselors with less than a doctorate but have recommended that up to sixty semester hours of graduate work, the exact amount to be determined by each state, be required.

### Accreditation of Counselor Training Programs

The major problem in the licensure issue, however, is that the counseling profession currently lacks an effective credentialing process, and as a result, its practitioners are restricted in their opportunities for practicing their profession. In the past, some attention has been given to the preparation standards and certification of counselors, but the emphasis has been on a recommended preparation program. The APGA Professional Preparation and Standards Committee was active in 1960, and standards for the preparation of secondary school counselors were developed in 1964. Yet, no procedure was developed for accrediting preparation programs.

The National Council for Accreditation of Teacher Education, which has been the official accrediting body for teacher preparation programs, has served as the primary structure for accreditation, although its practices have had little impact on the quality of programs. In 1973 the Association for Counselor Education and Supervision (ACES) approved a revised, expanded set of preparation standards that had been carefully formulated. In 1979 the Association for Counselor Education and Supervision began the implementation of a set of guidelines for the accreditation of counselor education programs, and the American Association for Counseling and Development is now administering an accreditation program.

This emphasis on accreditation of approved counselor training programs is of major importance in the credentialing process of counselors; still, such a procedure fails to provide the legal credentialing for the individual that licensure does. Therefore, the development of licensure standards and approved legislation for those licensure standards in each of the states is a major thrust of the counseling profession today.

### Standards for Licensure

Forester (1977) has defined some of the common methods used to credential practitioners of the profession. *Certification* is seen "as a process of recognizing the competence of practitioners of a profession by officially authorizing them to use the title adopted by the profession." Ordinarily such certification is granted by an agency or governmental body after checking the individual's transcripts for evidence that the applicant has completed the specific, required courses in acceptable preparation programs. *Licensure* is "a process authorized by state legislation that regulates the practice and the title of the profession." Because licensure is a legal process, it subjects violators to greater legal sanctions than does certification. The regulations governing licensure are generally far more specific and comprehensive, demanding greater training and preparation, than are the regulations regarding certification. *Accreditation* is "a process whereby an association or agency grants public recognition to a school, institute, college, university, or specialized program of study that has met certain established qualifications of standards as determined through initial and periodic evaluations" (p. 573). Often called "program approval," accreditation often acts to credential graduates of approved programs.

In a study that attempted to identify the kind of educational training necessary for licensure, Carroll, Griggs, and Halligan (1977) surveyed 1,556 ACES members in the United States. One part of their study asked, "In your opinion, which is the lowest educational level acceptable for being licensed in private practice?" The master's degree level was designated by 45.4 percent of the respondents, the doctorate by 41.6 percent, and other educational requirements were indicated by 13 percent. The suggested alternatives included:

1. BS with demonstrated experience
2. Post-master's degree in a specialized area
3. Thirty-six credits beyond MA
4. MA with specialization; e.g., family therapy
5. Two-year MA with supervision
6. Demonstrated experience; no degree designation
7. Supervised internship; no degree designation
8. Two years of clinical practice in an accredited agency
9. Licensure at doctoral level; certification below the doctorate

There is no reason to believe that the licensure issue will go away. Rather, recent events suggest that licensure will be required in more and more states, and increasingly higher levels of training will be required for applicants. The most important aspect, however, is the recognition that counselors need an effective credentialing process that will legitimize their professional standing.

The impetus for counselor licensure came from the Association for Counselor Education and Supervision, but by 1975 the American Personnel and Guidance Association had appointed a licensure commission and had begun work on developing resources for groups working toward licensure. In 1976 Virginia became the first state to pass a licensure law; by the summer of 1985, groups in fourteen other states had been successful in getting licensure laws passed.

### Pros and Cons of Licensure

Certainly the issue of whether counselor licensure is desirable or not generates a great deal of disagreement. Those who support licensing of counselors frequently give the following reasons for doing so: (1) one characteristic of a profession is that it monitors its own members and sets standards for its practice, which licensing would permit counselors to do; (2) licensure would grant increased dignity and prestige to counselors in diverse settings, including education, even though most states are expected to allow school counselors the option of choosing whether or not to become licensed; and (3) licensure would help protect the public's right to be served by a competent, qualified professional whenever counseling is desired.

Opponents of counselor licensure tend to focus on two issues: (1) the potential harm to the profession if licensing becomes more political than professional, with politicians deciding licensing standards; and (2) the potential effect of having licensure standards that reflect what "used to be" rather than what "needs to be"; such standards would serve to stultify rather than encourage growth and development in the training of counselors. Davis (1981), for one, argues that national certification provides greater freedom for counselors and greater protection for the public.

### National Board of Certified Counselors

Since 1982, the American Association for Counseling and Development has been developing a national registry of certified counselors. This system provides for professional recognition of competence by certifying an individual as a "national, certified counselor" when the individual successfully meets the professional standards established. These criteria include the following:

1. Master's or doctorate degree in counseling or a closely related field from a regionally accredited university,
2. At least two years professional counseling experience with a documented supervised counseling experience, and
3. Successful completion of a counselor certification examination.

In addition, certified counselors must show evidence of continuing professional growth and development as counselors in order to be recertified.

Similar certification procedures exist in order to be certified as a Certified Clinical Mental Health Counselor by the American Mental Health Counselors Association, as a Certified Career Counselor by the National Vocational Guidance Association, and as a Certified Rehabilitation Counselor by the Commission on Rehabilitation Counselor Certification.

## RESEARCH AND EVALUATION IN COUNSELING

### Need for Research

Remer points out that "a person cannot be a counselor, ethically or morally, without many of the skills and competencies engendered in learning about research, statistics, and testing. . ." (1981, p. 567). He goes on to suggest that counselors have an ethical responsibility to both their clients and the public to know the effects and limits of the tools and techniques they use.

Research efforts are necessary to determine the effects that counselors have on clients during counseling, to ascertain the value of various specialized programs on the behavior of clients (for example, drug education programs, and assertion training groups), to assess the needs of those with whom counselors work, and to provide information that will meet accountability requirements in schools and agencies.

### Purposes of Evaluation

Measuring the effectiveness of counseling continues to be a source of difficulty. Part of the problem is that many counselors see evaluation as a threatening process. The purpose of evaluation, however, is to provide new insights that will help counselors perform at higher and more professional levels. The counseling experience makes heavy demands on staff members, clients, and the community, in both financial and emotional terms. Consequently, it is necessary to determine the value of those counseling services by applying standards, and this process is evaluation. Thus, the major aim of evaluation is to ascertain the current status of the counseling service within some frame of reference, and then on the basis of this knowledge to improve its quality and its efficacy. Evaluation is the vehicle through which one learns whether counseling is doing what is expected of it.

### Difficulties in Evaluation

Certainly, most counselors accept that evaluation is one approach to bringing about self-improvement. Yet good evaluation studies in counseling effectiveness are relatively rare, for a number of reasons. The first and most fundamental problem is the difficulty of obtaining agreement on definitions of process and outcome that permit meaningful evaluations. Basically, counseling has no generally accepted goals or objectives. Instead, there are almost as many goals as there are researchers in the field. Some of these goals are almost completely nonoperational, in that they cannot be easily converted into measurable behaviors. Goals such as developing self-actualization, improving the client's self-concept, or reorganizing the client's self-structure are a bit difficult to translate into measurable behaviors. Traditionally, client self-reports, counselor judgments of improvement, improved grades, changes in test scores, and indices of behavioral change have been used as criteria for measuring client improvement. Each of these criteria, however, has definite weaknesses, either in terms of validity or in terms of showing long-term changes.

The weaknesses of these traditional criteria, along with the current emphasis on accountability, have placed a greater emphasis on behavioral criteria. Such an emphasis, while highly acceptable to behaviorally oriented counselors, is frequently rejected by counselors who believe that such emphasis on the specific behaviors is only a limited aspect of counseling and does not get at the important focus of the whole counseling process.

A second important problem encountered in measuring or evaluating counseling centers on the use of control groups. In any experimental design, an attempt must be made to isolate the effects of the treatment by designating a control group of subjects who are like the experimental group in every way except that they do not receive the treatment. Such control groups are best established by randomly dividing a single population into control and experimental groups. The presumption is that if change occurs in the group receiving treatment and not in the control group, the change can be attributed to the treatment. Control and experimental groups are generally selected to be as similar as possible on a large number of variables; they are matched in characteristics such as age, sex, IQ, and socioeconomic status.

In counseling research, however, the most relevant characteristics are the hardest to match. The most obvious relevant characteristic is motivation to enter counseling. Obviously a well-matched control group must contain individuals who also want and need the counselors' services. A serious ethical issue comes into play at this point. An individual who expresses a need for counseling does not wish to be assigned to a control group where no counseling help is provided. Such an assignment could well have a negative impact on the client and perhaps affect the validity of the results. In counseling evaluation, this issue is often resolved by utilizing a delaying tactic, keeping the control group subjects on a waiting list while providing the experimental subjects with counseling. After both groups are assessed for change, the control subjects receive counseling. Sometimes subjects in the control group receive very limited noncounseling contact to assure them that help will be received and to permit the counselor to determine if the need for counseling help is urgent.

Maintaining minimal noncounseling contact with the control group may also help eliminate the placebo effect. Some evidence indicates that some clients begin to show progress simply because they are in counseling, rather than because of what is happening during the counseling process. Providing limited noncounseling contact to the control group may help researchers distinguish between the improvement clients show as a result of the counseling and the improvement that occurs simply because they feel optimistic about being in counseling.

Another major problem in counseling evaluation is contamination of treatment effects. If a group of individuals who want counseling services are identified and half are selected to be a treatment group and half a control group, little can be done to prevent either of these groups from obtaining other outside assistance. This is particularly true if counseling is viewed primarily as a relationship; the therapeutic qualities of a counseling relationship are not necessarily confined to relationships that originate in professional settings. The control group, which presumably is receiving no counseling help, may also show improvement as a result of relationships established outside the counseling setting, thereby undermining the evaluative significance of the help the treatment group has received through counseling.

### Criteria for Evaluation

Blocher (1966) has identified four major types of criteria by which client improvement can be measured. These criteria include (1) social adjustment criteria, (2) personality criteria, (3) vocational adjustment criteria, and (4) educational criteria, along with other miscellaneous criteria.

Social adjustment criteria include changes in "adjustment" measures made by significant others in the client's life, such as parents or teachers. Sometimes more objective measures are used, such as increased participation in group activities or reduction in disciplinary offenses.

Personality criteria include subjective measures, such as changes in the kinds of self-descriptive adjectives the client uses in reference to himself over a period of time. Personality criteria also include changes in the scores attained on various personality tests, such as the Stevenson Q-sort or various personality inventories.

Vocational adjustment criteria may include improvements in the specificity of vocational plans as well as persistence or promotions on the job. In addition, vocational adjustment criteria may include clients' self-reports of job satisfaction or supervisors' reports of client performance on the job.

The most traditional educational criterion is increase in grade point averages of clients. Other measures that are sometimes used include a reduction in truancy or in the dropout rate and the correlation between grades and measured aptitudes.

Clients themselves provide a major source of information regarding counseling effectiveness. These reports may consist of subjective evaluations of improvement—statements such as, ''I seem to be getting along better with my friends'' or ''I'm not as uptight about taking exams as I was before.'' Although the client's subjective evaluation has limitations, often much can be learned from the client's perception of change. Unless the client is experiencing some satisfaction in the results of the counseling process, the likelihood of the client's continuing the process is very small.

The counselor's subjective report about the effectiveness of the counseling process is also important, although not ordinarily sufficient as the only means of evaluating counseling effectiveness. Experienced counselors learn to trust their own judgments about client growth during the counseling process, and such subjective evaluation can help them determine future courses of action during the counseling relationship.

In setting up an evaluation program, counselors must develop some sort of systematic approach that will give full recognition to those aspects they wish to emphasize. To do so, they must conceptualize three sets of experimental variables considered relevant in any comprehensive evaluation of counseling.

The first set of variables to be considered are those involved in the counseling situation, which can be categorized in terms of three subsets: counselor variables, client variables, and situational variables. *Counselor variables* include such factors as the counselor's age, sex, socioeconomic background, training, theoretical orientation, and institutional role. *Client variables* include the client's age, sex, socioeconomic background, nature of presenting problem, and expectations for counseling. *Situational variables* include the nature of referral and the institution or agency in which counseling occurs. Each of these input variables must be considered and controlled to determine if some individual counselors are helpful to some clients but are either useless or even harmful to others. The setting in which counseling occurs, the way in which clients are referred, and the clients' expectations are all extremely relevant. Failure to sort out these important variables could well mask the most important results.

The intermediate or process variables are also extremely important. What actually happens in the counseling situation—the kind of relationship established, the number of contacts, and the approaches used—provides valuable insights into the relationship that occurs during the process. Although these process variables are less important to the behavioral counselors, the process by which behavioral change is facilitated is an important variable for evaluation.

The third set of experimental variables are outcome variables. These include changes that have occurred in the client during the counseling process presumably as a result of counseling intervention. These changes must be relevant to the counseling goals established in the counseling situation. Such outcome variables may very well include differences in how clients feel, think, or behave; however, such outcomes must be evaluated to determine whether the counseling situation has succeeded in bringing about the desired change in the client.

## SUMMARY

Counselors must respond to the complex legal and ethical considerations that directly affect both the delivery of counseling services and the attitude of the public toward these services. As professionals, counselors must insist on a high level of ethical and legal behavior, on respected credentials of its practitioners, and on continuing evaluation.

Ethical obligations of counselors are stated in the ethical standards developed by the American Association for Counseling and Development and by the American Psychological Association. Both codes stress adherence to rigorous professional standards and to exemplary behavior, integrity, and objectivity toward clients.

Counselors are obligated to maintain professional levels of confidentiality, with three levels clearly differentiated. There is wide diversity among states as to the status of privileged communication for counselors, but few states provide the same degree of privileged communication for counselors that they do for ministers, lawyers, and medical doctors.

A recent trend toward states providing for counselor licensure has resulted in eleven states having licensure laws and most other states having groups working toward passage of such laws.

Despite the difficulties in measuring counseling effectiveness, research and evaluation are extremely important and a necessary part of ethical behavior for counselors.

## REFERENCES

American Association for Counseling and Development. (1981). *Ethical standards.* Washington, D.C.: Author.

American Psychological Association. (1981). *Ethical standards of psychologists.* Washington, D.C.: Author.

BLOCHER, D. H. (1966). *Developmental counseling.* New York: Ronald Press.

CARROLL, M. R., GRIGGS, S., and HALLIGAN, F. (1977). The licensure issue: How real is it? *Personnel and Guidance Journal, 55,* 577–580.

COREY, G., COREY, M. S., and CALLAHAN, P. (1984). *Issues and ethics in the helping professions* (2nd Ed.). Monterey, Calif.: Brooks/Cole.

DAVIS, J. W. (1981). Counselor licensure: Overkill? *Personnel and Guidance Journal, 60,* 83–85.

DENKOWSKI, K. M., and DENKOWSKI, G. C. (1982). Client-counselor confidentiality: An update of rationale, legal status, and implications. *Personnel and Guidance Journal, 60,* 371–375.

FORESTER, J. R. (1977). What shall we do about credentialing? *Personnel and Guidance Journal, 55,* 573–576.

GEHRING, D. D. (1982). The counselor's "duty to warn." *Personnel and Guidance Journal, 61,* 208–210.

KNAPP, S., and VANDECREEK, L. (1983). Communications and the counselor. *Personnel and Guidance Journal, 62,* 83–85.

McGUIRE, J. M., and BOROWY, T. D. (1978). Confidentiality and the Buckley-Pell Amendment: Ethical and legal considerations for counselors. *Personnel and Guidance Journal, 56,* 554–557.

REMER, R. (1981). The counselor and research: Introduction. *Personnel and Guidance Journal, 59,* 567–571.

SCHNEIDERS, A. A. (1963). The limits of confidentiality. *Personnel and Guidance Journal, 42,* 252–253.

STUDE, E. W., and McKELVEY, J. (1979). Ethics and the law: Friend or foe? *Personnel and Guidance Journal, 57,* 453–456.

TALBUTT, L. C. (1981). Ethical standards: Assets and limitations. *Personnel and Guidance Journal, 60,* 110–112.

# Appendix I
# AMERICAN ASSOCIATION FOR COUNSELING AND DEVELOPMENT

## ETHICAL STANDARDS, AMERICAN ASSOCIATION FOR COUNSELING AND DEVELOPMENT*

### PREAMBLE

*The American Personnel and Guidance Association is an educational, scientific, and professional organization whose members are dedicated to the enhancement of the worth, dignity, potential, and uniqueness of each individual and thus to the service of society.*

*The Association recognizes that the role definitions and work settings of its members include a wide variety of academic disciplines, levels of academic preparation and agency services. This diversity reflects the breadth of the Association's interest and influence. It also poses challenging complexities in efforts to set standards for the performance of members, desired requisite preparation or practice, and supporting social, legal, and ethical controls.*

*The specification of ethical standards enables the Association to clarify to present and future members and to those served by members, the nature of ethical responsibilities held in common by its members.*

*The existence of such standards serves to stimulate greater concern by members for their own professional functioning and for the conduct of fellow professionals such as counselors, guidance and student personnel workers, and others in the helping professions. As the ethical code of the Association, this document establishes principles that define the ethical behavior of Association members.*

*Ethical Standards* (revised), by the American Personnel and Guidance Association (since July 1, 1983, American Association for Counseling and Development). Copyright 1981 by the American Personnel and Guidance Association. Reprinted by permission.

*Formerly the American Personnel and Guidance Association.

(Approved by Executive Committee upon referral of the Board of Directors, January 17, 1981.)

## Section A: General

1. The member influences the development of the profession by continuous efforts to improve professional practices, teaching, services, and research. Professional growth is continuous throughout the member's career and is exemplified by the development of a philosophy that explains why and how a member functions in the helping relationship. Members must gather data on their effectiveness and be guided by the findings.

2. The member has a responsibility both to the individual who is served and to the institution within which the service is performed to maintain high standards of professional conduct. The member strives to maintain the highest levels of professional services offered to the individuals to be served. The member also strives to assist the agency, organization, or institution in providing the highest caliber of professional services. The acceptance of employment in an institution implies that the member is in agreement with the general policies and principles of the institution. Therefore the professional activities of the member are also in accord with the objectives of the institution. If, despite concerted efforts, the member cannot reach agreement with the employer as to acceptable standards of conduct that allow for changes in institutional policy conducive to the positive growth and development of clients, then terminating the affiliation should be seriously considered.

3. Ethical behavior among professional associates, both members and nonmembers, must be expected at all times. When information is possessed that raises doubt as to the ethical behavior of professional colleagues, whether Association members or not, the member must take action to attempt to rectify such a condition. Such action shall use the institution's channels first and then use procedures established by the state Branch, Division, or Association.

4. The member neither claims nor implies professional qualifications exceeding those possessed and is reponsible for correcting any misrepresentations of these qualifications by others.

5. In establishing fees for professional counseling services, members must consider the financial status of clients and locality. In the event that the established fee structure is inappropriate for a client, assistance must be provided in finding comparable services of acceptable cost.

6. When members provide information to the public or to subordinates, peers or supervisors, they have a responsibility to ensure that the content is general, unidentified client information that is accurate, unbiased, and consists of objective, factual data.

7. With regard to the delivery of professional services, members should accept only those positions for which they are professionally qualified.

8. In the counseling relationship the counselor is aware of the intimacy of the relationship and maintains respect for the client and avoids engaging in activities that seek to meet the counselor's personal needs at the expense of that client. Through awareness of the negative impact of both racial and sexual stereotyping and discrimination, the counselor guards the individual rights and personal dignity of the client in the counseling relationship.

## Section B: Counseling relationship

This section refers to practices and procedures of individual and/or group counseling relationships.

The member must recognize the need for client freedom of choice. Under those circumstances where this is not possible, the member must apprise clients of restrictions that may limit their freedom of choice.

1. The member's *primary* obligation is to respect the integrity and promote the welfare of the client(s), whether the client(s) is (are) assisted individually or in a group relationship. In a group setting, the member is also responsible for taking reasonable precautions to protect individuals from physical and/or psychological trauma resulting from interaction within the group.

2. The counseling relationship and information resulting therefrom [must] be kept confidential, consistent with the obligations of the member as a professional person. In a group counseling setting, the counselor must set a norm of confidentiality regarding all group participants' disclosures.

3. If an individual is already in a counseling relationship with another professional person, the member does not enter into a counseling relationship without first contacting and receiving the approval of that other professional. If the member discovers that the client is in another counseling relationship after the counseling relationship begins, the member must gain the consent of the other professional or terminate the relationship, unless the client elects to terminate the other relationship.

4. When the client's condition indicates that there is clear and imminent danger to the client or others, the member must take reasonable personal action or inform responsible authorities. Consultation with other professionals must be used where possible. The assumption of responsibility for the client's behavior must be taken only after careful deliberation. The client must be involved in the resumption of responsibility as quickly as possible.

5. Records of the counseling relationship, including interview notes, test data, correspondence, tape recordings, and other documents, are to be considered professional information for use in counseling and they should not be considered a part of the records of the institution or agency in which the counselor is employed unless specified by state statute or regulation. Revelation to others of counseling material must occur only upon the expressed consent of the client.

6. Use of data derived from a counseling relationship for purposes of counselor training or research shall be confined to content that can be disguised to ensure full protection of the identity of the subject client.

7. The member must inform the client of the purposes, goals, techniques, rules of procedure and limitations that may affect the relationship at or before the time that the counseling relationship is entered.

8. The member must screen prospective group participants, especially when the emphasis is on self-understanding and growth through self-disclosure. The member must maintain an awareness of the group participants' compatibility throughout the life of the group.

9. The member may choose to consult with any other professionally competent person about a client. In choosing a consultant, the member must avoid placing the consultant in a conflict of interest situation that would preclude the consultant's being a proper party to the member's efforts to help the client.

10. If the member determines an inability to be of professional assistance to the client, the member must either avoid initiating the counseling relationship or immediately terminate that relationship. In either event, the member must suggest appropriate alternatives. (The member must be knowledgeable about referral resources so that a satisfactory referral can be initiated.) In the event the client declines the suggested referral, the member is not obligated to continue the relationship.

11. When the member has other relationships, particularly if an administrative, supervisory and/or evaluative nature with an individual seeking counseling services, the member must not serve as the counselor but should refer the individual to another professional. Only in instances where such an alternative is unavailable and where the individual's situation warrants counseling intervention should the member enter into and/or main-

tain a counseling relationship. Dual relationships with clients that might impair the member's objectivity and professional judgment (e.g., as with close friends or relatives, sexual intimacies with any client) must be avoided and/or the counseling relationship terminated through referral to another competent professional.

12. All experimental methods of treatment must be clearly indicated to prospective recipients and safety precautions are to be adhered to by the member.

13. When the member is engaged in short-term group treatment/training programs (e.g., marathons and other encounter-type or growth groups), the member ensures that there is professional assistance available during and following the group experience.

14. Should the member be engaged in a work setting that calls for any variation from the above statements, the member is obligated to consult with other professionals whenever possible to consider justifiable alternatives.

## Section C: Measurement and evaluation

The primary purpose of educational and psychological testing is to provide descriptive measures that are objective and interpretable in either comparative or absolute terms. The member must recognize the need to interpret the statements that follow as applying to the whole range of appraisal techniques including test and nontest data. Test results constitute only one of a variety of pertinent sources of information for personnel, guidance, and counseling decisions.

1. The member must provide specific orientation or information to the examinee(s) prior to and following the test administration so that the results of testing may be placed in proper perspective with other relevant factors. In so doing, the member must recognize the effects of socioeconomic, ethnic and cultural factors on test scores. It is the member's professional responsibility to use additional unvalidated information carefully in modifying interpretation of the test results.

2. In selecting tests for use in a given situation or with a particular client, the member must consider carefully the specific validity, reliability, and appropriateness of the test(s). *General* validity, reliability and the like may be questioned legally as well as ethically when tests are used for vocational and educational selection, placement, or counseling.

3. When making any statements to the public about tests and testing, the member must give accurate information and avoid false claims or misconceptions. Special efforts are often required to avoid unwarranted connotations of such terms as *IQ* and *grade equivalent scores*.

4. Different tests demand different levels of competence for administration, scoring, and interpretation. Members must recognize the limits of their competence and perform only those functions for which they are prepared.

5. Tests must be administered under the same conditions that were established in their standardization. When tests are not administered under standard conditions or when unusual behavior or irregularities occur during the testing session, those conditions must be noted and the results designated as invalid or of questionable validity. Unsupervised or inadequately supervised test-taking, such as the use of tests through the mails, is considered unethical. On the other hand, the use of instruments that are so designed or standardized to be self-administered and self-scored, such as interest inventories, is to be encouraged.

6. The meaningfulness of test results used in personnel, guidance, and counseling functions generally depends on the examinee's unfamiliarity with the specific items on the

test. Any prior coaching or dissemination of the test materials can invalidate test results. Therefore, test security is one of the professional obligations of the member. Conditions that produce most favorable test results must be made known to the examinee.

7. The purpose of testing and the explicit use of the results must be made known to the examinee prior to testing. The counselor must ensure that instrument limitations are not exceeded and that periodic review and/or retesting are made to prevent client stereotyping.

8. The examinee's welfare and explicit prior understanding must be the criteria for determining the recipients of the test results. The member must see that specific interpretation accompanies any release of individual or group test data. The interpretation of test data must be related to the examinee's particular concerns.

9. The member must be cautious when interpreting the results of research instruments possessing insufficient technical data. The specific purposes for the use of such instruments must be stated explicitly to examinees.

10. The member must proceed with caution when attempting to evaluate and interpret the performance of minority group members or other persons who are not represented in the norm group on which the instrument was standardized.

11. The member must guard against the appropriation, reproduction, or modifications of published tests or parts thereof without acknowledgment and permission from the previous publisher.

12. Regarding the preparation, publication and distribution of tests, reference should be made to:
    a. *Standards for Educational and Psychological Tests and Manuals,* revised edition, 1974, published by the American Psychological Association on behalf of itself, the American Educational Research Association and the National Council on Measurement in Education.
    b. The responsible use of tests: A position paper of AMEG, APGA, and NCME. *Measurement and Evaluation in Guidance,* 1972, 5, 385–388.
    c. "Responsibilities of Users of Standardized Tests," APGA, *Guidepost,* October 5, 1978, pp. 5–8.

## Section D: Research and publication

1. Guidelines on research with human subjects shall be adhered to, such as:
    a. *Ethical Principles in the Conduct of Research with Human Participants,* Washington, D.C.: American Psychological Association, Inc., 1973.
    b. Code of Federal Regulations, Title 45, Subtitle A, Part 46, as currently issued.

2. In planning any research activity dealing with human subjects, the member must be aware of and responsive to all pertinent ethical principles and ensure that the research problem, design, and execution are in full compliance with them.

3. Responsibility for ethical research practice lies with the principal researcher, while others involved in the research activities share ethical obligation and full responsibility for their own actions.

4. In research with human subjects, researchers are responsible for the subjects' welfare throughout the experiment and they must take all reasonable precautions to avoid causing injurious psychological, physical, or social effects on their subjects.

5. All research subjects must be informed of the purpose of the study except when withholding information or providing misinformation to them is essential to the investigation. In such research the member must be responsible for corrective action as soon as possible following completion of the research.

6. Participation in research must be voluntary. Involuntary participation is appropriate only when it can be demonstrated that participation will have no harmful effects on subjects and is essential to the investigation.

7. When reporting research results, explicit mention must be made of all variables and conditions known to the investigator that might affect the outcome of the investigation or the interpretation of the data.

8. The member must be responsible for conducting and reporting investigations in a manner that minimizes the possibility that results will be misleading.

9. The member has an obligation to make available sufficient original research data to qualified others who may wish to replicate the study.

10. When supplying data, aiding in the research of another person, reporting research results, or in making original data available, due care must be taken to disguise the identity of the subjects in the absence of specific authorization from such subjects to do otherwise.

11. When conducting and reporting research, the member must be familiar with, and give recognition to, previous work on the topic, as well as to observe all copyright laws and follow the principles of giving full credit to all to whom credit is due.

12. The member must give due credit through joint authorship, acknowledgment, footnote statements, or other appropriate means to those who have contributed significantly to the research and/or publication, in accordance with such contributions.

13. The member must communicate to other members the results of any research judged to be of professional or scientific value. Results reflecting unfavorably on institutions, programs, services, or vested interests must not be withheld for such reasons.

14. If members agree to cooperate with another individual in research and/or publication, they incur an obligation to cooperate as promised in terms of punctuality of performance and with full regard to the completeness and accuracy of the information required.

15. Ethical practice requires that authors not submit the same manuscript or one essentially similar in content, for simultaneous publication consideration by two or more journals. In addition, manuscripts published in whole or in substantial part in another journal or published work should not be submitted for publication without acknowledgment and permission from the previous publication.

## Section E: Consulting

*Consultation* refers to a voluntary relationship between a professional helper and help-needing individual, group or social unit in which the consultant is providing help to the client(s) in defining and solving a work-related problem or potential problem with a client or client system. (This definition is adapted from Kurpius, DeWayne. Consultation theory and process: An integrated model. *Personnel and Guidance Journal,* 1978, 56.)

1. The member acting as consultant must have a high degree of self-awareness of his-her own values, knowledge, skills, limitations, and needs in entering a helping relationship that involves human and-or organizational change and that the focus of the relationship be on the issues to be resolved and not on the person(s) presenting the problem.

2. There must be understanding and agreement between member and client for the problem definition, change goals, and predicted consequences of interventions selected.

3. The member must be reasonably certain that she/he or the organization represented has the necessary competencies and resources for giving the kind of help that is needed

now or may develop later and that appropriate referral resources are available to the consultant.

4. The consulting relationship must be one in which client adaptability and growth toward self-direction are encouraged and cultivated. The member must maintain this role consistently and not become a decision maker for the client or create a future dependency on the consultant.

5. When announcing consultant availability for services, the member conscientiously adheres to the Association's *Ethical Standards*.

6. The member must refuse a private fee or other remuneration for consultation with persons who are entitled to these services through the member's employing institution or agency. The policies of a particular agency may make explicit provisions for private practice with agency clients by members of its staff. In such instances, the clients must be apprised of other options open to them should they seek private counseling services.

## Section F: Private practice

1. The member should assist the profession by facilitating the availability of counseling services in private as well as public settings.

2. In advertising services as a private practitioner, the member must advertise the services in such a manner so as to accurately inform the public as to services, expertise, profession, and techniques of counseling in a professional manner. A member who assumes an executive leadership role in the organization shall not permit his/her name to be used in professional notices during periods when not actively engaged in the private practice of counseling.

   The member may list the following: highest relevant degree, type and level of certification or license, type and/or description of services, and other relevant information. Such information must not contain false, inaccurate, misleading, partial, out-of-context, or deceptive material or statements.

3. Members may join in partnership/corporation with other members and-or other professionals provided that each member of the partnership or corporation makes clear the separate specialties by name in compliance with the regulations of the locality.

4. A member has an obligation to withdraw from a counseling relationship if it is believed that employment will result in violation of the *Ethical Standards*. If the mental or physical condition of the member renders it difficult to carry out an effective professional relationship or if the member is discharged by the client because the counseling relationship is no longer productive for the client, then the member is obligated to terminate the counseling relationship.

5. A member must adhere to the regulations for private practice of the locality where the services are offered.

6. It is unethical to use one's institutional affiliation to recruit clients for one's private practice.

## Section G: Personnel administration

It is recognized that most members are employed in public or quasi-public institutions. The functioning of a member within an institution must contribute to the goals of the institution and vice versa if either is to accomplish their respective goals or objectives. It is therefore essential that the member and the institution function in ways to (a) make the institution's goals explicit and public; (b) make the member's contribution to institutional goals specific; and (c) foster mutual accountability for goal achievement.

To accomplish these objectives, it is recognized that the member and the employer must share responsibilities in the formulation and implementation of personnel policies.

1. Members must define and describe the parameters and levels of their professional competency.
2. Members must establish interpersonal relations and working agreements with supervisors and subordinates regarding counseling or clinical relationships, confidentiality, distinction between public and private material, maintenance, and dissemination of recorded information, work load and accountability. Working agreements in each instance must be specified and made known to those concerned.
3. Members must alert their employers to conditions that may be potentially disruptive or damaging.
4. Members must inform employers of conditions that may limit their effectiveness.
5. Members must submit regularly to professional review and evaluation.
6. Members must be responsible for inservice development of self and-or staff.
7. Members must inform their staff of goals and programs.
8. Members must provide personnel practices that guarantee and enhance the rights and welfare of each recipient of their service.
9. Members must select competent persons and assign responsibilities compatible with their skills and experiences.

### Section H: Preparation standards

Members who are responsible for training others must be guided by the preparation standards of the Association and relevant Division(s). The member who functions in the capacity of trainer assumes unique ethical responsibilities that frequently go beyond that of the member who does not function in a training capacity. These ethical responsibilities are outlined as follows:

1. Members must orient students to program expectations, basic skills development, and employment prospects prior to admission to the program.
2. Members in charge of learning experiences must establish programs that integrate academic study and supervised practice.
3. Members must establish a program directed toward developing students' skills, knowledge, and self-understanding, stated whenever possible in competency or performance terms.
4. Members must identify the levels of competencies of their students in compliance with relevant Division standards. These competencies must accommodate the para-professional as well as the professional.
5. Members, through continual student evaluation and appraisal, must be aware of the personal limitations of the learner that might impede future performance. The instructor must not only assist the learner in securing remedial assistance but also screen from the program those individuals who are unable to provide competent services.

6. Members must provide a program that includes training in research commensurate with levels of role functioning. Para-professional and technician-level personnel must be trained as consumers of research. In addition, these personnel must learn how to evaluate their own and their program's effectiveness. Graduate training, especially at the doctoral level, would include preparation for original research by the member.

7. Members must make students aware of the ethical responsibilities and standards of the profession.

8. Preparatory programs must encourage students to value the ideals of service to individuals and to society. In this regard, direct financial remuneration or lack thereof must not influence the quality of service rendered. Monetary considerations must not be allowed to overshadow professional and humanitarian needs.

9. Members responsible for educational programs must be skilled as teachers and practitioners.

10. Members must present thoroughly varied theoretical positions so that students may make comparisons and have the opportunity to select a position.

11. Members must develop clear policies within their educational institutions regarding field placement and the roles of the student and the instructor in such placements.

12. Members must ensure that forms of learning focusing on self-understanding or growth are voluntary, or if required as part of the education program, are made known to prospective students prior to entering the program. When the education program offers a growth experience with an emphasis on self-disclosure or other relatively intimate or personal involvement, the member must have no administrative, supervisory, or evaluating authority regarding the participant.

13. Members must conduct an educational program in keeping the current relevant guidelines of the American Personnel and Guidance Association and its Divisions.

# Appendix II
# AMERICAN PSYCHOLOGICAL ASSOCIATION

## ETHICAL PRINCIPLES OF PSYCHOLOGISTS, AMERICAN PSYCHOLOGICAL ASSOCIATION

### PREAMBLE

*Psychologists respect the dignity and worth of the individual and strive for the preservation and protection of fundamental human rights. They are committed to increasing knowledge of human behavior and of people's understanding of themselves and others and to the utilization of such knowledge for*

*Ethical Principles of Psychologists* (revised edition), by the American Psychological Association. Copyright 1981 by the American Psychological Association. Reprinted by permission of the publisher.

This version of the *Ethical Principles of Psychologists* (formerly entitled *Ethical Standards of Psychologists*) was adopted by the American Psychological Association's Council of Representatives on January 24, 1981. The revised *Ethical Principles* contain both substantive and grammatical changes in each of the nine ethical principles constituting the *Ethical Standards of Psychologists* previously adopted by the Council of Representatives in 1979, plus a new tenth principle entitled "Care and Use of Animals." Inquiries concerning the *Ethical Principles of Psychologists* should be addressed to the Administrative Officer for Ethics, American Psychological Association, 1200 Seventeenth Street, N.W., Washington, D.C., 20036.

These revised *Ethical Principles* apply to psychologists, to students of psychology, and to others who do work of a psychological nature under the supervision of a psychologist. They are also intended for the guidance of nonmembers of the Association who are engaged in psychological research or practice.

Any complaints of unethical conduct filed after January 24, 1981, shall be governed by this 1981 revision. However, conduct (a) complained about after January 24, 1981, but which occurred prior to that date, and (b) not considered unethical under prior versions of the principles but considered unethical under the 1981 revision, shall not be deemed a violation of ethical principles. Any complaints pending as of January 24, 1981, shall be governed either by the 1979 or by the 1981 version of the *Ethical Principles,* at the sound discretion of the Committee on Scientific and Professional Ethics and Conduct.

*the promotion of human welfare. While pursuing these objectives, they make every effort to protect the welfare of those who seek their services and of the research participants that may be the object of study. They use their skills only for purposes consistent with these values and do not knowingly permit their misuse by others. While demanding for themselves freedom of inquiry and communication, psychologists accept the responsibility this freedom requires: competence, objectivity in the application of skills, and concern for the best interests of clients, colleagues, students, research participants, and society. In the pursuit of these ideals, psychologists subscribe to principles in the following areas: 1. Responsibility, 2. Competence, 3. Moral and Legal Standards, 4. Public Statements, 5. Confidentiality, 6. Welfare of the Consumer, 7. Professional Relationships, 8. Assessment Techniques, 9. Research with Human Participants, and 10. Care and Use of Animals.*

*Acceptance of membership in the American Psychological Association commits the member to adherence to these principles.*

*Psychologists cooperate with duly constituted committees of the American Psychological Association, in particular, the Committee on Scientific and Professional Ethics and Conduct, by responding to inquiries promptly and completely. Members also respond promptly and completely to inquiries from duly constituted state association ethics committees and professional standards review committees.*

### Principle 1: Responsibility

In providing services, psychologists maintain the highest standards of their profession. They accept responsibility for the consequences of their acts and make every effort to ensure that their services are used appropriately.

    a. As scientists, psychologists accept responsibility for the selection of their research topics and the methods used in investigation, analysis, and reporting. They plan their research in ways to minimize the possibility that their findings will be misleading. They provide thorough discussion of the limitations of their data, especially where their work touches on social policy or might be construed to the detriment of persons in specific age, sex, ethnic, socioeconomic, or other social groups. In publishing reports of their work, they never suppress disconfirming data, and they acknowledge the existence of alternative hypotheses and explanations of their findings. Psychologists take credit only for work they have actually done.

    b. Psychologists clarify in advance with all appropriate persons and agencies the expectations for sharing and utilizing research data. They avoid relationships that may limit their objectivity or create a conflict of interest. Interference with the milieu in which data are collected is kept to a minimum.

    c. Psychologists have the responsibility to attempt to prevent distortion, misuse, or suppression of psychological findings by the institution or agency of which they are employees.

    d. As members of governmental or other organizational bodies, psychologists remain accountable as individuals to the highest standards of their profession.

    e. As teachers, psychologists recognize their primary obligation to help others acquire knowledge and skill. They maintain high standards of scholarship by presenting psychological information objectively, fully, and accurately.

    f. As practitioners, psychologists know that they bear a heavy social responsibility because their recommendations and professional actions may alter the lives of others. They are alert to personal, social, organizational, financial, or political situations and pressures that might lead to misuse of their influence.

### Principle 2: Competence

The maintenance of high standards of competence is a responsibility shared by all psychologists in the interest of the public and the profession as a whole. Psychologists recognize the boundaries of their competence and the limitations of their techniques. They only provide services and only use techniques for which they are qualified by training and experience. In those areas in which recognized standards do not yet exist, psychologists take whatever precautions are necessary to protect the welfare of their clients. They maintain knowledge of current scientific and professional information related to the services they render.

a. Psychologists accurately represent their competence, education, training, and experience. They claim as evidence of educational qualifications only those degrees obtained from institutions acceptable under the Bylaws and Rules of Council of the American Psychological Association.

b. As teachers, psychologists perform their duties on the basis of careful preparation so that their instruction is accurate, current, and scholarly.

c. Psychologists recognize the need for continuing education and are open to new procedures and changes in expectations and values over time.

d. Psychologists recognize differences among people, such as those that may be associated with age, sex, socioeconomic, and ethnic backgrounds. When necessary, they obtain training, experience, or counsel to assure competent service or research relating to such persons.

e. Psychologists responsible for decisions involving individuals or policies based on test results have an understanding of psychological or educational measurement, validation problems, and test research.

f. Psychologists recognize that personal problems and conflicts may interfere with professional effectiveness. Accordingly, they refrain from undertaking any activity in which their personal problems are likely to lead to inadequate performance or harm to a client, colleague, student, or research participant. If engaged in such activity when they become aware of their personal problems, they seek competent professional assistance to determine whether they should suspend, terminate, or limit the scope of their professional and/or scientific activities.

### Principle 3: Moral and legal standards

Psychologists' moral and ethical standards of behavior are a personal matter to the same degree as they are for any other citizen, except as these may compromise the fulfillment of their professional responsibilities or reduce the public trust in psychology and psychologists. Regarding their own behavior, psychologists are sensitive to prevailing community standards and to the possible impact that conformity to or deviation from these standards may have upon the quality of their performance as psychologists. Psychologists are also aware of the possible impact of their public behavior upon the ability of colleagues to perform their professional duties.

a. As teachers, psychologists are aware of the fact that their personal values may affect the selection and presentation of instructional materials. When dealing with topics that may give offense, they recognize and respect the diverse attitudes that students may have toward such materials.

b. As employees or employers, psychologists do not engage in or condone practices that are inhumane or that result in illegal or unjustifiable actions. Such practices include, but are not limited to, those based on considerations of race, handicap, age, gender, sexual preference, religion, or national origin in hiring, promotion, or training.

c. In their professional roles, psychologists avoid any action that will violate or diminish the legal and civil rights of clients or of others who may be affected by their actions.

d. As practitioners and researchers, psychologists act in accord with Association standards and guidelines related to practice and to the conduct of research with human beings and animals. In the ordinary course of events, psychologists adhere to relevant governmental laws and institutional regulations. When federal, state, provincial, organizational, or institutional laws, regulations, or practices are in conflict with Association standards and guidelines, psychologists make known their commitment to Association standards and guidelines and, wherever possible, work toward a resolution of the conflict. Both practitioners and researchers are concerned with the development of such legal and quasi-legal regulations as best serve the public interest, and they work toward changing existing regulations that are not beneficial to the public interest.

### Principle 4: Public statements

Public statements, announcements of services, advertising, and promotional activities of psychologists serve the purpose of helping the public make informed judgments and choices. Psychologists represent accurately and objectively their professional qualifications, affiliations, and functions, as well as those of the institutions or organizations with which they or the statements may be associated. In public statements providing psychological information or professional opinions or providing information about the availability of psychological products, publications, and services, psychologists base their statements on scientifically acceptable psychological findings and techniques with full recognition of the limits and uncertainties of such evidence.

a. When announcing or advertising professional services, psychologists may list the following information to describe the provider and services provided: name, highest relevant academic degree earned from a regionally accredited institution, date, type, and level of certification or licensure, diplomate status, APA membership status, address, telephone number, office hours, a brief listing of the type of psychological services offered, an appropriate presentation of fee information, foreign languages spoken, and policy with regard to third-party payments. Additional relevant or important consumer information may be included if not prohibited by other sections of these Ethical Principles.

b. In announcing or advertising the availability of psychological products, publications, or services, psychologists do not present their affiliation with any organization in a manner that falsely implies sponsorship or certification by that organization. In particular and for example, psychologists do not state APA membership or fellow status in a way to suggest that such status implies specialized professional competence or qualifications. Public statements include, but are not limited to, communication by means of periodical, book, list, directory, television, radio, or motion picture. They do not contain (i) a false, fraudulent, misleading, deceptive, or unfair statement; (ii) a misinterpretation of fact or a statement likely to mislead or deceive because in context it makes only a partial disclosure of relevant facts; (iii) a testimonial from a patient regarding the quality of a psychologist's services or products; (iv) a statement intended or likely to create false or unjustified expectations of favorable results; (v) a statement implying unusual, unique, or one-of-a-kind abilities; (vi) a statement intended or likely to appeal to a client's fears, anxieties, or emotions concerning the possible results of failure to obtain the offered services; (vii) a statement concerning the comparative desirability of offered services; (viii) a statement of direct solicitation of individual clients.

c. Psychologists do not compensate or give anything of value to a representative of the press, radio, television, or other communication medium in anticipation of or in return for professional publicity in a news item. A paid advertisement must be identified as such, unless it is apparent from the context that it is a paid advertisement. If communicated to the public by use of radio or television, an advertisement is prerecorded and approved for broadcast by the psychologist, and a recording of the actual transmission is retained by the psychologist.

d. Announcements or advertisements of "personal growth groups," clinics, and agencies give a clear statement of purpose and a clear description of the experiences to be provided. The education, training, and experience of the staff members are appropriately specified.

e. Psychologists associated with the development or promotion of psychological devices, books, or other products offered for commercial sale make reasonable efforts to ensure that announcements and advertisements are presented in a professional, scientifically acceptable, and factually informative manner.

f. Psychologists do not participate for personal gain in commercial announcements or advertisements recommending to the public the purchase or use of proprietary or single-source products or services when that participation is based solely upon their identification as psychologists.

g. Psychologists present the science of psychology and offer their services, products, and publications fairly and accurately, avoiding misrepresentation through sensationalism, exaggeration, or superficiality. Psychologists are guided by the primary obligation to aid the public in developing informed judgments, opinions, and choices.

h. As teachers, psychologists ensure that statements in catalogs and course outlines are accurate and not misleading, particularly in terms of subject matter to be covered, bases for evaluating progress, and the nature of course experiences. Announcements, brochures, or advertisements describing workshops, seminars, or other educational programs accurately describe the audience for which the program is intended as well as eligibility requirements, educational objectives, and nature of the materials to be covered. These announcements also accurately represent the education, training, and experience of the psychologists presenting the programs and any fees involved.

i. Public announcements or advertisements soliciting research participants in which clinical services or other professional services are offered as an inducement make clear the nature of the services as well as the costs and other obligations to be accepted by participants in the research.

j. A psychologist accepts the obligation to correct others who represent the psychologist's professional qualifications, or associations with products or services, in a manner incompatible with these guidelines.

k. Individual diagnostic and therapeutic services are provided only in the context of a professional psychological relationship. When personal advice is given by means of public lectures or demonstrations, newspaper or magazine articles, radio or television programs, mail, or similar media, the psychologist utilizes the most current relevant data and exercises the highest level of professional judgment.

1. Products that are described or presented by means of public lectures or demonstrations, newspaper or magazine articles, radio or television programs, or similar media meet the same recognized standards as exist for products used in the context of a professional relationship.

### Principle 5: Confidentiality

Psychologists have a primary obligation to respect the confidentiality of information obtained from persons in the course of their work as psychologists. They reveal such information to others only with the consent of the person or the person's legal representative, except in those unusual circumstances in which not to do so would result in clear danger to the person or to others. Where appropriate, psychologists inform their clients of the legal limits of confidentiality.

   a. Information obtained in clinical or consulting relationships, or evaluative data concerning children, students, employees, and others, is discussed only for professional purposes and only with persons clearly concerned with the case. Written and oral reports present only data germane to the purposes of the evaluation, and every effort is made to avoid undue invasion of privacy.
   b. Psychologists who present personal information obtained during the course of professional work in writings, lectures, or other public forums either obtain adequate prior consent to do so or adequately disguise all identifying information.
   c. Psychologists make provisions for maintaining confidentiality in the storage and disposal of records.
   d. When working with minors or other persons who are unable to give voluntary, informed consent, psychologists take special care to protect these persons' best interests.

### Principle 6: Welfare of the consumer

Psychologists respect the integrity and protect the welfare of the people and groups with whom they work. When conflicts of interest arise between clients and psychologists' employing institutions, psychologists clarify the nature and direction of their loyalties and responsibilities and keep all parties informed of their commitments. Psychologists fully inform consumers as to the purpose and nature of an evaluative, treatment, educational, or training procedure, and they freely acknowledge that clients, students, or participants in research have freedom of choice with regard to participation.

   a. Psychologists are continually cognizant of their own needs and of their potentially influential position vis-à-vis persons such as clients, students, and subordinates. They avoid exploiting the trust and dependency of such persons. Psychologists make every effort to avoid dual relationships that could impair their professional judgment or increase the risk of exploitation. Examples of such dual relationships include, but are not limited to, research with and treatment of employees, students, supervisees, close friends, or relatives. Sexual intimacies with clients are unethical.
   b. When a psychologist agrees to provide services to a client at the request of a third party, the psychologist assumes the responsibility of clarifying the nature of the relationships to all parties concerned.

c. Where the demands of an organization require psychologists to violate these Ethical Principles, psychologists clarify the nature of the conflict between the demands and these principles. They inform all parties of psychologists' ethical responsibilities and take appropriate action.

d. Psychologists make advance financial arrangements that safeguard the best interests of and are clearly understood by their clients. They neither give nor receive any remuneration for referring clients for professional services. They contribute a portion of their services to work for which they receive little or no financial return.

e. Psychologists terminate a clinical or consulting relationship when it is reasonably clear that the consumer is not benefiting from it. They offer to help the consumer locate alternative sources of assistance.

### Principle 7: Professional relationships

Psychologists act with due regard for the needs, special competencies, and obligations of their colleagues in psychology and other professions. They respect the prerogatives and obligations of the institutions or organizations with which these other colleagues are associated.

a. Psychologists understand the areas of competence of related professions. They make full use of the professional, technical, and administrative resources that serve the best interests of consumers. The absence of formal relationships with other professional workers does not relieve psychologists of the responsibility of securing for their clients the best possible professional service, nor does it relieve them of the obligation to exercise foresight, diligence, and tact in obtaining the complementary or alternative assistance needed by clients.

b. Psychologists know and take into account the traditions and practices of other professional groups with whom they work and cooperate fully with such groups. If a person is receiving similar services from another professional, psychologists do not offer their own services directly to such a person. If a psychologist is contacted by a person who is already receiving similar services from another professional, the psychologist carefully considers that professional relationship and proceeds with caution and sensitivity to the therapeutic issues as well as the client's welfare. The psychologist discusses these issues with the client so as to minimize the risk of confusion and conflict.

c. Psychologists who employ or supervise other professionals or professionals in training accept the obligation to facilitate the further professional development of these individuals. They provide appropriate working conditions, timely evaluations, constructive consultation, and experience opportunities.

d. Psychologists do not exploit their professional relationships with clients, supervisees, students, employees, or research participants sexually or otherwise. Psychologists do not condone or engage in sexual harassment. Sexual harassment is defined as deliberate or repeated comments, gestures, or physical contacts of a sexual nature that are unwanted by the recipient.

e. In conducting research in institutions or organizations, psychologists secure appropriate authorization to conduct such research. They are aware of their obligations to future research workers and ensure that host institutions receive adequate information about the research and proper acknowledgment of their contributions.

f. Publication credit is assigned to those who have contributed to a publication in proportion to their professional contributions. Major contributions of a professional character made by several persons to a common project are recognized by joint authorship, with the individual who made the principal contribution listed first. Minor contributions of a professional character and extensive clerical or similar nonprofessional assistance may be acknowledged in footnotes or in an introductory statement. Acknowledgment through specific citations is made for unpublished as well as published material that has directly influenced the research or writing. Psychologists who compile and edit material of others for publication publish the material in the name of the originating group, if appropriate, with their own name appearing as chairperson or editor. All contributors are to be acknowledged and named.

g. When psychologists know of an ethical violation by another psychologist, and it seems appropriate, they informally attempt to resolve the issue by bringing the behavior to the attention of the psychologist. If the misconduct is of a minor nature and/or appears to be due to lack of sensitivity, knowledge, or experience, such an informal solution is usually appropriate. Such informal corrective efforts are made with sensitivity to any rights to confidentiality involved. If the violation does not seem amenable to an informal solution, or is of a more serious nature, psychologists bring it to the attention of the appropriate local, state, and/or national committee on professional ethics and conduct.

### Principle 8: Assessment techniques

In the development, publication, and utilization of psychological assessment techniques, psychologists make every effort to promote the welfare and best interests of the client. They guard against the misuse of assessment results. They respect the client's right to know the results, the interpretations made, and the bases for their conclusions and recommendations. Psychologists make every effort to maintain the security of tests and other assessment techniques within limits of legal mandates. They strive to ensure the appropriate use of assessment techniques by others.

a. In using assessment techniques, psychologists respect the right of clients to have full explanations of the nature and purpose of the techniques in language the clients can understand, unless an explicit exception to this right has been agreed upon in advance. When the explanations are to be provided by others, psychologists establish procedures for ensuring the adequacy of these explanations.

b. Psychologists responsible for the development and standardization of psychological tests and other assessment techniques utilize established scientific procedures and observe the relevant APA standards.

c. In reporting assessment results, psychologists indicate any reservations that exist regarding validity or reliability because of the circumstances of the assessment or the inappropriateness of the norms for the person tested. Psychologists strive to ensure that the results of assessments and their interpretations are not misused by others.

d. Psychologists recognize that assessment results may become obsolete. They make every effort to avoid and prevent the misuse of obsolete measures.

e. Psychologists offering scoring and interpretation services are able to produce appropriate evidence for the validity of the programs and procedures used in arriving at interpretations. The public offering of an automated interpretation service is considered a professional-to-professional consultation. Psychologists make every effort to avoid misuse of assessment reports.

f. Psychologists do not encourage or promote the use of psychological assessment techniques by inappropriately trained or otherwise unqualified persons through teaching, sponsorship, or supervision.

### Principle 9: Research with human participants

The decision to undertake research rests upon a considered judgment by the individual psychologist about how best to contribute to psychological science and human welfare. Having made the decision to conduct research, the psychologist considers alternative directions in which research energies and resources might be invested. On the basis of this consideration, the psychologist carries out the investigation with respect and concern for the dignity and welfare of the people who participate and with cognizance of federal and state regulations and professional standards governing the conduct of research with human participants.

a. In planning a study, the investigator has the responsibility to make a careful evaluation of its ethical acceptability. To the extent that the weighing of scientific and human values suggests a compromise of any principle, the investigator incurs a correspondingly serious obligation to seek ethical advice and to observe stringent safeguards to protect the rights of human participants.

b. Considering whether a participant in a planned study will be a "subject at risk" or a "subject at minimal risk," according to recognized standards, is of primary ethical concern to the investigator.

c. The investigator always retains the responsibility for ensuring ethical practice in research. The investigator is also responsible for the ethical treatment of research participants by collaborators, assistants, students, and employees, all of whom, however, incur similar obligations.

d. Except in minimal-risk research, the investigator establishes a clear and fair agreement with research participants, prior to their participation, that clarifies the obligations and responsibilities of each. The investigator has the obligation to honor all promises and commitments included in that agreement. The investigator informs the participants of all aspects of the research that might reasonably be expected to influence willingness to participate and explains all other aspects of the research about which the participants inquire. Failure to make full disclosure prior to obtaining informed consent requires additional safeguards to protect the welfare and dignity of the research participants. Research with children or with participants who have impairments that would limit understanding and/or communication requires special safeguarding procedures.

e. Methodological requirements of a study may make the use of concealment or deception necessary. Before conducting such a study, the investigator has a special responsibility to (i) determine whether the use of such techniques is justified by the study's prospective scientific, educational, or applied value; (ii) determine whether alternative procedures are available that do not use concealment or deception; and (iii) ensure that the participants are provided with sufficient explanation as soon as possible.

f. The investigator respects the individual's freedom to decline to participate in or to withdraw from the research at any time. The obligation to protect this freedom requires careful thought and consideration when the investigator is in a position of authority or influence over the participant. Such positions of authority include, but are not limited to, situations in which research participation is required as part of employment or in which the participant is a student, client, or employee of the investigator.

g. The investigator protects the participant from physical and mental discomfort, harm, and danger that may arise from research procedures. If risks of such consequences exist, the investigator informs the participant of that fact. Research procedures likely to cause serious or lasting harm to a participant are not used unless the failure to use these procedures might expose the participant to risk of greater harm, or unless the research has great potential benefit and fully informed and voluntary consent is obtained from each participant. The participant should be informed of procedures for contacting the investigator within a reasonable time period following participation should stress, potential harm, or related questions or concerns arise.

h. After the data are collected, the investigator provides the participant with information about the nature of the study and attempts to remove any misconceptions that may have arisen. Where scientific or humane values justify delaying or withholding this information, the investigator incurs a special responsibility to monitor the research and to ensure that there are no damaging consequences for the participant.

i. Where research procedures result in undesirable consequences for the individual participant, the investigator has the responsibility to detect and remove or correct these consequences, including long-term effects.

j. Information obtained about a research participant during the course of an investigation is confidential unless otherwise agreed upon in advance. When the possibility exists that others may obtain access to such information, this possibility, together with the plans for protecting confidentiality, is explained to the participant as part of the procedure for obtaining informed consent.

### Principle 10: Care and use of animals

An investigator of animal behavior strives to advance understanding of basic behavioral principles and/or to contribute to the improvement of human health and welfare. In seeking these ends, the investigator ensures the welfare of animals and treats them humanely. Laws and regulations notwithstanding, an animal's immediate protection depends upon the scientist's own conscience.

a. The acquisition, care, use, and disposal of all animals are in compliance with current federal, state or provincial, and local laws and regulations.

b. A psychologist trained in research methods and experienced in the care of laboratory animals closely supervises all procedures involving animals and is responsible for ensuring appropriate consideration of their comfort, health, and humane treatment.

c. Psychologists ensure that all individuals using animals under their supervision have received explicit instruction in experimental methods and in the care, maintenance, and handling of the species being used. Responsibilities and activities of individuals participating in a research project are consistent with their respective competencies.

d. Psychologists make every effort to minimize discomfort, illness, and pain of animals. A procedure subjecting animals to pain, stress, or privation is used only when an alternative procedure is unavailable and the goal is justified by its prospective scientific, educational, or applied value. Surgical procedures are performed under appropriate anesthesia; techniques to avoid infection and minimize pain are followed during and after surgery.

e. When it is appropriate that the animal's life be terminated, it is done rapidly and painlessly.

# AUTHOR INDEX

# SUBJECT INDEX

## A

AACD, 12
AASEC, 184–85
"ABC," rational-emotive, 83
Acceptance, 14–15, 121–22
Accreditation, 262–63
ACES, 264
Achievement tests, 228
Adlerian counseling, 48–50
Anal stage, 44
Anxiety, 62–63, 68
Anxiety, hierarchy, 91
APA, 12
Aptitude tests, 229
Assertion training, 92–93, 162
Assessment, 220–33
  purposes, 224–25
  types, 225–27,
Attending skills, 145–46
Authenticity (*See* Genuineness)

## B

Behavioral counseling, 86–93
Behavior change, 6–7
Behavior contract, 92, 95, 98, 161
Behaviorism, 30–31

Body language (*See* Nonverbal communication)
Buckley-Pell Amendment (1978), 260
Business and industry, consulting in, 250–51

## C

Career counseling, 203–19
Certification, 263
Change agent processes, 244–45
Classical conditioning, 30–31, 87
Client-centered therapy, 58–66
Client expectations, 9
Cognitive theories of learning, 31–32
Cognitive therapy, 101–2
Communication barriers, 122–24
Compensation, 43
Computerized testing, 230–32
Concreteness, 128–29
Confidentiality, 136–37, 257–59
Confrontation, 158–59
Congruence (*See* Genuineness)
Consultant skills, 237–38
Consultation, 176, 234–54
Consultation process, 238–40
Coping skills, 7
Core conditions of counseling, 125–31
Counseling, definitions of, 4–6
Counseling environment, 135–36